BLACK CATTLE

*The Sons of Japheth series:
about the Dutch and the slave trade
in the seventeenth century:*

*Black Cattle
On the Barbary Coast
Asiento
Banda Neira*

JOHN MEILINK
The Sons of Japheth
BLACK CATTLE

Original title: Kroesvee
First edition, 2019; second edition, 2022; third edition, 2023, the Netherlands
First English edition: 2025

Copyright © 2019/2025: John Meilink / Sons of Japheth Productions

Design and illustrations: John Meilink

Cover design: Ad van Helmond / John Meilink

Text guidance: Cocky van Bokhoven

Editing: Monieke Boonstoppel, Kate Smart, Naomi Nolte-Carrol

Literary agent in the Netherlands: Remco Volkers, Amsterdam

Cover illustration: fragment of The Cannon Shot (c. 1680), oil painting by Willem van de Velde the Younger (1633-1707)

Photo of John Meilink: Marco Bakker

ISBN Paperback/softcover: 9789083487120

ISBN Hardback: 9789083487137

All rights reserved.

No part of this publication may be reproduced, stored in an automated data file, and/or made public in any form or by any means, whether electronic, mechanical, by photocopying, recording, or otherwise, without prior written permission from the author.

Disclaimer: This book is set in a time when racism was the norm, and its content may be offensive to many. The views of the characters do not reflect those of the author.

BLACK CATTLE

"The old Noah drinks heartily from the fruit of the Vine which he himself has planted: He does not know the power of Wine, becomes drunk, lies down, and reveals his body, exposing his nakedness.
This is seen by Ham, who mocks and ridicules his old, disgraced Father.
Shem and Japheth discover this. They take a garment upon their shoulders, approach from behind, and cover their old, disgraced Father.
Noah awakens. He sees the garment and becomes aware of what has happened: the Spirit of God comes over him. He blesses Shem and Japheth, and curses Ham, saying: God shall enlarge Japheth, and he shall dwell in the tents of Shem. [...] Ham and his descendants shall forever be servants and slaves."

Genesis 9:18-29, according to the Dutch Minister Johan Picardt (1660)

"Get your facts first, and then you can distort them as much as you please."

Mark Twain (1835-1910)

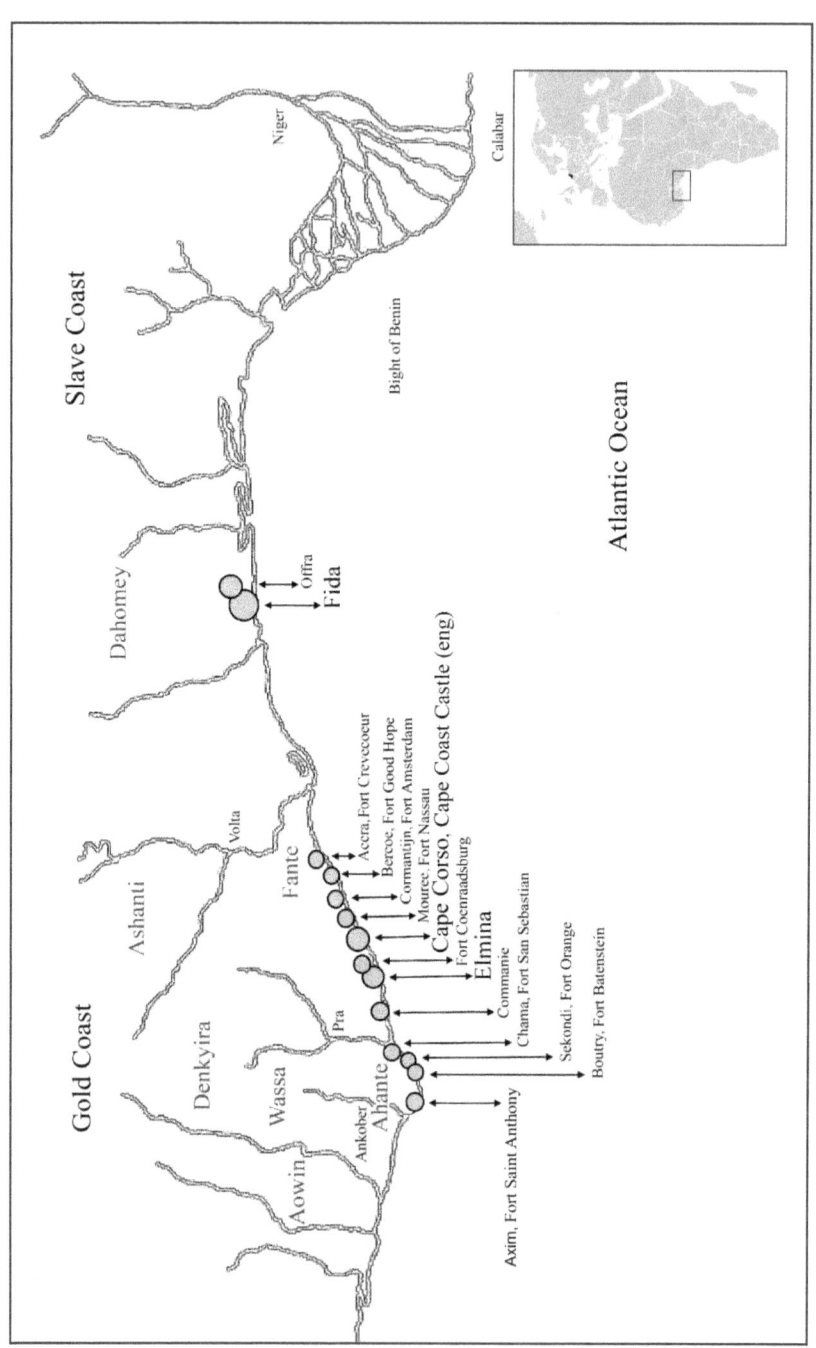

Map of the Gold and Slave Coasts in the 17th century, currently (from left to right) Ghana, Togo, Benin and Nigeria.

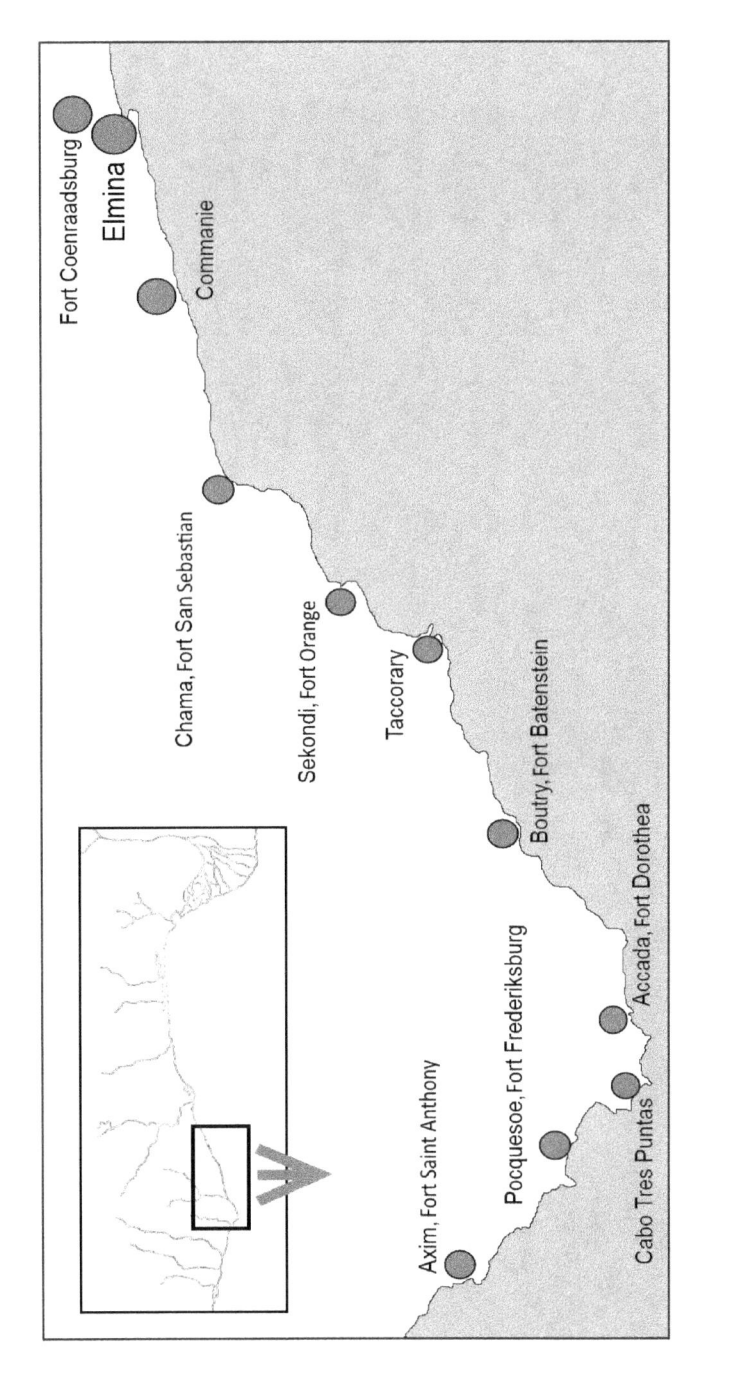

Contents

PROLOGUE 1

Part 1: Gold Coast

1 THE RAID 1
2 MUSSULMAN ALI BUYS SLAVES 6
3 NICHOLAAS SWEERTS ADMINISTERS JUSTICE 13
4 CALL FROM THE SHORE 21
5 NO WITNESSES FOR MUSSULMAN ALI 25
6 CHURCH AND BUSINESS IN ELMINA 28
7 THE TEMPTATIONS OF DUISTERBLOEM 34
8 THE SHEPHERD OF SOULS AND THE SMOOTH TALKER ... 39
9 VOYAGE TO POQUESOE 44
10 BACK: GILLIS GRAAUW 49
11 MUSSULMAN ALI SETS AN EXAMPLE 57
12 ARRIVAL IN POQUESOE 60
13 TRADE IS TRADE 64
14 DRUNKENNESS 71
15 BACK: ALDEMAR BURGHOUTSZ (1) 73
16 SWEERTS LANDS ON THE BRANDENBURG COAST 80
17 THE TAKING OF FORT DOROTHEA 86
18 BACK: NICHOLAAS SWEERTS 92
19 THE DYING ENSIGN 98
20 ATTACK ON FORT FREDERIKSBURG 102
21 REVENGE ON TACCORARY 110
22 BOMBA JAN 113
23 THE EXECUTION 124
24 MUSSULMAN ALI AND JASPER VOGEL 130
25 DUISTERBLOEM: MEDITATIONS IN THE DARK 136
26 THE WORM 139
27 BACK: ALDEMAR BURGHOUTSZ (2) 144
28 MUSSULMAN ALI DELIVERS HIS SLAVES 151
29 SCENE: ON WOMEN AND DISEASE 155

30 THE SLAVES OF ELMINA	157
31 BACK: ALDEMAR BURGHOUTSZ (3)	162
32 SWEERTS DISCOVERS CORRUPTION	169
33 ACTS OF JASPER VOGEL	174
34 THE EMBARKATION	180
35 BACK: BOMBA JAN MICHIELSZ	185
36 DUISTERBLOEM BANISHES THE DEVIL	189
37 SWEERTS, ABENA GYAN AND QUASSIE PATOE	192
38 VOGEL'S DISTRUST	197
39 BACK: ALDEMAR BURGHOUTSZ (4)	203
40 THE MEYBOOM ESCAPES	210
41 THE AMBUSH	222
42 SLAVES ON BOARD	228
43 QUASSIE PATOE AMONG THE AHANTE	234
44 THE SUFFERING OF MUSSULMAN ALI	240
45 FETCHING WATER IN CHAMA	245
46 BACK: ALDEMAR BURGHOUTSZ (5)	252
47 QUASSIE PATOE AND THE PORTUGESE	255
48 DUISTERBLOEM'S DECISION	259
49 THE SHARK	265
50 BACK: ALDEMAR BURGHOUTSZ (6)	270
51 DINNER IN ELMINA	277
52 BOMBA JAN'S DREAM	282
53 THE TEMPTATION OF QUASSIE PATOE	284
54 DEPARTURE	290
55 BACK: ALDEMAR BURGHOUTSZ (7)	292

Part 2: Du Casse

56 COASTAL SURVEY	297
57 A LANDING AT NIGHT	303
58 DU CASSE DIGS IN	308
59 BATTLE FOR COMMANIE	313
60 THE STORM	321
61 CONFRONTATION AT SEA	328
62 THE FALL OF BOMBA JAN	337

63 ON BOARD WITH THE DEVIL	343
64 RUINATION	347
EPILOGUE	351
NOTES	355
LITERATURE	363
ILLUSTRATION CREDITS	367
GLOSSARY	369

Important characters

Abena Gyan: concubine of Nicholaas Sweerts. Daughter of the king of Eguafo.

Aldemar Burghoutsz: (pronounce: 'Berg-hawts') skipper of the *Griffin*. Slave trader.

Anna Govers: the wife of Aldemar.

Bomba Jan Michielsz: overseer of slaves on the *Griffin*. Descendant of a Dutch grandfather and an African mother.

Gillis Graauw: boatswain on the *Griffin*.

Jean Baptiste Du Casse: French naval lieutenant. An ardent opponent of the Dutch. Commander of the two French warships.

Jasper Vogel: smuggler from Zeeland; skipper of the *Meyboom*.

Corporal Puteijn: Dutch soldier condemned to death.

Mussulman Ali: Arab slave trader operating on the West African coast.

Nicholaas Sweerts: director-general of the trading posts of the Dutch West India Company.

Reverend Duisterbloem: (pronounce: 'Dusterbloom' = 'Dark flower') minister at Elmina Castle.

Quameno Ewussi: enslaved resident of the village next to Elmina Castle.

Quassie Patoe: leader (ensign) of the auxiliary troops of Elmina.

* At the back of this book, you will find a glossary of terms.

This novel explores the Dutch involvement in the 17th-century Trans-Atlantic slave trade, with a focus on their rivalry with the English, who were their greatest competitors. Though the story is told from the Dutch point of view, it could just as well have been from the English side; the core of the narrative would remain the same. Both nations share the grim legacy of their history. By 1687, they had spent nearly a century crossing paths—whether in Europe, West Africa, the Americas or East Asia—trading in human lives. They were indeed true Sons of Japheth.

Prologue

⚓

The canoe bounces on the surf, tumbles over the swelling wave crests, held in check by eight black oarsmen. They paddle standing, in sync, and accompany themselves with shouts that are drowned out by the breaking water. Behind them, to the north, lies the West African Grain Coast, a dark green strip of land beneath a low, tattered cloud cover. It rains there: veils of water point in slanting, grey streaks toward the earth.

The last wave of surf rolls beneath them. The canoe takes the crest and then plunges straight down, sliding onto the ocean's swell. The men paddle alternately, with powerful strokes. Here, more than a mile from the shore, the sky is clear, with a setting sun in orange and red to the west.

Far outside the surf, they stow their paddles and tug at a thick bundle of fishing nets, unrolling them and casting them overboard, arm's length by arm's length. The canoe drifts with the current, dragging the net slowly behind it. An hour passes. The fishermen speak softly, passing gourds of water and palm wine among themselves. Far away in the north, thunder rumbles.

Then, on the western horizon, the masts of two ships appear, pyramids of sail, the canvas billowing in the wind, glowing in the last rays of the day. The men point. '*Abiessa*,' they say, raising three fingers to each other. Three-masters. Ships of the white men. Traveling in a line astern, they head east at a speed of six to seven knots toward Qua-qua-land or the Ivory Coast.

The fishermen wait. It takes a while before they can distinguish details; another hour passes slowly. The sun touches the horizon, and the eastern sky is already turning purple and blue, waiting for the night. Lightning flashes above the mainland, and a swarm of seagulls circles high in the air.

The ships pass them at a distance of five, maybe six cable lengths, high, massive hulks drawing a long wake through the water. They can see the gunports.

The men wave, but no one responds. All they hear is a ship's bell and the creaking of rigging. Then one of them recognizes a flag at the gaff peak, a long pennant fluttering forward: golden lilies on a blue field.

'*Fleurs de lis*,' he says, and suddenly all faces darken.

'Du Casse,' mutters another.

They suddenly make themselves small and thank Providence for the falling darkness; it is better not to be seen.

Part I
Gold Coast
November/December 1687

"I traded them for brandy,
For forks, beads, and knives;
I make eight hundred percent profit on that trade,
Even if half of them do not survive."

Heinrich Heine (1797-1856), The Slave Ship

1 The Raid

"(...) In Holland, there are many who think that parents sell their children here, that men sell their wives, or one brother sells another. Those with such thoughts are fooling themselves; for this has never happened except out of necessity or due to some crime; most of the slaves brought to us are people who have been captured in war and are sold by the victors as spoils. (...)"

From: 'Detailed Description of the Gold, Ivory, and Slave Coasts of Guinea', by Willem Bosman

⚓

The village is little more than a collection of round and rectangular huts, with pointed roofs made of cut grass mats. Well-maintained, though: neat walls of clay border the yards, with beautifully painted, arched gateways, every patch of ground carefully weeded and swept clean.

Surrounding it are small fields where millet and yams are grown, with an occasional old fruit tree here and there. And beyond that, stretching in all directions: the jungle, a patchwork of green. There is only one access road, nothing more than a path, muddy from the rain, winding southward from the village's central square deep into the forest.

The sun has just risen, casting a beer-coloured light over the land and creating long shadows; the rapidly rising heat evaporates the water that fell during the night. The forest steams.

Just another remote village, like so many others, far in the north of the Denkyira kingdom.

The woman lives in the hut farthest on the outskirts, halfway between a cassava field and in the shadow of a few fully grown ironwood trees. She was up early that morning because she had barely slept. Her baby had cried for half the night. Stomach cramps. Now that the sun is climbing above the forest, he is finally quiet, lying exhausted in the hammock near the entrance of the hut.

Still, she has no peace. A vague feeling of unease tingles in her stomach. Something is not right. It's not the baby; she knows that for sure—she can handle those cramps. Something else. Something... out there.

She steps out into the yard and feels the sun on her face. The humid heat is almost tangible. Oppressive. A faint mist hangs over the fields. Through the huts, she can see the other women waiting their turn at the water well on the central square. She puts her hands on her hips, her gaze gliding over the contours of the jungle.

Where are the birds, she thinks. It's too quiet.

Far away, on the other side of the fields, where the path disappears into the forest, she sees movement. A man? She squints, but it's gone immediately. Did she imagine it?

The uneasy feeling grows stronger.

She steps back, returns to the hut, and looks pensively at the baby, who is now fast asleep. He is only five months old, utterly helpless. Her first child. The love for him suddenly feels like a stone pressing on her shoulders. Is he in danger? Her father once told her that she had the Eye, that she could see where others were blind. But that was long ago; she hasn't thought about it in a long time.

On impulse, she picks up the baby, presses him against her chest, and steps out of the hut again. Her gaze automatically returns to the spot where she thought she saw the man.

At the back of the hut, the village's outer wall runs—a low structure of clay and branches. She follows the wall to a narrow strip of reeds.

"Woman, where are you going?" asks a raspy voice.

She is so startled that she almost drops the child. An old man stands in the shadow of a thatched roof. His black, thin chest is bare but covered with chains and pendants. She recognizes the village sorcerer.

"I don't know," she replies evasively. The sorcerer intensifies her unease. She dislikes him.

"Is the child sick?" he asks. His beady eyes study her. He tilts his head slightly, like a dog hearing something strange.

"No... yes," she stammers. "He has cramps."

He nods understandingly and attempts a smile. He stretches out an arm and says, "Give him to me. My medicine is good. I will heal him."

She presses the baby against her chest. The tingling in her stomach moves to her spine and climbs upward. Now, she is afraid. "No," she says, and with one hand, she reaches for the reed screen covering the opening in the wall. "It is nothing. I have to go."

The sorcerer takes a step forward. His face catches the sunlight, and she sees the scars on his face, embedded in lines and wrinkles. Old scars. Pockmarks.

"Where to?" he hisses, his eyebrows furrowed, pointing toward the emptiness of the field. "What is wrong with you? The child needs to be fed."

She has no answer. Yes, what does she want? To go into the jungle? Hesitantly, she places a foot in the opening of the wall. There is a voice in her head that keeps shouting the same three words: Save the child! Save the child! Not understanding, she looks at him. "There is danger," she whispers.

The sun climbs higher. The heat drives away the mists and shimmers, vibrating above the land. Crickets chirp in the tall grass. Where the path leaves the forest, movement is visible once more. Two black men emerge silently from the shadows of the trees. They wear long skirts of Beninese cloth around their waists, woven in blue patterns, and their bandoliers and muskets gleam in the sunlight. For a moment, they stand still, staring at the village. Hand gestures. Consultation. A third figure appears. A fourth. And then the forest empties: a large group of black warriors occupy the path. Now, there is sound too. Shouts.

In the village, ears are pricked.

The woman sees them first. A low moan of fear rises in her throat. The men are carrying firesticks, white men's weapons—no one in her village has firearms. Old stories suddenly flash through her mind, told endlessly by night fires. Old wives' tales, they seemed. But now it is different. "Slave raiders," she whispers. She turns her head and looks at the old man. "You didn't know," she hisses. "What kind of sorcerer are you?"

The old man is momentarily struck dumb. His eyes dart from the woman to the warriors in the distance. Slave raiders? "There is no war, woman," he says. "We pay tribute to the king. You have mud in your head." But his voice does not sound as certain as he would like.

She shakes her head. The child in her arms awakens, startled by her sudden movements and perhaps sensing her panic. It lets out a loud, drawn-out cry, its tiny hands clenched into fists. She is determined: no one will take her baby. No one will harm him. She squeezes herself hastily through the opening in the wall and runs into the field, in the opposite direction of the warriors, away from the village.

The warriors, forty in number, approach at a calm jog along the path, their weapons in hand. They are in no hurry; it is still early, already very hot, and the villagers have nowhere to go. At the first hut, they spread out, assegais and muskets at the ready. "Come outside!" they shout. "Wake up!" They beat on the clay walls of the houses, making as much noise as possible.

A few boys come out of their huts hesitantly, their faces still swollen with sleep. One of the intruders points toward the square with the well. "Go," he says with a grin, raising his assegai and giving one of the boys a teasing jab with the point. There's not much blood, it's just a small cut on the chest, bright red against black skin. The boy stares at it in surprise.

An older man appears, the father, holding a stick in his hand. "What are you doing with my son?" he asks indignantly. "Who are you? Go away. You do not belong here."

The warrior laughs. "It's nothing." He points to the stick. "Drop it."

"Go away!"

A second warrior approaches. He holds a musket and, without warning, strikes the wooden stock against the man's head. "Obey, *accaba*," he hisses, using the native word for slave. He kicks the man again. They laugh as his sons grab him by the arm and hurriedly drag him toward the square.

The woman looks over her shoulder. She hears shouts and cries and sees how men, women, and children are being herded together. Why aren't the men resisting? she thinks vaguely. They always think so highly of themselves. Panting and sobbing, she quickens her pace, struggling through the tall plants, the crying child pressed against her chest. The jungle still seems far away. Maybe two hundred steps. Sweat drips down her face. Onyame! God! Let me be on time.

"Look," says one of the intruders in the square. Between two huts, he sees a small figure running across the fields. He points. "*Aguane*. A runaway."

The man next to him curses. They have searched the houses and barns thoroughly; all the people are gathered at the well. It is rare for someone to escape.

"We won't catch up to her," says the first.

The other grumbles and stares thoughtfully at his musket. "How far?" he asks.

"Too far."

"How far?"

"Eight spear throws."

"Hm." The man with the musket reaches for the powder pouches on his bandolier, finds the powder horn, and pours the powder into the barrel. He inserts the wad, rams it down with the ramrod and primes the pan at the side with powder. Then, he attaches the match and closes the pan. Quickly, he places the fork rest under the barrel's end and carefully aims the musket. The distance has already grown—perhaps nine spear throws and quite a few feet more—but he is a good shot. Without taking his eyes off the target, he grabs his tinderbox and strikes a spark. The match hisses. He closes one eye and aims a little above the fleeing figure. The explosion makes his ears ring, and the musket slams hard against his shoulder. It takes a second. Then, they see a puff of dust appear in the distance, right next to the runaway.

"*Eééh?*" his companion exclaims in admiration.

But he himself is disappointed. "Missed," he grumbles.

The figure reaches the edge of the forest and disappears.

2 Mussulman Ali Buys Slaves

"And worship God and associate nothing with Him, and show kindness to parents, relatives, orphans, the needy, the near neighbor who is a stranger, and the near neighbor who is a relative, and to the companion, the traveler, and to those slaves whom your right hands possess."

From: The Quran, Surah 4:36

⚓

The tent does not look very comfortable from the outside. In fact, it appears worn, with frayed corners and conspicuously stitched-up tears. It has been raining for two days, and the broad leaves of the palms hang over the canopy, dripping with water. But appearances are deceiving. Inside, there is peace and warmth, with dry rugs covering what is essentially the jungle floor. Deep trenches drain the water away. The camps of Mussulman Ali are always remarkably efficient.

He himself sits cross-legged in the main compartment, the central area screened off with translucent cloth. The scents of essences fill the space, reminders of home. Oils. Coffee. Dried fruit.

He is a small, tough man, with a face like dark leather. Brown eyes. Sharp. Shrewd. Dressed in an old, comfortable kaftan. Beside him lies a small pile of green *qat*.

"Who?" he asks.

The servant before him bows and apologizes, for Mussulman Ali does not like to be disturbed, and his punishments are merciless.

"No name, *efendi*, but he says it is important."

Mussulman Ali spits a wad of qat into the brass spittoon before him. He reaches beside him, makes a fresh ball of the leaves, and puts it in his mouth. He closes his eyes, feeling new energy flow through his body. But he is also irritated. "Important to whom?"

"He speaks of slaves, *efendi*."

Slaves. He nods. His men are reliable. They would not disturb him for nothing, if there wasn't an indication of some importance. "Fine," he says in a weary tone. "Let him wait."

He sighs, lets his chin drop to his chest. Outside, the rain falls, and the water splashes against the cloth. A steady, soothing sound.

A visitor. A man who has found him, he thinks. Is that troubling? He has set up his camp in the shadows of a deep valley, out of sight of Denkyira spies. Lookouts are posted on the surrounding hilltops. At the slightest sign of danger, he will have his tents taken down. But it is difficult to remain invisible. There are always eyes and ears. In the forest. In the grass of the fields. The owl always hears the mouse.

Time for the midday prayer: *Salat al-Dhuhr.* He calmly and serenely performs the minor ablution, cleans his teeth with a twig, moistens his beard, and turns toward the northeast. "Glory be to You, O Allah, and praise be to You; blessed is Your name, exalted is Your majesty; there is no god but You."

Without haste, he completes the rituals. Slaves are important, but nothing is more important than God. *Allahu Akbar.*

The trader is black as pitch, with an almost blue undertone, shining like metal. A big man, coarse in build, coarse in face, with a broad jaw and a grin stretching from ear to ear. Mussulman Ali knows the type: not very smart, probably very violent. A bull. As he enters the tent, the atmosphere changes. But Mussulman Ali does not move a muscle and reveals nothing of his contempt.

The trader grins, in a way that is more awkward than offensive, and leans forward, offering Mussulman Ali the fingers of his right hand. His clothing is clean and new, striped blue and white, the traditional cotton imported by the Dutch from the Qua-qua coast. Around his neck and wrists hang the usual solid gold rings.

A dressed-up monkey, Mussulman Ali concludes with a downward curl of his lips. Dolled up and dusted off. He ignores the outstretched fingers and gestures for the other to sit on the rug before him. "*Salaam Aleikum*," he says softly.

The trader nods importantly, but there is no understanding. He knows nothing of etiquette. Instead, he starts to speak. A torrent of words. Political gossip. Insults about white men. Insults about black men. Trivial news. Mussulman Ali listens only half-heartedly, thinking and chewing his qat.

"Slaves, efendi. *Many* slaves," the trader finally concludes his speech.

At last.

Mussulman Ali opens his eyes. "Slaves? How many?"

The trader chuckles and leans forward slightly. His voice is a deep bass. "*Cinqüenta* men, *sessenta* women."

He still uses the Portuguese words. This also irritates Mussulman Ali. The Portuguese have been irrelevant in this region for decades. Does this black donkey think the Dutch and the Portuguese are the same?

Nevertheless, the number of slaves mentioned is excitingly high. His merchant mind quickly makes a few favorable calculations.

He shifts the ball of qat with his tongue from his right cheek to his left and calmly continues chewing. "How many children?"

"Maybe twenty."

He hesitates. If you do not work on consignment for the king, you are considered a free-trader, and you must be extremely careful, as the king has no appreciation for clandestine trade from which he does not profit. Then, you could suddenly find yourself hunted. Moreover, the political power centers are shifting. The Ashanti tribes are becoming more powerful, and the Denkyira are doing everything they can to maintain their influence. It would be very foolish, Mussulman Ali thinks, to choose the wrong side now.

"Where was the village?" he asks suddenly. "And what happened to the rest of the men?"

The trader purses his lips and furrows his heavy brows. "Just a village, *efendi*, far away from here, to the south, over the hills." He makes a sweeping gesture with his arm, causing his bracelets to jingle loudly. "Some of the men wanted to fight. We shot them. The village was burned, and what remains is for the vultures and Pataku, the hyena. The women barely lament, so I think there were few babies."

Mussulman Ali nods. Babies are worth nothing and always cause trouble. They get sick and die, and then the mothers cry, and before you know it, you have to keep them moving with sticks and clubs. No, he is more concerned about possible witnesses: people who escaped from the raiders and told their story in the villages. "Did anyone get away?"

The trader shakes his head almost indignantly. "No, no, *efendi*, no witnesses, never."

"I don't want people from here."

"Of course not."

Mussulman Ali sizes up the other man: his eyes look defiant and far too self-assured. Maybe I should capture this pig-eating monkey myself and sell him, he thinks, and see if he remains so arrogant then. These types always show up again. They do business for a while, act as if the world belongs to them, and are then found with their heads cut off by the side of the road. The thought pleases him. "*Eééh*," he exclaims, in the African manner. Mussulman Ali grins, and the black man immediately grins back, his dark eyes following every movement.

On the other hand, he considers, there is hardly any trade at the moment. There has been peace for too long. So fifty good men and sixty good women come as a gift from heaven. He lets out a deep sigh and decides he cannot afford to refuse, that he will pay the merchant. "Can you bring more people?"

The black man laughs and puffs himself up. "Of course. If you pay well, with muskets …"

Muskets, yes. But not too many, Mussulman Ali thinks. The hinterland is mine, not this unclean dog's who thinks he can compete with respectable merchants. I'll drop his name here and there; surely there's someone who would take offense. But not as long as he brings me negroes. I can always say I didn't know where they came from, that he lied, this filthy baboon who probably wipes his ass with his right hand—if he wipes it at all.

He gestures to one of his men, who is keeping an eye out behind him. "Bring tea, Mohammed."

The trader laughs and slaps his hand on his thigh. He knows now that the deal is sealed. "You and I," he says in a confidential tone, leaning forward slightly, "we are going to make a lot of money."

Mussulman Ali nods. In his mind, he sees the black man in heavy chains aboard a Dutch ship on the ocean, vomiting over himself, without a gun, without freedom, without a future. That is much better than a quick death, he thinks with satisfaction. *Allahumma.*

The jungle is dense, dark, and wet. For two days, the woman has cautiously headed north. There are villages nearby, but she avoids the paths, she doesn't trust them, the raiders could be anywhere. With the child on her back, she stumbles onward, past trees and bushes, over muddy ground and sharp grass. The child is very ill now. It hangs limp in its cloth. That worries her, but perhaps it has also saved her life, for the sound of a crying baby carries far and could attract attention. Occasionally, she offers her breast — she is still producing enough milk, fortunately — but the child drinks barely at all. It is too weak. She knows she must be quick. Otherwise, it will be too late.

The gunshot echoes endlessly in her mind. She knows nothing of white men's weapons. She suspects that the weapon housed a spirit sent after her, like a dog set on an intruder — hence the howling, the sound of a flying, crazed fly-demon. That thought is almost unbearable. Her fear is so great it feels like a lump in her throat. She would rather hide deep in the forest and crawl into a hole, her back against the wall. But she must warn the king's warriors in Abankeseso and beg for help so that they can stop the raiders and free the people from her village. Where have they been taken? She has never seen a white man, but the stories are clear enough. White men are devils who live on enormous boats, dwell on the Great Water, and prey on people. Her world has suddenly gone mad.

Oh, if only she does not encounter a leopard or — worse still — hyenas. That thought heightens her fear even more. Sobbing, she continues, the dangling child like a doll on her back.

Mussulman Ali, whose real name is Ali bin Fahrad Al-Fulan — though hardly anyone knows that — leaves his tent and steps into the open space between the trees. The sun is unrestrained here, and for a moment, he is blinded. He pauses and waits for his eyes to adjust.

On the other side of the clearing, his men have set up a corral made of bundles of branches. They stand in a loose circle around it, weapons in hand. After all these years, they have become very skilled; he has had to give hardly any instructions.

"The slaves are waiting outside the camp, *efendi*," says one of his overseers.

He nods and looks up. In one of the trees, a family of African grey parrots is quarrelling, making a tremendous noise. "Let them in."

The overseer shouts a command, and suddenly, everything is in motion. From the path across the clearing, the unmistakable, rhythmic sound of human footsteps echoes.

Mussulman Ali sees them appear: a throng of grey-brown figures, shackled, tied together with split branches, the ends of which clamp around their necks. His men drive them into the corral with practiced efficiency. There is no violence. The slaves are tired. They have been walking for days. They are freed from their primitive bonds, fastened with iron shackles at their wrists and ankles, and tied together in groups of four with ropes.

"Give them water," he orders.

They sit on the bare, earthen floor, and Mussulman Ali walks among them, his hands behind his back.

He observes and inspects their bodies, notices every imperfection, every scar, and estimates the value of each one. They are fine slaves, he thinks. Good-looking people. Hard workers. But now he has a problem. They are clearly Denkyira. "They are speaking Twi," one of his men had reported. "Maybe they come from the north, somewhere near Abankeseso."

Isn't that where the king is currently residing? he wonders. His gaze lingers for a moment on a young woman. She sits bent forward, her face toward the ground, her skin covered in dust and dirt, but he can tell that she will fetch a high price. He nods approvingly. Her nakedness does not bother him, it is not a temptation. She is *ahl al-fatrah*, an ignorant one, barely a person.

Yes, he thinks as he continues walking, they were probably taken from a small village somewhere deep in the jungle. That means he cannot sell them to the Dutch. The Dutch have made a treaty, they don't want any trouble with the black king.

He rubs his beard thoughtfully and turns his face to the southwest. Somewhere out there — far away — lies the ocean. His mind works quickly. There is always a solution, he knows. Above him, the African grey parrots are still quarrelling, their wings beat against the leaves, and small feathers float down. Fort Fredericksburg, he decides calmly. The Brandenburgers buy anything offered to them. They won't ask questions.

He signals to his overseer.

"Make sure the slaves get enough rest," he says. "We leave at sunrise tomorrow."

"To where, *efendi*?"

"Pocquesoe."

The overseer puffs out his unshaven cheeks. "That's a long journey."

"Yes," Mussulman Ali replies. "A dangerous trip. But the profit will be great, Ahmed. God willing. The Brandenburgers pay more than the Dutch or the English."

The sun burns on his keffiyeh. It is time for prayer again. *Salat al-'Asr*. Time for God. God is great. Only God can make everything go well.

3 Nicholaas Sweerts Administers Justice

"(...) The Blacks around Elmina, in fact, lead a double life. Their family ties are complex and contrary to our own: the right of descent follows the mother's line. This does not mean that the women have any say, for rights and functions are transferred from the man to the sister's son (and not—as one might expect—from the woman to the daughter). It goes without saying that this principle constantly gives rise to disputes.
Moreover, there is a second family bond along the male line: that of the factions or the asafo companies. Fathers, sons, nephews, and uncles have united into close-knit, well-trained, and armed militias, whose purpose is to protect the castle and the settlement against enemies. Elmina currently has six of these asafo companies and they have been formally recognized by us after swearing loyalty to the Company. Each of them has received a Dutch Prince's flag with the faction's number on it.
The problem, however, is that each asafo considers the others to be inferior. This leads to mutual hostility and provocation. They are full of themselves and behave arrogantly and aggressively, sometimes even against the whites. That is unacceptable. We have, therefore, denied their sorcerers, who play an important role, access to the castle."

From: Letters of Director-General Nicholaas Sweerts to the Directors of the Dutch West India Company, Autumn 1687

From the ocean, Elmina Castle is recognizable from afar: a gleaming white spot amid the beach, rocks, and coconut palms. As one gets closer, tall lime-washed walls come into view, curtain walls and bastions together forming a long rectangle, with main and auxiliary buildings, parapets, and sea-facing cannons within, and at the highest point, the Dutch flag, fluttering in an unceasing breeze.

The public counter is located on the ground floor, next to the courtyard, on the riverside of the castle.

As on most mornings, Director-General Nicholaas Sweerts, the highest official of the Company, is in session. The room is besieged by all sorts of people: blacks, whites and mulattoes, merchants and villagers. Everyone is walking and talking over each other despite the desperate attempts of his clerks to bring order to the chaos.

He himself sits on a wooden platform against the back wall of the room, on a seat that is rather ostentatiously decorated with carvings — he always feels a bit self-conscious about it — facing the common folk, guarded by two soldiers and flanked by a Company clerk, who sits at a small wooden desk, sweating as he records the complaints.

The director-general is a stocky, square-built man with a pear-shaped head, a stern face, and greying red hair that falls in a ponytail over his stark white collar — his *col vide*. He sits there sullenly, irritated by the commotion. "Next!" he barks at his provost, a tall, thin Dutchman in a light blue coat standing to his left. "And for heaven's sake, make them shut up."

"Silence!" the provost promptly roars into the hall.

That only helps for a moment, the complainants keep coming. Sweerts sighs. Most of the disputes are trivial: people deceive and steal from one another, and they all lie. After a while, it starts to bore him, which is bad for his mood. He looks up at the provost, who is managing the register. "Get on with it, man."

The provost reads aloud solemnly: "The asafo Enyampa contests the enslavement of this native, excellency," he says.

Some space has been cleared in front of the platform, and in the middle of it stands a sturdy, stark-naked black man. He is shackled at the wrists and ankles, and his chains make a heavy, rattling sound, but he stands proudly upright, with an indignant look in his eyes and his chin slightly raised.

Sweerts frowns. "Everyone would contest their enslavement if given the chance," he mutters impatiently. "Is the slave property of the Company?"

"Yes, sir, he has been in the men's house for a few days now."

"A fine specimen, I must say."

"However, the asafo Enyampa claims that he belongs to them."

"Aha." Sweerts inspects the slave. "Why is he not branded?"

"The asafo requested a postponement, sir. The chief chirurgeon honoured the request. Pending investigation."

"That is very kind of the chirurgeon, but I didn't know he had a say in this."

The provost makes a sour face. "Indeed, he does not."

"If the slave has ties to the Enyampa, then why is he standing here in chains before me?"

"There is talk of a crime."

"By the slave?"

"No, sir, by the person who sold him as a slave."

"And who is that?"

"We do not know."

"That sounds rather confusing," Sweerts concludes. "Where is the ensign of the asafo?"

The packed crowd in the office respectfully parts as Quassie Patoe, the ensign of the Enyampa, makes his appearance. Quassie Patoe is jet black and generously smeared with palm oil, giving his skin the same sheen as a cast twenty-four-pound admiralty cannon, and he has clearly taken great pains to present himself as stately as possible. His attire is extravagant: a *kente* cloak with bright colours and fringes that artfully drape over his left shoulder, a headdress of ostrich feathers, gold bracelets and necklaces, a small shield of elephant hide, and a long Dutch snaphaunce*, undoubtedly given to him by the Company.

Sweerts nods to him graciously, impressed by such splendour, while the ensign makes a slight, almost courteous bow.

"*Ackie*, Excellency Sweerts."

"*Ackie*, Ensign Patoe. What is the matter?"

"The black man here is family of the Enyampa."

"Then why is he imprisoned?"

"He was ambushed in the interior, far beyond the hills, by a gang of criminals who then abducted him and sold him as a slave to the Company in Sekondi."

"Did he not protest at the time of the sale?"

"There are many who claim they are not slaves, excellency, as you yourself just remarked; who would believe such a claim?"

Sweerts must admit that this is true. "Is he a trader?"

"He is, and he always faithfully pays his toll to the Company. He is respected by his family, both the male and female lines. He has wives and daughters, all of whom are also free citizens, and an eldest son who is already with the asafo."

"That sounds respectable."

Quassie Patoe touches the black man beside him with a single finger, doing so with visible reluctance, for the man reeks of hell after his stay in the prison house. He says in Twi: "Tell the white man who you are, *bebiny*."

The black man takes a deep breath, swelling his chest to appear even more imposing. "My name is Quameno Ewussi of the Enyampa," he says. "And I was a free man until I was unexpectedly ambushed." He points to his forehead, where, amid the dirt and dried blood, a large bump is visible.

Quassie Patoe grins with raised eyebrows at the director-general, as if to say,

---

* Snaphaunce = a more advanced version of a musket (rifle), equipped with a flintlock.

"See?" He leans nonchalantly on his snaphaunce and makes a sweeping gesture toward the people around him. "There are at least twenty people here who can confirm all of this. If you like, we can call them forward."

"No, no, spare me the testimonies," says Sweerts hastily, waving his right hand. "I believe the ensign of the Enyampa well enough." But he is annoyed. "You know," he says in a reproachful tone to the imprisoned black man, "that you must not venture into the interior without an escort, don't you? Have you never heard of the Ashanti on the warpath? And of the Wassa, who might abduct and sell even your old mother? Can't you listen to the advice of the men from your asafo? Are you stupid?"

"Not stupid," replies Quassie Patoe. He winks at the director-general and makes a vulgar gesture. "He was only following his manhood, Excellency Sweerts. There are outside women involved. Naturally."

Sweerts looks at him impassively. Quassie Patoe wears a gold plate on a chain around his neck. There is no motif on it, it is not an image or symbol, just a roughly cast rectangular block of solid gold, an ornament in the most basic form. And although Sweerts himself has made a career out of earning as much money as possible and claiming his share from every angle, it irritates him. Because, by God, this black beach king is very arrogant. "How much did the Company pay for this man?" he asks the provost.

"Forty-eight guilders in cowrie shells, sir."

"Forty-eight guilders is a lot of money."

"A whole lot of money, but if sold in the West, he would fetch at least two hundred and fifty guilders. It has been determined by the chirurgeon that he suffered from yaws in his youth, so he is now immune. Every plantation would want him."

"Hmm. Is the Company in any way to blame for this transaction?"

The provost flips through his papers. He shakes his head. "Not that I know of, sir. The merchant at Fort Orange claims to have acted in good faith — he had no reason to suspect anything was amiss with the sale — after which the slave was transported by canoe to Elmina."

"He was the only one?"

"Business is bad. Also in Sekondi."

Sweerts supports his chin with his right thumb. With the nail of his index finger, he absently scratches at a half-healed tropical sore next to the corner of his mouth. He thinks: I'll be damned if I let the Company pay for this. We need more negroes, not fewer. "Quassie Patoe," he says, "I acknowledge that this man should not have been sold as a slave."

Quassie Patoe smiles. "You are a wise man, Excellency Sweerts."

"Nevertheless, it appears the Company acted within its rights."

"*Eééh?*"

"So, you may have him back if you pay two hundred and fifty guilders."

"What?"

"It would be unfair for us to suffer losses due to the conduct of a band of native swindlers. That must be compensated first. We will consider him a pawn. After the amount is paid, he will be immediately released. But until then, he remains in the men's house."

Quassie Patoe no longer looks as affable. He purses his lips and frowns angrily. "Where is a man like him supposed to get two hundred and fifty guilders?"

"That is not my concern." Sweerts turns to the slave, who has been following the conversation with a look of disbelief: "Can you come up with that amount?"

The slave shakes his head angrily. "Of course not."

"Your family?"

"No, sir."

"Can the asafo guarantee it?"

"The asafo is not a lending bank," Quassie Patoe interrupts hastily. "And these are hard times."

Sweerts signals to his provost. "I do not wish to be insensitive," he says. "Is there no alternative?"

The provost furrows his brow and thinks while tapping the rolled paper against his cheek rhythmically. After a few seconds, he says, "He could exchange his place with another healthy male slave between fifteen and thirty-six years old. Perhaps the asafo Enyampa can arrange for that?"

Sweerts nods in agreement. "Very well. The asafo provides another native or pays the stipulated price. If not, then we are sorry, and he will go on the ship."

Quassie Patoe has too much dignity to argue, but his eyes blaze with anger. "A harsh judgment, excellency Sweerts."

"Well, it can't be helped," says Sweerts coolly. He leans back and rubs his eyes wearily. "That's it. No more palavers. I have a splitting headache."

But the day is far from over. He takes a light déjeuner in his office upstairs in the main building, where the thick walls keep out the heat and the open windows let in some draught. Cold poultry and a glass of diluted wine, while a chief clerk reads his schedule to him.

"A delegation from the Denkyira has presented itself, Excellency. They urgently request an audience."

"The Denkyira?" He furrows his brow. "Envoys of the king?"

"So it seems."

He grimaces. Unexpected delegations mean trouble, as he knows from experience. As if his life weren't complicated enough already.

The sun shines unobstructed on the courtyard, but a large sail has been stretched out to provide some shade. Underneath it, he has his seat placed on a small platform of wooden planks, covered with a rug.

Arrogant beggars, he concludes as he observes the three Denkyira envoys before him. They are beautifully dressed, with long cloths around their waists and the traditional *batakari* over their upper bodies, onto which leather pouches with amulets are fastened. The one in the middle wears a gray wig that undoubtedly once belonged to a fashion-conscious white. Perhaps an Englishman? Bought? Traded? Stolen? He doesn't want to think about it. "Greetings, sirs," he says in Dutch and immediately after in the Twi language: "*Aoro deie.*"

He looks at the gifts they have brought for him, laid out on a mat: a bag of gold nuggets, a live, bound piglet, and some traditional daggers and knives. At least that's practical, he chuckles to himself, for he was once given an ostrich as a gift, which was quite embarrassing, as he had no idea what to do with it (eventually, he had the nasty beast secretly put down).

He gestures for them to sit while sweat streams down his back, and he dabs the tropical sore at the corner of his mouth with a handkerchief. "Bring us some corn brandy," he orders gruffly, and a few company slaves fill small glasses.

They enjoy it. They chuckle at him amiably, rocking on their haunches. Two, three rounds are emptied in quick succession, and Sweerts exchanges the usual pleasantries. Is everything well with King Amponsem? Certainly, they reply, followed by a long salvo of praises. He nods occasionally, drinks his corn brandy moderately, and waits for them to get to the point.

Eventually, they do. There is a brief silence as the three look at him. They are startled when one of the cannons on Jago Hill announces the noon hour. Sweerts grins; artillery always makes an impression on the natives. The dull thud is felt beneath their feet. Then, the man in the middle, the one with the wig, asks if he is aware that there are poachers at work in the interior.

"Poachers?" Sweerts leans forward in his seat. "You mean slave raiders?"

The man with the wig nods. "Villages in the kingdom have been raided, and people have been enslaved, even near Abankeseso, where the king resides. Not just *any* black people, but Denkyira."

"That is serious," Sweerts admits. "Are the poachers white men? Zeelanders?"

"They are black. Filthy pimps from the Ashanti or Fante, or unscrupulous goat-screwers from the north. There is only one witness, and that is a woman who escaped at the risk of her own life, losing her child in the process. An infant. Just imagine. A heartless crime."

Sombrely, they accept another glass of corn brandy and toss it back solemnly. "But the raiders are not important," one of the other Denkyira remarks. "They will be caught and punished; it is only a matter of time. Their balls will be stuffed up their behinds, their pricks in their mouths, and then it will take a long time for them to die."

Sweerts listens without expression. "Then what is the problem?"

The man with the wig lowers his voice. "Rumour has it that the slaves were sold to the Arab known as Mussulman Ali. Do you know him?"

"Yes, of course." Sweerts snorts. "Who doesn't know him?" He looks at his handkerchief and concludes with disgust that his sore has started to fester again.

"Does Your Excellency perhaps suspect that Mussulman Ali will want to sell the slaves to the Dutch?"

That question is impertinent. He looks up, irritated. "Do you think that we have anything to do with this? That I have carried out these raids?"

"The treaty between Denkyira and the Dutch is carved in stone," adds the man with the wig. "Everyone knows that, black or white. Friends do not deceive each other."

"No," Sweerts agrees, thinking of the gold supplies that keep him and the Company afloat. His expensive wool coat is now drenched with sweat. He tugs at his moustache and says, "You can be assured that the Company keeps its word. We do not buy slaves who have been stolen from the Denkyira."

They smile compliantly. Of course, they agree. It is an old treaty, after all. But the king would be very disappointed if these unfortunate subjects were to end up on a white man's ship.

I can well believe that, he thinks. On an English ship, perhaps? Unlikely. They would have to pass through Fante territory. The Portuguese? No, they wouldn't dare approach the coast. The Zeelanders? Hmm. That could be possible. He stares pensively ahead. The Brandenburgers, he decides silently. That Arab is heading to Pocquesoe.

4 Call from the Shore

"Your Honours,
We may speak of a crisis if we no longer have a sufficient supply of cowrie shells or — as they are called by the Blacks — boesjes. The supply of slaves is already minimal, but now we face the problem that we cannot make our payments properly; the Blacks hardly wish to accept other means of payment. The rate of forty guilders per slave is currently at a price of twenty pounds of boesjes, which amounts to about ten thousand shells. The last supply dates back nine months. Our holds are almost empty. I have nevertheless heard through the grapevine that some ships of the Dutch East India Company called at the Maldives last autumn and have returned home safely. Thus, the auction in Amsterdam might be supplied with cargoes of boesjes. I would like to stress that Your Honours should secure the necessary stock in advance before the English or Zeeland smugglers place a bid and potentially seize them during the auction.
With respect."
From: Letters of Director-General Nicholaas Sweerts to the Directors of the Dutch West India Company, Autumn 1687

Gillis Graauw is brusquely awakened by a cannon shot fired from the castle: a dull *boom* echoing over the bay. He is immediately wide awake and jumps out of his bunk. Above him, he hears the voice of the second mate: "Boatswain! On deck!"

He slips on his clogs, buttons up his worn duffle coat, and instinctively grabs his half-pike. With clattering steps, he leaves the narrow alcove that serves as his sleeping place and squeezes his way along the gun deck past swaying hammocks and snoring, coughing, and mumbling sailors. Slanting, dusty beams of light break through the opened gunports. It reeks: the characteristic smell of men living on top of each other. Sweat. Alcohol. Someone has secretly relieved himself in the gutter — a daily recurring annoyance. He growls, climbs the ladder to the quarterdeck, and suddenly stands — blinking — in the full sun.

"Signal from the shore!" the second mate calls. "The big boss wants to speak to the skipper."

Graauw nods and lets his eyes adjust to the light. He glances at the hourglass next to the binnacle house*. Three double strikes of the ship's bell have already sounded; it is just seven in the morning. His square, hollowed-out face turns forward towards the waist deck and the forecastle, where the sailors of the watch wait for their relief. A few seagulls skim low over the deck, effortlessly balancing in the warm air, looking at him almost mockingly with their jet-black eyes.

"Lower the longboat," he orders while knocking the tip of his half-pike on the deck once. His stubby fingers brush along the scar that runs down the right side of his face, from forehead to chin. Big boss? His mind is still sluggish. That must be the director-general. He peers to port, and Elmina Castle gleams blindingly white in the morning sun. After weeks of doing nothing, this is the first time a signal has been given.

Finally.

The longboat drops flat onto the water, lowered by the deckhands. Graauw peers down. It's twenty-five feet from the railing to the sea surface.

The rope ladders are thrown over.

"Skipper on deck!"

He turns around. On the quarterdeck, the highest deck of the ship, stands the man he has sailed with for over thirty years, who was once his friend. Tall.

---

* Binnacle house = the enclosed space on a ship where the whipstaff (a long steering stick) was located and where no metal objects were allowed to prevent interference with the compass.

Angular. Dark blond hair tied in a ponytail and a too-old, almost deathly tired face, in which narrowed blue eyes look coolly and flatly out at the world.

"Longboat lowered, skipper," says the second mate.

A hand gesture. Casual. "Countersignal to the shore, I'm coming."

Skipper Aldemar Burghoutsz descends the companionways to the waist deck*. He is wearing a clean, white shirt with wide sleeves and a leather vest over it. His face is freshly shaven. He glances at Graauw. "Get in the boat," he says curtly.

Six rowers and a boatswain wait for orders. The longboat drifts away from the ship, catching the sun, swaying on the swell. Burghoutsz stands at the front on the bow, his legs moving with the water, his upper body straight and motionless. He inspects his ship, a flute with three decades of service, rounded shapes, a thick belly, and an inward-sloping upper deck. It is well-maintained, caulked and painted from top to bottom, scrubbed and polished, but it bears many scars: patched up like a worn coat, some repairs clearly improvised by a carpenter with imagination. The figurehead is painted in bright colors: the head of a bird with the body of a lion and small wings spread wide — a *griffin*.

The skipper looks and assesses. "The woolding on the lower mast is coming loose," he remarks critically.

Boatswain Graauw sits at the helm in silence, his lips pressed tightly together. Inwardly, he makes a note, for someone will pay for that.

"Good," mutters the skipper, apparently satisfied, though his eyes do not leave the ship. "Let's go."

Graauw nods to the rowers. "Pull." Six oars plunge into the water simultaneously. The longboat sets off, cutting through the milky green water of the bay, its bow aimed at the castle, half a mile away.

Fifteen minutes later, they reach the left bank of the river, right in front of the castle.

"Oars in," orders Graauw. He is already out of the longboat when they touch the dock, secures a line, and sends four rowers out of the boat. He designates the remaining crew as sentries. "You are not to go ashore. And don't let anyone into the boat." The others form the skipper's escort. He checks their weapons: a

---

* Waist deck (or waist) = the open, central section of a ship between the forecastle (forward part) and the quarterdeck (aft part).

few blunderbusses and two pistols. He trusts no one on this uncivilized coast. Grimly, he looks around, taking in the bustle of the mainland. People. Landlubbers. Blacks — many blacks. He would have preferred to stay aboard the ship, he fears the diseases that prevail on land, caused by the invisible but foul vapours from the swamps inland. The Dutch do their best to drain them, but it is long and arduous work, and in the meantime, the diseases continue to take a heavy toll.

Locals in crowded small boats shout at him boldly and loudly.

"Buy, sir, fresh *fufu*?"

"*Borodee*?"

"*Yam*?"

The yam roots are rinsed in the river, which stinks of dung and rotten eggs. A little further away, a small black boy, naked, urinates with a graceful arc into the same water.

Graauw shivers with disgust. He sticks as much as possible to a diet of Dutch food—ship provisions.

Across the way, a group of women wash clothes in the water. They beat the colourful fabric on flat stones with hard, rhythmic slaps accompanied by singing. Right next to them, a Company ship is being loaded with large bales of Arabic gum and barrels of lime juice destined for the Amsterdam market. The sailors shout at the black porters, who balance in a column on the gangplanks high above him, with their heavy loads on their shoulders. Unconsciously, they have begun to walk in time with the singing of the women doing laundry, making the entire scene look like a carefully choreographed dance.

"Move on," says the skipper. He turns around and walks off the pier toward the road to the castle, followed by Graauw and his four sailors.

5 No Witnesses for Mussulman Ali

"Tell the believing men to lower their gaze and guard their private parts, except with their wives or the slave women whom they possess; in that case, they are not to be blamed."

From: The Quran, Surah 23: 5-6

Where the jungle ends, the sun scorches. Tall grass covers the hills. The path is nothing more than a reddish-brown trail that, at night — when the rain breaks loose — turns into mud and is baked during the day. The long line of slaves thunders on in a synchronized rhythm, driven forward by the overseers. After a few days, the individuals have faded. Men, women, and children have become one; their bodies move in the same pattern. There is no talking. As they march, the group emits guttural sounds of fatigue, exertion and misery, and gradually — as if by itself — it becomes a song that drums along with their rhythm.

Mussulman Ali rides at the back on his small, mouse-gray horse. He is pleased, for ahead of him rushes a single organism. Moulded clay. His men are ruthless. At this pace, they will soon reach the coast.

As evening falls, he finds a place to set up his camp, deep among the trees, with only a few canopies of canvas stretched at eye level for shelter. No fires are lit. The slaves are herded together and tied to each other with ropes and chains: man to man, woman to woman. When the rain comes, they huddle even closer, drawing warmth from each other's bodies.

Mussulman Ali watches approvingly. The slaves protect themselves, and he protects them all. With loaded muskets, he and his men complete the *Salat al-Isha*, the night prayer, while the jungle moves around them, rustling in the rain, a thousand unseen night eyes upon them. He occasionally touches the stock of his gun. It reassures him. At the end, he murmurs to the angel on his left side: "May God accept my prayer." *Allah-i-takabel*.

But danger comes in many forms. He can never rest, must always be on his guard. In the morning sun, three of his men stand around a kneeling figure, whose hands are tied behind his back.

"He's the only one?" he asks.

His men nod simultaneously. "We searched carefully, *efendi*."

Mussulman Ali gazes around, over the treetops toward the green hills in the distance, as if he could disprove their words from here. Spies are an abomination to him. They appear everywhere, disguised as merchants or hunters. They lie behind bushes or rocks or in the ditch along a path, or you find them drawing water from a well. This one was disguised as a cowherd. He had three cattle with him, bells and all. It was a good disguise, Mussulman Ali admits.

He inspects the kneeling man, undoubtedly a spy of the Denkyira, even though he denies it. That is normal; spies always deny everything; they would even claim they don't have a mother. But if you let them go, they suddenly remember seeing an Arab on a horse leading a large group of captured blacks to the coast.

He grins. Not this time. He has outsmarted them. He will have the cows slaughtered, so tonight they will eat fine meat, undoubtedly at the king's expense, because those cows surely belonged to him. Mussulman Ali presses his heels gently against the flanks of his horse, and the animal obediently takes two steps back. He has had this little beast for a long time, which is remarkable because horses usually succumb quickly in this hot, humid climate. An Arabian thoroughbred would not last six months, but this unimpressive, tough little fighter bravely withstands the elements. He thinks: God Himself decides to whom He grants His strength; no human has a say in it.

The sun burns. It is hot. But the coast is not so far away anymore. Mussulman Ali nods to his men. "Make him disappear," he says quietly. He turns his horse and lets it calmly walk down the path while behind him comes the sound of protesting, fearful cries. Sometimes, it is necessary to be ruthless, he knows. He cannot take any risks.

Above him, a vulture caws. Out of nowhere, the large birds have appeared, and their shadows skim over the treetops. He grunts with satisfaction and thanks God for His help. Africa leaves no traces behind.

6 Church and Business in Elmina

"(...) The slaves from the tribes of the Gold Coast are undoubtedly of the best quality, but due to the absence of large wars and conflicts, they are scarce. Supply from the Denkyira and Ashanti circles is nil, except for occasional pawns, and even then, only with the explicit permission of their kings. The Wassa are hostile and unmanageable, so only a small amount is still supplied by the Ahante and the Aowin. Therefore, we prefer to transport mixed slave cargoes, that is, a bulk of second-rate black cattle purchased in Fida or Offra, supplemented with a cadre of Gold Coast slaves, who are assigned on board to oversee the rest. This relieves our people of much work and ensures better communication between white and black. The negroes of the Gold Coast are superior in every respect to those from Luanda or Angola, and to the saltwater negroes of the Tooth Coast or from Bonny and Calabar: they are more intelligent, more reliable, healthier, and undeniably much better built. (...)"

From: Letters of Director-General Nicholaas Sweerts to the Directors of the Dutch West India Company, Autumn 1687

⚓

Halfway along the castle is the main gate. People stand in line to get in, while on the other side, there is pushing to get out. Two soldiers try to maintain order, threatening with their pikes.

Burghoutsz and his escort shuffle inside. Through a portal, they enter the main courtyard, where the morning shadows still linger. The castle is a haphazard collection of buildings, erected by the Portuguese, but in the hands of the Company for fifty years now. They walk past the soup kitchen and the former Papist church — now both a trading house and a warehouse — where white and black men stand together in groups.

It is a daily routine: the white merchants sit at trestle tables strewn with papers, surrounded by black traders offering elephant tusks, dried Arabic gum, and ostrich feathers. They look splendid with their bracelets, gold chains, and colourful robes.

Boatswain Graauw eyes them distrustfully. In his view, Elmina is a world turned upside down; it is blasphemy to see so many blacks so free, debating with whites as if they were on equal footing. He points to a black man sitting naked in a corner, legs wide apart, showing a scrotum so swollen that he can hardly walk. "That's what happens when you drink wine from the chrysia palm," he says instructively to his oarsmen. "Don't be like them. They are Hamites."

He walks on with his head bowed, hands behind his back, longing for the peace and order of his ship.

At the end of the courtyard, against the main building, a pyramid-shaped, open structure has been built from heavy wooden beams. At the top hangs a bronze bell. A scarecrow in a black coat tugs on a rope, and the sudden, piercing sound silences all conversations.

The skipper makes an unhappy face. "I forgot the morning service," he says. He looks around, searching for a way out, but is stopped by an unyielding boatswain.

"Church is mandatory ashore, skipper. You don't want to get fined, do you?"

From his pulpit, Reverend Duisterbloem gazes down sternly upon his congregation, with the Europeans seated in the front benches and the few blacks standing at the back, all eyes fixed on him.

The reverend is not a man to be trifled with. He leads his flock — both the white and the black — with a watchful eye and zeal, and there is never any doubt about the righteousness and severity of his teachings. He knows his parishioners personally and in great detail, which, in his opinion, does not generally lead to optimism, for his sinners sin with great fervor, and it is certainly not limited to drunkenness and polygamy alone. In his long career, he has seldom seen so much concentrated immoral behavior, lechery, and hypocrisy as here on this spot on the African coast. But Reverend Duisterbloem did not come here by order of the Amsterdam Classis for nothing. He intends to make a clean sweep. There has been too much patience and tolerance for too long.

"Only fifty years ago," he thunders, pointing to the bare walls, "this castle was still a Portuguese den, stuffed with statues and paintings, for these are the tools with which the Catholic practices his apostate ways. But we have driven them from the coast."

Below him, he sees the stern, surly face of Director-General Nicholaas Sweerts. A hypocrite, he thinks, who almost openly lives in sin with a native mistress, a black woman from Eguafo.

Countless predecessors of the reverend have begged the Company to allow the wives to come to Elmina so they could support their husbands and put an end to whoring, but to no avail. And so, the relations with black women continue, undoubtedly to the anger of the Lord God Himself, and he is determined to bombard the Classis with letters, petitions, and laments. "For," he asks loudly, "are we better than the papists if we wallow in sin, in bacchanals and lust?"

He leans back for a moment and is aware of the coolness in the church. Outside, in his heavy black coat, it is almost unbearable, and the dried sweat of weeks bites into his skin, turning his armpits and groin into raw flesh that itches and stings. He quotes Corinthians: "Or do you not know that he who unites with a prostitute becomes one with her? For Scripture says: The two will become one flesh. But whoever is united with the Lord is one with Him in spirit. Flee from sexual immorality. Every other sin a person commits is outside the body, but the sexually immoral person sins against his own body. You know this: your body is a temple of the Holy Spirit who dwells in you, whom you have received from God. You are not your own. You were bought at a price. Therefore, honour God with your body."

But still, he thinks, even he must adhere to conventions; the director-general is a powerful and influential man, and one must not cross him, even if you have the support of God.

Indifference radiates from the pews. He sees the stubborn looks, the surliness. They don't like him, of course not, he is in their way. They see the service as *un service du Dieu par force* — a duty against their will.

Dig in your heels if you must, he thinks grimly, but decency will return. He has faced such challenges before: years ago, the Protestants in New York nearly forced him onto a ship back to Texel after they refused to contribute another penny to his upkeep.

"Children," he continues more mildly, "abstain from the sins of the flesh. In patria*, your spouses and little ones are waiting for you. What sorrow do you cause them, those who have been left behind with sometimes less than a few pence a week?"

The sun has now reached the dirty windows of the church, and a filtered beam of light suddenly falls upon the congregation below him. It is a daily occurrence. The church suddenly resembles a painting with rich colors that seem to reflect an almost esoteric composition.

"Behold," he says with awe, as always genuinely moved, his arms spread wide. "The hand of God."

And he recognizes the religious emotion in the eyes of the blacks at the back. The church is a beacon of light, an island in a sea full of sharks lurking from the depths. If the reverend knows moments of doubt, then this morning light is a reminder of his duty. It is not for him to falter. It is God's will.

The quarters of Director-General Sweerts are located right next to the inner courtyard, on the top floor of the government building. The hallways leading to his office are spotlessly clean, and the scrubbed wooden floors, polished with wax, shine and reflect. Two soldiers guard the door, and a few slave girls are busy with mops.

Skipper Burghoutsz waits to be announced. He sits on a bench against the wall, enjoying the coolness. In the hallways, only whispers are heard. The bustle from outside is muffled, the sound of the surf is barely discernible. Here is the centre of the Company's power; all trade along the African coast is directed from this place.

A company slave, dressed like a footman in dignified purple with a high white collar, opens the double doors to the governor's office. He nods politely to the skipper: "His Excellency is expecting you, sir."

Burghoutsz stands up, brushes some imaginary dust from his vest, and walks in.

Sweerts waits for him, seated behind his enormous teak desk, which is scattered with papers, sea charts, and bound books. He wears a coat of

---

* Patria = the homeland

broadcloth, a gleaming blue colour, with velvet buttons. "Burghoutsz," he says, searching through his papers, and it does not sound like a greeting. "You took your time."

The skipper remains unaffected, standing in front of the desk, hands behind his back. He is not offered a chair. They look at each other, sizing each other up.

Sweerts holds up a sheet of paper. "Look: a letter of complaint from the Amsterdam Chamber. There are hardly any slave ship skippers to be found." Burghoutsz always provokes irritation in him, there is nothing readable in the man's face. "And of those willing to make the crossing, most drop out after just one time." His fingers drum on the desk. "One time," he repeats. He smiles, but his expression shows no friendliness. "And then they lock themselves away in their cottages on Texel or Vlieland." He leans back in his chair and folds his hands over his belly. "It's a matter of personality, of course. Those who make the crossing twice have — hmm — a tougher shell, or so it seems. Yet, it weighs on their conscience. Is it guilt? Shame?" Now he grins. "Morally speaking, the enslavement of people may be less bearable than expected, despite all the justification from the church. It gets under your skin, so I've been told." He pensively picks at the tropical sore at the corner of his mouth. It has grown considerably. "But you, Burghoutsz, don't seem to be affected: three times you have delivered your slave cargo, and still you keep going — that is remarkable."

The skipper shrugs. He looks around the room. Paintings on bright white walls. Expensive tapestries. Everything radiates wealth. "Profit is profit," he concludes flatly, as if that explains everything.

Sweerts furrows his brow. "There are others. Ruthless bastards, every one of them. Not to mention those illegal Zeeland smugglers. But you are different, Burghoutsz. They say you are a just man. Your last passage was unfortunate. That must have been hard on you."

For a moment, those blue eyes light up. Irritation? That pleases him. He picks up another form from the pile and reads aloud: "Thirty-eight percent loss. Lost nearly all the women and children. And the survivors were in such a wretched condition that they were practically unsellable." He looks up: "You missed the trade winds."

Burghoutsz snorts. "My report is before you, sir. The doldrums lay unusually far south that year. No pressure in the glass, not a breath of wind. For four weeks, we drifted aimlessly. After that, we were so far off course that we lost another thirty days. We were spared nothing: scurvy, dysentery, and two cases of typhus."

"You were not blamed."

"Perhaps not. But I also lost a good number of my own men."

"And yet you are back."

"I want to make up for my losses."

"I have only three hundred slaves in the dungeons beneath the castle. That is over a hundred short of filling your holds. And their quality is visibly deteriorating; some have been there for three months." Sweerts pushes his chair back and stands up. "Doing nothing yields no profit. Not for me and not for you. We've only outfitted two ships from Offra this year. The Company wants us to increase the cargos to six hundred heads."

"Six hundred is far too many."

"The plantations are crying out for slaves."

"The English and the French settle for lower numbers, and their ships suffer a much higher loss."

Sweerts sighs. "In the summer, I lost a slaver near the Canary Islands to Saletian pirates. I must have a full cargo by the end of the year." He walks to the window, which is half-covered by a shutter. A narrow beam of sunlight sets his red hair ablaze. "There are a hundred and ten slaves on their way to Pocquesoe."

"To Fort Fredericksburg?"

"Illegally, it is claimed. Abducted by the Arab. The Denkyira have lodged a complaint with me, and I think Mussulman Ali will take the shortest route: those Brandenburgers will buy up everything he offers." He snorts indignantly. "I have no intention of granting them that advantage."

"You want those slaves?"

"A hundred and ten extra heads would complete your cargo."

"But it would also violate the treaty with the Denkyira."

"Yes. And that's why they must not know about it."

A brief silence. Outside, the ocean rustles. "What do you want me to do?"

Sweerts looks thoughtfully outside. Through the narrow gap in the shutter, he sees the canoes of the natives rocking on the waves. He says, "Go to Pocquesoe incognito. Find out what is going on. I want to know at all costs where those slaves are going."

"Incognito?"

"Leave your ship here. With a Dutch three-master, you'd scare everyone away there. Put on canvas trousers and have yourself dropped off near the Brandenburg fort unseen. No one will recognize you."

7 The Temptations of Duisterbloem

"And the Lord has blessed my master greatly, so that he has become a wealthy and well-known man. The Lord has given him many sheep and cattle, gold and silver, male and female slaves, and camels and donkeys."

From: The Bible, Genesis 24:35

⚓

Reverend Duisterbloem sits with his head bowed over his plate. The evening meal is, as always, meagre. On the plate is a salted herring and a raw, peeled onion, and in his left hand, he holds a crust of stale bread. He doesn't care. He does not like abundance. Besides, he isn't hungry. Hasn't been for days.

He mutters a prayer of thanks. He is alone, except for his black servant girl, who stands behind him with a jug of beer in her hand.

That servant girl bothers him. He snaps at her, even when she does nothing wrong. She was assigned to him by the Company, so he had no say in the matter. He has gone through quite a few servants: farmers' daughters in Holland, an Englishwoman in New York, and even for a brief time an Indian girl in Midwout[*], but he has never had a black servant, and he wonders if this is a new temptation. God does not make things easy for him, in his experience, though he is very devout and always tries to please Him. But the more he tries, the more God seems to test him.

Out of the corner of his eye, still with his head bowed, he sneaks a look at her. She is a young, tall, slender black woman with a proud demeanour and intelligent brown eyes.

At first, he managed to ignore her. Shortly after his arrival, he fell ill, as almost everyone does here — *febris biliosa putrida*, as the chirurgeons call it, or seasoning — and he paid more attention to his own misery than to her. She cleaned up his mess, changed his bed when he soiled himself again, and took care of his food and drink. Nothing out of the ordinary. Everything was fine. And afterward, well, he barely had time; he was home late in the evening and

---

[*] Midwood, Brooklyn, New York

gone early in the morning. His new flock consumed all his attention with all the crimes, sins, vices, diseases, and deaths.

But after the start of the rainy season, he was home more often, and that was when he began to suspect something.

The devil comes in many forms, he knows. It must be the devil because, in the Book of James, it is written: 'When tempted, no one should say, 'God is tempting me.' For God cannot be tempted by evil, nor does he tempt anyone.'

He raises his head. Takes a bite of the bread and gestures with his mug. "Beer," he orders gruffly.

She approaches him in silence and pours. He can smell her. It is a feminine scent. The scent of... lust. Yes. Her physical presence, so near to him, seems to generate electricity: the hairs on his neck stand straight up. And that is not the only thing: his erection is almost unbearable. It pains him, it itches, and he is ashamed. His desire rages like a storm through his mind. There are images, of himself, with his head between her black thighs. His manhood in her mouth. By God... the filth. The depravity. How can he defend himself? What does Satan want from him?

As she sets the jug on the table, her arm briefly touches his hand. Reverend Duisterbloem jumps up as if stung by a wasp, taking the table, chair, and utensils with him while the bewildered servant girl starts screaming.

In the cellar beneath the main building of the castle, there are five chests made of heavy wood, reinforced with thick iron bands. The lids lie beside them, waiting to be sealed with rivets and double locks.

The air in the room shimmers with heat. Against one wall stands a large brazier, smouldering red and yellow, with the blacksmith beside it, hammer in his fists. In the background, the silhouettes of silent, anonymous men: guards. Soldiers. They carry loaded guns.

Director-General Sweerts stares, mesmerized, at the contents of the chests. It is gold dust, mined in the interior of West Africa, in places the Denkyira carefully keep secret. The material is still raw, with a lot of impurities: sand, bits of stone, earth. Chests full of glittering grit, which will only be refined and smelted into gold in Holland. Nevertheless, its value is high. A lot has been paid for it. Cowrie shells. Bags full.

He turns, frowning, to the two clerks, who stand respectfully behind their folding table, and to the chief accountant, who serves as a witness. "Got it?"

The chief accountant nods obediently. "Yes, Your Excellency. Six hundred and fifty *marks**, four ounces."

Sweerts grunts with satisfaction. It is the result of four months of work — of negotiating and haggling, of talking and bribing, of deliveries here and there along the coast, from Akkra to Elmina, always in small quantities. "Those mining sites are sacred," he remarks. "They claim God Himself placed that gold there. Not *our* God, of course, but theirs."

"As you say, sir."

"But I'd give a lot to mine that stuff myself. It would save a lot of time."

"Completely agree with you."

The clerks write in their cash ledger and carefully check off the list. "Please sign here, Your Excellency."

Sweerts scans the lines, his index finger hovering over the paper. One hundred and twenty marks and a bit per chest. Two hundred and ninety-nine guilders per mark, total value 188,645 guilders. A fortune. He signs with the quill. "All right, seal them."

The papers are sprinkled with sand, then folded and tied with ribbons. One of the clerks melts the wax and carefully drips it over the paper and ribbon. "Your ring, sir, if you please."

Sweerts presses his seal into the hot wax. "*Our* God does not lay gold at our feet," he continues, licking the sore at the corner of his mouth with the tip of his tongue. "No, ours makes us toil in the sweat of our brow." He chuckles. "But the Company will be pleased, gentlemen. For a while. Only for a very short while. Because it is always hungry." He nods to the patiently waiting blacksmith, pointing at the chests: "Lock them up."

The late evening brings rain again. It streams along walls and windows, drips over the sills of his office, forming small puddles on the wooden floor. It is dark. He has only a single candle lit, but that is how he likes it so late in the evening when he can finally have some privacy. He gazes outside, his eyes searching the bay, looking for the return ship anchored there. Curtains of water obscure the view, but he can see the lights of the stern lanterns on board. There, on that Dutch ship, deep in the hold, lies his precious gold, tucked away between stacks of ivory and bales of baize, guarded by sixty soldiers and twenty-two pieces of artillery. Time will tell if that is enough, if no Turkish pirates appear along the way, or perhaps a Spaniard with enough courage.

---

* The 'mark' was used by the Dutch as a standard unit for gold, measuring 800 grams.

Danger is always lurking.

Through the rain, he sees the orange-yellow flashes of gunfire. Seven in a row. Only a moment later does the rumbling follow. Faint. Far away, for the rain drowns out everything. It is a farewell salute to him and the Company.

In response, the heavy thuds from the fort on Jago Hill sound behind him, a much heavier sound that reverberates through the floor. The lights at sea are moving. Very faintly, he sees the sails — tiny white spots in a vast darkness. There goes his vulnerable return ship, heading for Holland with two or three months of uncertainty ahead. The director-general realizes he is powerless. His cargo is at the mercy of fate.

At night, Burghoutsz wanders aimlessly through the settlement next to the castle. Beyond the district of the whites — with their typically Dutch brick facades — begins the domain of the asafo companies. The houses give way to huts and muddy paths; he slips and slides past fences of bundles of branches and round walls of clay. Chickens scatter from under his feet. Here and there, loose goats and pigs roam. There are sounds of singing. The rhythmic pounding of drums. The scents of exotic foods. In the flickering light of open fires, groups of young black men stand. As he passes, they look at him defiantly. Few whites dare to come here, but he tempts fate. It's not bravery or a need to prove himself, more a matter of indifference.

He buys palm wine and visits cockfights. The old ringmasters know him by now. They smile at him, encouraging him.

"This rooster will bring you fortune, *aene*."

But his favourite always ends up a bloody heap of feathers in the sand.

"*Eééh*," they shout, eagerly stuffing the cowrie shells of the white visitor into their pouches. "Better luck next time."

But he doesn't care.

On a whim, he buys *voacanga*, the seeds that bring hallucinations, and afterward he wanders dazed through the night, staring at swirling shapes and colours, at the spirits in the branches of the trees, listening to the intense rhythm of the drums, while the rain pours over his hot skin. He looks at all those black faces around him, small, large, beautiful, and ugly. Girls. Women. The supply is endless, and the voacanga sets his loins on fire. But it does not satisfy him, never, they are living dolls, and he makes mechanical movements, lying on a mat on the floor in a hut with a black pimp at the entrance. Sweat. Wet. Groaning. His body responds as it should, but his mind takes no part in it.

And after the haze, he ends up on the beach, searching for the wind and the smell of the ocean, his back against a rock, his face turned east, waiting for the sky to light up. And eventually, inevitably, there is the African sun, majestic and blood-red. For a moment, his gaze softens. Something of a memory breaks through in the closed spaces of his mind — images, shadows, old ghosts. But he quickly pushes it away, he has become very good at that.

8 The Shepherd of Souls and the Smooth Talker

"(...) It is particularly the beginning and the end of the rainy season that we fear the most, as these have a very detrimental effect on our state of health.
An analysis of the cases of illness during this season seems appropriate. It appears to me that the approach of our English neighbours, namely treatment with opium, emetics, bloodletting, brandy, and water, is too general, and this is evidenced by the unfortunate results they achieve. The new remedy calomel seems to provide some relief here and there, but it is available in such small quantities that we can hardly incorporate it into our treatment.
As for the form in which the cases of illness present themselves, they can be described as follows:
Severe, pressing pain in the frontal sinuses and lower back; intense pulsation of the arteries in the forehead and neck; great restlessness, insomnia, marked loss of strength; hollowed face and emaciation; pulse hard, very frequent, 160-180 beats per minute (in children no longer countable); much thirst, no appetite, pasty taste in the mouth, nausea, and tendency to vomit.
The most severe and dangerous cases occur in those who are addicted to strong drink."

From: Correspondence of Chief Chirurgeon Zacharias Augustijns to the Collegium Medicum of Amsterdam, September 1687

Beyond Elmina, across the Benya River, lies Jago Hill, with the brand-new Fort Coenraadsburg on its summit. High ramparts overlook the bay, guarding the Dutch interests, supported by enormous forty-two-pounder cannons.

The white walls shimmer in the heat of the midday sun, which stands directly overhead. On the high walls, there is no shade except under some old sails stretched over the ramparts with ropes, but even beneath those, it is stiflingly hot. The soldiers stand sweating on watch amid the heavy cast pieces and cannonballs stacked in racks, looking out over Elmina, the settlement, the bay, and the ocean. Most take it easy. They sit on low stools or lean against the heavy wooden gun carriages, drinking lukewarm beer from earthenware jugs. Coenraadsburg is a place of utmost boredom unless you are sick with dysentery or some other contagious disease, in which case you are laid down in the infirmary below, where you wait for recovery or — in many cases — death. The soldiers have grown blind to it; they have lost too many comrades to feel pity anymore. The sight of blood, filth, pus, and vomit numbs them. Even the stench is something they eventually get used to.

Around midday, they invariably see a black, crow-like figure climbing the hill toward the fort, his back bent, the inseparable Bible in hand. Reverend Duisterbloem is a dutiful visitor. Tirelessly, he enters the dim halls of the infirmary, where soldiers and Company officers lie side by side on mattresses and straw sacks, to offer comfort with God's word.

The misery before his eyes tugs like an iron hook at his soul: young men who should be in the prime of their lives languish here like emaciated, pale skeletons in the half-light, in spaces he has come to see as the antechambers of hell. There is virtually nothing to be done, and what is done does not help, except on rare occasions, which, in his view, is more a result of the fickle grace of God than the skill and knowledge of the chirurgeon and his assistants. The reverend does not have much faith in medicine.

"Have faith in God," he whispers to the men. "Believe in the Lord Jesus."

Their hollow-eyed gazes do not give him much hope. The patients are often too far gone, but that hardly dims his fire: every soul he can save is one. His long, thin fingers stroke fevered foreheads and gaunt, hollow cheeks. "Keep your courage, lad. It is not over yet."

Sometimes, there is a hand that grabs his arm, and he sees eyes seeking contact in a moment of clarity.

"Pray for me, Reverend."

"I pray, my son."

"For my children."

"Jesus will care for them."

The tears he sees are the tears of God. There is no peace in death so far from home. He lays the palm of his hand on a thin, labouring chest. Beneath it, the fever burns, and the heat radiates up his own arm. A heart gone wild. *Thump. Thump. Thump.* And spirits crawl along the ceiling.

Where is God?

"Go to sleep, boy."

"I can't..."

"Jesus is waiting." The reverend looks around and sees nothing but darkness.

Midday in Elmina.

Quassie Patoe, the ensign of the Enyampa, is leading his boys today, and, as so often, he has them parade on the square in front of the castle. He himself stands a little apart, one hand resting on a simple sundial that the whites once placed there. The sunstone indicates the time, they say, but that is one of those typical white assertions because Quassie Patoe doesn't even know what time is. Whites talk in hours and minutes, but that means nothing to him. It's almost midday now, he thinks, glancing at the sun with a knowing look; nearly time to eat, to take a nap, and perhaps to tickle one of his wives. He grins lustfully at the thought.

His young warriors perform aggressive, rhythmic dances, with spears and shields clattering in time and arm and ankle bands jingling, stomping on the hard clay. Their war cries, filled with filthy, vulgar insults directed at the other asafo companies, the mulattos, the locals, and even the whites, ring out loudly and sometimes even threateningly. It's a good batch, this generation, Quassie Patoe judges with satisfaction, and he should know, for he has trained many of these young lions. Their ostentatious aggressiveness is not merely a means but a fundamental goal, an expression of independence and solidarity. It is political, you might say, just like the Dutch Prince's flags they carry, bearing the Company's mark and the number six in the white field, the number of the Enyampa. If he trains his boys well and makes them strong, clever, unbeatable warriors, it is possible to stay ahead of the Allade and Assamfoe, numbers four and five. And then he himself remains the most important man in Elmina.

Of course.

Quassie Patoe wipes some sweat from his gleaming chest. It is time to rest, he decides. He looks around and is about to call his lieutenants together when he sees a black woman approaching out of the corner of his eye.

He starts. His eyes search for a way out, but his boys are watching him. They have seen the woman too, they know who she is, and all eyes are on him. If he makes a run for it now, he will lose face.

He turns around so that he faces her. "*Ackie*, sister," he greets her.

Quameno Ewussi's wife is panting. She had walked quickly because Quassie Patoe is hard to approach — he has not responded to her requests for a meeting — so when she suddenly saw him standing there on the square, she seized her chance. "Where is my husband?" she asks, without greeting him.

"*Eééh?*" Quassie Patoe feigns surprise. He smiles. His eyes scan her body. She is a beautiful woman, he thinks. Still in good shape, despite many children. He likes them sturdy. His own wives are sturdy too. "We did not succeed, sister," he says in a regretful tone.

"You have money; you must pay."

"There is no money. There is never money. Only the whites have money."

She places her hands on her hips, a stubborn look on her face. "You must see to it that he is released. He belongs to the Enyampa. He is family."

Quassie Patoe nods. He keeps smiling. But he thinks: Why won't she leave? Why does she keep nagging? Why doesn't she accept her fate? He says: "We are doing everything we can, sister."

"I spoke to the white boss. He tells me that Quassie Patoe has not made contact."

That is a painful statement. Quassie Patoe looks at his lieutenants, who have gathered around them and are listening attentively. "I have had many discussions," he replies calmly. "With important people and chiefs, to see if there is any gold to be freed up. Day and night, I have been working. The whites do not accept cowrie shells, goats, or copper wire. They want gold. But how can you repay two hundred and fifty guilders? That is a lot of money. No one dares take that risk. People do not want to suffer losses." He now sees something of despair in her eyes. He thinks to himself: It can't be helped. The sun will simply rise again tomorrow.

"Then you must replace him," she says hoarsely. "There are plenty of negroes in the forest. Or in the villages along the river. The white boss will accept that. He said so himself."

Quassie Patoe furrows his brow. He looks meaningfully at his lieutenants.

"Who then?" he asks. He points to one of them. "You?"

The lieutenant makes a dismissive gesture. "No, ensign."

"No?" He looks around, searching. Points to another. "You, then? Will you take Quameno Ewussi's place?"

"Of course not."

They all shake their heads and lower their eyes.

Quassie Patoe places his hand on the woman's shoulder, but she angrily shrugs him off. Tears well up in her eyes. Anger gives way to sorrow.

"No one goes on the boat willingly, sister. There are no slaves, not from here, nor from Akim or Acani, from Adam or Aquamba. The whites can barely get slaves themselves. They fight over them, the Dutch and the English and the Brandenburgers. And the French! The Portuguese!" He waves a finger in front of her nose. "Or do you want to sell free people from the village? Would that not be just as unjust for them as it is for you and your husband now?"

Now he has her where he wants her. He sees it in her shoulders, which suddenly slump. He sighs, looks at his lieutenants again, and spreads his hands helplessly. "I'm sorry. I have pleaded for him, but the whites give nothing away. They have no feelings, like we do." He stares for a few moments at the tricolour flags on the square, fluttering cheerfully in the sea breeze. Red, white, and blue.

9 Voyage to Poquesoe

"(...) For some time now, we have been dealing with the difficulty that the traders of the Ashanti do indeed regularly offer slaves from other tribes, but they increasingly wish to be paid in weapons. This creates an impasse. The Ashanti will use these against the Denkyira and the Aowin; they have decided to seize power in the interior.

It is difficult for us to determine our position in this matter: a war will certainly yield us more slaves, but on the other hand, it will decimate gold production. And vice versa, as we have experienced for some time now.

Gold takes precedence over slaves!

We have, therefore, consistently refused the blacks offered by the Ashanti in Elmina, accepting the calculated risk that they will sell these to the English at Cape Coast Castle. So be it. But the supply is also being hampered because the kingdom of Wassa apparently considers itself strong enough to threaten the inland trade routes; we receive more and more reports that merchants are being attacked, robbed, and sometimes even murdered. We have reported this before, but in the meantime, the gold supply to Axim has also been endangered. This is intolerable. We will have to take measures, if necessary, by force.

Thus, the 285 slaves we currently have in storage have, for the most part, been brought in from Akkra and Sekondi, and to a lesser extent from the factories at Commanie, Mouree, and Bercoe."

From: Letters of Director-General Nicholaas Sweerts to the Directors of the West India Company, autumn 1687

"Welcome aboard," says the skipper of the Dutch hooker as Burghoutsz and Graauw climb aboard. He surveys his new, unfamiliar passengers with undisguised curiosity. "Take two men to Pocquesoe, said the director-general. But he didn't mention who you are." He's a tall, gaunt fellow, much younger than Burghoutsz. His blond beard flutters in the wind. "You're the skipper of that slave ship that's been lying in the bay for weeks. I'm surprised to see you here."

Burghoutsz looks around with bloodshot eyes. The hooker is a small two-master, a coastal trader used by the Company as a workhorse. "So am I," he merely replies. His unshaven face is gaunt.

"Vloet's the name," says the skipper without extending his hand. His voice is nasal; where his right nostril used to be, there is now just a hole surrounded by scar tissue. A messy tuft of nose hair sticks out defiantly. "At your service." He stands wide-legged on his aft deck, one fist on the tiller. His eyes shift to Gillis Graauw, who stands sullen and stocky in his duffel coat. "And you are?"

"He's my assistant," says Burghoutsz.

Graauw grunts an inaudible greeting, shuffling his rough clogs across the deck.

"Whatever you say," Vloet chuckles. "A real lackey." He clears his throat and points to the hatch on the foredeck. "This is a shabby little boat, gentlemen. I'm afraid there's no guest quarters, so you'll have to bunk with the crew." He whistles through his fingers and gestures frantically towards the long bowsprit. "On deck! Get that anchor up!" And upwards, where a few sailors are hanging in the main mast: "Make sail, lads, we're leaving. Loosen those seizings, goddammit. Move!"

The hooker is sluggish and slow, but she plows steadily forward, with the wind slightly ahead of the beam, causing the rigging to sing and the bow wave to splash over the sides. Elmina disappears to leeward, and now only a bright green coastline remains, stretching far to the west.

Burghoutsz uses his spyglass. The ocean is empty. No ship in sight.

"We're staying close to the coast," Vloet explains. "I've got no guns except for two rusty swivel cannons, so at the first sign of trouble, we'll try to escape into shallow water. If necessary, I'll run the whole thing aground. They say Du Casse is in the area."

"The French pirate?"

"A bona fide *capitaine de vaisseau* by now, sir, he's got his privateer papers from the king himself. This autumn, he took an English three-master near Axim. You can bet he's got his sights set on Dutch ships."

Burghoutsz peers through his spyglass, following the curve of the horizon. "He wouldn't dare come here. Sweerts has a cruiser and two frigates in service."

Vloet looks at him mockingly. "I had a cousin on Gorée, off the coast of Senegal. When Du Casse attacked in '77, he was heavily outnumbered, but he slaughtered every Dutchman, even after they surrendered. We never heard from my cousin again." He crosses himself and glances at the sky. "I tell you: that man is the devil."

At noon, the sun is shot. "Four knots and a fathom," says Vloet, still holding the wet log board. "We won't go much faster with this tub of a ship. But we've passed Commanie." He watches a fishing canoe bobbing on the swell a few cables' lengths off the port side. The native fishermen wave, and he grins back maliciously. "Black devils. They'd slit your throat with a smile." He turns to Burghoutsz, who is leaning against the railing, smoking a pipe. "With any luck, you'll be near Pocquesoe tomorrow morning. Are you going to tell me what you're up to?"

Burghoutsz calmly exhales smoke. "Taking stock."

Vloet glances at him, opens his mouth to make a comment, then shrugs and looks up. His eyes slide along the foresail of the main mast, and he gives the tiller a little pull. "Ease those sheets!" he shouts forward, where a couple of startled men jump into action. He spits overboard and peers at Burghoutsz from beneath bushy eyebrows. "You mean spying."

"None of your business."

"No, I'm just a former Batavia sailor, second mate on an East Indiaman with three hundred souls on board, dishonourably discharged for drunkenness and insubordination. Believe me, I'm not proud of it. Since then, I've been rotting away on this damned coast. But sometimes, a man could use some help."

"How'd you get that hole in your nose?"

Vloet defiantly tugs at the tuft of nose hair now sticking straight out to the side. "Mutiny. They caught me, and stuck a red-hot sail needle into my face.

Would've hanged me if I hadn't had a papist skipper. Catholics believe in forgiveness, you know. Anyway, they kicked me out, and besides the West India Company, no one else will have me. They pay poorly, too. By God, how poorly they pay!" He grins, makes a dismissive gesture, studies the sky, and tastes the wind. "Southeast by east. It'll rain within three glasses, mark my words."

An hour and a half later, dark cloud formations swell. They drift low above the water, overtake the hooker, block out the sun, and let through no more light than a few green, diffuse Jacob's ladders. The rain comes quickly, a tropical downpour drenches the ocean, with heavy drops falling almost straight down, hampering the wind, which now blows in gusts, erratic and unpredictable.

Vloet struggles with the tiller. "Hardly any pressure on the rudder!" he shouts, soaked to the skin while trying to keep an eye on the coast. "Watch that bowsprit, sir!" Even with full sails, the boat just manages to stay into the wind.

A clap of thunder shatters the silence. The hooker struggles through the bubble-covered water, now making no more than one or two knots, a slow shadow between the veils of rain.

Evening. Apart from those on watch, the crew takes shelter in the cramped quarters of the forepeak, with Gillis Graauw as a silent, sullen guest of honour. Shoulder to shoulder, seven men sit around the mess while the cook sets out a meal of boiled peas and fried mackerel.

With wooden spoons, they hungrily scoop from the shared pot.

But the cook doesn't eat. He stands hunched under the low ceiling, studying Graauw with intense interest. Graauw has his own spoon. Before eating, he habitually taps his hardtack on the table—to shake off any worms. "You, sir, are a seaman," the cook concludes.

Graauw looks up. His gray eyes gleam in the dim light from the single deck prism above. "So what?"

The shipmates fall silent, their movements frozen. They stare at him suspiciously.

Graauw, unfazed, takes a bite, chews, swallows, and leans back, his gnarled fingers gripping the edge of the table. "Your deck hasn't been scrubbed in weeks," he says quietly. "The woolding on the anchor cable is worn out, and there's not a drop of tar on the rigging. Loose lines. Swinging blocks. And I'd bet your keel is fouled from stem to stern. This is a damn sloppy ship."

More silence. No one eats. Only the sound of rain on the deck.

"Damn it," says the cook finally. "A real boatswain. Just what we needed."

As darkness falls, the clouds form a solid blanket, and the rain falls steadily. The wind picks up, shifts a degree or two to the east, and now blows more abaft than beam. With tightly stretched sails, the old hooker finds its resolve and new strength. The blunt bow pushes the water foaming ahead.

Vloet and Burghoutsz sit in the cramped skipper's cabin at the stern of the boat. There's barely any room: a small table and two nailed-down wooden stools, and when they sit opposite each other, their noses almost touch. On the table, a storm lamp holds a flickering candle, casting light on a map of the coast.

"Listen," says Vloet, tapping on the map. "I'll drop anchor by the fort, on the village side. They know me, I come there often. Sometimes, they have some trade for me. Mostly wood. Or dried fish. You're just a merchant traveling with me. Maybe you rented some cargo space. Maybe you're buying ivory. Or fruit. It's all good, merchants are coming and going all the time." He winks. "The Brandenburgers are our friends, you know? Since last year, there's been a treaty."

"Sweerts has a very different opinion on that."

"Of course. That fort is nothing more than a cover for Zeelanders to bypass the Company's monopoly. Are you interested in slaves?"

Burghoutsz's face grows suspicious, and Vloet snorts disdainfully. "Do you think I'm an idiot?" He points a finger: "What else would a slaver like you be doing here?" With his right hand, he reaches for a leather wine pouch hanging from a nail in the wall behind him. "It's hotter in here than on the gun deck of the *Ruyter*, damn it." He noisily gulps down the wine, eyeing Burghoutsz slyly from under his eyebrows. "But I'll tell you something: if it's about tricking those Brandenburgers, I'm your man."

At night, they lie in their hammocks in the crew quarters, swaying in sync with the rest of the crew, while the rain pounds relentlessly on the deck. The air is humid and hot, and they can feel the moisture on their skin. No one sleeps deeply. From afar, the rumbling of thunder can occasionally be heard, and above, the faint ringing of the ship's bell.

Gillis Graauw hears everything. Displaced from his own ship, he cannot sleep, lying wide awake in an unfamiliar darkness, listening warily to the sounds around him as outside the hooker stubbornly cuts through the swell.

10 *Back: Gillis Graauw*

After a life full of hardships and violence, he looks older than he is. Short, stocky, and wiry, his face is dominated by a long scar on the right side, running from forehead to chin—the legacy of an exploding powder room. His eyes watch the world with suspicion, always ready to strike with half-pike, fists, or knife. Only at sea does he find peace. The ship is his home; there are no press gangs or constables, no women to belittle him, no temptations to get him into trouble.

Waterland, 1649
Little Gillis sits on the step in front of the house. He's a funny-looking kid, much too skinny, with wild hair that sticks out in all directions.

"Go," says Sis, who stands next to him, even though she isn't his sister—not that Gillis is old enough to understand that. He stands up right away. He looks up to Sis, and he'll do anything for her.

He runs across the street and disappears among the people. The gentleman is easy to spot, even for a boy so small. He's large and plump, with a huge plume on his hat. Little Gillis weaves confidently between legs and skirts. The gentleman wobbles a bit, his path far from straight. That's from the krak*, Gillis knows. Sis told him so. Men sit in taverns and drink krak, and then they're drunk and don't pay attention.

He follows the gentleman around the corner and into an alley. It's much less crowded here. You need patience, Sis says, but when the moment comes, you've got to be quick, Gillis.

And he is. Quick as water. With a sly little loop, he edges along the walls and suddenly, clumsily, bumps right into the gentleman.

"Whát?" The man staggers, stumbling toward the wall with both hands out, barely managing to catch himself. "You damned monkey!"

But little Gillis is already gone. He's tucked the heavy purse under his shirt. No one will notice, Sis says. Sis knows everything.

Mother is less fun. She snaps at him because, during the day, she lies on the straw mat, fully dressed and worn out, and doesn't want to be disturbed. She has no patience, and if he's a bother, he gets a slap on the head. "Get lost, you little brat." Sometimes, he hates her. Then he feels something in his gut, something that wants to burst out. He glares at her while shielding his head with his arms.

"What are you looking at, you little wretch?" she laughs nastily, and then he gets a few more slaps. "That Gillis of mine," she sometimes says, "he's a fierce one, he'll end up beating someone to death one day."

In the evening, she disappears, dolled up and trailing the scent of cheap perfume. He, Sis, and the boys then lie on the same straw mat, under a piece of old canvas cloth that serves as their blanket. There isn't a house, just a simple wooden shack built onto another hovel. The plank walls are thin, and the roof leaks when it rains, but it's not bad—they almost never go hungry, and all those young bodies together generate plenty of warmth.

Gillis enjoys talking with Sis a little more before bed, doing math games. "One plus one is two."

"And three plus ten?"

He strains his brain. "Go to hell," he says. *Sis can always come up with something he doesn't have an answer for.*

---

* Krak = Dutch slang: corn brandy or Dutch gin

She giggles. "You're just a dumb little brat."

Mother comes back in the morning with bloodshot eyes and reeking of gin. Other smells, too: sweat, smoke, and stale beer. Then she laughs and talks to herself while kicking him and the other kids out of the shack. "Get out and earn your bread."

And that's how the day begins.

The country houses of the rich line the Amstel River. In winter, they are usually deserted. With a small group, they stroll along the dike, Sis leading the way. It's very simple, Gillis knows. Sis points out a house, and then they spend some time watching. "Keep a good eye out, Gillis," she says. Is anyone home? Are there guards? Are the guards drunk? (very often, they are).

Sis makes the call. "Go inside," she orders.

He's still small enough to slip through the bars of the gates most of the time. If not, they give him a boost. And if there's no dog, he just walks right in (he doesn't care for dogs). Every house has its weak spots. If there are guards, a door is usually left open—that's actually the easiest way: throw a little stone, wait, and by the time the guard goes to check, he's already inside. Or he takes the basement window: tap the glass, and hop. Slip-slide, easy as that.

The houses are beautifully furnished. Rugs on the floors and the scent of polish. Porcelain lining the walls. Paintings everywhere. Sometimes, he can stay inside for an hour just because he enjoys it. "Don't steal anything big," Sis always says. "Little things, Gillis. Gold or money, or jewellery." He knows. He has all the time in the world.

Look, a dollhouse. It fascinates him. He kneels there, soaking in the details. So finely made. A man, a woman, a servant. Three floors. Rooms with beds just like real ones. And in the attic, there's a girl. She's playing with... a dollhouse! It almost takes his breath away. He's so absorbed in it that he loses track of time. Only when he's yanked up roughly by his hair does he snap back to reality.

"None of them are any good," says the bailiff, pointing at Gillis and his mother. "That little rascal steals whatever he can get his hands on. The whole family's the same: rotten to the core."

"And the father?" asks the magistrate from behind his desk.

"Unknown, sir. As I mentioned, the mother is a whore, already banished from Amsterdam, and now they roam around Waterland, hungry for loot. There's a whole gang of other children with them, too."

The magistrate sighs. "Always the same story." He leans forward, looking at them sternly. "You are a disgrace to your family, madam."

Hands on her hips, she glares back defiantly. "A body can't live on air."

"You're incorrigible. And your son is a thief."

"He ain't never hurt nobody."

"If he stays with you, he's bound for the gallows, that's certain." He looks at the boy, seeing nothing that gives him hope. Already looks mean, he thinks, the wickedness oozes from him. "Does he go to school?"

"No money."

"My patience is at an end. I am revoking your parental rights."

"Wha'?"

"He's going to the orphanage. We'll see if they can make a decent human being out of him."

They stare at him, standing in a circle around him. There's no way out.

"You're the smallest," says Beanstalk, the leader. "So you do everything we say, got it? Everything."

Gillis doesn't look back. He stares at the floor. The dormitory is large, with rows of beds along the walls, each bed shared by three kids under a horse blanket. He doesn't know any of them. He misses Sis.

"You gotta greet us, bow to us, to all of us." Beanstalk gives him a shove. "Bow."

Gillis looks up. "I don't bow," he says calmly. "To no one."

That causes laughter. The boys around him giggle, but Beanstalk just glares and smacks him across the head. "Bow."

Gillis stands firm. He gets hit again. His head spins. Something stirs in his stomach, trying to break free, and at the third slap, he springs forward like a coil. His small fists fly, but they don't do much damage.

Beanstalk sneers, "You're a nasty little wretch, aren't you?" He throws Gillis to the floor and starts kicking him. The others join in. Gillis curls up into a ball and lets them. No big deal. A little pain. His nose is bleeding, and that'll pass. But the anger in his belly burns.

Gray days, black nights. By day, sailcloth is stitched with needles and marlinspikes, and by night, the dormitory becomes a Roman arena, there are always tensions. Gillis keeps to himself as much as possible, but Beanstalk never lets him rest. "Bow, you little scumbag."

Gillis doesn't bow.

And takes his punishment.

He just needs to grow a bit bigger and stronger. Not much, because size and strength aren't what matter most, he's discovered; some of them already shrink back when he looks them straight in the eyes.

In the winter, the evenings are long. By mid-afternoon, darkness crawls over the ceiling of the dormitory, filling the corners and gaps. Outside, snow falls; inside, the never-ending struggle rages on.

"Bow."

"No."

The first blow. This time, he blocks it. His arms and wrists have grown stronger from stitching sails with the needle.

Beanstalk looks up, surprised. "Are you fighting back, you little rat?" The fists come one after the other. Against his head. Against his nose. Into his liver. Gillis resists in silence. Blood runs down his cheek, and his left eye begins to swell. But the rage in his gut pulses steadily. He's waited, just like Sis once advised him. *When the moment comes, you have to act fast, Gillis.* In his sleeve rests the sail needle, carefully sharpened, its triangular point razor-sharp, with a block of wood as the handle. He's been working on it silently for weeks.

Báng! His head spins, but he shakes it off. Beanstalk grows overconfident. Maybe his arms are getting tired.

Gillis seizes the moment. The needle slips from his sleeve, and he doesn't hesitate. His opponent's face twists in shock as he grabs his throat, where a ragged hole has opened up. Blood spurts out. Slowly, he staggers back, eyes wide, with Gillis trailing like a fighting dog behind him. *Keep going. Revenge. Retribution.* The needle flashes again, easily slicing through the nerves of the defending fingers. Easy. Just like that. The boys shout for him to stop, but Gillis grins and doesn't hear them. He's only just begun.

Amsterdam, 1651

The Rasphuis. That's where they put him. The prisoners are labourers, sawing brazilwood into fibres. Gruelling work. The food is bad, the days are long. Big men break under the conditions, unable to withstand them. Gillis runs errands in the courtyard, he's far too small to operate the large twelve-bladed saws. He walks there among murderers, rapists, and madmen, passing men being heavily flogged and overseers who prefer to strike rather than speak. It's a strange, sinister world covered in red dust; the stuff creeps into hair and clothes, into pores and skin folds.

Sometimes, parents come by with their children. They use him as a lesson.

"Look, that's what happens when you grow up to be worthless."

"You're going to hell," says a rich boy with chubby cheeks.

Gillis looks back coldly. He's been in hell for a long time already. If he could, he'd do something to that boy because the anger in him is always simmering.

Once, he gets a real visitor. Sis. She had to pay a stiver* for the privilege.

She cries when she sees him. "How are you, Gillis?"

He shrugs, staring at the ground. He's as thin as a rake, with sunken cheeks and hollow eyes, his hair and face covered in dark red dust.

"Are you coming to get me?" he asks.

"No, of course not. You almost killed that boy, Gillis." She shakes her head. He's only ten years old; his age is the only reason they didn't hang him straight away. "It's a miracle you're still alive."

"You're still my sis."

"I'm not your sis." She bites her lip.

Sudden anger flashes in his eyes. "Yes, you are," he says softly. A tear rolls down his dust-covered face. It mixes with the brazilwood powder and looks like blood.

"Where is mother?"

"She's disappeared. They chased her out of Waterland. I don't know where she is."

He says nothing. He doesn't miss his mother, but he misses Sis. With Sis, everything was better. He often thinks about those warm nights under the old canvas cloth. Back then, everything was good. Now, everything is wrong. Is she abandoning him? Sis? He wipes away the tears with his sleeve.

"I have to go." She stands up. Her mouth tightens a little. "The magistrate says you might go to sea. With the Admiralty. They're always looking for new sailors. And there's a war coming with the English."

That means nothing to him. He looks at her. "Will you come back?"

"I don't know, Gillis."

The North Sea, spring of 1652

Up and down. The powder monkeys handle the ammunition because they're small, fast, and don't have to duck. The powder magazine is all the way down in the belly of the ship, hidden in darkness and foul air. The master gunner is a shadow behind a small window with small square panes. Gillis waits in a line of soot-covered children. When it's his turn, bags and bandoliers are slung over his shoulders.

"Move it!" A boot pushes him on, and off he goes again. Always running because

---

* A stiver (Dutch 'stuiver') was a coin worth 1/20th of a guilder

if you're slow, you'll feel the cat.

Above, the rumbling and thunder never cease. Explosions. The whistle of cannonballs. A roaring bosun drives him forward. When he reaches the upper gun deck, he can barely make out his path. Thick, yellow-brown smoke billows in the passageway. The sharp stench of saltpetre burns in his nose. Shadows of men. The wooden deck, covered with an inch of sand, is a dark red mess of blood and water, guts, and limbs. The sounds pound in his ears. Shouting. Screaming. The barking of 32-pound cannons. After every shot, the guns jerk violently backward, barely restrained by their breeching tackle.

"Number four! Ammo!"

He rushes forward, paper cartridges clutched in his hands.

The gunners have no patience. They grab, shove, take what they need, and roughly push him out of the way again. In the harsh, smoke-filled beams of light from the gunports, he sees them toil, their bare bodies black as pitch, with bright red burns on their arms and legs. No more faces. No more individuals. Living ghosts. The heat is unbearable.

Bóóm!

Flying debris. The ship suddenly heels over. He falls and slides across the planks like a projectile, grabbing hold of a rope in blind panic.

"Aaaaaaaaaaaaawwww!" someone howls.

He scrambles to his feet, clutching the damp woollen firecloths hung around, checking his legs, arms, belly, and chest. No blood. No breaks. Not a scratch.

"Get that body out of here!"

Four powder monkeys pull together at the slippery arms, but dead bodies are stubborn and don't give easily. Panting and sniffling, they manage to drag the corpse towards the opening to the hold. There, they pile them up, just like dolls. *Don't look, Gillis*, flashes through his mind. *They say dead eyes are dangerous.* Instead, he sneaks a glance outside, inhaling a brief breath of fresh air. The sea is unrecognizable. Smoke. Ships everywhere. Burning. Firing. The enemy trailing in a long line to leeward. English. Dozens of cannons. Above him, the screech of grapeshot and the sharp clicks of canister shot. Men in the rigging, struggling with shredded sails.

A smack hits the back of his head. "Get below, you!"

With eyes streaming from the smoke, he pulls himself back into the suffocating chaos. Down again. Along the narrow companionway into the hold. There's only one candle burning in a niche near the powder magazine—no more light allowed here; too dangerous. He waits. The line grows shorter, even powder monkeys die. There's no time to think. Just as it's his turn, another explosion rings out, deeper, heavier this time. Different. Sharp, successive blasts of splintering wood, followed by a prolonged, groaning creak, like the death cry of a wounded beast. Three, four more thuds midship. The planks beneath his feet vibrate so violently that he nearly loses his balance. Somewhere above, a distant scream, muffled. A yellow-green, unnaturally bright flash of light flares behind the niche. The small square panes shatter into fragments, and sudden heat scorches his skin. Wood splinters shoot through the darkness like arrows, and one of them slices through the skin of his forehead, ripping open the right side of his face down to his chin. Immediately afterward, there's a high-pitched, hissing sound as all the air is sucked out of the hold. The ship tilts. Little Gillis tilts with it, spinning through the pitch-black darkness. Somehow, his fingers find something to grip. He recognizes the steps of the aft ladder, now on their side. Beyond them, a sliver of daylight. With rasping breaths, he claws and scrambles across the planks toward the narrow stairs leading up to the deck. Fresh air fills his lungs. Behind him comes a deafening roar, like that of a lion, and it takes him a moment to realize what it is: the onrushing water.

11 Mussulman Ali Sets an Example

"No believer should kill another believer except by accident. Anyone who kills a believer by accident must set free a believing slave and pay compensation to the family of the deceased unless they forgo it out of charity. If the deceased belonged to a people at war with you and was a believer, then freeing a believing slave is enough. If he belonged to a people with whom you have a treaty, then compensation must be paid to his family, and a believing slave must be set free."

From: the Quran, Surah 4: 92

⚓

A few miles north of Pocquesoe, Mussulman Ali finally orders the group to stop. His scouts discover an open, well-concealed spot in the forest, close to a stream of fresh, clear water. He personally inspects the location, carefully prodding the ground with a stick, searching for ant nests or snakes, and tasting the water from the stream, which winds westward toward the Kpani River—following it would naturally lead to Pocquesoe.

It is a satisfying spot: to the north lies the territory of the Wassa, which he has deliberately avoided—the Wassa are ruthless marauders—and to the east and west lie the scattered kingdoms and tribal alliances of the Ahante, most of which are allied with the Dutch. Danger is everywhere, he knows, but he has reached his destination unnoticed after a week of hardships. After offering a prayer of thanks to God—*Insha'Allah*—he turns to his patiently waiting overseers and declares, "We make camp here."

The slaves sit huddled together on the bare ground. They are exhausted, dusty, and sweaty. But he has lost no one, and not a single one is injured.

"You are strong," he says encouragingly, searching for the right words. "Tired but healthy. You will rest. There is fresh water. There is food." He points to the blue sky. "It will rain soon, but tonight you will stay dry. You will build an enclosure of branches and twigs, with waterproof cloths above."

He senses their sullen apathy and crouches down, wiping the sweat from his face. "You no longer need to walk or run. That is over. It is safe here."

For a fraction of a second, he catches the gaze of one of them, a large man in the middle of the group. He recognizes that look. Hostility. Maybe pride. He says, "You feel you've been treated unfairly, but that is a useless thought. This is your fate. No one will come to rescue you. You are no longer Denkyira." His eyes remain fixed on the man in the middle, whose gaze has now shifted to the ground. A sturdy, muscular black man, he thinks. Probably a good worker, worth a high price. But in every profession, there are rules, and unwritten laws that must be followed. He knows the chaos that arises when authority is not absolute, when there is even a hint of doubt.

"Accept your fate, children. Obey and live," he says, briefly closing his eyes and kneading the moist red earth with his fingers. Then he motions to one of his overseers. "Untie that man, Mohammed."

"Yes, *efendi*." The overseer strides purposefully into the group of slaves. He points to the large, muscular black man in the middle. "This one?"

"Bring him here."

With a hammer, the slave's wrist and ankle chains are removed, and he is forced forward.

Mussulman Ali wearily rises to his feet. He sizes up the prisoner, who is a full head taller than he is. "Look at me."

The eyes turn in his direction. Mussulman Ali sees a flash of anger, a smouldering fire. No, he thinks, I was not mistaken.

"Resistance is a contagious disease," he says patiently, as if addressing a group of children. "It's not always visible, but it must be cured immediately so that you aren't infected." In a lecturing tone, he quotes from the Surah: "Surely, with us are heavy chains and a blazing fire, and food that chokes, and a painful punishment."

He steps aside and nods to his overseer.

His men know exactly what to do. The *Spanish buck* is effective: a thick stick is placed horizontally behind the slave's knees, his legs bent over it and bound at the ankles, his arms looped beneath the stick and tied together at the wrists. He is quickly curled into a ball on the ground, unable to move. The anger is gone from his eyes, replaced by fear.

The overseer grabs his cat, a piece of rope with nine ends, each tipped with a knot. As he begins to strike the bound man, Mussulman Ali silently watches the group of slaves. Their shock feeds his satisfaction; it is a lesson that must be learned.

"This is a good *kraal*," he says as the afternoon fades into evening and the shadows grow longer. The slaves stand in the centre beneath the stretched tarpaulins, freed from their iron chains but still bound together in groups of five with rope. They have worked well and obediently, he thinks. The fence is sturdy and tight, high enough to keep them in and intruders out.

Around him, the jungle teems with a cacophony of sounds: monkeys, birds, and insects. Above the treetops, the sky darkens. "Cleanse yourselves in the rain," he calls out. "Drink and eat when you're clean. There is enough for everyone."

He turns and walks toward his tent, hungry and longing for sleep. On his way, he steps casually over the beaten slave, who is still trapped in the Spanish buck on the ground. As the rain begins, thin streams of blood drip from the man's body.

12 Arrival in Poquesoe

"Slaves, in reverent fear of God, submit yourselves to your masters, not only to those who are good and considerate, but also to those who are harsh. For it is commendable if someone bears up under the pain of unjust suffering because they are conscious of God."

From: The Bible, 1 Peter 2:18-19

⚓

In the morning, the sky is clear and washed. The ocean below glistens blue-green in a steady easterly breeze that occasionally sends white caps dancing on the waves. The hooker makes an easy four knots, powered by the main and topsail.

Since sunrise, Gillis Graauw has been perched high in the mainmast's topsail yard, his spyglass fixed on the land. Along the starboard side, barely a nautical mile away, the cliffs of Cabo Tres Puntas pass slowly by. There is no sign of human presence to be seen.

Directly below him, the topsail catches the sun, and the light is so bright that he can make out every fold and tear in the canvas. He glances down and, through the sails, catches glimpses of the long, continuous deck, with Burghoutsz standing alone at the very front, legs apart, hands resting on the railing. Graauw harbours no illusions: now that the skipper has allied himself with the big shot at the castle, those slaves will eventually end up in the hold of the *Griffin*, whether they like it or not. But at what cost? After two triangular voyages, he knows all too well that this fish comes at a high price; the last passage was hell for everyone, and he is sure the skipper has not revealed the true reason for it.

Just below him, two sailors appear, climbing nimbly along the ratlines. He nods curtly to them, watching as they disappear behind the mainsail, out of sight.

No, it wasn't just bad luck, because *before* they ended up in that deadly doldrum, they had spent three days chasing a Moorish privateer, a brigantine that had suffered severe damage. An easy prize, Burghoutsz had predicted. But during an exceptionally dark night, they had lost sight of it. The ship had vanished like a ghost, never to reappear—probably sunk—and only then did they realize that this pointless pursuit had taken them hundreds of miles off course. That's why they had missed the trade winds. It was sheer greed.

The memory is painful. He knows the skipper is a stubborn man, by God, he listens to no one—hasn't for a long time, not since that fateful spring of '69— and Graauw's own anger had been great. He had seriously considered punishing Burghoutsz—God knows there were enough men who agreed with him. But mutiny is a capital offense, and he couldn't betray the only friend he'd ever had.

"Village to leeward!" a voice shouts below him. Skipper Vloet is at the helm, pointing to starboard. On the coast, a beach comes into view, and just behind it, a cluster of huts, with wisps of smoke from cooking fires being blown westward by the wind.

"You can't see it from here," Vloet says, grabbing Burghoutsz's arm, "but beyond the village, there's a path running along the lagoon into the interior. It eventually ends up a few miles away at the back of the fort. That's strategically interesting; a small group of soldiers could approach unnoticed at night."

Burghoutsz looks at him. "Are you a military man too?"

"Man, against my will. In Java, we always had a shortage of musketeers because the white lads were dying off in droves. I was simultaneously a helmsman, cook, soldier, and executioner. We cleared quite a few villages of rebellious—uh—elements."

"Could a small group of soldiers steal a batch of slaves?"

"And lead them along that path, back to the village?" Vloet winks and taps his forehead. "Suppose a few empty barges were waiting for you on the beach. You'd load those blacks on board and disappear into the night in no time. No one would be the wiser." He laughs and runs his fingers through his hair. "You and I don't think so differently, skipper."

Fort Frederiksburg is an impressive sight, it sits like a massive, thick pimple on Manfro Hill, a promontory surrounded by cliffs and rocks jutting into the sea. Four massive corner towers guard the coast, and from the parapet, the Brandenburg flag with its red eagle soars into the sky. Beside it, seen from the ocean on the left, the mouth of the Kpani River glistens in the setting sun, with the native settlement of Pocquesoe on its banks, and on the other side stretches the Ehunli Lagoon, a long strip of brackish water running parallel to the coast.

The hooker approaches from the west, with the wind slightly abaft the beam, rounding Manfro Hill in a wide arc. "Careful!" warns Vloet, his eyes fixed on two rocks jutting from the water like teeth. He directs the hands up the main mast, where the topsail has already been taken in. There are two reefs in the mainsail, which flaps softly in the dying wind.

"Slowly, boys, ready to go about."

The rocks are notorious. But the weather is fair, the ocean calm, and the hooker drifts unscathed into the bay. Now they can see the ships clearly: canoes of all shapes and sizes, a Brandenburg yacht, a few small boats with lateen sails, a brig flying the English flag and to port, a little farther off and straining impatiently at her anchors, a Zeeland pinnace.

"The *Meyboom*. A contraband runner," Vloet explains, one hand on the helm. "Smuggler from Vlissingen." He nods towards Burghoutsz, who stands at the railing with Graauw. "If you had come with your own ship, she'd have fled already. Has a mortal fear of Dutch men-of-war with a gun deck." He spits disdainfully overboard. "Those Zeelanders feel right at home under the eagle's flag."

Burghoutsz studies the pinnace. A sleek ship, well-rigged, with a clean hull, in the prime of her life. Undoubtedly fast. One gun deck, ten ports on each side, possibly two chasers on the gallion*, maybe two more copper eight-pounders aft. A bona fide pirate. "Sweerts would kill to catch that one," he says.

"Indeed. But she's as slippery as an eel, and her skipper, a guy named Vogel, is a clever bastard. You've got to watch out for him. He's not right in the head."

"Hm. What do you think, Gillis?"

Graauw shrugs. "I've heard of him," he mutters. "A dangerous lunatic." But he looks approvingly at the ship, which shows all the signs of a well-disciplined crew.

"Four fathoms, skipper!" a sailor shouts from the tip of the bowsprit. Vloet nods, turns the helm to leeward, and the hooker falls off. On the foredeck, the scraping of the anchor line can be heard. "We've arrived, lads." He squints towards the surf, from which an armada of canoes is paddling toward them. "Here come the bumboat traders," he says. "Watch your purses. Thieves and hucksters, every one of 'em."

---

* Gallion = the section of the ship between the forecastle and the bowsprit

13 Trade is Trade

"(...) I admit that the Africans, especially those from regions where the strongest are found, are more suitable for colonial agriculture than the natives of the West Indian islands or the American mainland. Indeed, even more so: he suffers no harm from leaving his homeland to settle in a foreign land with a similar climate because he is a slave both in his own country and overseas, and the increased labour he must perform is offset by certain enjoyments that compensate for the suffering of displacement and labour.

The barbarity that seemingly resides in the slave trade, or rather: in the transportation of serfs (for that is what the slave trade essentially is), can only be attributed to the whites to a limited extent, as the trade in slaves among the negroes in Africa far surpasses that of the whites, both in number and in the scale of relocations, for more than nine-tenths are slaves in their own land. This latter fact is a natural consequence of their mindset, which holds that a child is considered the saleable property of the parents, that the woman is the slave of the man, and that the children of a female slave belong to the one to whom the mother belongs. (...)"

From: Travels and Description of the Gold Coast of Guinea, by J.A. de Marée

⚓

"*Scheisse!*" The Brandenburg head merchant knocks over his bowl of food. Salted meat rolls across the table, and hot grease drips over the edge onto his lap, staining his woollen coat and breeches. "*Verdammt.*" He dabs at the stains with a handkerchief. "*Entschuldigung*," he says to Mussulman Ali. "I am very clumsy."

Mussulman Ali does not respond. His smile had already been on his face when he entered the dim room. Awkwardly, he sits on a wooden chair, his hands on the table, while the smell of salted pork fills his nostrils. *Haram*, he thinks, unclean. He struggles to suppress his disgust.

"Slaves, huh?" asks the head merchant again. He tosses the chunks of meat back into the bowl and licks his fingers. "What kind of slaves?"

"Fine blacks," says Mussulman Ali, now suppressing a rising nausea. He has declined wine and beer and sips sparingly from a small bowl of hot water. "For the honourable prince, for Frederick William."

The head merchant looks at him, puzzled for a moment, then begins to chuckle. "You're a cunning fox, aren't you? Where are these slaves? And where do they come from? I bet they're donkas, right? Circumcised troublemakers that nobody wants."

"No, no, not donkas," says Mussulman Ali irritably because the *kafir*, in all his ignorance, insults the circumcision commanded by God to the Prophet Ibrahim. "It's a secret, a delicate matter. One mustn't speak of it."

"Aha?" The head merchant leans forward slightly. His shoulders move as he speaks. "Did you steal them? Are they from the *Holländer*?"

"Yes, the *Hulandi*. And the Denkyira. It's all the same."

"How many?"

"A hundred and ten."

"That's considerable."

Mussulman Ali spreads his hands. "There's a lot of money involved." His eyes wander around, and inwardly, he is still amazed at the stone structures the whites build. The new main building of Fort Frederiksburg is an impressive structure with thick walls that keep out the heat.

"We can't afford trouble with the cheeseheads," the chief merchant grumbles, his expression suddenly serious. "There's a treaty, *verstehst du*?" He takes a bite of his salted meat, chews thoughtfully, and then leans forward, his voice dropping to a whisper: "I can't do business with you openly, *Herr* Ali."

Mussulman Ali smells fat, salt, and something else, something even filthier—it is written in Al-Maidah: *Why do their rabbis and scholars not forbid them from sinful speech and consuming unlawful food?* —but he does not recoil, his smile remains as if carved from stone. "Perhaps, *efendi*, an intermediary might be of service," he suggests.

"A ruse?"

"The Hulandi need not know."

"They must know nothing."

Silence again. The merchant weighs his options.

"There is a Zeelander," he finally says. "Jasper Vogel. A smuggler from Zeeland who just happens to be anchored here. You could hand your slaves over to him, and he could then, later on, out at sea and out of sight of Dutch eyes, deliver them to us."

"That's a very clever plan," says Mussulman Ali, feeling like a puppet master. Everything is preordained. In his mind, the verse resounds: *These are the ones whom Allah has cursed, and with whom He is angry, and He has turned them into apes and swine and worshippers of false gods.*

The merchant smiles benevolently. "What binds us is our hatred for those arrogant bacon-eaters. Are you sure you won't have some salted meat?"

"No, thank you. It's a matter of faith."

"The transfer cannot take place in Pocquesoe. Under no circumstances."

"Of course not. I know just the place."

It hasn't been a fruitful day. Nothing but wandering through the narrow paths and alleys of the village, past the vendors' stalls, the taverns, the houses and huts, up the sloping road to the fort and the guard at the gate, where Brandenburg soldiers stubbornly block the entrance. By evening, they return to the beach with no more knowledge than they had in the morning.

Gillis Graauw squats down on the sand, his gaze sweeping over the sea and the ships lying just beyond the surf. In the rapidly fading light, he can barely make out skipper Vloet's hooker. A small light flickers in its mainmast. "What now?" he asks.

Burghoutsz paces in front of him. As the day progressed, he became more and more irritable and started drinking. Palm wine. Gin. Rum. Glass after glass. His voice is still steady, but his steps are occasionally uncertain. He looks up at the fort, looming high on the hill, overlooking the ocean. A dark shape. Massive. Inaccessible. "I'm not giving up," he growls. "There must be someone here who has heard or seen something."

"Maybe the Arab went somewhere else."

"No, by God, he's nearby, I can feel it." He shakes his head and rubs his stomach. "Let's get something to eat. I saw a cookhouse nearby."

Back along the beach, Gillis Graauw following behind. To the left and right, the fires of the native fishermen, and the smell of fried fish. Separate from them: white men, merchants, traders, shady characters. Jugs of drink pass from hand to hand. Sounds. Laughter. A cacophony of voices and languages. A barking dog. And beneath it all, the constant thrum of the surf. Night falls as if God is throwing a blanket over the world.

At the edge of sand and rocks stands a long open structure made of wooden poles. *Seestück*, says the sign in dripping Gothic letters. Beneath the roof of palm leaves stands a bar made of driftwood, with a native clay oven behind it. Two sweaty black men are stirring pots. The smoke wafts through the open space, keeping the mosquitoes at bay.

Burghoutsz and Graauw choose a table in a far corner and order Spanish mackerel with bread, beans, and beer.

The innkeeper is a big man with a bald head. He brings their food and eyes them suspiciously. "I don't know you," he says with a heavy German accent. "Are you *Holländer*?"

"Yes," answers Burghoutsz. "We're from Offra."

"Really?" The innkeeper wipes his greasy hands on his apron. He points toward the surf. "That hooker out there sails to Elmina, if I'm not mistaken. I heard you were on board."

"We're not with the Company. We happen to know skipper Vloet. He was kind enough to give us passage."

"Are you looking for trade?"

"Whatever is available."

"Do you have money?"

"Plenty."

The innkeeper tilts his head and shows a faint smile. "People are very particular here. Cheeseheads aren't trusted."

Burghoutsz shrugs, grabs his mug, and takes a sip. The beer is sour and warm. "Slaves," he says flatly. "That would interest us."

"Slaves are scarce. There's peace."

"Sometimes you hear things. We're *not* particular." The skipper rummages in his pockets and pulls out a leather pouch. As he places it on the table, the contents jingle. "Someone who could put us in touch with a trader would earn a generous commission."

"Why would anyone want to do business with you? *Everyone* is desperate for slaves."

"If you pay enough, anything is available."

The innkeeper shakes his head. "There's nothing here for you." He walks back to his bar, where a group of white customers stand silently, drinking.

When it starts to rain, water streams down the edges of the tavern's roof. Under it, the air is thick and oppressive, mixed with the sour smell of wet clothes. Men—white men—take shelter from the rain, gathering at the bar and around the tables. They smoke heavily from long clay pipes and the smoke hangs dense and pungent among them.

Burghoutsz keeps drinking steadily, glaring morosely into his glass. Among empty plates and food scraps stands a wicker-covered demijohn of gin. He seems to have forgotten his surroundings. Sweat trickles down his neckline. Occasionally, he mutters something unintelligible, and from time to time, he glances absently at Gillis Graauw, who has pushed his chair back and is silently watching, barely drinking, waiting for whatever is to come.

A man in a red velvet suit appears. He places his hat, adorned with a striking ostrich feather, on the bar. The other customers step back, making respectful room for him. The man downs a glass of rum. He talks. He laughs. His eyes dart around the room until his sparkling gaze fixes on Burghoutsz.

Gillis Graauw senses the tension. Here comes trouble, he thinks grimly.

The man in the red velvet suit begins to walk towards them. His stride is smooth, almost nonchalant, and a long knife dangles from his right thigh. He stops just in front of their table and looks down at them with a smile. "On deck!" he calls out, his boot tapping against a table leg.

Burghoutsz slowly raises his head. His bloodshot eyes seem vacant, turned inward, it takes a moment before he shows any sign of awareness.

"I've heard," the man in the red velvet suit drawls, "that you're looking for trade." He speaks Dutch with a heavy Zeelandic accent.

"It's the guy from that contraband runner," mutters Gillis Graauw.

A dismissive gesture. "You're selling me short, sir. Trading ship is the proper term. De *Meyboom*, from the anchorage of Vlissingen, at your service. My name is Vogel." He gives a mocking bow and turns back to Burghoutsz. "Permission to come aboard, captain."

"I'm not a captain, I'm a merchant."

"Yes, sure." He grabs a stool and sits down opposite them. Leaning forward, his voice drops to a conspiratorial whisper. "I bet you command a ship working for the Dutch Company. What are you doing here? Asking foolish questions, assuming every native is an idiot. There wasn't a single Brandenburger who wanted to talk to you."

"I'm from Offra."

"Yes, and my mother is Sultan Suleiman's favourite concubine." He gestures towards the bar: "Bring brandy, by God, we're thirsty!"

Burghoutsz stares at him stubbornly. "I've got my own gin." He grabs the wicker bottle by the neck and pulls it towards him. "What do you have to offer?"

"I've got what you want."

"And what do I want?"

"Slaves."

"You have slaves?"

They size each other up. They're probably the same age, but Burghoutsz's face is far more lined. "Why would you have slaves when the Brandenburgers don't?"

Vogel smiles, but his eyes are hard as stone. "You're drawing the wrong conclusion, my good man. Who says that? No one. Let me tell you a little story." He scoots his stool closer as the innkeeper brings fresh glasses and a pitcher. Vogel waits until the man has left. He glances at Gillis Graauw, who is still sitting off to the side. "Does he drink too? What is he, a bodyguard? I'll give you a Spanish dollar if he's not your boatswain."

He fills three glasses and winks at Graauw. "To your health, *uncle**. A good bosun is worth his weight in gold, right?" His light eyes glitter like a cat's and then shift back to Burghoutsz. "You, sir, are here because the Denkyira have complained to your boss. One of their villages has been plundered. Where did they go, huh, all those innocent blacks?" He nods, pleased with himself. "Imagine this," he continues. "An Arab slaver with an illegal batch to sell. Big money, big profits ahead, but who can he sell to? He has only one place to go: Pocquesoe. Fort Frederiksburg. And that's why you are here."

---

* Uncle = a title typically used between Dutch seasoned sailors to address each other

Burghoutsz stares half-drunk at the table. His thoughts swirl like shattered fragments in his head. Is it a trap? Vogel exudes danger. He feels the piercing gaze of Gillis Graauw, Gillis who trusts no one. Never. He downs another glass, but the alcohol has lost its kick. "Go on," he says hoarsely.

"The Brandenburgers aren't stupid. They know full well: if they openly trade those slaves, they'll offend the Dutch. That's dangerous because the new treaty is their only foothold in West Africa." He leans back, fingers touching his chest. "So they come up with a plan: they approach me." He taps his forehead. "They say: Vogel, you unscrupulous, dirty smuggler, if you buy the slaves from that Arab and secretly take them to the open sea, we'll take them off your hands. Nobody sees a thing, the Dutch are none the wiser, *alles klar*, right?"

Burghoutsz snorts. "If that's all true, then why are you here?"

"Good question." Vogel crosses his legs. He's wearing expensive boots with fashionable butterfly ties. "I thought to myself: those Brandenburgers are a thorn in Sweerts' side, he'd love to cut them off. And he'd rather have those slaves himself. That would kill two birds with one stone, wouldn't it?"

"And?"

"Well, with your permission, I bet your boss is willing to pay a lot more than they are."

"You gave them your word."

"Ha! My word!" Vogel places his elbows on the table, revealing forearms covered in brightly coloured tattoos. Green dragons. Teeth. Scales. Claws. "I work for myself. I look after my own interests. But something's needed for that. *A fait accompli.*"

"A what?"

"Block access to Fort Frederiksburg, don't let any ship in or out. With your frigates, that should be a piece of cake. Tell me, how can the Brandenburgers take those slaves off my hands then, hm?" He flashes his teeth, they're remarkably intact for a man of his age. "I'd be forced to sell my cargo to you. What else could I do with all those people on my ship? You don't really think they're going to complain to Sweerts, do you? Ah, lads, an advance payment would be greatly appreciated. Didn't you place a little bag of money on the table?"

14 Drunkenness

"Consider Cham and his descendants—though they have become mighty nations—how much has slavery nonetheless prevailed among them! Have not most Africans generally been slaves of their kings? Is not a large part of them still, to this day, enslaved by the Turks? Are Congo, Angola, Guinea, Monomotapa, and Bagamidri not slave nests, from which so many are dragged away and sold far and wide, and used for all kinds of slave labour?"

From: Brief Description of Some Forgotten and Hidden Antiquities of the Provinces and Lands Located Between the North Sea, the IJssel, the Ems, and the Lippe, by Reverend Johan Picardt.

⚓

Night. The ocean has a dull metallic sheen, the sky is gray, and a warm wind blows from the south.

Gillis Graauw stands upright at the bow as the rented canoe bumps softly against the side of the hooker. He whistles up to the deck. "Ahoy, mates, lower a bosun's chair."

Shuffling sounds above.

"Why?" comes a gruff voice from above. "Can't you climb?"

Graauw looks at the motionless form at the bottom of the canoe. "It's the merchant," he says. "He's out cold."

Grumbling curses. Footsteps and indistinct muttering. Then, the commanding voice of skipper Vloet: "Make that rope fast."

Squeaking and creaking.

Graauw reaches for the dark shape of rope and plank that slowly descends. With the help of the rower, he lifts the unconscious Burghoutsz onto the chair and ties him securely.

"All right, hoist him up."

He climbs up himself via the rope ladder.

Vloet looks down at the motionless man at his feet. "Completely out," he says. "Drunk to his keel. Is he always like this?"

"Sometimes," Graauw replies.

"Is he a problem?"

"No. Let him sleep. He'll be right as rain in the morning."

"That would surprise me." Vloet gives Burghoutsz a nudge in the side with his foot, crouches down, and seems to study him intently. "I once knew a Marine lieutenant," he says thoughtfully. "That was back in '78, I think—claimed he'd spent a night with a talking fulmar off the coast of Nova Zembla." He chuckles. "The stupid bird was supposed to have flawlessly quoted passages from the Bible. I'm not judging, wonders never cease, but what I mean is: that lieutenant was the same sort as this one here."

Graauw looks at him, not understanding.

"All misfortune, I mean."

They both stare at the unconscious figure.

"You don't know anything," Graauw growls.

Vloet shrugs. "Maybe not," he says as he stands up and brushes some imaginary dust from his coat. "But I can tell you, mate, I'm very good at recognizing a man who's teetering on the edge, whose joy in life is no brighter than the flame of a snuff candle."

Gillis Graauw drags Burghoutsz to the aft cabin and gently lays him down in the narrow space between the table and the back wall. An old coat serves as a pillow.

Burghoutsz mumbles something. A thin stream of saliva drips down from the corner of his mouth. "No," he suddenly croaks. "Don't let them go!" His eyes snap open, wild and frenzied in the darkness. "Cowardly bastard!"

Graauw sighs. "Go to sleep, skipper."

Burghoutsz turns his face towards him. For a brief moment, there's a flicker of awareness. "Gillis?"

"I'm here."

"Where are they, Gillis?"

Graauw shakes his head. Any answer will only lead to more despair. Even in the dim light, he can see the pain twisted on his skipper's face.

15 *Back: Aldemar Burghoutsz (1)*

A dark-haired, cheerful boy with an open gaze, growing up in Enkhuizen. Narrow streets, small houses. The Zuiderpoort and the Westerkerk. The ever-present influence of the East India Company and the Noorderkwartier, the supreme council of the herring fishermen. A harbour full of ships with the Zuiderzee beyond. He is the only child in the family to survive past infancy; three little brothers and a sister are taken by smallpox and sudden infant death syndrome. Perhaps that's why he finds no peace on land and quickly seeks the vastness of the water, joining his father on the herring buss, a nine-year-old in his tarred trousers, doing the dirty work, six to eight weeks at sea, living the rough life with the fishermen.

The North Sea, 1650
The herring busses are bulky and round, heaving heavily on the swells of the Scottish coastal sea, with sails furled and masts lowered. The uncles skilfully shoot the nets, attaching them to the main rope, net after net, until a wall nearly a mile wide hangs in the water. Now, it's just a matter of waiting for the fish.

Aldemar sits on the port-side bench with a basket between his short legs, gutting the herring that was caught earlier. He's getting the hang of it: inserting the knife into the lower jaw, making a cut, and then, in one smooth motion, pulling out the entrails. The uncles keep an eye on him, as they pass by, they give him a nod of approval.

He grins. The uncles are kind, but they sometimes play cruel tricks: "Aldemar, go ask your dad to come check on the 'dockside dolly' in the galley. Tell him it's urgent." In his innocence, he follows the order and is stunned when he gets a sharp slap on the head. The men burst out laughing. A 'dockside dolly' is not a dolly. He has no idea.

Another herring goes into the barrel. He places them neatly—upright, tails down, side by side—until not even one more can fit. After each layer, he throws a few generous handfuls of salt on top. It burns his skin because the cold and seawater have left his fingers covered in cracks and sores. "It'll pass, little man," his dad said, so he grits his teeth. A sailor doesn't complain.

His father stands at the stern, manning the tiller, a broad-shouldered man in a canvas jacket. Behind him, the sea rises and falls wildly, and a half-dozen armed convoyers from the Admiralty are in sight; if the English come, they'll need to get away quickly.

"Is it their fish then?" he had asked.

"No, but they're scoundrels. They'll seize all the herring and throw us in jail. Last year, they hanged Harmen Heithuizen over a spiny dogfish."

His face falls. He doesn't want to go to jail, and he certainly doesn't want to be hanged. Now and then, he scans the water himself. Just in case. Every little bit helps.

Enkhuizen, 1657

In winter, there is no fishing, and Bible lessons are given in the church's vestry. He sits at a bare wooden table, his head bent low, reluctantly reading from his catechism booklet, memorizing the questions and answers by heart.

His nose nearly touches the paper.

Oral examination:

"What is the pope?"

"The Antichrist."

"Who dwells in the papist church?"

"The idols."

"What are they?"

"Big dolls."

"What do they do there?"

"They stand and flaunt themselves."

"Very good." The minister looks pleased and studies him for a moment. "You've got brains, Burghoutsz. What do you want to be when you grow up?"

He hesitates. Pride is frowned upon, but lying is a sin. "A captain on an East Indiaman, Reverend," he whispers.

"That's a dangerous profession. Many East Indiamen never return. Why don't you stay with your father and take over the herring buss later on?"

Aldemar shrugs; herring doesn't interest him. He wants more.

"If you wish to be a captain on the high seas, then God has inspired that in you, boy. It's His plan for you. If God gives you a ship, you must use it in His name. Against the Spaniards, the Portuguese, and all other papists in the world. For God is with us, do you understand?"

"Yes, Reverend," he replies, barely audible.

"As long as we remain God-fearing, hardworking citizens who live according to the Bible and attend church daily, God will protect us. By fire and sword."

Aldemar nods. He understands that. He secretly sees himself standing on the quarterdeck of his ship, the Dutch flag flying high, his rapier in hand. But then something occurs to him.

"And the blacks, Reverend?"

The minister looks up, surprised. "The blacks? What about them?"

"Am I supposed to protect the blacks too?"

"As long as the blacks are under our care as if they were our children, you must protect them, for that is also God's will."

"Are blacks also people, do they have a soul, like we do? And do they go to heaven?"

The minister taps his fingers on the table. "If blacks convert to the true faith, they will receive a soul, and God will take pity on them. That is why we must not sell them to Catholic traders, to spare them from papist superstition. It is our duty to bring the slaves to the true religion."

"Do the papists also keep blacks?"

"Yes, but that is a sin."

Aldemar's face shows genuine surprise. "Aren't all people equal in the eyes of God, Reverend, as Jesus preached?"

The minister shakes his head sternly. He says, in a tone that allows no contradiction, "The all-governing providence of God is the cause of the different fates of the descendants of Ham, Shem, and Japheth, the sons of Noah. Thus, Noah's prophecy is fulfilled: that Ham's descendants shall live in servitude, Shem's descendants in exile, and Japheth's descendants are blessed with prosperity, power, and knowledge. This explains the division between blacks, Jews, and whites."

"Am I a descendant of Japheth?"

"Of course. Son of Japheth, son of Noah. And a Dutchman on top of that." He looks at the boy triumphantly. "It is divine Providence that has determined the fate of peoples and individuals, their happiness or misery, their freedom or slavery."

Aldemar glances at the wall clock. The hands are barely visible in the gathering darkness. And he's not entirely sure he understood the minister.

"If you want to be a captain, you'll have to go to school."

"Yes, Reverend."

"I'll have a word with your father."

Amsterdam, Winter 1660

Frost in the air. The streets are snow-covered, the cobblestones along the canals slippery and almost impassable. On the Oudezijds Voorburgwal, across from the Oude Kerk*, a horse has slipped into the canal along with its cart. A crowd has gathered, men and women with caps on, sliding and laughing along the street.

The cart is hanging halfway over the quay wall, with the shaft in the water, and beneath it, the horse is fighting for its life, its flailing hooves shattering the thin layer of ice.

Aldemar Burghoutsz, fifteen years old, stands on the sidelines, his navigation books under his arm, staring in fascination at the scene. It's early in the morning, and the candles in the street lanterns are still burning. He has to get to his classes at the nautical school of Abraham de Graaf on the Niezel, next to the Witte Ruit. Being late will lead to repercussions, but a horse is drowning in the canal, and there's been blood, and the more details he knows, the better his story will be when he tells it to his classmates. He decides to stay just a little while longer. Just a few minutes.

Two constables from the city guard approach the scene of the accident. They call out to a few small boats, struggling through the ice with their fish baskets on their way to the market. Ropes are thrown. There's shouting and yelling, and everyone thinks they know best. By now, the horse seems to be tiring. It stops its frantic movements, barely keeping its head above water. It is still tied to the shaft straps and makes a plaintive, groaning sound, eerily like a human voice, piercing to the bone. Two small boats work together and throw ropes around the animal's neck. Long knives cut the harnesses free. The boatmen curse as the icy water numbs their

---

* The Oude Kerk ("Old Church") was originally a Catholic church named after Saint Nicholas, but was converted into a Protestant house of worship in the late 16th century. It is the oldest church in Amsterdam, dating back to the 13th century.

hands. The horse now lies motionless in the water.

Aldemar sighs: he really has to get to school now, or there'll be trouble. Reluctantly, he slides on his worn-out shoes over the snow-covered cobblestones down the Oudezijds towards the Lange Niezel, flailing his arms and legs to keep his balance while behind him, the horse is being pulled from the canal with combined efforts. It's already dead.

In winter, the evenings are long and dark. In his unheated attic room on Zwartlakensteeg, he studies late into the night by the light of a single candle, wrapped in a woolen blanket yet still shivering from the cold, while the wind howls over the bare roof tiles above his head. He lives on stale bread, and a chunk of cheese, and occasionally a salted herring, for his monthly stipend is meagre, and he needs money for books, paper, and ink.

The studies are demanding and cover a wide range of subjects: navigation, cartography, latitude and longitude measurement, and the use of angular measuring instruments. Mathematics. Physics. His head spins with it all.

But he perseveres. He is a good student, and he longs for the sea. Amsterdam is the centre of the world, private nautical schools are springing up like mushrooms, and students are flocking in. Five thousand sea vessels fly the Dutch flag worldwide, and the commercial sector is clamouring for skilled sailors. Those who pass can find *work. And pass he will.*

On Oudekennissteeg, across the bridge, lies Govers' bakery. To earn a few extra coins, he sometimes helps the millers from Amstelland, who pole the heavy sacks of flour through the canals on flat-bottomed boats. He hauls a wooden handcart over the cobblestones, which is no easy task, as the stones are uneven. It's cold, but sweat glistens on his forehead each time he has to get the cart moving again.

The miller grumbles, "Hurry up, boy, for God's sake, we've got more to do."

"Yes, yes."

The bakery has a shop. The daughter of Govers works there, and every time he passes the half-frosted shop window, he tries to catch a glimpse of her. He's not very good with girls. And in the big city, they're different from those in Enkhuizen. Bolder. Sometimes even sharp-tongued.

But Anna is different.

Anna brings light.

Late in the afternoon, he's done, and with his hard-earned coins, he appears in the bakery. It's warm and bright, and the smell of fresh bread makes his stomach growl.

"Hello, Aldemar."

"Hello, Anna."

He can't look at her for too long—that would be improper, and he doesn't want to make a fool of himself. But their eyes meet, and he feels himself blushing. She has brown eyes. Chestnut coloured hair.

"Succade bread, Aldemar?"

"Yes," he answers hoarsely. "And pretzels."

He points. The pretzels are dusted with powdered sugar.

Baker Govers appears in the shop and fiddles with a breadbasket. "Burghoutsz," he greets. "Is the flour in the cellar?"

"Yes, baker."

"How is school?"

"Good."

Govers winks. "Here's your bread."

He takes his groceries, and her fingers brush his for just a moment.

On the last, blank page of a book titled Treasure Trove of the Great Art of Navigation *by Cornelis Lastman, he has scrawled in clumsy handwriting: "Anna." Underlined. Beneath that, a date: "the 28th day of slaughter month." Double underlined. And below that, at the very bottom, in very small letters: "Kissed." Circled.*

The Oude Kerk is Amsterdam's living room, and on winter days, it is packed to the rafters. The poor seek refuge from the cold, for outside, a bitter wind blows and wet snow is falling. They huddle inside, clad in rags, stamping their feet, pushing and shoving, taking possession of the many corners and the spaces beside the white pillars, spreading their pitiful blankets or cloaks on the stone floor and sitting close together. There are stray dogs shamelessly wandering among the people, begging for scraps. Cheerful women sell currant buns and white bread from shoulder bags, always wary of the Church Council's disciples, for whom these excesses are an abomination. It's Saint Nicholas Day, and the Oude Kerk has an indelible connection to the past, a centuries-old devotion to the Bishop of Myra—something the Calvinists can't seem to eradicate—so the poor have secretly placed their shoes in niches and corners – eagerly waiting for the generous Saint to put something in them – hidden from the sight of the city regents.

Aldemar loves coming to the church. It's more pleasant than his attic room and certainly safer than the heady, alcohol-soaked atmosphere of the taverns. But above all, it's the perfect place to meet Anna Govers. There, they sit on the gravestones of famous Amsterdammers, sharing bread and small mugs of beer.

Aldemar talks endlessly. He has visions: of the world, of the sea, and of Dutch men-of-war.

Evening. Darkness. Hand in hand over the slippery cobblestones of the canal and Zwartlakensteeg. Sneaking around the back of the courtyard. The snow falls in thick flakes, and the wind plays with the roof tiles. Up the creaking stairs. He puts his finger to his lips: the landlord is strict. There's no light. They find his attic room by touch. He lights a stub of a candle, and she takes in the humble surroundings. Books. So many books. A hunk of stale bread on a tin plate. Worn shoes in a corner. Under one leg of his rickety desk, he's stuffed pieces of paper.

His bed is unsteady, and the blanket is damp and smells like him. They are still clumsy, and nothing is as she had imagined. But the world outside suddenly feels far away.

16 Sweerts Lands on the Brandenburg Coast

"Indeed, we are aware of last year's agreement with the Brandenburgers, which acknowledges their presence in Accada and Poquesoe, but I won't beat around the bush: Fort Frederiksburg is a thorn in my side. And we are not the government. The competition with the English requires all our resources, yes, all our effort and dedication, and currently, our resources are thinner than ever. We are certainly not looking forward to the rise of a Brandenburg trading power.

Maybe we can no longer drive them from the coast due to that accursed treaty, but that doesn't mean we have to give them free rein. Let the States-General deal with their complaints. Meanwhile, I will continue to do what we must: we will make their lives miserable, as we have successfully done before."

From: letters of Director-General Nicholaas Sweerts to the Directors of the West India Company, autumn 1687

Six days later, the Dutch cruiser *Westsouborgh* is sailing at full speed on a favourable beam wind, reaching speeds of seven knots or more at times. It is three bells[*] into the forenoon watch, and Nicholaas Sweerts stands on the ship's quarterdeck, facing forward.

He hadn't hesitated after receiving Burghoutsz's report. Decisiveness, that's what matters, he knows. And besides, his hands are itching. Now that it has been confirmed that the Brandenburgers have purchased slaves and dared to defy the Company, he can finally take action.

To starboard, a faint line of coast is visible in the far distance. That's as he ordered: keep the land in sight, but don't get too close—no one needs to see the Dutch heading towards Cabo Tres Puntas, although very little remains secret in this small part of the world. They sailed in a wide arc around busy Commanie, then passed close along the coast by the Dutch factories of San Sebastian, Orange, and Batenstein.

He savours the fresh air and the wind, and even the ship's rolling feels almost pleasant, though he's always a bit afraid of getting seasick. Fortunately, the

---

[*] Sailors measured time counting 'glasses': the ship's bell was rung next to an hourglass that took thirty minutes to run out.

ulcer at the corner of his mouth has healed; that might be a good omen, he thinks. He looks aft, where his two frigates follow in line, heeling slightly over the water, their bows cutting through the waves, the Company flags fluttering in the wind—a sight he finds both magnificent and imposing.

The ship vibrates under his feet, the mainsail is taut, and the spray sparkles like gemstones in the sunlight. Above the mizzenmast, high in the sky, a frigate bird gracefully follows their course.

It's a matter of making an impression, he thinks the following morning as he stands on the quarterdeck in full view and dressed in his best attire. Below him, in the waist, the delegation from the Ashanti tribe has arrived, led by three of their kings, flanked by advisors, tribal chiefs, and a few warriors. He sees crowns made of ostrich feathers and caps of monkey hide, expensive *kente* cloaks, and arms, wrists, and ankles adorned with rings of solid gold.

But despite all that opulence, they seem somewhat overwhelmed, as it is their first time aboard a Dutch cruiser—the three masts towering high above them—and from the yards, tops, and rigging, they are being watched by silent white seamen. Along the railings on both sides, Dutch soldiers are lined up neatly, their buttons and cuirasses polished, their snaphaunces, pistols, swords, and knives clearly visible. An ensign shouts a few commands, and the men stomp their heavy boots on the deck, which always makes a strong impression. To windward of the cruiser, the two frigates float like comrades in the water. A short while earlier, the saluting shots were fired, and the gunpowder smoke still hangs like low-lying clouds. He can smell the saltpeter.

Sweerts raises a hand to get their attention. The three kings—who the crew has already nicknamed Caspar, Melchior, and Balthazar—take a few tentative steps towards him, but since he is standing on the quarterdeck, they are forced to look up at him.

"I warmly welcome you," he calls out in his best Guinean while thinking: hypocrites, you Brandenburg bootlickers. He looks each of them in the eye and says, "I have summoned you here to seal our friendship, which has lasted for a long time. The Ahante are a great people. We know this. Friendship between great peoples is important."

He thinks: but you catch more flies with honey than with vinegar. So, I won't hang them from the main yardarm. I'll give them brandy and feast them until they're sick of it themselves, those godless thieves, but after that, their complaints will stop. He continues, "That is why we need to talk today, to resolve our differences, because there are also Ahante who want to take a different path, who no longer value our friendship, who are misled by the sweet words of strangers and thus endanger the peace."

He sees the concern in their eyes because they know very well that they need him to stand against the Fante, their ancient, estranged brothers in the east. "Yes, true friendship," he repeats, meanwhile glancing to starboard.

A little over a thousand feet away, beyond the surf, lies Taccrama, a small, unremarkable village with ramshackle huts and buildings, where the common folk of the Ahante have gathered, a coalition of black tribes united under their three kings. Large fires burn there, and the people dance, clap, and sing—the sound carries far over the water. He can see the warriors, tall men with spears, shields, and clubs, and here and there, a musket. They bellow their war cries and call upon their ancestors.

Good, he thinks, as he plucks a louse from his collar and crushes it between his thumb and forefinger. It makes a faint popping sound. Go ahead, fill yourself with your *nsafufuo,* and eat your *kenkey* until your belly bursts, but after that, you can storm the walls of Dorothea and Frederiksburg. That's what we're here for.

In the evening, he plays *le grande*, the supreme leader, mightier and greater than them all: the white ruler of the Company. The galley glows yellow with blazing fire, and the cooks roast beef, chicken, and fish. French wine and Schiedam gin flow freely. The three Ahante kings sit in the waist deck, surrounded by servants and vassals. And he himself stands above them on the quarterdeck, untouchable, gracious, a paragon of true Christian civilization.

Lanterns hang in the masts, on the yards, and on the stern gallery. The cruiser rides lazily at anchor, with soldiers and weapons on deck and open gunports on every side—a floating castle of light.

Yes, he has them all wrapped around his finger. Convinced of his superiority, they will fight for him. For him and the Company. He raises his glass. At a moment like this, he feels no contempt for them, for they form the exotic, grand backdrop to this play, this drama, one might say, in which he is the leading actor, in which everything revolves around him.

Emperor Sweerts.

By noon the next day, the *Westsouborgh* rounds the headland near Accada, and, accompanied by her two Dutch frigates, cautiously enters the small yet picturesque bay of Ezile. Almost immediately, the sails are set back, and the cruiser comes to a halt in crystal-clear waters, with barely a fathom and a half beneath her keel.

To starboard lies the crescent-shaped beach, with the mouth of a small, winding river beside the headland. The beach is scattered with canoes, and in the shallow water, a few longboats and a yacht are bobbing about. Further inland, on a natural rise amidst lush, vibrant green vegetation, rises a small, triangular fort still under construction: Dorothea, a Brandenburg outpost located two miles east of Cabo Tres Puntas.

Sweerts stands at the rail of the quarterdeck, taking in the scene. The beach is bustling: it appears the yacht, a small single-masted vessel undoubtedly from Pocquesoe, is being unloaded. Longboats shuttle back and forth with building materials, and black porters climb the dirt path to the outpost. But as soon as the *Westsouborgh* is spotted, the scene seems to freeze: all faces turn towards the three Dutch warships in the bay, and a sudden tense silence falls, broken only by the heavy splash of the cruiser's anchors.

Sweerts wipes the sweat from his forehead. The sun is blazing, and the sea breeze offers little relief. To the east, low-hanging clouds are visible; rain is on its way. He looks to the right, a cluster of huts along the river mouth marks the village of Accada.

The master gunner, an older man in a black coat, steps onto the quarterdeck and salutes. "All pieces are ready to fire, sir, the cartridges filled, and the shot racks stacked. With your permission, the starboard ports can be opened."

Sweerts nods. He's leaving nothing to chance, although he doesn't expect a single shot to be fired. "See to it that your men are kept in check," he says. "Nothing happens without my approval."

"Of course not, sir."

On the waist deck, the soldiers stand ready. Their snaphaunces and pistols are loaded, their faces set grim and perhaps a little eager; maybe soon they'll finally get the chance to crack a few skulls again.

Sweerts beckons to Vermeulen, the ensign, who stands near the mainmast, looking pale. Ensign Vermeulen, Sweerts knows, has been suffering from the *trots* for a week. No small matter, he admits to himself. He rarely has trouble with diarrhoea. An iron stomach. Always has.

"You're coming with me, sir," he says without a trace of sympathy. "Choose two men who can keep their wits about them when things get tense. We're going to pay those Brandenburgers a visit."

Meanwhile, the boatswain bellows that the longboat is to be lowered. The deckhands handle the tackles. With combined effort, the heavy boat is hoisted over the side until it touches the clear, light-green water. From the deck, fish can be seen coming to investigate. Some crewmen toss bits of ship's biscuit into the water. The fish dart forward hungrily.

"Off-board!" the boatswain shouts.

Sweerts clumsily descends the side ladder, followed by his escort. The ensign and the two soldiers stumble, bumping awkwardly against the ship's side, encouraged mockingly by the sailors at the rail, who—traditionally—harbour a dislike for them.

"Turn your arse to the sea, peg-leg, not to the sky."

"That's how your sweetheart looks from above, too."

Laughter fills the deck. The ensign, already feeling miserable, presses his lips together tightly, but Sweerts, already in the boat, waves impatiently with his hands. "Hurry up, by God, we don't have all day."

Finally, everyone is on board. The rowers push off and row out of the cruiser's lee. The longboat has a single mast, and the quartermaster, in command, hoists the triangular sail, which immediately catches the wind and propels the group swiftly toward the shore.

They pass the Brandenburg yacht. Several white sailors stare at them from the deck with astonished expressions. "Ahoy, lads," calls a voice with an unmistakable Zeeland accent, "what's going on?"

The soldiers in the boat snicker. "That German must have studied in Vlissingen."

But the director-general's face shows a stubborn expression. "Shut your traps, men," he growls. He finds it inappropriate that one Dutchman, through a foreign venture, is trying to outmanoeuvre another. That reeks of unfair competition.

The boat scrapes along the bottom as the sailors jump overboard and drag it onto the sand.

Sweerts disembarks, and after four full days at sea, the solid ground feels strange even to a landlubber.

17 The Taking of Fort Dorothea

"Slaves must recognize their master's authority in everything and strive to please him. They must not talk back or steal from him but show that they are completely trustworthy. Then, in everything they do, they will adorn the doctrine of God our Savior."

From: The Bible, Titus 2:9-10

On the beach stands a group of four white men, each dressed in dark breeches and doublets, white stockings, and high shoes. They wait for him, surprised, perhaps even a little irritated.

"Sir," they greet, stiffly doffing their hats. "What brings you here? And with such an escort, no less?"

Sweerts nods to them, then turns his head and glances back at the ships in the bay. They lie in formation, with their starboard sides facing the shore. "Don't worry," he reassures them. "I'm merely conducting an inspection along the coast."

"That may be," says one of the Brandenburgers, a square-built fellow with a snow-white beard, his doublet trimmed with gold braid. His eyes shift suspiciously between the director-general and the Dutch ships. "But this is Brandenburg territory."

Sweerts spreads his hands, feigning confusion. "Our nations have signed a treaty, sir."

The man with the white beard, apparently the leader, lets out a cynical laugh. "Diplomacy may have done its job, sir, but with all due respect, you have always fought us tooth and nail, even capturing two of our most valuable ships last year; we have little reason to embrace you as yet."

The other three men nod gravely. It's clear they don't know what to do. But Sweerts smiles at them. "That was before the agreement," he explains reassuringly. "Didn't we return the cruiser *Wappen vor Brandenburg* early this year? And pay compensation? Things are different now. We've become allies. That's how politics works."

Fort Dorothea is a compact, triangular fortification built only four years earlier.

The walls are thick, made of heavy stones, but the Brandenburgers have decided on further expansion and reinforcement. Watchtowers have been constructed on each corner of the three walls, overlooking the sea, and batteries are planned to be placed on the broad ramparts between them. It's all still under construction, with black labourers bustling back and forth with materials while a few white overseers try to keep the work on track.

Sweerts walks through the gate, accompanied by his bodyguard and the four Brandenburg merchants. They enter a narrow courtyard dominated by a heavy stone building in the German style, its masonry reinforced here and there with horizontal yellow beams of mangrove wood. Five soldiers are stationed at the entrance.

Scarcely any firepower, he thinks. He has made the climb up the road, which is flanked by thick underbrush, in good spirits, with a faint smile on his lips. He hasn't encountered a single soldier. And those five at the door aren't much of a force, even though they're armed with brand-new snaphaunces. He concludes that there is no significant defence to speak of.

The stone building serves multiple functions: warehouse, living quarters, slave house, and barracks, as is often the case with many smaller trading posts along the coast. But this one is very solidly built, he has to admit. Many of the old company forts consist of little more than rotten beams and planks, barely holding things together. There's no money for luxurious constructions like this. But that damned Frederick William apparently has plenty of funds.

The Brandenburg merchants open the door and beckon him inside. "A refreshment, with your permission, *Herr* Director General?"

"Of course, gladly," Sweerts says politely. He has his hands clasped behind his back. It is a fine fort, he sincerely thinks. The courtyard is cool, and they've left the enormous ironwood trees standing, their tall canopies providing a wonderfully soothing shade. Those Germans can certainly build, he has to give them that.

By evening, he returns. The longboat is much fuller than on the outward journey because he has invited the merchants for an early meal. He mentioned that fresh herring had arrived last week, straight from the Great Fishery in Amsterdam, gutted, salted, and of the finest quality. The Germans are eager, despite their initial mistrust, but *Herr* Sweerts has been the epitome of courtesy. He showed great interest in the little, brave fort, admired its solid construction, and complimented them on the materials used. He even remarked that *they* were better builders than the Dutch. In fact, he went as far as to say that if *they* had built the Dutch forts along the coast, the Company would be in a much better position; just look at the deplorable state of Batenstein and Orange.

They thawed a bit under this flattery and wisely kept silent. *Herr* Sweerts probably doesn't know that the architect of Fort Dorothea is a Dutchman.

But the new friendship is a welcome change in relations, as they are accustomed to looking over their shoulders, always vigilant, always scanning the sea and horizon, constantly expecting to see frigates emerge. There's not much flexibility in the Dutch spirit in their experience, the Company seizes Brandenburg ships, confiscates trade, and threatens the Ahante tribes, who have been doing business with them for a few years now.

But now there is peace. There's no denying it: even the West India Company must bow to the gentlemen regents in The Hague. They suspect *Herr* Sweerts has been put on notice because even he is not above the law. The animosity between nations is never personal. It's politics, simply business.

As they pass the German yacht, still anchored off the beach, Sweerts invites the skipper, who is watching them from the rail with suspicion.

"Come aboard as well, sir, you're welcome. We have fresh herring."

The men let the longboat drift alongside.

The skipper consults with the merchants in German. They shrug, they've already been won over. "Everything is fine, *Herr Kapitän*. You can come along without worry."

Sweerts himself is helpful as the man climbs down. He almost pulls him aboard. "Good," he mutters. "Now we have everyone."

The longboat continues its course. There is little wind, and what there is comes from the land, so the sail offers little help.

"Row," orders the quartermaster, standing at the stern, one foot on the gunwale. He glances at the sky, now heavy with clouds the colour of molten lead. The first raindrops begin to pelt down.

"The weather's going to get rough," someone mutters. The men dip their oars into the rowlocks and find their rhythm quickly.

They approach the *Westsouborgh*, and the Brandenburgers crane their necks, the ship is like a castle on the water. The muzzles of the cannons protrude from the gunports.

The longboat swings around to the stern. They have to duck under the thick line of the stern anchor, taut as a violin string.

The merchants stare up at the faces peering down at them from the rail. They are not friendly faces, and they suddenly feel a sense of foreboding. But Sweerts waves away any threat. He gestures impatiently for the sailors to drop the side ladders. "Hurry up! The herring is waiting."

Ah, yes. The merchants hail from Emden, where the herring has been brought in by the fishing fleets for as long as anyone can remember, just like in Holland. They'd get up in the middle of the night for it.

Aboard, Sweerts' smile disappears like snow in the sun. With a stern face, he points to the ensign, who has been almost invisible during their trip ashore, still struggling with his bowels. "Give me your cutlass, Vermeulen."

The sword is a bit rusty, and that irritates him. He points the tip forward towards the five invited guests. "You are under arrest," he says curtly.

The merchants open their mouths but are too shocked to protest. The soldiers on deck form a circle. The looks they're giving now are very menacing.

Sweerts stands ramrod straight, his back rigid, left hand on his hip. The tip of his cutlass just brushes against the chest of the German skipper. "Are you armed?"

"No, but if I had known …"

"Dagger? Knife? Dirk?"

"No."

"Pistol?"

"No."

"If you're lying, I'll have you executed, you can count on that."

The skipper remains silent, flabbergasted.

"Take them to my cabin," Sweerts orders the ensign. "Search them and lock them up. Serve beer, herring, and white bread, as I promised. I keep my word. They won't lack anything. No harm will come to them. But make sure they don't escape. Station four of your men at the door."

"Yes, sir." Ensign Vermeulen stares at him, suddenly with his eyes glazed, shoulders slumped, upper body swaying gently back and forth as if he wants to rest his head on Sweerts' chest but keeps changing his mind because it wouldn't be appropriate.

Sweerts looks back, bewildered. The ensign's eyes have the expression of a dead man. "Man, what are you doing?" He grabs him by the upper arms and shakes him.

There's a sound of escaping gas, the stench of rotten eggs and excrement. He looks down and sees blood-red diarrhoea. The ensign collapses to his knees, clinging to him like a child to its mother.

"By God!" He signals to the soldiers, who are watching the scene in shock. "For God's sake, do something!"

They rush over, grab the ensign, and pull him away. The diarrhoea splatters onto the deck. The ensign mumbles incomprehensible words, sounding as if he's drunk. He falls to the planks, hits his head, and loses consciousness.

The ship's chirurgeon comes running. "The bloody flux," he diagnoses quickly. "Get him below deck."

The soldiers drag the man away, leaving a red-brown trail behind.

Sweerts watches them go, suddenly furious. His triumph is gone; the Brandenburg prisoners have utterly forgotten him as they stare, horrified, at the blood.

It's starting to rain steadily now. Within minutes, the decks are glistening with water.

Sweerts waves up to the top of the main mast, where a signalman hangs from the topgallant. He's a young deckhand, casually gripping the yard with one hand, his left foot on the footrope. He waves back cheerfully, gives a thumbs-up, and then pulls out a red flag and sets it in the wind. The flapping fills the silence, and all eyes turn to the flickering cloth.

Sweerts looks at the shore. Behind the village, at the edge of the jungle, there's suddenly movement. A large group of Ahante warriors appears, armed with spears, shields, and muskets.

The action is well-coordinated: they swiftly and silently encircle the village of Accada, and the inhabitants are too stunned to resist. Not a single shot is fired. Barely fifteen minutes later, the small army, perhaps three hundred men strong, moves along the beach towards the bay and the path leading to the fort. The workers and slaves on the beach watch them with open mouths.

Fort Dorothea is overwhelmed. There are pistol and musket shots, shouting, yelling, and utter confusion. Sweerts narrows his eyes. The coast blurs as the rain intensifies. The sea now seems to be boiling.

He sees the Brandenburg yacht lifting anchor and hoisting its mainsail. In the curtain of rain, it's no more than a triangular shadow. "Damn, she's making a run for it!" he growls. "Master gunner, give her a warning shot."

The gunner runs to the main hatch in the waist and bellows down into the gun deck.

"Upper deck battery! One shot! Across the bow!"

The crew is ready. Sweerts hears them shouting and cursing. With tackles, they pull one of the cannons inside and load it. The powder monkey places the cartridge, and the iron ball is rolled into the barrel with a ladle, then covered with a wad of cotton waste.

"Aim!"

The cannon is secured, and the men wedge the breech against the carriage. At a furious pace, they fasten the breeching rope.

"Ready to fire, sir!"

"Fire to starboard!" shouts the master gunner.

The explosion shakes the cruiser. There is a terrifying, whistling sound as the shot rapidly moves away. Just ahead of the yacht's bow, the cannonball bounces three, four times across the surface of the sea, creating spray in its wake.

The message is received; within five seconds, they see the yacht hastily drop its mainsail.

"That'll teach them," says Sweerts, who is also impressed. "If they try that again, we'll hit them for real."

18 *Back: Nicholaas Sweerts*

A stocky, unattractive man with lank red hair and a hard face. Everything about him seems square. His green eyes are set a bit too close together, his nose is short and blunt. Thin lips, with corners that seem to turn downwards. Because he is not very tall, he has adopted the habit of standing overly straight, hands behind his back, which gives him a challenging, almost offensive posture. He appears to be unapproachable. But deep down, there is insecurity; despite his ambitions, there are rungs on the ladder he will never be able to climb. His father is a simple clerk at the Chapter of Oudmunster in Utrecht. Just a middleman.

⚓

Utrecht, Spring 1644
"Our Nicholaas wants to move up in the world," says his mother, pointing with her crooked sail needle. A stout woman, smelling of sweat and stewed cabbage. Her eyesight is failing, and there is little light in the stuffy front room, so she is always bent over, her nose close to the sailcloth. "Thinks he's going to make it big. I always say: know your place. A donkey will never become a horse." Her mocking laughter will haunt him for the rest of his life.

Young Nicholaas attends the Dutch Reformed school. He is a good student; while the others are idle and cause trouble, he diligently learns his ABCs.
　Question: "What does God require of us?"
　Answer: "To love Him above all and our neighbours as ourselves."
　Q: "Can we do that perfectly?"
　A: "No."
　Q: "Why not?"
　A: "Because we are corrupt."
　Reading. Writing. Arithmetic. Most students leave the classroom when they are ten or eleven years old, for small hands are needed to supplement family incomes. But not Nicholaas, he wants to become a learned man, someone with status. Maybe even an officer in the States Army. Or at the Admiralty.
　The teacher furrows his brow. "An officer?"
　"A lieutenant, sir."
　A bony finger lifts his chin. "Listen, lad: noblemen, regents, and patricians

become officers. A lowly runt like you does not."

Everything is a competition. Being first is what matters. He's not popular, but his square, solid body commands respect.
"Arm-wrestle, Sweerts? For a penny."
He's spent an entire day hauling at the meat market for that money, but he doesn't hesitate for a second. "Fine. Bring it on."
In a dead-end alley, not far from the Ammunition House, the local kids gather, forming a circle around him and his opponent, a fourteen-year-old boy who is a head taller than he is. They sit at a crate, right elbows on the wood, with candles burning on either side.
"It's not fair," says Jansje Jansdochter, who lives two doors down and has only one eye. "Nicholaas is only twelve."
He grunts stubbornly and places his penny on the crate.
Right hands clasped. Tension in his biceps. He is determined. Suddenly, he knows exactly what he wants to be. He feels the strength in his forearm, pushing down, teeth clenched. He snarls at his opponent, "I... will... be... a merchant."
"Look at that," says Jansje, surprised. "The big one's burning his hand."

At the Latin school, he learns commercial arithmetic and bookkeeping. French is the international language, and Latin forms the foundation of erudition. For the first time, he meets young men from a higher class. They are polite but distant. Sometimes, he overhears their comments: "Sweerts? Il est un pauper." It irks him, but he looks down on his own equals. They—the high and mighty—have what he wants: power and connections, the means to make something of life. Merchant class. Mercator sapiens.
He throws himself into his studies but soon realizes that without initial capital, he can't make any real progress. The university? No chance. The best he can hope for is a life as a lowly clerk at a trading house. Or worse—God forbid—at the Chapter, perhaps at a standing desk right next to his father, in the same stuffy room, year after year. Do this. Do that. Until you drop dead. What will they say then, those arrogant bastards?
"Sweerts? Il est un serviteur."
The realization makes him rebellious ("I'll show them"). He takes pleasure in petty, malicious pranks: vandalizing their property, sending slanderous notes to the rector ("Van Drielenburch is a sodomite, we've all seen it!"), spreading rumors and lies. Sometimes, in the evenings, in the taverns, and when he's drunk—which

happens often—he tries to pick fights with them, but they're too clever, too nimble. They've learned to avoid him.

"Sweerts? Il est une douleur dans le cul."

Goddammit. He knows very well that he's making a fool of himself.

Girls? By the time he's seventeen, his face is covered in severe acne, and he has limp, greasy red hair. But it's not just that, what truly makes him unattractive is his bad temper, his constant dissatisfaction, and his complete lack of humour.

"You bore me," complains even Fijtje Fuller, who's never been too picky about boys, while he—grim-faced—tries to take her behind her father's piss-smelling vats in exchange for a few coins. He doesn't reply. It's always the same. His lust takes over, and he shoves and pushes and waits for the uncontrollable, exhausting explosion between his thighs. It's impersonal, and Fijtje is insignificant. She could have been someone else. It wouldn't have mattered to him.

Yet, the longing lingers. On one rare occasion—New Year's Eve—he is briefly allowed to step into the stately home of the Junius family in the Ridderschap Quarter. It's just a fleeting glimpse, a peek into that other world. He feels out of place, like a cat in a strange warehouse. But then he sees her—Wijnanda, the sister of his classmate Justus—sitting at the harpsichord in the side room, her slender fingers playing a melody that everyone knows except him. He can't take his eyes off her. There is no seduction, not in that house, everything is decorum, and she wears a modest black bodice of velvet and lace. Yet he sees through it all, sees her naked and beautiful, and lustful desires surge through him. A muse. It will haunt him for weeks, even months, stirring the raw broth of his mind and prompting clumsy attempts at poetry:

> 'Your eyes, Rose of Dawn, set me ablaze,
> Your golden-blonde hair confounds my heart.'

It is nonsensical. Unattainable. He is Pan, ugly and stubborn, and she the nymph Syrinx. Wijnanda Junius will never know who he is. And in the corridors, people talk about him: "Have you seen Sweerts? By God, it was horrendous, you can't be seen anywhere with someone like him, he looked like a lecherous bear."

His father's sigh. "What's wrong with a stable job for life, son? In modesty, as God intended."

He despises his father. His father's status. "I want to get ahead."

"Do you think they will accept you? They close ranks. You'll never be one of them."

"I am my own man."

"With what? Who will give you credit? Who will vouch for you?"

"There has to be a way. I'll find one." Stubbornness. Quick temper. He ends up wandering the streets at night, but he has an idea.

Amsterdam, 1656

With great difficulty he managed to wheedle some pocket money out of his father for a journey that would take six days there and six days back. Under his arm, wrapped in waterproof oilcloth, he carries his Sunday best, his finest shoes. Frost and light snowfall slow his progress, frost-covered meadows stretch out on either side as far as the eye can see. He sleeps in barns, buys meagre meals—stale bread and cheese, simple fare—and walks endless hours along a half-frozen river Vecht. Then, Amstelland: windmills in a white world, peat cutters, and towboats. The east wind is sharp, cutting through his coat and scarf. And finally Amsterdam—the Leidse Gate, people everywhere, through Leidsestraat to Koningsplein, the Rokin, the Dam—where he gawks at the construction of the new town hall—the canals, the ships and—unmistakably—the smell of the sea.

On a scrap of paper, he has scribbled the name of a street. "De Rapenburg?"

"The West India Warehouse?"

He is exhausted, chilled to the bone, but to be sure, he embarks on a reconnaissance mission. Yes, there it is, across the drawbridge where the Oude Schans flows into the IJ: stately, with steps and gables, four stories of stone, and to the left, in the fading afternoon light, the IJ quay.

He grins. At last, he feels a hint of satisfaction and affirmation ("I am my own man").

In a dark, shabby inn, he eats his first hot meal in six days (gruel with fat and fried bacon), rents a bed—there are four in one room—and falls asleep immediately.

Heavy, black beams support the ceiling of the West India Warehouse. Where stacks of ivory once lay, now stand tables and desks, benches and lecterns. Applicants are to report at the counter, but he doesn't have to wait long. Besides him, there are no other candidates.

The interview proceeds more smoothly than he had anticipated: his school certificates are excellent, and the recruiter—referred to here as the 'acquisiteur'—even makes an effort to remain friendly. Perched atop a high table, he towers over Nicholaas, casting a condescending glance at his worn Sunday coat. "I see a recommendation from the canons. The Chapter of Oudmunster is exceedingly wealthy, so I've heard. I'm surprised to see you here."

Nicholaas pulls a face. His limp red hair is tied back in a ponytail, making his pear-shaped head appear even larger. "I'm not a churchman."

"The Chapter is secular if I'm not mistaken?"

"I want to become a merchant."

Furrowed brows. "Merchant at the Company is a very high position, young man. Accessible only to the most dedicated employee, after a life full of sacrifices."

"But not impossible." He grimaces, realizing it might have sounded too presumptuous. "I mean, I'm willing to work hard."

The recruiter nods solemnly. "I admit: the West India Company has no barriers regarding status or rank; an ambitious man can go far. The most Honourable Monsignor Valkenburg himself is the son of a basket maker." He taps his nose. "Perhaps that's the difference with the East India Company, no? Are you healthy?"

"Fit as a fiddle."

"The climate is no trifle."

"I've never been sick a day in my life."

"The living conditions are abysmal. The local population can be hostile. Can you handle a sword? And you know nothing of the sea."

"I adapt quickly, sir. I'm determined."

He hears the scratching of a quill on paper. The recruiter is writing with a goose feather pen. "Very well." He leans forward and looks sternly at Nicholaas from his elevated position. "Assistant undercommis, that's your starting rank. Fourteen guilders a month, with deductions for board and lodging. And you'll pay for the journey yourself."

Seven months later, he sets foot on Elmina soil for the first time. The Gold Coast. Guinea. Gold. Slaves. Ivory. The scents. The colours. The heat. The humidity. Blacks of every kind and stature. He is instantly enchanted. Nothing is like in Holland; those who can hold their ground can gain status and wealth. Anyone can, yes, but God knows: they are few and far between. Healthy, sturdy young white men wither away within months. But he stays upright. The African air seems favourable to him; he rarely falls ill, suffers neither yellow fever nor elephantiasis, the bloody flux or yaws. Stubborn and tenacious, he works on, from sunrise to late into the evening, listening and learning, currying favour with superiors, lashing out at inferiors, patiently waiting for his rivals to fall by the wayside, and he steadily rises in rank: from assistant undercommis to senior commis, from merchant to provost, and— yes—in June 1684: director-general, the highest position on the West African coast.

He, Nicholaas Sweerts.

19 The Dying Ensign

"But if your servant says to you, 'I do not want to leave you,' because he loves you and your family and is well off with you, then take an awl and push it through his ear lobe into the door, and he will become your servant for life. Do the same for your female servant."

From: The Bible, Deuteronomy 15:16-17

⚓

The atmosphere in the grand cabin of the *Westsouborgh* is grim. The stern windows let in barely any light. Outside, the rain is pouring down, the sky is heavy and dark, and candles have been lit inside. Seated around the large table are the Brandenburg merchants and the skipper of the German yacht, with Sweerts at the head, flanked by his captain, a few officers, and midshipmen.

"The game is up," says Sweerts, his hands on the table. "The Ahante have taken your fort."

There is no response. The merchants press their lips together and stare grimly ahead.

"It has gone on for too long," he continues. "We have been too tolerant. That smugglers' fort was an annoyance. Let's be honest: most of your people come from Zeeland. From Vlissingen, sir!" He taps his fingers on the tabletop. "Your five soldiers were taken prisoner on the spot. One of them is wounded because he resisted. He fired his pistol. Then the Ahante fired back. According to the chirurgeon, he has a pierced lung."

Still no reaction.

He understands, but he's still angry. Ensign Vermeulen's condition is dire; the chief chirurgeon has predicted he probably won't make it through the night, and that's a setback, even if Vermeulen wasn't very good at his job. Sweerts shivers, he can still smell the stench of excrement in his nose. And to make matters worse, his ulcer has reopened, he feels warm fluid dripping into his beard. "Your wounded soldier has been brought aboard," he continues. "We will treat him to the best of our ability. But during the night, we will sail on to Frederiksburg. And we will take that too. We will no longer tolerate Brandenburg settlements along the coast." He looks at them one by one. "As for you, we will hold you hostage aboard until your governor surrenders." '

"*Herr* Niemann will never bow," one of the merchants protests.

Sweerts snorts. He makes an authoritative gesture toward one of the servants in the background. "Bring me a handkerchief." He points his finger menacingly at the man who dared to speak up. "Governor Niemann is a fool if he resists. We will not leave a single stone of your fort in one piece." He glances thoughtfully at the rain-soaked windows. "Frederick William wants to be the head of a seafaring nation. It's the fancy of a spoiled child. Do you think Dutch supremacy was achieved in a day? Or that the English merely decided on a whim to sail all the world's seas?"

He stands, and the servant hands him a clean handkerchief. He dabs at the wound. Yellow stains on the white cloth. Disgusted, he turns away. This day has brought him no satisfaction despite the progress he's made. "We have also taken in ten of your black labourers. They will be transported as slaves to the West. As compensation for expenses."

One of the merchants looks up in astonishment. "What expenses?"

"For our campaign, sir. By God, do you think waging war is free?"

He hurries two decks down and enters the crowded gun deck of the cruiser. Darkness, interrupted only by the occasional, carefully guarded storm lantern—there's a great fear of fire. Men everywhere. Talking. Lying down. As they see him, silence falls. Hammocks sway along the ceiling, from side to side, with the guns securely lashed down in their breechings in between. The air is stale. Greasy. Salty. He ignores the surprised faces, elbows his way forward towards the galley—where there's a bit more light from the smouldering coals in the ovens—and finds a space near the sick bay, which is screened off by canvas.

"Where's the chirurgeon?" he snaps.

"Sir?" The ship's master chirurgeon appears, a bald man wearing an indescribably filthy apron. He pulls aside the canvas. "After you."

Sweerts steps into the sick bay and immediately notices the change in stench. Now it's sickness. Blood. Faeces. Death. He suppresses a shudder. "The ensign?"

The hammock in the corner.

Ensign Vermeulen has aged decades in a few hours. Sunken face, sallow skin, hollow eyes. A vein throbs visibly on his parched forehead.

"I've given him *Peruvian bark**," the chirurgeon explains, clearly uncomfortable. "But it's not working. The flux has perforated his intestines." He absently wipes his apron, leaving a brown-red streak behind. "The bleeding won't stop. I fear the worst."

"Is he conscious?"

"Off and on."

Sweerts leans forward. Two beady eyes stare back at him, burning with fever.

"Grass," the ensign croaks.

"Grass?"

A faint hint of a smile. "There." The ensign lifts his hand, but it falls back immediately. "Meadows."

"He's hallucinating," says the chirurgeon behind him.

Sweerts sighs. Reluctantly, his fingers touch the ensign's shoulder. He feels the heat immediately. "Vermeulen," he says, "can you hear me?"

The head turns towards him. The ensign slips back into reality. "The plan is sound, sir," he whispers. "Burghoutsz was right. You must carry it out."

"But who's in command?"

"The sergeant."

"The sergeant is an idiot."

"Let him." He closes his eyes. "Get the men ashore beyond Crema. They can march all night."

---

* Peruvian bark = quinine: an antipyretic

Above them, the ship's bell strikes three times. "All's well!" the watch calls down through the main hatch.

"You have to go," says the chirurgeon. "He's too weak."

Sweerts dismisses him. "Vermeulen?"

The stench of faeces suddenly becomes overwhelming. Thin, brown clots splatter onto the floor beneath the hammock.

"You have no choice. I'm finished." The ensign makes a harsh, cackling sound in his throat. "I got Marie van de Hoeve pregnant. In '81. God forgive me. She never said a word. Never." His eyes now shine like cold stars. "She was a good woman, but I didn't want to be tied down. I had to run." His hand reaches for Sweerts. "I'm dying, sir! In this godforsaken place."

Sweerts avoids the hand and steps back. He holds his handkerchief to his nose. "I'm sorry, Vermeulen."

The hand flails in the air like a fish out of water. "I'm cursed," he moans, writhing in his hammock, which now sways back and forth. New splatters of blood hit the planks. "My God." A deep sigh. Rattling breath. "Marie!"

"It won't be long now. Fetch the ship's chaplain," the chirurgeon orders.

20 Attack on Fort Frederiksburg

"And the Lord said to Moses on Mount Sinai: 'You may buy male and female slaves from the nations around you, or from the foreigners residing among you and their descendants born in your land. They will be your property. You can bequeath them to your children as inherited property and make them slaves for life. (...)"

From: The Bible, Leviticus 25:44-46

⚓

Morning. The coast of Pocquesoe. Apart from a few small yachts and some canoes, the sea is empty. Word has gotten ahead of the Dutch, and illegal traders have quickly made themselves scarce. Even the fishing canoes lie unused in long rows on the beach.

The indigenous inhabitants have gathered, and there is a tense atmosphere as the *Westsouborgh* and the two frigates approach the coast unimpeded. People point and gesture. They are uneasy. A group of warriors stands indecisively and helplessly at the water's edge, spears and bows in hand, while the three ships sail in line, the cruiser leading, with open gunports.

The four Brandenburg merchants are sent ahead in the longboat, equipped with instructions. The boat drops them off on the beach, and the group climbs the hill dejectedly, with slumped shoulders, following the path that leads around the back to Fort Frederiksburg.

The gate is closed.

On the curtain wall between the two bastions facing inland, soldiers stand ready with muskets. "What do you want?" they ask suspiciously.

"Don't you recognize us?" shouts the spokesperson for the merchants, calling up to them. "We are Brandenburgers."

"Have you defected?"

"No, no, we were taken hostage by the Dutch. Sweerts sent us to deliver a message."

"What message?"

"Get *Herr* Niemann. It's for his ears."

There's some deliberation. The merchants wait patiently, but the gate remains closed.

"What do you want?" a voice calls down a little later in unmistakable German.

The merchants crane their necks. Governor Niemann, in his shirt sleeves, looks down at them with a stern expression from the curtain wall. "What were you doing on that Dutch cruiser?"

"Fort Dorothea has fallen, sir. The Dutch have taken it. There was shooting. People were wounded. They captured us."

Governor Niemann curses. "There's a treaty," he says.

"Director-general Sweerts is determined," the spokesperson calls back. "He seems beside himself. He wants you to surrender. He wants to occupy Fort Frederiksburg."

"And if I don't comply with his demands?"

"Then he will bombard the fort and the village. He threatens murder and mayhem, sir, he won't be reasoned with."

"Hmm." Niemann looks at his men. He counts twenty-five heads, that's all: a sergeant, a corporal, a handful of soldiers, and a few black auxiliaries. Plus eleven craftsmen, two chirurgeons, and a constable. Civilians.

His cannons have no carriages. We're not ready yet, he thinks. It's too soon. But damn it, it's a good fort, solidly built. And his men worked hard through the night.

"I will not bow to Dutch threats," he says resolutely. "If Sweerts wants to fire, let him. We'll see what happens. Tell him we will resist to the last man."

The merchants nod. That's more or less what they expected. "May we come inside, sir?"

The governor looks down at them disdainfully. "Of course not. You have been designated as messengers. So take my answer back to him at once."

The sergeant inspects his troop, which consists of a section of European lads divided into four squads, supplemented by five black mulattos from Elmina and the three hundred-strong group of Ahante warriors who had conquered Fort Dorothea and the village of Accada the day before. The indigenous warriors still look fit enough, but the whites present a pitiful sight. They have marched half the night, stumbling over unfamiliar terrain, along forest edges, and through dense, tough vegetation, cursing and sweating in the oppressive heat, soaked by downpours and covered in mud. The sergeant himself is not in much better shape. He leans on his snaphaunce—he had tried in vain to keep it dry— his lungs labouring, gasping for relief. His feet ache, his calves feel like lead and the straps of his cuirass and the weight of his bandoliers have chafed raw, red patches on his shoulders. Mosquitoes swarm in thick clouds around his head.

He squints at the sky and the sun. It's good that the rain has finally stopped, he thinks, so the guns and pistols can dry, but the heat will only get worse.

"How much farther?" he asks the guide, a jet-black Ahante who hasn't left his side all night.

"Very close," the guide responds obligingly, gesturing vaguely to the south.

Yeah, right. The sergeant sighs and wipes his sweaty, pockmarked face with a cloth. He's a veteran who's been in Guinea for a long time, with a lean, wiry body and skin that resembles wet leather.

When they were put ashore last night, a few miles back as the crow flies, he had been nervous, fearful of the responsibility. But now, exhaustion and lack of sleep have banished all doubt. All he wants is for this hellish task to be over as soon as possible. His mission is simple: reach the rear of Fort Frederiksburg undetected, wait for the ships to appear off the coast, and, while the Brandenburgers seek cover from the artillery fire of the ship's cannons, launch a surprise attack. The director-general had looked him straight in the eyes for a moment before departure. "Failure is not an option," he had said. The sergeant curses the death of the ensign Vermeulen. Just his luck. Anyway, if he pulls this off today, he can expect a reward, maybe even a promotion; after all, there's now a vacancy.

He straightens up. "Come on, men," he says. "We have to keep moving."

They march quickly down an old game trail. The ground is muddy and slippery. Every now and then, someone slips. Suppressed cursing. Branches and low undergrowth. They hack their way through with sabres and cutlasses. No one speaks. There is only the sound of equipment clattering against itself.

To their left lies the lagoon, its muddy brown water glistening in the sunlight. White pelicans drift on the surface. On branches above the water, cormorants perch, watching for mullet and tilapia. The guide has warned them emphatically about crocodiles. And in the trees, small monkeys scream like curious spectators, accompanied by equally noisy parrots.

A hut is visible among the green of the guava bushes. Naive residents who aren't cautious: a thin plume of smoke rises above the treetops and can be seen from miles around. The black guide presses a finger to his lips. To their left, the water of the lagoon laps against wooden posts and a long, dugout canoe that's been pulled halfway up the narrow beach.

The sergeant nods. Sweat pours down his face. His blonde hair, already thinning, sticks to his skin in wet, greasy strands. They haven't been detected yet. That's good. Despite everything, they've made little noise. Their biggest advantage is the element of surprise, remaining unseen until they reach the fort. His forefinger slides across his throat, from left to right.

The guide gestures to the five mulattoes. They silently rise and, crouching low, move quietly through the bushes toward the hut.

Waiting seems endless. The sergeant grimaces. He glances over his shoulder, where the Ahante warriors are squatting along the edge of the path, seemingly without a care in the world. Suddenly, a muffled cry sounds from behind the leaves. Then another. The second sound is higher-pitched. Perhaps a woman, the sergeant thinks. Or a child. When the mulattoes return a moment later, one of them holds a bloodstained knife in his hand.

"Just a few fishermen," he whispers.

"Any problems?" the sergeant asks.

The mulatto grins and shakes his head. "Not anymore."

They're right on time.

As they reach the base of the hill and see the grey walls of the fort towering high above, a distant rumble echoes. A muffled *boom*. A faint whine. And a dull thud on the other side of the hill.

"It's starting," the sergeant says to no one in particular. "Ship's artillery."

They lie hidden in the underbrush among the trees, still invisible, stretched out in a broad, single line of men. To their right, the huts of the village are visible. Chickens. Goats. And black figures darting back and forth like tiny dots. *Boom*! Another shot. *Boom*! *Boom*! Those are carronades, he thinks. The Germans won't know what hit them. He glances along the line again. The five mulattoes lie right next to him, their muskets at the ready. "Patience, lads," he says. "Give it time."

They wait for the impact of the cannonballs. The ground trembles as the heavy thirty-six-pounders hit the walls. In the air, bits of stone and debris fly up.

The ships sail in line ahead along the beach and Manfro Hill, with the *Westsouborgh* leading the way. The sea is deep here, though the reefs near the hill are treacherous, but there is enough water to approach closely.

First barrage: the two gun decks on the starboard side fire almost simultaneously. The cannons erupt with plumes of smoke and showers of sparks, expelling their ammunition with a deafening roar. The wind is to windward, so the gunpowder smoke drifts away from the ship, and the sparks don't touch the sails. The cannonballs shriek through the air: a wailing, screaming, terrifying sound that makes the hair stand on end.

The people on the beach vanish as if by magic. *Boom. Boom.* Heavy, trembling impacts on the hill and the fort. Earth and stone seem to explode. Even entire trees are hurled into the air, splintered and broken. The frigates follow one by one, each with two battery decks. New explosions.

Sweerts watches from the quarterdeck, fascinated. The power of the artillery fills him with a sense of might and satisfaction. He smells the saltpetre, and yellowish smoke lingers low over the water. With each thunderous blast, he flinches.

"Forward!" orders the sergeant once he is sure the ships have ceased firing. While they lay on the ground, they loaded and checked their snaphaunces. No taking chances. He's a veteran for a reason; there's nothing worse than a gun that misfires. That's lesson one, dammit.

He stands up and waves to his squads. The Ahante warriors lie farther ahead. Not all of them have firearms. Most carry spears. That's fine, he thinks. They're deadly with those.

The rear of the fort is just a little over four hundred paces up the hill. That's also where the only entrance is. The hope is that the Brandenburgers are so preoccupied with the bombardment at the front that the gate is left almost undefended. They don't have many soldiers.

The sergeant urges them to move faster. If we're spotted, it's over, he knows. Then we'll never make it inside.

They run up the slope in a wide, spreading line, backs bent low. But the terrain at the back is open, with only some low brush and the occasional palm tree. Human figures appear on the parapet. He curses. We've been spotted already, he thinks grimly. Should he have known better? Would the ensign have done better? Sweat stings his eyes. He's underestimated the Brandenburgers' resourcefulness; they've made makeshift carriages from palisade wood. A cannon barrel emerges on the left tower. He can see the muzzle clearly. Something stirs inside him. Unease. Fear.

"Run! Faster!" he barks at his men. He sees the uncertainty in their eyes. They're following *him*, not the Company, not the director-general. It's *his* responsibility. By God. Just two hundred paces left. He sees puffs of smoke from the wall. Musket fire. But it's still too far. You couldn't hit an elephant with a musket at that range. Breathing is difficult now, in this heat, and uphill no less. His lungs are on fire. The muscles in his legs scream in protest, it feels like he's wading knee-deep through mud. He sees the muzzle flashes. In his direction. No doubt about it. He thinks: grapeshot, they're using grapeshot. The screech of the projectile fills his ears, and then it's like something is yanking at his clothes. The hail of shot and shards shreds through the hot air. And that's it. His body is torn to pieces, he's dead before he hits the ground, reduced to strips and chunks.

The fort now lies to port. Sweerts peers through his spyglass at the shore, his face tense. And he's astonished: after all that violence, Frederiksburg stands as unscathed as before. The thick walls seem to mock him. He sees a few scrapes and traces of impacts here and there, but that's about it, despite the felled trees and burning underbrush.

"Why isn't it in ruins?" he asks the captain standing beside him.

"It's solid," the captain replies stoically. "Stone. Masonry. A wooden ship can be blown apart with a single hit, but not those walls. They're well built."

Sweerts growls like a dog. From the hill, the faint sound of musket fire can be heard. "That's our men!" he shouts. "Provide support. Enfilade, man, by God! Another barrage."

"Aye, sir."

The assault on the rear of the fort comes to nothing. The Brandenburgers have closed the narrow gate, and the defenders on the parapets, hardly hindered by the artillery fire from the sea, have a clear line of fire. Their muskets may not be very accurate, but the barrage of grapeshot against the broad line of advancing men is devastating. The warriors are powerless with their spears and shields. The slope seems to have an invisible wall, pushing them back every time they try to move forward. The cannons spew canister shots, thinning the line. A dozen attackers sit or lie on the ground, bewildered by their own vulnerability, by the blood flowing so abundantly onto the grass. No one has prepared them for the power of shell fragments. There is no battle. There is no one against whom they can use their spears or muskets. They stare at each other and into nothingness, stunned and full of fear.

It doesn't last long.

The Dutch call them back. Their eyes are hollow. Four white men lie like shapeless heaps among the churned earth. "Get out! Get out of here!"

The Ahante seek refuge, leaving behind their dead and wounded as they flee down the hill in long strides, away from that wall of ripping, killing metal, jeered at by the Brandenburgers on the fort's walls.

"We could, of course, tack again!" shouts the captain of the *Westsouborgh* because, after all that cannon fire, everyone is half-deaf. "And then fire a third barrage, a fourth, and a fifth, but it won't get you anywhere! It's pointless! You're just wasting powder and shot!"

Sweerts bites his lower lip. His ears are ringing. The captain is, of course, right, but the defeat feels like an open wound. The threat itself should have been enough, there was no reason for resistance. The Brandenburgers' combat strength is negligible; they have no ships to relieve themselves. Just one bastion defying him and the entire Company, one goddamned stubborn German!

He irritably sticks his fingers in his ears, maddened by the whistling in his head. Fine, he thinks, I don't have enough soldiers to take the fort, so be it. "You're right!" he yells at the captain, making a cutting gesture with his hands. "For God's sake, don't rub it in."

The thundering stops immediately, and the ship falls silent. The thick, stinking clouds of cordite drift away slowly.

He casts a dark look at the four Brandenburg merchants, huddled together on the quarterdeck like whipped dogs, terrified. "Your governor is an unreasonable man!" he bellows.

"Yes, director-general!"

He would love to hang them from the yardarm as a deterrent, it would undoubtedly give him some satisfaction, but nothing more than that. It would only make *Herr* Niemann more resolute.

His eyes survey the coast and the surf. He thinks: well, let him rot in his impregnable hole. It is as Burghoutsz said, we control the sea, no ship can get in or out. I'll leave my two frigates here and then let them try to collect their slaves. Let them come out with empty stomachs, and we'll be waiting.

His irritation fades. He has learned to be pragmatic.

21 Revenge on Taccorary

"(...) We intend to establish some plantations on the other side of the Benya River, to be called 'the Nation's Garden,' for the cultivation of vegetables and fruit for the white population. However, we must acknowledge that the soil and climate at the level of Elmina cannot compete with the abundance in Axim, where large quantities of rice, sweet potatoes, Indian corn (milho), and abromenades are harvested. The latter are a type of peculiar potato: they grow in clusters on the fibrous roots of a herb, with stems as thick as a finger, ending in two or three oval leaves. Once this crop is planted, it becomes difficult to eradicate, as it grows like a weed, tastes unpleasant (soapy), is not easily digestible, and somewhat resembles frozen potatoes."

From: Correspondence of Chief Chirurgeon Zacharias Augustijns to the Collegium Medicum of Amsterdam, October 1687

Days pass. Cool mornings with scattered cumulus clouds far to the west, the ocean swells with smooth, undulating slopes, like ancient, weathered mountain ranges, deep blue in colour. Occasionally, a petrel high in the sky, and groups of dolphins swimming ahead of the bow for a while. In the afternoon, the scorching sun bakes the decks. The *Westsouborgh*, now alone, sails close to the wind back towards Elmina.

A few miles past Fort Orange, on a promontory shielding the mouth of a sandy freshwater stream, the Brandenburgers hold yet another small settlement: Taccorary. It is all quite modest: a low palisade wall surrounding a wooden blockhouse and a sawmill, inhabited by a single merchant and guarded by six soldiers and a couple of unimpressive three-pounder cannons. The tiny settlement leads a secluded existence. It was built three years ago on the remains of a dilapidated fort, which was captured from the English by the

Dutch over twenty years earlier and subsequently neglected and forgotten. To the south of the ruin, remnants of a bastion still stand, now flying the flag with the red eagle.

Sweerts stands on deck, staring intently at that defiant banner. He hasn't forgotten Taccorary. Earlier this year, the place suddenly drew attention when the *Compagnie Française de Guinée* landed there, intending to establish a French trading post right next to the Brandenburgers. This provoked his displeasure, and he didn't hesitate to ruthlessly drive them back into the sea with the help of land troops and frigates, where they retreated with their tails between their legs.

I haven't been thorough enough, he now realizes. I should have not only crushed those Frenchmen but also beaten the Brandenburgers to a pulp. They didn't lift a finger to help us.

He is acutely aware of the tension among his soldiers, who have yet to see battle but have still suffered losses. Below deck lie five dead, including the ensign and their sergeant, the latter stored in gathered body parts under a folded piece of sailcloth. The men stand in sullen, silent groups. Even the sailors, who usually seize every opportunity to belittle them, now wisely keep their mouths shut. The atmosphere is volatile, and Sweerts knows he must act before things spiral out of control.

Perhaps he can kill two birds with one stone. Taccorary, he decides, must be destroyed. Let them also feel what it's like to lose people.

At dawn, the longboat is lowered. Two squads of soldiers sit cramped on thwarts and gunwales. Not a word is spoken, everyone is staring straight ahead, the barrels of their muskets pointing skyward. The soldiers themselves take up the oars, there is no room for anyone else. But it isn't far: in the twilight, they can see the mouth of the freshwater stream, and they row with grim determination.

The sea is dotted with sandbanks, the water shallow. They startle large flocks of storm petrels and gannets, which chatter in protest. On the boundary between salt and fresh water, they spot the dorsal fin of a small shark, cutting circles on the surface as it hunts. The coast draws near quickly. Mangrove trees anchor their gnarled roots in the ground. The sand gives way to mud, and in the clear water, small, colourful fish are visible. A few mampams rest on the shore: lizards with red, blue, and gray stripes running along their bodies.

"Don't touch them," someone warns, "or you'll die a horrible death."

Some soldiers quickly cross themselves.

The longboat scrapes onto the eastern shore, and the soldiers jump out. They run up the bank, through tall grass and rain-soaked shrubs. The palisade wall is not very high and nowhere near as sturdy as that of Frederiksburg or Dorothea. The Brandenburgers are still asleep. There is no sound except for the muffled clatter of equipment.

The men reach the gate unseen. With pikes, they pry at the cracks and gaps. The double doors begin to give. They pull and push with all their might. The wood snaps quickly, sounding like a gunshot. Only now do the Brandenburgers wake up.

But it's already too late. The Dutch storm into the yard. Two half-dressed guards appear in the doorway of the blockhouse and are mercilessly cut down. They charge inside. There's a scuffle and shouting. A shot. Another. A guard is dragged outside, screaming and begging, and promptly dispatched. Then comes the merchant. He is a short, stout man with a large, pointed moustache. He staggers out in his nightshirt. "*Was ist los?*" He nearly slips in the blood of his own guards. Sweat drips from his nose and chin. But he gets no answer.

The soldiers spit at him, kicking him across the yard. He is thrown onto the dirt floor. Heavy boots kick at his neck, his ribs, and his backside. He wraps his arms around his head and wails and screams.

"Shut him up!" someone shouts.

The butt of a musket smashes against the back of his head a few times. That silences him.

A cutlass opens his belly. The bright red of his blood contrasts sharply against his pale white skin. A few men emerge from the blockhouse, carrying small barrels of gunpowder.

"Remember the sergeant, boys."

"Right, no mercy."

The contents of the barrels are enthusiastically poured over him.

Sweerts stares at the shore, his lips pressed tightly together. Above the headland, a thick, grey plume of smoke rises. The sun has not yet fully risen, so he can clearly see the flames leaping from the blazing blockhouse. It burns like a torch. Further away, along the faint outlines of a path, he sees dark figures fleeing in panic toward the hinterland.

He nods with satisfaction. That will teach them. Damn Germans. Let's see how many more slaves they can take in now.

22 Bomba Jan

"(...) From Ashanti to Benin, it is the vultures who are left to devour those condemned to death. The black people hold a great fear for these birds; they are untouchable, and no one will harm them. Specially appointed individuals feed the creatures, and they are held in very high regard; no one is permitted to watch them as they perform their duty."

From: Correspondence of Chief Chirurgeon Zacharias Augustijns to the Collegium Medicum of Amsterdam, November 1687

Bomba Jan Michielsz stands proudly upright in the canoe, which is skilfully paddled towards the *Griffin*. The salty, warm wind plays through his frizzy hair, now showing a few grey streaks. Bomba Jan is enjoying himself. Life is good, and the future promises more adventures. He nods contentedly at the two rowers. Because he is missing his two front teeth, his broad face with its large, flat nose has a friendly, trustworthy appearance.

The rowers laugh cheerfully in return. They handle their paddles with playful ease, catching the waves at just the right moment so that the canoe's bow keeps steady contact with the water.

Bomba Jan grunts approvingly. He recognizes skill. He is a large man with an enormous chest, but he stands firmly and confidently in the boat, perfectly balanced on his elastic sea legs. At his feet is a large sea chest, four and a half feet long, one and a half feet wide, a beautifully crafted piece made from African padauk, darkened to a deep black over time.

The canoe reaches the ship. High above him, the crew has gathered along the railing. They recognized him long before, waving at him—many of them have shared a middle passage with him. "Bomba Jan!" they call out cheerfully.

He waves back, his grin stretching from ear to ear.

The side ladder is thrown down, and the crew throws him a rope so he can secure his chest.

Bomba Jan climbs up and lets himself be helped aboard.

Hands are shaken. They clap him on his broad shoulders like brothers and ruffle his hair. Bomba Jan looks around, taking in the familiar scents. He recognizes everything. Nothing has changed. His fingers rest on the railing, feeling the heartbeat and soul of the ship, it flows through him like a sip of grog, warming his throat and stomach. "*Eééh.*"

The boatswain approaches him. Bomba Jan lowers his head, suddenly all humility; he holds the boatswain in a respect bordering on fear. "*Ackie*, boss," he greets, standing there like a child caught in the act.

Boatswain Graauw is a head shorter. His mouth is a lipless line. He gazes at Bomba Jan with hard, light-grey eyes. "There you are again, Bomba Jan," he says without much friendliness.

Bomba Jan nods silently.

"The skipper's been waiting for you."

"Yes, boss."

Bomba Jan is sweating bullets. He finds the boatswain to be an unpleasant white. He still remembers much from the last voyage. There had been dark days. *Very* dark days. Bomba Jan shudders. Some memories he had already pushed away.

"Come along then," the boatswain says at last, turning on his heel.

Bomba Jan sighs in relief. He sneaks a wink at the crew, his grin back in place like the sun breaking through a cloud. Obediently, he follows the long path to the cabin, deep in the aft of the ship.

The boatswain knocks on the door. "Go on in, he's expecting you."

Bomba Jan opens the door.

The skipper is seated at the large table, hunched over a stack of sea charts, with his back to the stern windows. The light streaming through them is greenish-yellow.

"*Ackie, aene.*"

Burghoutsz looks up. His gaze is tired, and there are dark circles under his eyes. "Bomba Jan. How was Amsterdam?"

Bomba Jan hugs himself and blows out a puff of air. "Cold!"

The skipper nods. "Did you see snow?"

In his mind, Bomba Jan sees the city. There was a morning when *everything* was white. Streets and rooftops. His breath looked like smoke. He had slipped and fallen on something so strange that it almost frightened him. He held it in his large, calloused hands until they went numb. But if you held it long enough, it turned into water. Just like that. You could drink it. Slurp it up. Pure magic. But the people around him laughed at his amazement. "No need to be scared, Bomba Jan," they had called. "It's just snow."

He says, "No one here believes me, *aene*. The old men in the village claim I've lost my mind. Because I skated on water as hard as stone. From Amsterdam to Alkmaar." Bomba Jan shakes his head in bewilderment, he can hardly believe it himself. That winter felt like a dream, he sometimes thinks, as if Onyame had taken him and shown him feverish visions, like when you're very ill and on the brink of death. But the whites know the truth, they know it was all real. They live in that strange, cold world, where even the paths are made of stone— something those babbling old men in the village can't comprehend despite all their bluster. He chuckles; ever since he was chosen as bomba, his status has skyrocketed like a comet.

The skipper asks, "When did you come back?"

He thinks for a moment. "The trees turned green, and the days grew longer. I sailed to the sea, to an island where many ships were anchored. I got on board. I earned money. One hundred and twelve guilders." Yes, he thinks with satisfaction, when I returned, I was a rich man. I bought two wives and a goat right away.

The skipper says, "A new journey is underway, Bomba Jan. We need you. You're the best bomba."

He swells with pride and nods solemnly. "Yes, *aene*. Are we going to Offra, to fetch slaves?"

"No, this time, we're going straight to the West."

"But... the dungeons aren't full!"

"There will be more, don't worry."

He looks concerned. "No *donkas*, aene, no *bad* slaves?"

"No, no donkas. People from the Gold Coast. But you mustn't speak of this, Bomba Jan."

Bomba Jan closes one eye and tilts his head slightly. His face turns serious now. He understands. Yes. More or less. "I will keep silent," he swears.

The skipper points to the table, where a piece of paper and a small burlap pouch lie. "Two months' pay, twenty-two guilders, to be paid in advance by the Company." He places the paper in front of the big man. "Sign here."

Bomba Jan leans forward. He takes a quill and dips it into the inkwell. There are marks on the paper. White men's marks. He can't decipher them. But he sticks the tip of his tongue into the gap where his front teeth used to be and, with great concentration, makes a wobbly cross.

The mulatto quarter is located next to Elmina Castle, a cluster of huts and wooden houses close to the wet moat and the western defensive wall. Bomba Jan squats in front of his hut. It's Sunday, a day when the white men take their rest—a habit he has gladly adopted, though the reason behind it escapes him. He doesn't think much of the white man's god, whom the black population mockingly calls Jan Compan.

It's one of his last days on land, and that makes him see his surroundings with a sharper focus, as if his spirit is already beginning to say farewell. He knows from experience that sleepless nights full of longing will inevitably follow once he's at sea, and it's good to remember the coconut palms and bombax trees, the beach, the hut, the village, and, of course, his two wives.

Bomba Jan chuckles. Buying those wives was a good move. He had thought it over for a long time; it wasn't an impulsive act. A young one and a slightly older one—that's what he had decided. The younger for his desires, the older because she is experienced and can manage a household and teach the younger one a thing or two. It has worked out well. They are pure-blooded Akim with manners and dignity, and the bride price was reasonable. They don't argue too much, though they are still women, and bickering goes on all day long. That's just how it is, there's nothing he can do about it. But at night, they are compliant and obedient, and their bodies are warm. The older one is a bit plump, which has pleasantly surprised him. Just thinking of her can arouse him, even now, while it is still morning. But the younger woman boosts his status, and that is worth a lot, too, especially in the village.

Bomba Jan takes a sip of his beer, resting in a wooden cup at his feet. The beer is bitter and strong, just as it should be—not that weak stuff the white men drink—and he feels a pleasant buzz in his head. His large body sways slightly, balancing on the balls of his bare feet, enjoying the sun that's not yet too hot. Unconsciously, he starts to doze, a smile playing on his lips. Time passes. He feels fingers against his hand. "Wake up, Bomba Jan."

Bomba Jan looks up.

Quassie Patoe, the ensign of the asafo Enyampa, towers over him, hands on his hips, legs spread wide, a grin on his pitch-black face. "What are you dreaming about, Bomba Jan?" he asks.

Bomba Jan winks. "White women."

"White women? *Eééh*." Quassie Patoe curls his lips downward. "White women stink."

"Not rich white women," Bomba Jan says, thinking of Amsterdam. "They wear pomanders." He gestures invitingly. "Have a seat, Quassie Patoe."

Quassie Patoe shrugs. He has no idea what a pomander is, and Amsterdam is an abstract concept to him. Of course, he has heard of all those white villages like London, and Lisbon, and Paris, but they don't evoke any images for him. He's never been farther than Commanie. He does understand why Bomba Jan feels differently: Bomba Jan isn't a true black Akim but a mulatto with white blood in his veins. It must be that white blood that leads him to end up on white ships. But Quassie Patoe himself has no desire to travel, he is perfectly content with his own little piece of earth.

He squats down, finding his balance while his eyes take in the yard: the hut is well-maintained, the earthen floor swept, the vegetable garden watered and weeded. There is a goat in a pen of woven branches, and plump chickens roam around. Bomba Jan, he decides, has things well under control.

"What can I do for you?" Bomba Jan asks. "Perhaps you'd like something to drink?"

Quassie Patoe looks at the cup of beer and nods.

Bomba Jan gestures to his wives. The older woman nods to the younger one. The younger woman steps out of the hammock, grumbling, and disappears into the hut.

"A favour is what I ask," says Quassie Patoe, getting straight to the point. "On behalf of the asafo Enyampa."

Bomba Jan immediately becomes cautious. He knows very well that the asafo people look down on him. They don't like blacks with white names. White names are unpronounceable (he knows a mulatto called Grootgrutter). "If I can," he says carefully, "I will help."

"It's about Quameno Ewussi, who is pawned."

"The slave?"

"The man who isn't branded yet."

"The slave."

"He stands as security for two hundred and fifty guilders."

"Then he must be paid for."

"There aren't two hundred and fifty guilders."

"Not with the asafo?"

"The asafo aren't going to put down two hundred and fifty guilders for a negro foolish enough to wander into the hinterland alone. Besides, he could never repay us."

"Aha."

"Nevertheless, something has been collected..."

"But not enough."

Quassie Patoe looks annoyed. "No, not enough. Of course not. A few reed mats, chickens, and goats. Twenty spans of Portuguese roll tobacco. All sold on the market. About forty guilders altogether. They gave it to me. They said: Quassie Patoe, you're the ensign of the Enyampa for a reason. Go to the bomba of the white ship and see what you can do." He spreads his hands. "I'm doing what I can. So here I am." He rummages under his robe and pulls out a small pouch. "In stivers, guilders and pieces of eight."

The pouch is placed between them.

Bomba Jan hears the sound of coins. It's music to his ears, but his pleasant buzz is gone. He doesn't like where this conversation is going at all. "What am I supposed to do with forty guilders?" he asks. "The *aene* will laugh at me first and then tie me to the mast."

Quassie Patoe shakes his head sympathetically. "You don't have to pay off the debt, but you could make sure Quameno Ewussi doesn't go on the ship. You're one of the few blacks allowed near the prisoners, Bomba Jan. You could make sure he falls ill and is declared unfit."

"Ill?"

"A few seeds of Kombe poison, like the sorcerers use. It'll make him struggle to breathe and unable to move his arms and legs. Not too much, he mustn't die. The sorcerers know exactly how much to give; there's a good..."

"For forty guilders?"

"What?"

Bomba Jan feels his anger rising. Of course, they despise him, that's nothing new, but the ease with which they want to exploit him ignites his fury. He looks at Quassie Patoe and sees him for what he is: a braggart. But there's more—a layer of cold calculation. Quassie Patoe won't hesitate to do whatever it takes to achieve his goals. He wants to become the *tufohen*, the commander of all the asafo companies.

But Bomba Jan won't get his fingers burned. He says, "The white man's medicine man will see through it. He's an old, crafty chirurgeon and knows all the tricks."

"No, no," sputters Quassie Patoe, waving his hand dismissively. "Kombe poison is invisible. No one will know. Only you and me. And Quameno Ewussi, of course."

As if I were a child, Bomba Jan thinks. He believes I'll sell my soul for that bit of money because, in his eyes, I'm just a dumb half-blood, like the house slaves of the Akan or the wretches who survive on handouts from the mulatto fund.

He points to the massive gold amulet around Quassie Patoe's neck, and the golden bracelets and rings. "That *chika* is worth a lot. Much more than two hundred and fifty guilders."

"That's personal property."

"With its value, you could buy Quameno Ewussi's freedom right now. You could keep him as your own slave, make him work for you. You could even take his wife."

"I don't want a slave," says Quassie Patoe, irritated. "And my *chika* has nothing to do with Quameno Ewussi."

"Then I ask for two hundred and fifty guilders," says Bomba Jan. "For two hundred and fifty guilders, I'll give him Kombe poison."

Quassie Patoe looks incredulous, his mouth falling open a little. "What do you mean?"

"Why should I ask for less than the Company? If they catch me, they'll flog me and hang me. That's a lot of risk for forty guilders."

"So you're refusing."

Bomba Jan leans back and feels the pounding of his own heart. He suppresses the urge to strike Quassie Patoe. That would be unwise. People are watching; they have ears and eyes. People *talk*. "Bomba Jan Michielsz is an *Akrampafo*," he says in a hoarse voice, though not without pride. "A free citizen with white blood. No one tells him what to do. He has his own house and his own family, and he is in the service of the Company. He has earned a hundred and thirty-four guilders. When he dies, he is entitled to a funeral, a wooden coffin, three gun salutes, and a flag flown at half-mast. Who is Quassie Patoe to come onto Bomba Jan's land and criticize him and ask him to do things he himself doesn't dare to do?" He shrugs. "The pawn stays where he is," he decides, "unless the asafo Enyampa pays two hundred and fifty guilders to the Company."

There isn't much left to say. From the corner of his eye, he sees his youngest wife approaching with a full cup of beer in her hands. He makes a dismissive gesture with his hand. "Quassie Patoe doesn't need it any longer," he growls angrily, "he is just about to leave."

Quassie Patoe stands up. His face is a tight mask, but he maintains his calm and dignity. He even nods briefly to Bomba Jan's youngest wife. "Whites choose whites," he hisses. "Even when they look like blacks."

The conversation with Quassie Patoe has left Bomba Jan upset. Lost in thought, he leaves his house, crosses the bridge towards Krabbenberg, and walks along the old lane lined with stately silk-cotton trees toward the Dutch cemetery. He knows the graveyard like the back of his hand because he often comes here to think or find peace, but also because this is the only place that connects him to his past.

Almost at the back, between low white walls, half-hidden under a cluster of trees, stands a simple, grey gravestone with a nearly faded inscription: *Michiel Michielsz, 1601-1643*. He can't read the letters, but as a child, he was told who this was: his grandfather, a poor, insignificant, white assistant clerk from Ransdorp, Waterland, who came here when the Dutch drove the Portuguese from the coast in '37, and who succumbed to malaria six years later. Bomba Jan never knew him. He can barely imagine having a white ancestor because he knows he looks no different from the other blacks. His skin might be a shade lighter, but that's not unusual either; 'black' is only a relative term, as the locals come in all colours: black, brown, dark, and light.

He crouches by the gravestone and brushes away some moss. The stone is warm from the sun but still damp from the night rain. His fingers trace the inscription as if the touch could bring him closer to the mystery. When he was in Holland, he didn't find a sense of belonging. He saw strange white people in a strange, cold land, and as a black man, he was often little more than a curiosity. How could he have roots in that distant soil?

And yet, Quassie Patoe does not see him as one of them, and the Akan tribes do not see him as one of them. Bomba Jan is neither black nor white. What, then, is Bomba Jan?

He looks up as he hears footsteps beside him. The tall figure of Reverend Duisterbloem looks down at him intently: "Are you a *tapoeijer*, a mulatto?"

Bomba Jan stands up. The reverend reminds him of Akrampa the vulture, with his drooping shoulders and his black suit. He doesn't trust those white sorcerers; they're humourless men who always seem to be angry. "Yes, sir."

The reverend looks at him sternly. "A half-blood is the work of the devil. An abomination in the eyes of the Lord. Do you believe in God and in Jesus Christ?"

Bomba Jan believes in Onyame, not in Jan Compan. But he attends mass faithfully every morning because he doesn't want to be fined. "Of course, sir."

"Jesus is the only hope for salvation," the reverend nods. He points to the gravestone. "Your progenitor burns in hell. He was tempted by the devil when he slept with a black woman."

Bomba Jan hardly listens. If that almighty white god hates mulattoes so much, he wonders, why then does he allow white men to mate with black women?

The reverend puts his hands on his hips, a faintly mocking expression on his face. "Mulattoes often forget that they are still like Ham, the son of Noah. Ham wants to return to the father, he wants to be like Japheth. He crawls. He writhes. But the curse cannot be undone. A black man cannot become white. Never!"

In a gloomy mood, Bomba Jan has taken to drinking. Aimlessly, he has roamed from one black tavern to another, filling himself with palm wine, staggering along the old path to the hinterland, past scattered huts and miserable little fields, where the influence of the whites diminishes with every step. Now, late in the afternoon, he has approached a tiny village, and the alcohol hums through his head.

Ahead of him, a bit away from the settlement, stand the dog kennels, row upon row, with the bitches and their puppies, the pups bred for the Akan feasts. Whites don't eat dogs, Bomba Jan knows. Whites are crazy. He laughs, stumbles along the path, his legs like rubber and his feet moving of their own accord. Beyond the path lies a field covered in tall grass, and among the stalks stands a vulture: bald-headed, wings lazily spread. The vulture waits. It's eyeing the young dogs or perhaps waiting for the slaughter remains. With its waddling gait, it hops back and forth, beak forward, neck bent, like a deformed killer, its eyes suspiciously fixed on Bomba Jan.

"*Akrampa!*" shouts Bomba Jan with a slurred tongue, and he's not entirely sure what he sees: is it really a vulture, or is it that reverend? Are the two perhaps one and the same? Shaking his head, he takes a few hesitant steps forward. He's now so drunk that he can hardly stand. "Are you a spirit or a man?" he slurs.

The vulture watches. Its black eyes flicker. In the heat, its long wings seem to quiver.

Bomba Jan loses his balance. His heavy body thuds to the ground, sunbeams dancing in golden streaks through the grass. Mosquitoes and flies buzz around him. He hears the vulture nearby, rustling in the grass, and his foggy mind vaguely registers the danger. He swings a heavy arm around him.

Even the dogs have now noticed the bird of prey. They whine and bark in their cages, jumping against the walls.

Bomba Jan mutters incoherent words. The vulture stands beside him, its claws in the soft ground, its wings spread. Its beady eyes stare coldly at him.

"What do you want?" His voice cracks, feeling his own vulnerability. "I'm nothing. I'm just a half-blood, you said it yourself!"

The dark grey beak hovers before his nose. Along its jagged edges, sharp as knives, are dried pieces of meat. A foul stench wafts toward him. The vulture tilts its head. Wrinkled, red skin flaps tremble. In the cages, the dogs snarl. Bomba Jan feels dizzy. He turns onto his belly and crawls on hands and knees toward the cages. "It's not my fault!"

The vulture twists its neck, its head thrust forward. The heat ripples above the grass. For a moment, Bomba Jan feels the touch: the hard, horn-like beak scrapes over his shoulder. He looks back into dead eyes, into an inky, distant depth. There is nothing there but cold and darkness. He begins to cry.

The dogs in the cages seem to have gone mad. Their howling, barking, and growling alarm the village. He hears people shouting. The wings make a flapping sound. Shadows above his head. There it goes. Bomba Jan follows the contours in the sky. The vulture rises, lifting on the warm wind.

That evening, four armed mulattoes open the door to the large dungeon in the courtyard of Elmina Castle. Their half-white faces peer at the bound black men, who are huddled together in the darkness on the encrusted floor. The air in the dungeon is heavy, almost tangible. A sour stench takes their breath away. They curse and wave their torches, causing the light to dance over the black men. They don't want to go inside unless they have to, as there are excrements and other filth on the floor.

"Quameno Ewussi?" they call impatiently. "Quameno Ewussi?"

Quameno Ewussi stands up immediately. In the yellow light of the torches, his face looks surprised but hopeful, and also relieved. He raises his hand. "Here I am!"

"Come with us," barks one of the mulattoes.

Quameno Ewussi squeezes through the tightly packed men.

Outside, it is dusk. Thick clouds drift overhead, and the stones of the courtyard are wet from the rain. Quameno Ewussi fills his lungs with fresh air. The wind is blowing. He can smell the ocean, and the sound of the surf is like music to his ears. His heart fills with joy. Finally, there is justice.

An old white man with grey hair is waiting for him by a brazier. "Quameno Ewussi?" he asks.

Quameno Ewussi eagerly nods and smiles at the old man. He recognizes him: it's the chief chirurgeon of the castle, a kind of medicine man who examines the slaves and gives them potions when they're ill.

Two of the mulattoes grab his arms. Quameno Ewussi feels the weight of his chains, but he willingly lets himself be pushed forward. The old man probably wants to check him over, make sure he's not injured or hasn't caught some disease in that filthy pigsty from hell. "I feel fine," he says.

The chirurgeon picks up an iron rod from the brazier. At the end of the rod is a branding iron, glowing yellow. The mulattoes pin his arms down. Quameno Ewussi can't move.

"It didn't work out," the chirurgeon says regretfully. "No one wants to pay for you."

Quameno Ewussi stares at him in disbelief. This can't be true, he thinks. He has a wife. He has children. He feels fear rip through him like a cold shiver. "No, no," he pants. "I am Quameno Ewussi of the asafo Enyampa. I am a free man."

"Not anymore," the chirurgeon says curtly. He makes an impatient gesture as it's late, and he's been invited to dine with the head merchant at the castle. It has to be quick, so this time, there's no liquid wax to dull the pain.

Quameno Ewussi writhes, but he's trapped in an iron grip.

"It's a mistake!" Now, he feels the heat.

"It will be over soon," the chirurgeon says soothingly.

The fire touches his chest. Quameno Ewussi roars in pain and rage as the mark of the Company is seared into his skin.

23 The Execution

"(...) And before he could draw his sword, the white man was struck from behind by a javelin, causing him to fall from his hammock. Then, several more wounds were inflicted upon him, after which he gave up the ghost. The enraged negroes did not stop there but severed his head, which later adorned the headman's great drum, with the jawbone on display. And since the unfortunate man had an unusually beautiful, red-blonde head of hair, they fashioned from it a fly-whisk, as they usually do with horse or ox tails.

We describe this event in detail and with all particulars to demonstrate the cruelty of the negroes towards their enemies. And alas! If only it could end here; but we will be compelled to depict more scenes of their unpleasant nature! (...)"

From: 'Travels and Description of the Gold Coast of Guinea,' by J.A. de Marée

The Company's provost* stands before the iron door of the prison cell, trying to adjust to the darkness. Only a little light filters through the narrow air vents high in the outer wall. The stench is barely tolerable.

"Corporal Puteijn," he calls out to the cell door, "it's time."

From behind the peephole, he vaguely sees something move, and he gestures to the two guards. "Get him out."

He tries to breathe shallowly as the door creaks and groans open. The two guards, armed with pistols and cutlasses, enter. He hears the clinking of chains. A moment later, a pitiful figure emerges with slumped shoulders, dressed in

---

*The provost was responsible for law enforcement, justice, and maintaining order in overseas settlements.

black knee-breeches and a torn, filthy undershirt. Shackles on his neck, wrists, and ankles are linked together, so he can only shuffle along, his hands out in front of him, his face turned to the floor.

The provost sighs and curses the task he must perform this morning. "Corporal Puteijn," he says without much conviction, "today your sentence will be carried out, as decreed by the Council of Elmina."

The prisoner does not respond. His long, greasy hair hangs over his eyes.

"Do you understand me, boy?"

He feels the urge to give him a sip of water or a word of comfort or—God forbid—a pat on the head, but that would, of course, be inappropriate. Life is harsh. There are rules. And this boy has broken all of them.

"Alright," he decides, "let's go." He turns and walks out of the prison area with stiff steps, followed by the prisoner, flanked by the two guards.

Outside, the sun glares off the stone floor of the courtyard, momentarily blinding him. He blinks his eyes and sees dancing yellow and red circles. Slowly, the world comes back into focus: the blue sky, the castle, the spectators along the three open sides of the square, the wooden scaffold in the middle, with the sergeant of the guard and two soldiers beside it, and on top of the scaffold, the gallows, the motionless rope with its noose, and the waiting executioner.

Out of the corner of his eye, he notices Reverend Duisterbloem with his sharp, stern face. The man is clutching a Bible and muttering inaudible prayers. The provost ignores him. He dislikes the cold-hearted, fanatical pain-in-the-ass. But perhaps the feeling is mutual. Duisterbloem doesn't even glance his way. The reverend takes up a position behind the prisoner with a self-righteous air and begins whispering his prayers into the boy's ear. The boy doesn't react. He stands utterly still, waiting for what's to come.

The provost turns and walks with his entourage toward the scaffold. Somewhere, a drummer begins to beat his drum. It irritates him, though he knows it's all part of the procedure. The spectators stare at him silently. They have removed their hats. On the parapets, the soldiers look down on him, snaphaunces in hand. No one speaks, but the tension and anger among them is palpable; Corporal Puteijn is one of theirs, and the provost is just a lousy civilian.

He glances around once more, just to be sure, not wanting any incidents. This must proceed in an orderly fashion. It's bad enough as it is. Near the carpenter's workshop on the far side, he spots two company slaves peering curiously in their direction. Damn it. His small group reaches the scaffold. The provost stops just a yard away from the sergeant. The sergeant salutes. The provost whispers, "There are two nigger slaves over there, watching the execution of a white man, sir. Get rid of them. Now!"

Director-general Sweerts stands on the balcony of the main building, his lips tightly pursed as he gazes down at the scene. All the Europeans are required to be present, including the crews of the Dutch ships. Anyone who fails to show up without a valid reason can expect a hefty fine. So they are all there, standing two to three rows deep, waiting in the scorching sun for him to give the signal. Sweerts despises executions, not because he feels any aversion to the death penalty, but because it means that someone under his command has stepped out of line, that he hasn't enforced discipline strictly enough. It fills him with both anger and shame.

So he lets them wait down there, in the blazing sun and heat, sweating and grumbling, because he holds them all responsible for what is about to happen. Every now and then, he sees a face looking in his direction, and he makes sure to stare back with the intensity of a general spoiling for war.

He watches as a sergeant leads the condemned man up the steps to the scaffold. He doesn't know Corporal Puteijn personally—a face among many. The Company is a refuge for the destitute. He thinks grimly: for Germans, country bumpkins and other wretches who still have grass between their teeth.

Puteijn was not a bad man, his scribe had explained, but he was typical of the type: illiterate, rough and impulsive. It often happens like this: the climate and the long time away from home make men restless and quick-tempered.

It has cost him a lot of effort to smooth things over; not only did the corporal, in a fit of rage and drunkenness, stab a white merchant to death, but he also killed two black traders who were under the protection of the king of Denkyira. Such traders are highly regarded.

The drummers roll their drums. The provost stands on the scaffold and reads from a piece of paper. It is inaudible, but Sweerts knows exactly what is being said.

The provost glances up and sees Sweerts in his blue coat standing on the balustrade. He rolls up the sentence, hurriedly stuffs it under his coat, and turns his head towards the executioner. "Get on with it," he says as evenly as possible and involuntarily takes a step back as if trying to distance himself from his own complicity.

The executioner is a big man. He wears a leather hood over his head, concealing his face, along with heavy gloves and an apron. He walks over to the boy without hesitation, grabs him from behind, lifts him effortlessly and throws him belly-down onto a wooden barrel lying on its side. The barrel rests on a rope, the ends of which have been split into two loops. The executioner expertly wraps these loops around the corporal's wrists and ankles and pulls them tight. The boy groans briefly. Now, he lies helpless, like a trussed pig, defenceless against whatever is to come.

The provost has personally selected this executioner, having sailed to Fida for the purpose. The man is the only one on the coast who rents his services to the Dutch, English and Brandenburgers alike. There is no conflict of interest when it comes to torture; in that regard, all Europeans are the same.

First, the lashing must take place. A hundred lashes is a lot, too much, he thinks, but Sweerts had insisted and would not relent; the boy is to be made an example for the others, and the provost understands that. The executioner had shown him his arsenal: did the provost want the cat with iron points or with leather knots? He shudders. The Dutch use a wet rope for lashing, not iron. What's the point of hanging a dead man?

The executioner rips the boy's shirt and trousers off, the sound of tearing fabric echoing painfully through the crowd. The spectators on the sidelines seem to flinch momentarily. There are murmurs as the executioner pulls out the cat-o'-nine-tails and holds it up. He dips the ropes into a bucket of water. The dripping, wet cords splash water onto the wooden planks of the scaffold. He takes aim, the nine cords swishing through the air, followed by sparkling arcs of water in the sunlight, and the first lash lands with a crack like a gunshot. The boy's head jerks up. He lets out a cry that expresses more surprise than pain, but his bare buttocks are already marked with thick red welts.

The provost shrinks back. From his position, he has a clear view of the scene, and he doesn't dare look away—not under the watchful eyes of the director-general, who is undoubtedly observing him.

Second lash. Third. The condemned boy has recovered from his shock. His cries now unmistakably convey pain. But the executioner maintains a steady, relentless rhythm, seemingly keeping time with the strikes of the clock. After the tenth lash, the cat is dipped into the bucket again. The water dripping off it is tinged with a faint pink hue.

After a hundred lashes, Corporal Puteijn's buttocks are unrecognizable. Halfway through, he stopped screaming. Blood and faeces drip down his thighs onto the scaffold, filling the air with a sickly, metallic smell that attracts flies. The executioner pants slightly, sweat pouring from beneath his hood, making a faint squelching sound as he moves. He glances at the provost, waiting for the signal to continue, but the provost just stands there, his shoulders slumped, face pale as if he were seasick. It happens often, the executioner knows. He throws the cat into the now empty bucket, removes his gloves, and unties the loops around the convict's wrists and ankles. The boy doesn't move but is still breathing. The executioner pulls his trousers back up, covering the bloody mess on his buttocks. It's not fitting to hang someone stark naked, with his genitals exposed to everyone.

Reverend Duisterbloem watches as the executioner drags the boy toward the noose. Hé feels no shame or unease. In his view, the condemned is receiving his just punishment, and it should be witnessed by all. He steps forward, holding the Bible demonstratively in front of him, and prays loudly so that everyone can hear the words God spoke to the sons of Noah: "And I will demand an accounting for the life of another human being!"

The executioner shoves him aside indifferently. The noose is placed around the boy's neck.

The provost flinches at the sound of the trapdoor slamming open. The condemned plummets like a stone, and the noose makes a sickening, snapping sound.

    The boy's legs twitch momentarily. Urine drips from his feet, splashing onto the stone floor of the courtyard. No one speaks. The rope creaks. The sun blazes. The provost lowers his eyes. Death walks there now, he thinks, an invisible spectre collecting that boy's soul. He shudders and thinks of the big cup of corn brandy he'll need later. More than one. A man needs to be able to sleep.

24 Mussulman Ali and Jasper Vogel

"O Prophet! We (Allah) have made lawful for you: your wives to whom you have paid their bridal gift, and those whom your right hand possesses of those slaves whom Allah has given you as spoils of war."

From: The Quran, Surah 33:50

The narrow beach lies in a sheltered bay, almost invisible from the sea, protected by a palm-covered promontory. Mussulman Ali is squatting with his bare feet in the warm sand, his elbows resting on his knees and his caftan slightly pulled up. He has safely reached the coast with his clandestine cargo of slaves and can now rest and gaze at the sea. He likes to watch the sea. The sea has something mysterious about it, sometimes it's friendly and kind, but often it shows its true nature and is deadly and harsh. Today, Mussulman Ali has noticed that it is in a gentle mood, wearing its light green coat, and the whitecaps in the surf further away look peaceful. Beyond them bobs a small ship with three masts.

The Dutch gave all types of ships a name, as he learned early on. They have dozens, and it's hard to distinguish one from the other, but if you don't recognize a particular type, you can certainly count on their derision.

He chuckles softly. He learns very quickly and is always ahead of his competitors. *Masha Allah.* The ship beyond the surf is a pinnace. It is the *Meyboom.* All whites regard a ship as a woman. He has long gotten over his astonishment at this.

Perhaps it's because the whites never see their own women. Mussulman Ali knows very few white women, and *they* are all filthy whores. He shudders and feels sorry for the infidels, for their women apparently cannot meet their expectations, otherwise they would not take black concubines, whom they treat like old rags and discard after a while. He thinks lovingly of his own three wives, who are neither white nor black but pure daughters of Aminah bint Wahab, *Allahu Akbar.* They run his household, cook his food, repair his tents and play with his manhood. He grunts contentedly, scratches his crotch, lost in pleasant, sensual memories, and spits a wad of qat into the sand.

A launch boat detaches from the ship. Mussulman Ali stands up and adjusts his caftan, making himself presentable to receive his guest with dignity. He raises his right hand, and immediately, five of his men appear from the edge of the forest behind the beach. They are armed with snaphaunces and pistols, carefully loaded, and their expressions are grim and resolute. Mussulman Ali nods approvingly. His men do not carry fake guns like the blacks in the interior, who believe that everything that comes from the whites is good. But the whites only give away what is worthless or when they get something better in return. He bought his snaphaunces for a fair price, paid with gold, and therefore, they are of unquestionable quality.

He looks at the boat, which is slowly manoeuvring around the promontory and heading for the inlet. There are five men in it, four rowing and one sitting at the stern. From here, Mussulman Ali can see his wide-brimmed hat. "Keep your distance," he says to his men. "But make sure the infidels can see you."

These are different kinds of Dutchmen, he knows, Dutchmen who recognize no laws, who are not bound by the rules of the Company, and who are enemies of the soldiers and merchants in the forts. Dangerous men. Mussulman Ali respects them. He is a dangerous man himself. And the leader, the one with the wide-brimmed hat, is in his eyes a true *djinn*, a demon from hell, who knows neither God nor law and is on earth to take possession of innocent people.

The launch boat approaches the shore. The white djinn waves to him. Mussulman Ali waves back, but with his lips tightly pressed together. Under his caftan, he carries a long, curved and razor-sharp knife, and his fingers briefly touch the hilt. Just for reassurance. *Alhamdulillah.*

The white djinn has piercing, light-coloured eyes that seem to look right through you. This is a disconcerting thought, thinks Mussulman Ali, who is sitting across from him. He sees a dark red velvet vest, a white lace collar, and a wide-felt hat. On that hat is a huge ostrich feather, black and white, swaying in all directions in time with the movements of the white djinn, who cannot seem to sit still for even a moment. Mussulman Ali has never seen such glowing eyes before, though he is now used to white men's eyes, but his are like glass, sparkling and crackling as if an unearthly fire burns behind them, and that is probably the case. He suppresses a shiver and prays silently to the Almighty, who will protect him from this barbaric hellhound, *Audhu billah.*

Mohammed, his personal servant, pours hot tea into small earthen cups. The steam rises almost straight up; it is windless here under the trees. Around them, the beach stretches out, with the forest edge behind and the sea before them and the launch boat—out of earshot—where the four rowers sit. The light is fading. Evening is near. But he can see the barrels of their muskets.

"That is a very, very large sum of money," says the white djinn in the coastal lingua franca; he speaks with a rough accent, although his voice is strangely melodious. He looks at Mussulman Ali intently, as if searching for every thought in his head, and his finger pointedly gestures toward the chest of money at his feet.

Mussulman Ali nods obediently and smiles. He knows that smiling puts the white men at ease. His father, the first Mussulman Ali, had taught him this when he said, "Never show your true face, Ali bin Fahrad Al-Fulan. If you are afraid, put on your mask, and do the same if you are angry, sad, or hopeful. If you don't, they will see right through you. They will devour you whole." Mussulman Ali remembers this lesson well. Over the years, he has perfected several masks. But he does not dare to look yet at the wooden chest placed between him and the white djinn.

The chest holds the payment for his goods, a fortune in coins because he insists on being paid in money, not in cowrie shells. Cowries are for the locals, for the blacks and mulattoes, not for an Arab trader like himself. If the white djinn does not cheat him, there will be enough coins to pay for a hundred and ten slaves. That is more than enough to tempt the white djinn; he might think it worthwhile to hack Mussulman Ali into pieces and take off with both the money and the slaves. But he has taken no risks. His men stand ready, and he only has to give a signal for the bullets to start flying. He is not foolish. He will not be deceived.

The white djinn laughs as if he has clearly understood those thoughts. He raises a finger and waves it around while his eerie eyes survey the guards.

Mussulman Ali reaches for his teacup and slurps. The tea is sweet, with plenty of sugar. The whites like that, too. Smiles and sweetness. "Yes, much money for many slaves," he agrees once more.

But what about the other way around? A sly voice whispers at the back of his mind. What if Mussulman Ali were to shorten the white djinn by a head and run off with both the money and the slaves himself?

Lalala, he thinks, admonishing himself, though he has to admit that thought was indeed tempting, if only for a moment. The white djinn is certainly being very arrogant, sitting here calmly drinking tea with him and the chest of money between them while his own men remain behind in the boat at the water's edge. Surely, they have their guns loaded, but still, if Mussulman Ali were to act quickly and mercilessly, he could overwhelm them and be gone between the hills before they could do anything about it. Then he could sell the slaves to the *al'Inglizia*—the English—in Fida or Cape Coast Castle and make a double profit.

Eééh.

He drinks his tea and decides against that idea. No, that would be very unwise. He would betray all trust. They would put a bounty on his head in all the coastal kingdoms and hunt him down mercilessly, and he would have to flee beyond the Great Desert in the north. Besides, he has the nagging suspicion that he cannot kill the white djinn, that the bullets would pass right through him and come out the other side without causing any harm at all.

"Very good slaves," he says again, just to break the silence and cut off these terrible thoughts. *La ilaha illa Allah, Muhammadun rasulullah.*

The white djinn nods. He barely touches his tea, playing with a twig instead.

"Have you suffered losses, Mussulman Ali?" he asks cheerfully, and when he grins, he reveals a white, even set of teeth, which is quite unusual for most whites his age—he must be in his thirties—have hardly any teeth left. "I didn't come here for nothing, did I?"

Mussulman Ali shakes his head. "For nothing? No, of course not," he says kindly, still with that frozen smile on his wrinkled, sun-baked face. "A few children fell ill on the way. That was to be expected. Young children are always difficult to transport. Everyone knows that."

"Rotten fever?"

"Dysentery."

"How many?"

"Four." Mussulman Ali remembers how he had the children taken from their mothers. There was no point in dragging them along, as it slowed the caravan down terribly, but of course, the women did not understand that. Life isn't always rosy. He did his best to make the little ones better with extra water rations and bloodletting. But it usually doesn't help, and that was the case now as well, so there was nothing left to do but leave them behind in the forest. He is convinced there is no merciful way to leave the sick behind. Only God is merciful. If God wills it, He will send Pataku the hyena, and then it will be over quickly. *Inna lillahi wa inna ilaihi raji'un.*

He gestures with his hand toward the treeline, and immediately, there is movement visible. Someone shouts a command in Arabic. Mussulman Ali notices the white djinn stiffen ever so slightly, an almost imperceptible reaction, but it pleases him; it makes the other seem just a little more human. "There is no cause for alarm," he says softly.

The colourless eyes flash in his direction. Anger? No. No emotion. But probing for mockery in his voice. Or any other reason to slit Mussulman Ali's throat. This devil will never be my friend, he thinks. Never. *Subhan'Allah.* He now notices that the white djinn has painted forearms and wrists. Another devilish habit. Someone once told him that such men have been to the ends of the earth. The images depict green, writhing dragons with enormous jaws and teeth that seem to move with the muscles of the white djinn. Perhaps he has indeed slain dragons in those distant lands, Mussulman Ali thinks. That's far, far removed from his own origins, and although he himself is far from home, he shudders at the thought of venturing to the edges of the world.

Yes, the whites are restless and never satisfied.

He waves his hand again, and from the shadows beneath the row of trees, two naked figures emerge—a man and a woman, two specimens from his black stock. The chains on their ankles clink. The blacks are used to each other's pace: they automatically synchronize their movements and cross the beach in a sort of shuffling step. The white djinn rises. He wears black velvet pantaloons and knee-high boots with butterfly flaps.

The man and the woman now stand before them, bowing their heads to be inspected. The male slave is tall and straight, with broad shoulders that droop slightly. This irritates Mussulman Ali. It's unnecessary since he's fed his slaves well on the journey and has barely beaten them. He taps the male slave reproachfully with his fingers, showing him how to stand up straight with his shoulders back.

Meanwhile, the white djinn pinches the breasts of the female slave and grins lasciviously at Mussulman Ali. "Young," he says.

"Strong," Mussulman Ali replies as he watches the white djinn feel the skin of the female slave. He had them washed and rubbed with goat fat that afternoon so their skins shine in the late light and had their frizzy hair rinsed with palm oil and vinegar, and for those with grey hair, he had it dyed with a paste of charcoal and unripe figs. Beauty sells, Mussulman Ali knows. He doesn't make mistakes. Never.

The white djinn seems fascinated by that dark, shining skin. He can't take his eyes off it. Perhaps he doesn't often encounter black women, Mussulman Ali thinks, since this trickster with his fast pinnace is more of a gold smuggler than a slaver: it's clear that he doesn't really know how to inspect negroes. That's foolish because Mussulman Ali could have sold him worthless goods. He shrugs. If the white djinn wants to mate with the merchandise, that's his business. It's not his concern what the whites do with the slaves after they've paid him, but the market isn't happy with slave women who unexpectedly give birth to mulatto children after the purchase. Mulattoes bring shame; it undermines white supremacy in the New World. It's not like here: here, pigs mate with dogs and vice versa, and no one is shocked anymore. This old world is sick.

He stares at the money chest, now sitting unattended in the sand. Suddenly, he's had enough of this infidel. *Astagfirullah*. It's time to do business.

25 Duisterbloem: Meditations in the Dark

"Slaves, obey your earthly masters with respect, reverence, and sincerity, just as you would obey Christ."

From: The Bible, Ephesians 6:5

In the cellars beneath Fort Coenraadsburg, it is always dark and cool. The air smells damp, and in the darkness, the echo of dripping water can be heard. The hollow spaces are divided by rusty iron bars, which groan and squeak as they open. In the corners, centipedes, cockroaches and woodlice crawl silently, and bats hang from the ceilings, shoulder to shoulder, their delicate wings draped like black cloaks around them.

Reverend Duisterbloem stares at the six corpses lying side by side on wooden trestles, illuminated only by a single lantern. He has already recited the prayers for the dead, holding the cross in his hand, the Bible under his arm. His murmuring has now ceased, and the silence descends upon him like an avalanche. In the desolation of the cellars, the normal world feels like a different reality.

In the darkness, anything is possible.

The reverend is distressed. He has seen many corpses before—he is used to it—but this time, the sight of these six bodies wrapped in coarse cloth weighs heavily on his mind. The prayers do not help. The words have been repeated so often that they seem to have lost their meaning, so often that he recites them without thinking, like a nursery rhyme. But the Bible is the word of God, and where does he find the audacity to rattle off His words so carelessly? Is it the devil again trying to tempt him?

He is tired. Tired of thinking. Tired of doubting and of his own weaknesses. Exhausted by the throbbing lust in his body, the constant fantasies. His head spins, and obscenities crowd out the holy texts: copulate. Fuck. Screw. Shag. For God's sake!

People are talking about him. His skin is grey as ash, and his emaciated appearance suggests the worst. Is he ill? They avoid him, are afraid of him. Yet here, in the darkness, he finds a sort of peace.

The six dead men, all of whom he knew in life, have suddenly become silent companions. They do not argue, do not mock him, do not despise him. It is a strange kind of friendship he feels, a connection he cannot explain and that God could not possibly approve of. Tomorrow morning, he will bury them in unmarked graves, for they were poor wretches—except perhaps the ensign, who is rumoured to have saddled a married woman with child. Ah, what a lot: one murderer, an adulterer, and four anonymous soldiers. The Company will honour them perfunctorily with volleys fired from the castle's ramparts and a Dutch flag at half-mast, but after that, they will be insignificant, quickly forgotten victims. Swept away like crumbs from a table.

Duisterbloem shakes his head in confusion. Psalm 65 says: "Silence waits for You, O Lord, in Your holy dwelling."

In a sudden impulse, he unfolds the coarse canvas shroud that wraps the sergeant. There's not much left of the man. He is barely recognizable as a human. Rough chunks of dead flesh hastily gathered together. The flesh is dark red, raw, and shredded. It looks as if—as if an entire person has been undone. He shudders. Why does he want to see this? Is it a form of self-punishment? He recalls something someone once said to him, long ago, at the university: "You, with your own congregation, Duisterbloem? In Holland? Never. You're far too radical. You'd drive everyone away. You can go convert the blackies."

With his long, thin fingers, he touches the cold, dead skin. The chill feels surreal. He looks at the face. The blonde hair. The half-grown beard. There is nothing peaceful about the sergeant's expression. He looks exhausted, with hollow cheeks and bags under his eyes. The blue lips are tight, even grim. Scars.

It is the face of someone who has suffered greatly. As everyone here suffers, in Africa, or in the New World, or in the East. The suffering is immeasurable and all-encompassing.

Too radical? Yes. At the Latin school, he was already criticized for his rigid nature: "Grotius was *against* slavery, Duisterbloem. Read up on it for once!"

That debate is marginal, but it exists. It irritates him. He has inherited the views of Udemans and Usselincx: "Christians may enslave Muslims and heathens, provided they are taken as prisoners in a just war or purchased from their parents or other rightful masters for a fair price."

But the young like to debate, to be contrary, even though they will ultimately always bow to the pragmatism of the Dutch mercantile spirit. He himself prefers to quote the Dutch preacher Picardt: "In summary, Europe is a queen over Asia, Africa and America."

And so it is. But this does not make him well-liked. He is too black-and-white, without a sense of humour or perspective. Someone once said, "You're a bore, Duisterbloem. There's no fun with you."

He looks up, and in a far corner, near the barred door, where the light of his lantern barely reaches, he sees his father. His face is square and angular. Dark eyes look at him reproachfully. He holds his breath, fervently hoping that there will be no voice, but the face slowly turns toward him.

"God does not love idlers," his father's dead mouth whispers.

He obediently shakes his head. No. He remembers his father's leather belt, who was a beloved preacher, who did have his own congregation in Soest and who preached from the pulpit every week. His belt was the voice of God. Some memories are permanent; now and then, when it's cold and wet, the thick, cord-like scars on his back itch. He lowers his gaze, gathers courage, and looks up again.

There's nothing there.

The darkness is black and impenetrable. Almost tenderly, he folds back the canvas, covering the sergeant again. Later, a few assistants will sew the shrouds shut.

Above him, the bats squeak. And across the walls slide the shadows of naked women's bodies; he hears their lustful panting, their wantonness.

26 The Worm

"(...) I tell you: every day is the same. After the call for 'all hands,' we have five minutes to get up, get dressed, and come on deck. And if anyone takes longer, the boatswain with the cat-o'-nine-tails is always there. Inboard and outboard, fore and aft, above and below deck, the rails and sides are rinsed, scrubbed, and scoured with scrubbers and sailcloth, and the decks are strewn with sand. Small hand-stones, called 'psalm books,' are used to scrub the tighter spaces and corners. This takes a few hours, after which the pump is manned, and all the sand is washed away from the decks and sides. The scrubbing must be finished before mealtime, and meanwhile, the crew is busy filling the water cask, and the cook scrapes the wooden tubs from which the crew eats. When all is done, the captain appears on the quarterdeck, and then the crew eats. Half an hour is allowed for breakfast. (...)"

From: **Letter of an able seaman to his father in Rotterdam, winter 1687**

Skipper Burghoutsz stares at the coast of Elmina. On the beach in front of the castle, a careening barge* has heeled a Dutch yacht onto her port side. A

---

*Careening barge = a heavy flat-bottomed vessel used to tilt ships on their side so that maintenance can be performed on the keel and hull.

swarm of black figures bustles around the hull, dark with clinging barnacles and limpets. They attack the unwanted growth with caulking hammers and scrapers. Heavy kettles filled with pitch and tar stand on roaring fires, and the smoke wafts thick and greasy over the water; the smell reaches all the way to the *Griffin*.

But this barely registers with him. He has more pressing concerns, for his steward is suffering from the guinea worm. This isn't unusual; almost everyone in Elmina, whether black or white, succumbs to the worm sooner or later. That's why he usually ensures that his crew goes ashore as little as possible, minimizing the risk of catching diseases from the African coast.

Yet here they are with the third case this year. Good sailors are hard to come by, so Burghoutsz has summoned the chief chirurgeon of Elmina aboard, who is widely regarded as the expert in the matter due to his years of experience.

The chirurgeon has laid the poor steward on his back on the deck, fully exposed to the bright sunlight, as it's well known that the worm is most inclined to emerge when it's warm. The patient's bare, gaunt, white torso is held down by two sailors while the chirurgeon, a chubby old man with a worn-out wig on his head, bends over him, assessing the situation.

The worm, a thin ribbon beneath the skin of the abdominal area, moves very slowly and ends in a swollen, fiery red blister just above the navel.

The steward looks at his own belly with horror. He's in pain and in danger: the worm's exit could lead to life-threatening infections, as everyone knows. It all depends on where the creature chooses to emerge and, more importantly, whether it remains intact, as a worm broken into pieces means severe trouble for the patient. "Get it out, sir," he pleads, panting like a workhorse. "Please."

The chirurgeon nods reassuringly. Despite the unusual location—most worms exit through the legs or feet—he doesn't consider this a particularly complicated case. "We'll do our best, sir. I can promise you some skill and experience," he says, giving the patient an encouraging look. "Once, I had to pull a worm out of an eye—*that* naturally caused permanent damage. Just like that poor clerk back in '82, or thereabouts, whose scrotum had swollen up to the size of a pig's bladder. And then there are cases where the legs and feet become so swollen that walking becomes impossible, accompanied by horrific inflammations resembling leprosy, with rotting tissue and all." He chuckles reassuringly. "Yes, the worm chooses its own path, and if you're lucky, there's only one because some poor souls are tormented by several at once."

He squats down and examines the blister on the steward's belly. A yellowish fluid seeps out. In the middle, there's a tiny opening behind which something white moves. He gently taps it with the nail of his index finger. The steward flinches and lets out a startled cry.

"There's the head," he announces to the audience, which consists of the entire crew standing in a circle around him, jostling for a better view. "The creature wants to come out. It's full of eggs and wants to deliver them to the outside world."

The onlookers shudder. They've heard and seen it several times before, but the sight is so horrifying that it disgusts them anew every time.

"Give him some rum," the chirurgeon orders. "And a piece of rope, for between his teeth."

It must be the water, he thinks, it's not because of foul vapours or the hand of God, as they claim. I may only be a humble chirurgeon, but I am certainly competent enough to determine that this is the only explanation for why there is no difference in contamination between the crews aboard the ships and the blacks on land: they all drink from the same source. He clamps a piece of rope between his patient's teeth, rummages in the leather bag beside him, and takes out a pair of iron scissors. "You mustn't break the head," he explains, "and the hole has to be big enough."

He is a large, heavy individual. Without ceremony, he sits down on the steward's pelvis so that the man can't move. "Hold him down tightly, lads," he says to the two sailors, pinning the patient's arms.

He leans forward until his nose almost touches the blister—he has to because his eyesight is no longer what it once was—and gently inserts the tip of the scissors into the small hole in the middle, very carefully, so as not to touch the worm, and then he makes a tiny cut in the skin. The steward starts moaning and writhing, but the chirurgeon's weight keeps him in place. Another snip on the other side of the hole. His tongue sticks out slightly, and beads of sweat glisten on his forehead. From the inside, he presses the split skin outward with the tip of the scissors. There's some blood, but not much. The hole is now considerably larger, and the worm's head, barely distinguishable from the rest of its body, suddenly protrudes.

The crew holds its breath.

The chirurgeon takes a small pair of forceps from his bag. He is proud of his instruments. Many of them he forged himself. The jaws of the forceps are ridged for a better grip, and the head of the worm is smooth, but you mustn't squeeze too hard; the creature must not be harmed, not even the slightest scratch, because as soon as you grip it too roughly, it will brace itself and try to retreat into the host's body. Then you're in serious trouble. That causes excruciating pain for the victim. You don't mess around with the worm, for God's sake.

"Bite down on your bit," says the chirurgeon. "Hard."

The steward's face is as white as a dishcloth, but he nods obediently and bites down so hard on the piece of rope that his jaw muscles crack.

The chirurgeon wriggles the forceps into the blister. The worm reacts, pulling back a little. The jaws of the forceps slip behind its head and clamp on. The chirurgeon feels resistance as the creature braces itself. "Now we wait," he says. "Patience. Pray to God. Drink a flagon of brandy. Let the earth spin around the sun." He stays seated like that while the steward makes a groaning, almost whimpering sound. His eyes are as wide as saucers.

Finally, a bit of give; the creature relaxes slightly. Now, the chirurgeon begins to pull very gently, very gradually. Under the steward's skin, the worm's movement is clearly visible: it's as if a finger is scratching from the inside.

"By God," someone mutters. "It's coming loose."

The chirurgeon shakes his head. It's not that easy. It always goes slowly, in increments. In segments, he thinks. A few inches of slack—that's what he hopes for today. He's had patients where it took four weeks for the worm to emerge.

With his free left hand, he reaches into his bag again and feels around for a thin, rectangular wooden block. Meanwhile, he continues to apply pressure. The worm's head is now out of the blister, and slowly, a piece of its body appears. It's pure white, like a thick strand of cotton. The chirurgeon pinches it between his thumb and forefinger and pulls on it as if it were a piece of string. He drops the forceps back into his bag and wraps the first segment of the worm around the wooden block. Bobbin lace, he thinks. Tatting. He turns his head and meets skipper Burghoutsz's eyes. "It's going well," he says. "Piece of cake. That steward of yours will be back on his feet in no time, mark my words."

Logbook of the Griffin, Saturday, December 6:

"Day 47 at the Elmina anchorage, 5°5'N, 18°6'W. The unrest is growing; there have been disputes among the crew. I took firm action and had all hands busy lowering the masts and yards, taking down and re-rigging the main and fore stays. The chirurgeon is doing his best for the steward, who is having bouts of fever. So far, thirty inches of the creature have been removed from his body, but

inflammation might be setting in.

The carpenter, being the oldest on board, played the role of Saint Nicholas in the evening and handed out gingerbread, much to the crew's delight. This has significantly improved the mood."

27 *Back: Aldemar Burghoutsz (2)*

Father has sailed out, and mother no longer sleeps. Admiral De Ruyter must cut the English down to size.

⚓

Amsterdam, 1662

In the summer, the wealthy leave the city because the thick, brackish water in the canals is fouled by faeces, urine and decomposing waste; the stench is unbearable. On hot days, people prefer to stay inside with shutters closed, holding perfumed cloths to their noses. However, those who can afford it escape. The wealthy have ostentatious country houses in Amstelland or along the River Vecht, where they flaunt their riches.

Aldemar Burghoutsz walks with his girl along the Nieuwe Vecht, the Wael and the Nieuwe Wael, where return ships are docked in long rows along wooden quays. No stench here, only the scent of the sea. He laughs at Anna, his arm motioning to encompass the whole world, all oceans. "Look," he shouts. "Everything is connected, that is where I want to go."

She smiles indulgently, understanding his ambitions, but is also troubled by them. The sea gives much but always demands recompense. Every Dutchman knows that.

Master de Graaf not only runs his own navigation school but is also an examiner of helmsmen at the chambers of the East and West India Companies in Amsterdam. His own students are openly given preferential treatment. Not that Aldemar lacks knowledge—he has studied day and night and passes with flying colours.

"What now, boy?" asks de Graaf. "The East?"

Of course. He wants to see the Spice Islands. But that means being away from home for two years, and he has Anna now. He doesn't quite know how to reconcile his longing for the sea with her. It's the first real complication in his life. So, he has thought about it. "I'm going to the Zaan River, master."

"The timber trade?"

"Maybe. That seems like something I'd enjoy."

In the Baltic Sea trade, he would be home more often. There, he can also learn his *craft, and it gives him time.*

Master de Graaf nods approvingly. "I'll provide you with references," he says. "I know a few skippers who sail to Russia and Poland."

The Zaan area. The industrial heart of Holland. Aldemar arrives by ferry, traveling up the river from the Northern-IJ. Shipping companies, shipyards and windmills line the riverbank.

The ferry moors at the Beer Quay, on the border with the Klauwershoek. Aldemar shivers. It has been raining all day, and a sharp, cold wind sweeps without hindrance over the waters. There's hardly any shelter on the boat.

The old ferryman points to a building along the waterfront: "There's an inn, lad, grab a grog and something to eat."

Aldemar shakes his head. He has neither time nor money. He has to return to Amsterdam this afternoon. "Where does shipowner Gijsen live, sir?"

"Gijsen?" The ferryman frowns at him. A drop of snot hangs from his nose. "What's it to you?"

"I want to sign on, sir."

"Do you have papers?"

Aldemar nods. "From master de Graaf, on the Niezel. With a recommendation."

"Helmsman?"

"If God wills."

"Hm." The ferryman, with his weathered, square face and white stubble on sunken cheeks, examines Aldemar with piercing blue eyes. "Gijsen has an East Countryman[*] anchored off Texel. A rear-loader. Timber. Riga. The skipper is still looking for hands. Hard work in the cold, boy. Is that a problem?"

"I'm willing to work hard, sir."

"You'd better." The ferryman sizes him up one more time, those sharp blue eyes searching for any flaws. He nods, seemingly satisfied. "Come along, I'll take you to the skipper."

They head to the west side of the river. Due to lack of space, the houses are built along narrow paths that run perpendicular to the Zaan and the dike. Each path is its own little community, lined with ditches and small, simple homes made of

---

[*] East Countrymen = English translation for Dutch 'noordsvaarder' (north trader), referring to ships that typically traded with the Baltic. The Baltic trade was highly significant for both England and Holland during the 17th and 18th centuries, as both nations relied on timber and grain from the region. In England, the trade route to the Baltic was commonly referred to as the East Country trade, in Holland as the 'mother trade'.

overlapping planks with neatly crafted facades. Willows droop next to the entrances. Beyond the houses stretch endless meadows and marshlands. It's still raining. Large puddles have formed along the path.

The ferryman knocks on the door of the first small house. "Wait here."

Aldemar hides within his cloak, hands in his pockets, shivering from the cold. His long hair sticks to his head. He smells the water of the Zaan, dirty and foaming along the banks. In the background, he hears the sounds of hundreds of sawmills, the most advanced in the world. He suddenly realizes that he is now further from home than ever before. In West-Zaandam.

Clogs off. Now standing in his socks in the tidy kitchen, his hands behind his back. Water drips generously from his clothes onto the scrubbed wooden floor, which makes him feel a little ashamed. The black stove against the tiled wall radiates heat, which he eagerly soaks in.

Skipper Rijkjan is a big man with hands like shovels and gray hair tied back in a long ponytail that glistens with macassar oil. He looks sternly at Aldemar from the other end of the kitchen. "Do you have a family?" *he asks in a low, raspy voice.*

"Yes, skipper. Mum and dad."

"What does your father do?"

"Herring fisherman, in Enkhuizen."

"Do you have a girl?"

He blushes. "Yes."

"We can't use homesickness, boy." *Skipper Rijkjan quickly glances at his certificate and seaman's book.* "You were a good student, but you still have a long way to go. I've got cabin boys who are drier behind the ears. Not everything is in books."

"I'll do my best, skipper."

"The timber trade is hard work. We have no room for provosts, chirurgeons, gunners, preachers or passengers. We're not the VOC. Fifteen heads on board, and that's it. Work until you drop. We sail out, pack the holds full and go back. Time is money. Shipowner Gijsen doesn't like to waste it." *The skipper looks him straight in the eyes.* "Discipline is strict, lad. Once you're on board, you do as I say; there's no turning back."

"I understand."

"Do you want to come along or not?"

"Yes, skipper."

"We leave in a week. Make sure you're on board. You can catch the ferry at the

Texel Quay in Amsterdam."

It is early in the morning, the spring sun shines brightly, and the waves on the IJ glitter in the sharp light.

People are already standing in line, and Aldemar is among them, with a knot in his stomach and a duffel bag slung over his left shoulder. With his advance payment, he can afford the ferry service to Texel; for just a few coins, you can get on board. The ferry is an old barge, which usually sails across the Zuiderzee to the Texel Roads twice a week, but in the spring, when the Easter fleet of the East India Company is about to depart, the number of crossings is doubled.

The passengers sit in the open air. There's no luxury; in bad weather, the deck is covered with a sail. Aldemar finds a spot by the side, near the port leeboard, leaning his back against his bag. There he sits, in the middle of the rough seafaring folk. He hears countless dialects, and there are many German and Danish lads on the boat.

"Wohin gehst' du?"

"Til Batavia, på Bruinvis. Og du?"

"Cádiz, Spain."

The sailors read each other's ship's articles and shout at one another.

"The East India Company pays better, mates. It's right here in black and white!"

"And that boor of a boatswain said: 'You can manage with just one leg too.'"

"Mate, in Bantam, I've got myself a sweetheart. I bet she's waited for me."

He hears all these exotic names. Java. Makassar. Accra. Elmina. The Sound. Livonia.

The ferry hoists sail with the wind at the port stern. He hears the IJ streaming past the sides. Seagulls screech in the air.

Amsterdam slowly fades from sight.

After a full day of sailing, they finally leave the Zuiderzee behind. Through the Texel Stream and the Balg, they reach the Moscow Roads and see the lights of 't Schild. In the falling darkness, he can just make out the silhouettes of ships at anchor. Masts wherever you look. Lanterns are being lit. The ferry skipper lowers the sail, and the sailors use poles and oars to slow down, with critical comments from others. Everyone is awake now, and sounds of rustling abound: in the dark, people search for their sea chests and other belongings.

"Keep an eye on your stuff, men."

The skipper swears and curses to keep the passengers in check. "Goddammit, get out of sight, stay seated, you bunch of idiots!"

They are not the only ones: ferries arrive from Hoorn, Delft and Enkhuizen. The small boats jostle for space, bobbing in the water.

"Out of the way! Get out of my wind!"

't Schild has no harbour, so they have to moor by the dike. The ferry scrapes over the bottom. "Disembark!"

Aldemar clutches his duffel bag tightly.

The main road runs parallel to the dike. On the landward side are houses, inns and taverns. To the left, at the end, lies the Kollegat, the red-light district where sailors seek their entertainment. Rows upon rows of water barrels are waiting for the ships bound for the East Indies, strictly guarded by VOC soldiers. The brown, iron-rich water from Texel's wells is sacred: it will remain drinkable until the Cape of Good Hope.

Porters, loaders, skippers and merchants shout over one another. A group of sailors, arm in arm, sing a bawdy drinking song at the top of their lungs. Horse carts rattle by. There are traders, prostitutes, loafers, thieves and tourists. Everyone's in a hurry, everyone has somewhere to be.

Aldemar stands there, feeling lost. He is hungry and thirsty. As he walks along the fronts of buildings, he reads the signs hanging outside. It's equally busy everywhere, so he randomly steps into an inn. The common room is packed, the air reeks, and it's stifling hot. After a long wait, he finally manages to get some rye bread, a slice of cheese and a mug of beer for far too much money. With difficulty, he finds a place for himself along the wall, where the men lie side by side in long rows. There are no rooms left. Texel is overwhelmed.

But gradually, the noise dies down. Night falls. Aldemar lies on his back, using his duffel bag as a pillow. Around him, snoring, mumbling and whispering. Occasionally, the door opens, and a ship's provost enters, looking for crew members who are still missing.

"Lijsken Janszoon?"

"Present, boss!"

"Come with me! The boat's down by the dike."

Another checkmark on the muster roll.

The Roads of Texel are the largest in the world. The yachts, pinnaces and flute ships are anchored from Nieuweschild to the southernmost tip of the island, flanked by merchant ships and vessels from the West India Company. Around them, the frigates of the Admiralty and the warships of the VOC, vigilant, scanning for Dunkirk privateers. And far off in the distance, like tiny dots on the horizon, the English, always keeping an eye on what the Dutch are doing.

Aldemar stands on the dike, clutching his duffel bag tightly. A fresh east wind blows into his face. "The wind is steady," said the seasoned seamen, and they know beyond doubt the fleet will soon set sail.

By late morning, the dunes begin to fill with tourists. They settle comfortably in the grass and on the sand, sitting on blankets and stools, carrying baskets of food and jugs of beer or brandy. There's chatting and laughter, and a cheerful excitement fills the air. When the first East Indiaman lets her halyards run—and fresh new sails unfurl—cheers erupt cautiously.

"The Purmer, under skipper Rijkjan?' Aldemar asks.

The old man chews thoughtfully on his pipe and scratches under his woolen cap.

'The Baltic Sea?'

'Yes, sir, from shipowner Gijsen of Zaandam.'

'That'll be further back. Near the Moscovian Roads. Just keep walking down the road.'

He walks, duffel bag over his shoulder. To his right lies Gallows Hill, where two corpses dangle from frayed ropes, their hands tied behind their backs, with bloated, grey-white faces and empty eye sockets. On the horizontal beams sit well-fed crows. A group of scruffy boys throw stones and clumps of earth at the bodies. Each time they hit one, they cheer triumphantly.

The longboats wait at the bottom of the dike for passengers. Aldemar stands at the top, looking down at them. 'The Purmer?' he asks.

One of the sailors looks up. 'Here, lad. What do you want?'
'I'm the new ship's apprentice.'
The sailor sizes him up from head to toe and laughs scornfully. 'You're no sailor. You're a hatchling, fresh out of the egg.'"

On the Merchant Roadstead, the sails are hoisted one after another. The rhythmic singing of the sailors rings out across the water:

> *"We eat beans with vinegar,*
> *Over the salty sea.*
> *The bacon is for the captain,*
> *Over the salty brine sea, over the salty sea."*

The sails flap. A large topsail slackens for a moment, then fills with wind again. "Brace!" shout the boatswain's mates. The yards adjust to the wind, the canvas tightens, and the first ship starts to move. On the beach, people cheer and applaud. The sailors continue to sing.

> *"Then we call upon Neptune,*
> *Over the salty sea.*
> *Neptune, do not let us perish,*
> *Over the salty brine sea, over the salty sea."*

From the Marsdiep, the VOC warships sail in formation, already at full speed. Their white bow waves crest, flags fly high, and gunports are open. As they pass the Texel Roads, one by one, they fire their cannons in a farewell salute to the people left behind, to Holland and to the Companies. The thunder of the cannons echoes across the sea and land, joined by the heavy guns of the Admiralty ships. The sounds of 32- and 36-pounders fill the air. Onshore, people wave and cry, watching as the merchant ships—mainsails, topsails and topgallants fully rigged—turn away from the land and gather speed, joining their heavily armed war companions. With one final cannonade, they disappear toward the North Sea.

The Easter fleet has set sail.

28 Mussulman Ali Delivers His Slaves

"O believers, let your slaves and those among you who have not yet reached puberty ask your permission before entering your presence at three times: before the dawn prayer when you take off your garments for rest at noon, and after the night prayer. These are three times of privacy for you."

From: The Quran, Surah 24: 58

⚓

Mussulman Ali thinks saying goodbye is difficult. Look at them: the men on the left, the women and children on the right. They are tired but not exhausted, not broken, not even the children. They are strong people, a good race. Not rebellious like the Komenda, who are known for causing problems and inciting violence, forcing the white masters on the plantations to bring out their whips and floggers to set examples. No more Komenda, say the traders, both the *Hulandi* and the *Inglizia*, though that's not always possible, for slaves don't grow on trees, sometimes you have to settle for what's available. But these people, clandestine or not, will become good workers and produce many generations. It's just a matter of time. Perhaps one day, they will say, long after I'm in the ground, that those fine bloodlines were once supplied by the house of Fulan. That would be an honour.

But things are thinning here. The whites want too much. There are hardly any Arab brothers left in this part of the land, so maybe I should return to the roots of our trade and head east, to the Swahili peoples or to that beautiful, flourishing island of Zanzibar, and join the old caravans north, far away from these white gluttons who spoil the trade with their barbaric ideas.

Ah, those women with their beautiful bodies: strong, lithe, and full of grace. If they're smart, they'll convert to the faith of the whites. That's better for them. God will surely forgive them. God knows the whites are full of shit. You don't get filthy just by pretending as long as you don't actually believe in a man-god on a cross like the white pig-eaters do. No, God understands everything as long as you're sincere.

Let's hope they have a prosperous voyage. And that it goes quickly, so they don't have to suffer too much aboard that little ship. The money was good, the profit fair. For that, I thank God. Without God, nothing is possible. *Bismi'llah ir-Rahman ir-Rahiem.*

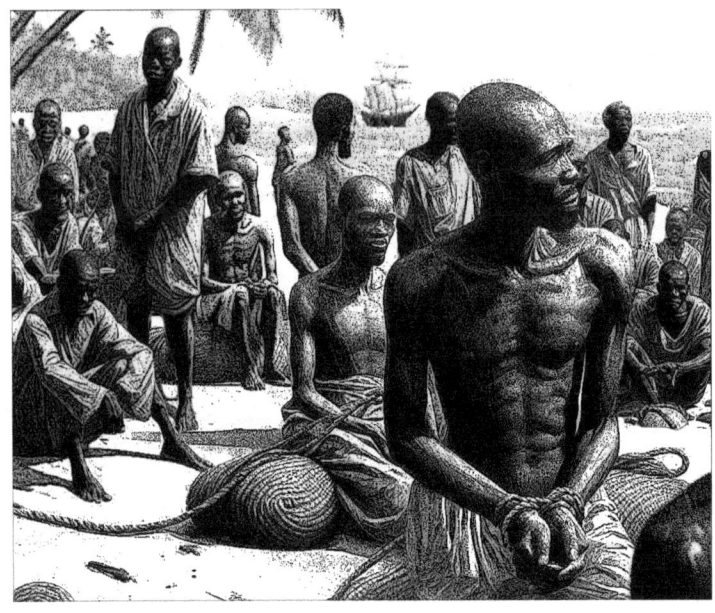

The orange sun hangs just above the horizon, casting a streak across the ocean. In the fading light, flocks of storm petrels and shearwaters are visible, flying hurriedly as if an inaudible call is urging them home.

The *Meyboom* cautiously sails into the bay, trying to enter against the wind, heeling to leeward, with double-reefed lower sails, under the warning cries of the lookout, who continuously measures the depth of the water. Along the sides and at the masts of the pinnace, lanterns have been lit, their glow illuminating the calm water in the bay.

Skipper Vogel stands on the shore, the tips of his precious boots in the salty water, his hands on his hips. With a critical eye, he follows the approach of his ship, slightly concerned that the keel might run aground, though the bay is reasonably deep, and he has confidence in his helmsman. About five hundred feet from the shore, the last sails are taken in, and the pinnace immediately begins to drift back. A voice bellows, "Anchor down!"

The ship tugs and slowly swings with the current, the anchor rope goes taut, and a new command rings out. The kedge anchor is thrown out.

"Veer out!" shouts the helmsman from the quarterdeck.

The men let the hawser run out. The *Meyboom* turns nicely broadside to the shore and then comes to a stop.

The skipper nods, pleased with his ship, his crew and himself. This is a good spot, he thinks. That damned little Moor knows his business, that much is certain. I've been scouring these coasts for two years, but I never knew about this bay. "I'd bet," he says confidentially to the four men in the boat, "that even the natives couldn't find this place."

From De *Meyboom*, the sloop is being launched. The carpenters have made some modifications. The middle thwarts have been removed and replaced with partitions, allowing more blacks to be crammed in. The embarkation needs to be fast, that's his order; he doesn't trust the situation, he doesn't trust anyone. "Before you know it, those filthy fellows over there will be shooting us down and running off with both the goods and the gold," he continues, pointing behind him to where the Arabs of Mussulman Ali are guarding the group of slaves. "Those bloody Moors. You can never figure them out; their faces are always smiling and you never know what they're thinking or what they're planning. I could've sworn that heathen was trying to trick me, but he had no idea there was a loaded four-pounder at the bottom of the boat, ready to fire and blast that whole miserable gang to pulp."

He laughs, and his men laugh along. "We would've given them something to remember, skipper."

Yes, he thinks with satisfaction, and if I had the chance, by God, I would have slit that mussulman's throat myself with the knife hidden under my shirt.

But everything went smoothly. Nothing happened, and the merchandise is what could be expected. Perhaps not the full number that was promised, but there's always some loss, and even that little dark swindler can't help that.

"Damn," he mutters to himself. "If things keep going this well, we can rest on our laurels for a while."

The sloop approaches quickly. Vogel looks at the sky, which is quickly darkening. "Come on, hurry up," he calls impatiently.

De *Meyboom* is not built to accommodate so many people, but he had benches constructed, and a women's house set up on the aft deck. It won't be for long, he hopes, so the hardships will be bearable. For a brief moment, he considered to ignore all agreements altogether. He could just take the entire cargo and sail straight to Gorée at Cabo Verde, where the French buy up every black slave they can get. But the pinnace is too small, it would lead to far too much loss, and he would also have to stock up on extra provisions and water.

Yes, and before you know it, someone catches wind of it, and then you'd have to shoot your way through lines of privateers and Dutch Company ships, and with all those slaves on board, your fast pinnace becomes top-heavy, and just try slipping away then. He shakes his head. No tricks, Vogel, he thinks. Not this time.

The sloop hits the beach. The boatswain and half a dozen sailors jump ashore. They carry cat-o'-nine-tails and bullwhips.

"Good." Vogel turns around and waves to Mussulman Ali. Mussulman Ali nods in understanding. He cautiously walks backward, away from the blacks, followed by his guards. The barrels of their snaphaunces point to the ground.

"Wait until they've disappeared into the trees," Vogel warns. He smiles kindly at Mussulman Ali. "Goodbye, boys, and thanks again!"

The group of helpless, bound blacks on the beach is left alone. They stand motionless together. Silent. Staring at the ground. "That's not a cheerful bunch," he chuckles. "Drive them on, lads. Get them on the boat."

29 Scene: On Women and Disease

"(...) The primary cause of the unhealthiness of this coast is that it is lined from top to bottom with a multitude of high mountains, between which one sees, in the morning, a thick, foul-smelling, sulfurous vapor or mist rising, especially in watery areas and near small rivers. This vapor spreads and descends upon the earth in such quantities that it is almost impossible not to be infected by it, particularly since, at that time, we are still fasting, and our bodies are thus more susceptible. (...) It further mixes with a vile stench caused by the negroes, due to their custom of letting their fish rot for five or six days before eating it and because they allow everyone to relieve themselves around their homes, as well as throughout the entire village."

From: Correspondence of Chief Chirurgeon Zacharias Augustijns to the Collegium Medicum of Amsterdam, December 1687

Two Dutch soldiers are sitting at ease in the shade in the courtyard of Fort Coenraadsburg. Under the watchful eye of a corporal, they are polishing their cuirasses, which show traces of rust every morning.

Soldier 1: "I just thought of somethin'."

Soldier 2: "Wot's that?"

Soldier 1: (Counting on his fingers) "Twenty-seven bleedin' months. That's how long it's been since I seen a white lass stark naked."

Soldier 2: "Aye." (Thinking, scratching his bare right foot, which is severely swollen from an infection) "Yeah, that's a hell of a long stretch, that."

Soldier 1: "I'd give up a month's pay for a bit o' white skirt."

Soldier 2: "Ain't no point wishin', mate. Closest white tarts are in Fida, an' they're bloody French. Best stick to the black girls."

(They polish in silence for a while. With ointment, they make the metal plates shine.)

Soldier 1: "Ya think God's punishin' us? With them diseases? For layin' with blackies?"

Soldier 2: (Shakes his head, picking at the dark spot in the middle of his infection) " Blacks ain't got no souls, mate. God don't give a toss if you shag 'em or not."

Soldier 1: "Then why are all our lads droppin' like flies?"

Soldier 2: "How the hell should I know? Ask the reverend."

Soldier 1: "Honestly, mate, every time I go at one of them curly-haired lasses, I get the shivers."

The corporal: (Sitting on a stool, laughing) "Bugger me, you sure coulda fooled me, private, 'cos you fuck like a bloody rabbit."

Soldier 1: (With a sour face) "Yeah, well, damn it, corporal, I just don't get how somethin' that feels so good can make you so sick."

30 The Slaves of Elmina

"Let all who are under the yoke of slavery regard their masters as worthy of full respect so that God's name and our teaching may not be slandered."

From: The Bible, 1 Timothy 6:1

⚓

Logbook of the Griffin, Wednesday, December 10:
"*Day 51 at the roadstead of Elmina. Despite careful attention, the steward, who had been infected by a malignant native coastal worm, died during the middle watch around 5 bells due to complications. His entire abdominal area was swollen and inflamed. This afternoon, after sunset, his belongings were auctioned off at the main mast. Proceeds: 18 guilders and 12 stivers, which were handed over to the provost of Elmina for dispatch to the homeland.*

We have finally received permission to embark the slave cargo from the castle. Thank God."

It rained all night, but in the morning, the sky cleared up. When the sun breaks through, the heat is immediately back to its usual intensity, maybe even worse, as the moisture still lingers in the air like vapor. The walls of Elmina Castle show damp spots, and mold grows in the shadows. Cloths are draped over the windows of the soldiers' quarters on the main square to ward off mosquitoes, which thrive in the many stagnant puddles and pools, just like the black flies, whose bites are painful.

Skipper Burghoutsz sits on one of the upper steps of the side stairs leading to the square, flanked by his first mate, the ship's chirurgeon and the chirurgeon's three assistants.

Below them, in the courtyard, a group of male slaves is being aired. They stand naked together, blinking in the bright daylight. Although they all wear ankle and wrist shackles, they are not chained together in groups, allowing them to move independently. Burghoutsz had requested this. It's a good practice to observe the male slaves before embarkation.

"There are always troublemakers," he explains to his ship's chirurgeon, who is relatively young and inexperienced. This is his first voyage on the triangular trade. "I want to know who the leaders are and whether they have any capability."

The ship's chirurgeon nods in understanding. He has a red, wispy beard and sunburnt skin. His nose is covered with a thick scab, on which he has applied some kind of ointment. For protection, he wears a straw hat. He points to a large, broad-shouldered black standing slightly apart from the rest, looking around with a thoughtful yet intense gaze. "Like him?"

Burghoutsz observes the slave. The man briefly makes eye contact with a second slave. The second man approaches as inconspicuously as possible. They are forbidden to speak, but their body language betrays a primitive, silent form of communication.

No one else notices it, not even the many sentries who stand nervously in a circle around the group, their pistols and cutlasses ready in hand. They don't like it at all that the slaves are not chained together. For safety, two more squads of soldiers stand on the parapets high above them. The barrels of their snaphaunces are clearly visible.

"The crossing takes long enough," continues Burghoutsz, ignoring the tension of the soldiers. "He who is locked up starts thinking. He has nothing else to do. Maybe he'll convince himself that escape is possible." He keeps looking at the slave. "Some skippers separate the leaders so they can't plot among themselves. But I think differently. If you keep them together long enough, they'll start quarrelling."

"Well thought out," nods the ship's chirurgeon, scratching his nose. For him, this journey is one big new adventure.

"They always quarrel," grumbles the first mate, who sits one step higher. He waves his hand irritably in a futile attempt to chase away the flies.

Burghoutsz continues: "So I chain the leaders together and place them in the rearmost, lowest cages of the orlop deck*. That undermines their authority, and they can do the least harm there."

Meanwhile, a third slave has joined the other two. The three now form a small group. They stand with their backs to each other, each looking in a different direction, ignoring each other so conspicuously that it almost seems unnatural. The leader lowers his head, holding his hands in front of his mouth casually, as if wiping his face, but anyone paying close attention can see that his lips are moving. His eyes scan the surroundings, and for a brief moment, he and the skipper look directly at each other.

Burghoutsz has seen enough. "You're right," he decides, giving his chirurgeon a pat on the knee. He signals to Bomba Jan, who is strolling among the slaves and points to the slave he has been observing. "Mark him, Bomba Jan."

Bomba Jan nods. He knows the procedure. He carries a wooden bucket filled with a grey, foul-smelling substance, a mixture of sulphur, talc, white lead, fish oil and plant tar, used to prevent ship hulls from becoming encrusted. He dips a brush into the concoction and walks without hesitation toward the slave.

"Your back," he says gruffly. He makes a turning motion with his hand. "Turn around."

The black man looks at him, uncomprehending. The other two shuffle away discreetly, knowing that being singled out is never a good sign.

"Easy now," Bomba Jan soothes. "Nothing to worry about." He quickly walks around the slave and draws the brush across his back, leaving a greasy streak of gray paint. "Now I know who you are," he grins. "That stuff won't come off anytime soon."

Food is brought in. It's in a barrel rolled in by mulattoes, and it contains salted pork. The slaves are given a wooden bowl and must stand in line. The first slave

---

*Orlop deck = an extra, lowered deck between the gun deck and the hold, used for storing gear or as living quarters for soldiers or slaves.

looks into the barrel. He recoils when he sees the meat. It's submerged in brine, and the smell is repulsive.

The chirurgeon chuckles. "He's picky."

"No," says Burghoutsz calmly. "He thinks it's human flesh."

The small inner courtyard of the castle lies a bit farther back, beyond the governor's quarters, bordered by warehouses and the women's slave pit. The floor is paved with cobblestones, smoothed over the years by countless bare feet. The female slaves—separated from the men and awaiting their embarkation—are confined in the pit, but they must remain healthy, so they are regularly aired in the small courtyard under the watchful eyes of a few soldiers.

The assistants of the company clerks herd the group together, which also includes a significant number of children. Buckets are drawn from the well in the centre of the courtyard, and the water is poured over the apathetic women amid laughter and jeering.

Meanwhile, company slaves are ordered to clean the prison floors. The stink is overwhelming, and the flies are innumerable. The buzzing sometimes drowns out the constant background sound of the surf. With water, brooms and scrubbing brushes, faeces, vomit, and urine are removed, after which the walls and floors are sprinkled with vinegar, as is done on Dutch ships. When the fly infestation becomes too severe, sometimes a bit of gunpowder is spread in the pit and ignited, so the filth burns, and the sharp cordite fumes bring some relief.

The chief chirurgeon of the Company inspects the merchandise and determines the losses: the unfit, the injured, the sick and the dead. He has the female slaves pass before him, carefully inspecting the fresh brands, which often become infected. That is a major concern. He is furious when the prison isn't properly scrubbed. Raging at the company slaves and sub-clerks, he threatens them with hell and damnation, and the entire cleaning operation has to be done over again.

It is the women who benefit from this unexpected reprieve. Now, they are allowed to stay a little longer in the courtyard. Despite the sun, anything is better than remaining in that suffocating dungeon where they are crammed together.

They silently eat from their wooden bowls of barley porridge and gaze around, their eyes fixed on the tall, swaying tops of the coconut palms rising above the walls, hoping for something that will never come: deliverance.

31 *Back: Aldemar Burghoutsz (3)*

$$\frac{\theta}{2} = tan(w/l)$$

⚓

The Baltic Sea, Spring/Summer 1663
The Purmer is an old ship, a rear-loader with removable cargo ports at the stern, allowing entire tree trunks to be loaded. The ship is well-maintained: the wood of the dark, rounded hull gleams in the sun and the rigging is taut.

Skipper Rijkjan looks down from the quarterdeck and sizes up the new hand, who has clumsily climbed aboard. His expression is stern. "You finally made it, you brat?"

"Yes, skipper." Aldemar bows his head and feels the swell beneath his feet.

"Do you have your books with you?"

He nods.

"Put them in the cabin at the back. I want to see you studying every evening."

The crew makes a colourful impression. The uncles have names like Cross-eyed Jan, Fat Driek, Janus the Crow and Four-fingered Gisbert. Nicknames are sacred. If you don't have one, you're still a grommet, and grommets have damn few rights. Aldemar is a grommet. He quickly learns that the unwritten laws on board are strictly enforced. There's no room for error, the sailors are tough, and any rule-breaking gets punished on the spot. The boatswain assigns him to the mess of Red Rick, an English-able seaman with carrot-orange hair and a god-awful accent. Red Rick eyes him sideways. "Let's see yer hands, lad."

Aldemar shows his palms.

"Lookie here! We got ourselves a girl on board!" Red Rick bellows. "Not a damn speck of callus on them hands!" He grabs his crotch and grins wickedly. "We eat up young lasses like you, boy," he growls. "Have a lot of fun with 'em at night, we do."

The first mate comes to Aldemar's rescue. "Knock it off, Red Rick, or you'll feel the cat."

"Just havin' a laugh, sir," Red Rick winks at Aldemar.

Gillis Graauw ain't no grommet. As a cabin boy, he's been sailing for a while now.

He's a small, wiry kid of thirteen with ash-blonde hair, light grey eyes, a face full of freckles and a pale complexion. A ropey, white scar runs down the left side of his forehead, past his left eye and down his cheek. He sits in the same mess as Aldemar. Gillis seems happy he finally has someone lower in the pecking order. "What's yer name?"

"Aldemar."

Gillis shakes his head. "Can ya climb?"

"What?"

"Climb. Up the rigging."

Aldemar stares upward. Way above him, the flag flaps at the gaff peak. A flute ship ain't no herring buss.

The waves are high, and the wind howls. Ropes pulled taut, singing, then slackening again. The Purmer pounds and bucks on the water. When the ship dives into the troughs, the bow spray crashes over the deck, foaming and cold. The mizzen rigging trembles as if a hundred men are beating it with sticks. Aldemar is hanging forty feet up, and the world around him spins and sways. The mizzen has come alive and does what it pleases, with long, stomach-churning swings from side to side. He clings on. The rain slashes at his face, and the drops sting his skin. His hands have been numb for a while.

"Get over the top!" Red Rick bellows, hanging about ten feet away from him, one hand gripping the rigging, the other waving wildly in the air. He points to the flapping topsail, which needs to be taken in. Aldemar grabs hold of the wet wood. The crossjack is slick from the rain. He hesitates. His shoe slips on the rope. "I can't do it!" he yells.

Red Rick shows his blackened teeth. The mizzenmast swings back to starboard, the wood groaning and creaking like a wounded beast.

A dark blur shoots past Aldemar. Gillis Graauw moves up like a monkey. Nimbly and barefoot, he climbs over the crossjack and leaps onto the lower yard, grabbing hold of shivering, soaking deadeye. He reaches out a hand, and Aldemar gathers his courage. "Come on!"

He makes a little jump. For a split second, it feels like he's going to fall, and his heart skips a beat, but then he feels Gillis's strong fingers grip his own. "Get yer foot on the rope!"

Four, five men spread across the lower yard, loosening the seizings. Above them, on the crossjack yard, two men tug at the sail.

"Haul it in!" Red Rick roars.

Aldemar grabs the seizing. His half-dead fingers fumble with the knot. The lower yard wobbles in the wind, but he keeps his balance. Around him, the grey sea churns. He glances at Red Rick. The Englishman is singing a song, most of it lost in the wind. His red hair sticks to his head in long, wet strands. He yells, "Lovely weather, eh?"

After three days, his body is broken. Every muscle screams for rest, and the pain is unbearable. His hands are raw, and the salt bites into his flesh.

Gillis hands him his oorlam. "Rum's good for ya."

The drink warms his throat.

"I'll never make it."

"Course ya will."

Gillis rubs his young-old, freckled face. "Nothin' to it."

Old ships are like sieves. Water seeps in through cracks and gaps, collecting in the bilge, forming a sloshing, oily soup that gradually spreads and weighs the ship down, so the pumps are always running. The watch on duty works in pairs at the pump well, lit by a single lantern. The plunger is pulled back and forth with a crank, and the water gurgles through the heavy leather valves. Swish, thump. Swish, thump. Hard work.

While they pump, Aldemar and Gillis practice the procedures. "Midships?"

"Third mate..." Aldemar pants. "... sailor on the main halyard and bowline..."

"Behind the foremast?"

"First mate..."

"Mizzen sails?"

"Second mate... let go the fore and main braces to leeward... one man windward on the crossjack, three others to leeward... two on the main topsail and topgallant braces..."

"Pump, quit jabberin', Burghoutsz!" Red Rick bellows from above the hatch.

Grommets do the work no one else wants to do. Dikkie, the cook, pulls him out of his hammock early in the morning and recites a familiar rhyme: "Fresh from the galley, silly fool, rise from your cot, refresh your gruel."

Disgusted and still half asleep, Aldemar steps into the large tub by the galley, filled with salted chunks of pork and seawater. With his bare feet, he kneads the meat. Rancid fat squelches between his toes.

"Come on, lad," Dikkie grins while stirring a pot of barley. "Gonna be a feast tonight."

Mealtime. Each mess consists of seven men sharing utensils and pans. Sailors sit with sailors, carpenters with carpenters. The deckhands serve from large, steaming kettles. Groats and pork fat. Hardtack. Salted herring. "Say grace first," orders the mess leader of the day. The Lord's Prayer is rushed through. "...who art in heaven, hallowed be Thy name..." Amen. The crew attacks the food like a pack of hungry wolves.

Aldemar isn't hungry, eating in tiny nibbles.

"Ya gotta eat, boy," Red Rick says. His eyes gleam with mischief.

"I'm not hungry."

"If ya don't eat, ya can't work. And if ya don't work, Red Rick's gonna get a thrashing."

Cross-eyed, Jan speaks up for Aldemar. "He's been doing well so far, Red Rick."

Red Rick points with his knife. "He'd better, Cross-eyed Jan. 'Cause if Red Rick gets a thrashing, he sure ain't gonna be celebrating."

Skipper Rijkjan isn't one to budge, either. "Burghoutsz! To the cabin!"

In the lantern light, Aldemar sits in a corner at the large table, bent over his books, while the skipper, the officers and the boatswain drink their corn brandy.

"Prepare a navigation report[*], Aldemar."

"Aye, skipper."

"And be finished by morning this time."

"I'll do my best."

The second mate glances at him like he's invisible, then turns to the others and says, "Ever tell ya that story 'bout the Hottentot with three tits?"

During the middle watch, he finds peace. The sailors are in their hammocks, the officers have withdrawn to their cabins, and the skipper is below deck. The night is dark and moonless, with the rolling, pitch-black Skagerrak beneath the boat. Denmark lies to starboard, but there's not a light in sight. The first mate stands by the mizzen. He's a calm fellow, built like an ox, with curly brown hair and a square jaw. He calmly smokes his pipe, and Aldemar is allowed to handle the whipstaff[†] in the binnacle house.

"No more than ten degrees off midships, Burghoutsz, remember that. Keep an eye on the upper topsail."

"Aye, sir."

The whipstaff is alive. Aldemar feels the ship's tremble. He feels it when the mainsail is trimmed a notch or two. He feels it when the bow gives a soft smack on the water. He forgets his fatigue. The Purmer responds to his hand. Far ahead, he hears the bow wave splashing. "Is she holding steady, sir?"

"She's holding steady, Aldemar."

The Sound is the gateway to the Baltic Sea, the source of Dutch prosperity. At its narrowest point, the passage is only two nautical miles wide. To starboard rises Elsinore and the castle of Kronborg. Here, passing ships must lower their sails and pay tolls to the Danish king.

The Purmer lowers the sloop, skipper Rijkjan must report to the toll office. On the outbound journey, they're carrying barrels of Bordeaux wine, each of which will be taxed at a value of one hundred guilders.

Aldemar looks out over the railing at the sea. The merchant ships are lined up side by side in the grey water, and more than half fly the Dutch flag. Danish warships guard the passage: anyone who doesn't pay is unceremoniously fired upon.

---

[*] Navigation report = daily calculation of a ship's position based on course, speed, and time.
[†] Whipstaff = a vertical lever used to steer the ship before the invention of the wheel.

The Sound baptism is a rite of passage for every grommet. Aldemar is officially getting his sea legs. Beyond Kronborg Castle, he stands stark naked in a tub on deck, and Red Rick slathers him from head to toe with lard. Dikkie the cook shaves his head. Shivering and trembling, he stands there, smiling through gritted teeth. The uncles have done their best; the herring has been rotting in lukewarm water for days, green with slime and full of maggots. Neptune is invoked: "Accept this offering!"

Then the fish goes over his head. Aldemar gags and the uncles cheer, raising their oorlams: "Now you're a sailor, laddie!"

In Riga, they're loading unsawn pine. The *Purmer* is moored at the quay and the cargo port on the port side is removed. The crew uses cranes and tackles to stack the long logs in the hold. It's heavy and dangerous work. Aldemar grits his teeth against the pain from blisters and splinters while the sailors curse and swear, spurred on by the skipper.

"Up! Push! By God!"

The tackle squeaks and groans. Suddenly, a rope snaps and the heavy beam shoots into the hold like a missile. The sailors scramble for safety, but in the half-dark, climbing over the logs makes it hard to move quickly. The beam crashes down with heavy, dull thuds. Janus the Crow takes a hit and slams unconscious against a beam. His rough head bleeds profusely.

"Drag him topside. Hurry the hell up!"

They lay him on a coil of rope in the waist. The Crow is as white as a sheet, completely still. His arms hang limply at his sides. The crew stands around him in a circle, jostling for a better view. "Damn, he's not gonna croak, is he?"

Dikkie, the cook who spends his days in the galley, steps in as a makeshift chirurgeon as best he can. He pulls out a small box with mysterious tools: needles, pliers, knives, ointments and bottles. He cuts away the hair and dabs the deep head wound with seawater.

"I can see his skull!" shouts Red Rick.

Aldemar watches the scene with horror.

"As long as he's bleedin', he ain't dead," Dikkie reassures them. With needle and thread, he stitches up the wound. Not very neatly. Every time he pulls the thread tight, the onlookers shudder. But the bleeding stops. With a bit of showmanship, he slathers the wound with an ointment made of fat and boiled marigold. Then, he wraps the patient's head in an impressive bandage.

Janus the Crow opens his eyes. "Where am I?" he slurs, his tongue thick. He's cross-eyed now, just like Cross-eyed Jan. "I've got a pain in me noggin."

"Goddamn, Dikkie, you've got skills!" shout the sailors. They slap him on the shoulder, and Dikkie blushes with pride.

32 Sweerts Discovers Corruption

"The slave who knows his master's will but does not get ready or does not do what his master wants will be beaten with many blows."

From: The Bible, Luke 12:47

It is immoral, thinks director-general Sweerts, sitting at the massive desk in his office, as he slowly feels his anger rising.

It is evening, and it is dark, but he has not yet lit a candle. Below, outside in the courtyard of Elmina Castle, the sounds gradually fade. A man strides hastily toward the main gate, undoubtedly on his way to a late supper. Sweerts pays no attention and stares at his desk. On it sits a wooden chest, the type used by most sailors and soldiers. It contains the personal belongings of the unfortunate Corporal Puteijn, whom he had quietly buried that morning in the Dutch cemetery across the river. It had been an unremarkable ceremony. There was no stone, no epitaph, and the minister confined himself to a few hastily mumbled psalms. After all, the deceased had been a convicted murderer, and

God would surely know what to do with him—no man needed to add anything. The grave had already been dug, and the body, wrapped in Dutch canvas, was laid in without much ceremony, and that was that.

The chest initially contained nothing special. The usual trinkets of a soldier: tin eating utensils, cutlery, a worn-out Bible, a tinderbox, a razor, a pipe, a tobacco tin, and so on. There was also a pouch of stivers worth just under fifteen guilders. Not much to speak of—except for one thing, and that's the source of his outrage. Corporal Puteijn apparently had more to him than one might expect, because in a hidden drawer in the bottom of the chest, Sweerts found a leather pouch filled with gold dust. Gold. *Chika*, as the locals call it. After recovering from the shock of the discovery, he secretly weighed it. Then came the second surprise: the gold was worth around four hundred guilders. For a corporal earning barely twelve guilders a month, that's a fortune.

It was enough to raise his suspicions.

Everyone knows that corruption carries severe punishments. While the Company might turn a blind eye to misconduct now and then—even the directors know that West Africa is hell for whites; the English even call it *the white man's grave*—self-enrichment must be stamped out completely. If, *if* any profit is made—and God knows that's no easy task—then it belongs to the shareholders.

Self-enrichment, yes. Bribery? His gaze wanders around the room. Everything is in shadow now, even the paintings on the wall: dark rectangles against a backdrop of deep gray.

Puteijn was a wretch. Paupers are always looking for easy solutions, that much is obvious, but to curb missteps, there are officers and a provost, a director-general... damn it, he—Sweerts—hadn't been paying enough attention, and in the end, it's *his* responsibility.

He plays with the pouch of gold, feels its weight, and lets it thud onto the desk.

Alright, Puteijn had found a source. Was he a thief? Maybe. But that murder now seems different. That can't be a coincidence. Two black traders and a white man. An angry, drunk corporal. They had a quarrel. Why? Was he not paid? Or not paid enough? Or not on time?

Now he has something.

Yes, Puteijn must have worked for them. At least for the white man. The white man was a Zeelander. And what do those Zeelanders want?

Slaves.

He sits up straight, staring at the chest.

Is there trading going on behind his back?

The lid is open. He puts the pouch back, not in the hidden drawer, but right on top.

There it lies.

It burns in his mind.

Two hours later. In the tower room of the castle, he lies on his bed, dressed only in a nightshirt, hands folded under his head.

Abena Gyan, his concubine, sits beside him. She dabs the sore at the corner of his mouth with a damp cloth. "It's swollen," she says, her voice carrying a husky tone he finds very appealing.

He makes a face and looks at her. There are few people he trusts. It comes with his position. Yet, he has a soft spot for her. "It'll go away." Damn sore. "What's bothering me is that corporal we hanged." He grimaces as she rubs a herbal paste into the sore. It smells foul. "He was part of a conspiracy. I found *chika* in his chest."

"Really?" She furrows her brows, two perfect arches on a smooth, finely carved face.

"I suspect a group of soldiers is secretly transporting slaves," he continues. "It's possible those two murdered Denkyira traders were involved."

"The Denkyira?" She purses her lips, which are very lovely. Aside from a jingling collection of gold bracelets, she's completely naked. "Their king is a thief. Everyone knows that."

He snorts. "Arponsem?" he asks. "Is he involved? Have you heard anything?"

She shakes her head, sets the cloth aside, and lies down on her side. "The Denkyira are untrustworthy pigs. How many times do I have to explain that to you?"

He chuckles. She is more than just a black concubine. By Guinean standards, he is even formally married to her since her father is the king of Eguafo, and he willingly gave her to him, complete with official ceremonies. It's what you might call a political marriage, for by aligning himself with Abena Gyan, he secured the loyalty of many locals. And with him, the Company.

"It would be insane," he says, "if I were clandestinely buying slaves stolen from Arponsem while he secretly organizes transports and sells them behind our backs."

"The fox deceives the wolf."

"It violates the treaty!"

"And who does he sell them to?" She lifts her head, very arrogant, fully aware of her high birth; Eguafo is the cradle of the Guans, the first inhabitants of the coast. "Certainly not to my father," she says firmly. "He honours all treaties."

"Yes, yes." He thinks: speaking of thieves, your father is the biggest swindler on the Gold Coast. But he agrees with her; Eguafo has nothing to gain from illegal trade.

"The Brandenburgers then?" He shakes his head. "No, the naval blockade has proven effective. Since I left those two frigates behind, there hasn't been a single Zeeland smuggler on the coast. Not there and not at Fort Dorothea." That, he believes, is at least one thing he's accomplished.

Abena Gyan stretches like a cat, and from his viewpoint, her smooth, perfectly shaped legs seem to go on forever. "Even those two Denkyira could never have organized a transport through Wassa land on their own," she suggests. "It must be someone from outside, someone neutral. A middleman between the Denkyira and the whites."

He nods. That's well thought out. "Do you think the Ahante will stick to the treaty?"

"Of course," she answers confidently. "Except for those monkeys in Pocquesoe. They're criminals and thieves cast out from their own villages. They say the Brandenburgers support them. They'll try to bypass your blockade."

That irritates him. "Maybe."

Her fingers stroke his neck. "Quassie Patoe," she says.

"What?"

"Everyone knows Quassie Patoe. And he has neither a conscience nor loyalty."

He waves his hand dismissively. "Quassie Patoe wants to become an ensign of all the asafo companies. He gains nothing by opposing me."

"Maybe he thinks he's smarter than the white boss." She giggles. "Quassie Patoe is an Enyampa. They descend from goat-humping baboons. Honestly."

"You don't think much of your own people."

"Yuck. Even the most beautiful tree has dead branches."

He scratches his belly. Outside, he hears the first raindrops falling.

Abena Gyan pulls up his nightshirt and begins stroking his chest. It stirs a reaction, and sensual feelings course through his body.

He glances at the two black pages standing by the bed, waving fresh palm leaves to provide some cool air. It must be a strange, decadent sight. Who would believe such a thing back in Holland? What would they say? What would his own father say?

It amuses him. He thinks she may be intelligent and sensible, but she's also a spoiled brat. He says, "When I was waiting to embark, I once took a short trip around the island of Texel, just for fun. Many retired captains live there, they drink their rum in the inns, and if you feel like it, you can listen to their stories. But I didn't believe them. I thought all those tales were exaggerated. But now I know it was the truth. Beyond Europe, everything is different."

She looks at him for a few seconds, shaking her head, a mocking smile on her lips. "White people are backward," she finally says. "Big boats, small brains. Didn't I teach you to wash your genitals so you don't stink like all the others?"

He grins. Now, she's lifted his spirits. Soon, he decides, I'll interrogate Quassie Patoe.

The rain pours down fiercely. God, he thinks, three, four more years, and my pockets will be full. Then I can finally go back to Holland and think about a little country house along the river Vecht. Let them say again that I had no chance, those arrogant nobles with their superior airs, because damn it, I'll be a regent myself by then.

Grumbling, he turns on his side. Her belly is at the level of his head.

I wish she could come with me to Utrecht. But you can't exactly show up with a black woman, though I'd love to see their faces. Maybe as a housemaid. But she's too proud of that. Too temperamental. She'd cause trouble. Sweerts, they'd say, turns out to be a parvenu after all.

"What are you thinking about?" she asks.

"You."

"You only think about the Company." She pouts.

He has no illusions. In patria, everything would be different. She'd start to bore me, or I'd grow irritated with her, and then I'd be stuck with her. He runs his tongue along her belly, and she lets out a soft giggle. Her skin tastes a little salty. He reaches the edge of her pubic hair.

Abena Gyan spreads her long legs. Her fingers push his head down. "Be careful," she giggles. "You're smearing the medicinal herbs."

Sweerts rubs his nose through delicate, jet-black curls. It blocks out his thoughts.

33 Acts of Jasper Vogel

"Rejoice in the presence of the Lord your God at the place He will choose as a dwelling for His Name—you, your sons and daughters, your male and female slaves, the Levites in your towns, and the foreigners, the fatherless, and the widows living among you."

From: The Bible, Deuteronomy 16:11

⚓

The *Meyboom* lies at anchor behind a narrow spit of land, not far from several sharp cliffs jutting out above the water, just east of Boutry, where the Dutch Fort Batenstein is located. A row of trees almost completely hides the pinnace so that—except for her three masts—she is barely visible from the ocean.

Skipper Vogel leans against the taffrail* of his ship and surveys the activity on the aft deck, where a wooden hut with a flat roof has been constructed: the daytime quarters for the female slaves and children. The structure is only temporary and barely finished, but it shields the naked women from both the sun and the lustful eyes of the crew. He's not prudish, but trouble between slaves and crew is something he can't afford. Sexual relations aboard a ship inevitably lead to envy and jealousy and thus to quarrels, fighting and knife-play. Worse still, people could die. And that's not going to happen. Not on his ship. So he made a personal proclamation in front of the entire crew: anyone caught in lewd behaviour, whether with women, men or children, would be tied to the mast. That is to say, they will be flogged until their skin comes off, and he'll do it himself, with great pleasure. And that's enough warning; they know exactly who he is.

But he still feels uneasy because bringing women on board is bad luck—everyone knows that—and the pinnace is overloaded. It's a good, fast ship. He knows her from bowsprit to rigging, but with all these souls on board, she's hard to manoeuvre. He has posted a double watch, and there's always a boy in the crow's nest of the mainmast; at the first sign of trouble, he'll weigh anchor.

---

* Taffrail = the upper part of the stern, often richly decorated

Meanwhile, a large part of his cargo is seasick. That's another problem he hadn't considered in his inexperience: the slaves are landlubbers. They've never been at sea. The *Meyboom* hadn't even left the bay when the heavy, sluggish swell of the ocean took hold—and that's when it started. The sour smell of vomit now seems to cling to them. The mess sloshes through the scuppers on the deck and soaks into the wood, the rope and everything else it touches. The boatswain has put the slaves who aren't sick to work with vinegar, brooms, mops and water, but the stench lingers, and to make matters worse, there's barely any wind.

He considered putting at least the women and children ashore for now, but Burghoutsz had been very clear: no one must see those slaves, so don't let them off the ship. Witnesses are dangerous, so stay on the open sea if possible. If they're spotted, the whole deal could be called off because the Company takes no risks with the Denkyira.

He takes a deep breath. Restlessness courses through his body. Irritably, he paces back and forth, carefully avoided by his crew.

An hour or so later, he looks up, annoyed, as commotion breaks out in the hold. Shouting. Running footsteps. Someone curses. He walks to the railing of the quarterdeck and sees, on the port side of his ship, two naked black men jumping overboard. "Well, goddamn..."

His crew gathers and peers down. Two black heads with frizzy hair surface. One of them turns his face toward the coast, the other gasps and sputters, flailing his arms. That one can't swim, he thinks, and he yells, "Do something, for God's sake!"

But he knows: his own men can't swim either. They look at him helplessly. Even the boatswain spreads his hands in frustration. "I can't, skipper," he stammers, his face red.

Instead, someone aims a musket at the struggling black man.

That's not the plan.

"Put that down!" Vogel shouts.

But the shot rings out before he can stop it. The blast roars, and the sailors all duck their heads at once. The gunpowder smoke billows across the deck. "Uh!" cries the man in the water. A bright red cloud starts to appear around him. His body convulses, then suddenly goes still, floating with arms and legs outstretched, slowly rolling forward, face down. Small fish come curiously to investigate. They dart sharply back and forth, drawn to the blood.

Cursing, swearing, and stumbling, the skipper pulls off his boots. In his stockinged feet, he runs to the portside railing, pushes off and disappears into the depths.

The other slave has a good head start, but Vogel is a better swimmer. With long strokes, he cuts through the water. His anger fuels his strength. He knows this is all his own fault. He should have taken precautions. Slave ships hang nets or canvas along the sides to catch escapees immediately, or they throw meat or fish scraps overboard to attract sharks; only an idiot would jump overboard then.

The surf lifts him up, broad, rolling walls of water follow one another. He can see the slave's head ahead of him, below him, then rising as Vogel descends again. Meanwhile, his arms keep churning. His muscles grow heavy. It's not fast enough. The slave's head is nearing the shore. That makes him even angrier. Cursing and gasping, he pushes his body to the limit. The waves break. Foam bubbles past him, and he gets salt water in his mouth. He feels the bottom, then is lifted again. About ten meters ahead, the slave tries to stand. A wave knocks him over again. They're both exhausted. But now Vogel feels sand under his feet. He tries to stand, takes two staggering steps and falls forward. Another wave picks him up and hurls him forward with great force past the slave, who stares at him in shock, wide-eyed.

Vogel scrambles up the beach. The black man wobbles on his legs like a drunk. He shouts something, but it's incomprehensible. Vogel waits for him, arms hanging and chest heaving. "Come on, you black bastard," he pants.

The slave looks left, then right, and starts running. But Vogel throws himself forward and grabs a leg. They tumble over each other in the wet sand. Now, his anger explodes. His fists pound wet flesh. The slave is too tired to fight back. He curls up into a ball. Vogel keeps hitting. He sees blood. A top lip tears. An eyelid swells. But it's over quickly. His body is too exhausted, his arms too heavy. He collapses forward, gasping for breath, faces down in the sand.

A group of sailors, led by the boatswain, follows him in the sloop. When they reach the shore, they find him sitting cross-legged, waiting for them, with the unconscious slave behind him. The boatswain cautiously calls out from the boat, "All well, skipper?"

He looks back silently. But his eyes gleam and spark. Now that he has his breath back, he's in control of his body again. "Throw that nigger in the boat," he orders in a low voice.

The boatswain senses his anger. He knows his skipper. Someone will pay.

Back on board, he's wearing only canvas trousers. His upper body is wiry. Green, tattooed dragons crawl across his chest and back, with open jaws full of teeth and forked tongues. Spread wings. As he moves, they move with him. He strides across the deck. His men stand together by the forecastle. Some quickly cross themselves when they see him like this.

"The drowning man?" he asks.

The boatswain shrugs. "Sunk."

"Who fired the shot?"

Silence.

"Who?"

The boatswain looks unhappy. "It was a mistake, skipper. A young lad. He'll be punished."

"Who?"

"He's already in the brig."

Vogel growls. "Bring him here."

The young sailor doesn't dare look at Vogel. His eyes are downcast. He trembles. Snot covers his lips and chin. He knows there will be no mercy.

Vogel stares at him intently. "Why did you do it?" he asks. "Who told you that you could fire?"

The boy can't answer. Only some stammering comes out. That makes Vogel even angrier. "Do you have any idea what a slave costs?" His hands itch. He feels the dragons on his body; they seem to want to crawl out, and it hurts his skin. Sometimes—when his rage becomes uncontrollable—he can hear them. Then there's no turning back, it must be satisfied.

"From the yard," he orders.

A little later, the sailor stands barefoot in the main yard, his hands tied behind his back, a blindfold over his eyes. Two older sailors hold him steady. A long rope has been tied around his ankles, and a hefty chunk of lead hangs from the rope. The young sailor looks like his legs are about to give out, and it's clear he's crying. His body trembles like a leaf in the wind. The sailors on deck hold their breath, but they're also relieved, knowing the skipper has spared them and there will only be one victim. *Better him than us*, they think. They glance upward and no one says a word.

Vogel stands motionless, a carafe of rum in his hand. The rum is hot and sharp in his throat. He feels the boy's fear. He nods. The boatswain shouts upward, and the two sailors don't hesitate: one little push and the boy is off. In complete silence, he falls from the yard, the rope trailing behind him in a graceful arc. After two agonizingly long seconds, there's a hard, flat smack on the water. The rope snaps taut with a whistling sound, and he disappears beneath the surface. The sea closes over him.

Silence again.

The two sailors in the yard wait for a signal from the skipper. Vogel sways slightly. He drinks his rum. And again. The rope is still in the water. The wind gently toys with some sailcloth on the foremast. It flutters briefly. The steady ticking of the reef points. Somewhere, a seagull screeches. He drinks his rum and keeps his eyes closed, but he sees the red in his mind, which slowly seems to recede, and the pain in his skin fades away. He knows the boy is unconscious; he won't even realize that Death is swimming around him. He takes another sip and listens to the wind. The rum hums in his head.

"Pull him up," he finally says.

Grim but calm, he stands on the quarterdeck, gazing out over the ocean. He is alone and lets no one near him. He had the recovered slave tied to the mast and personally, in the presence of men, women and children, flogged him until he bled.

But now his men are sullen, their expressions dark, and they keep getting in each other's way. He gave the boatswain a clear signal: be strict, don't give an inch, because trouble will brew before you know it. Anyone with nothing to do has been sent ashore to forage. Anything will do: fish, turtles, mussels, coconuts or eggs. As long as they stay busy. And meanwhile, he waits until he sees a sail on the horizon, until Burghoutsz's *Griffin* appears, as agreed.

But by God, don't let it take too long.

He shakes his head and promises himself this is a once-in-a-lifetime thing. He feels trapped. This kind of trade isn't for him. Gold, that's their game: buy it, load it and get the hell out. Back to Vlissingen. Like the wind. Yes, that's a good thought. He holds onto it.

34 The Embarkation

"Everyone knows: slave traders are sorcerers and cannibals. They steal the souls of their fellow humans and carry them away across the ocean. White men devour black men, strip them of limbs and organs, and process them into oil, cheese, red wine, gunpowder, and black leather. They are beheaded, and their skulls and brains are boiled and sold as medicine, and their blood is used to dye the coats of the white soldiers so they will fight more bravely."

From: Traditions of an akomfo, sorcerer of the Akim

⚓

It is the first watch, three bells have struck. The *Griffin* lies anchored and motionless in the bay of Elmina, brightly lit with lanterns, their reflections shimmering on the water.

Burghoutsz stands on the quarterdeck, a pistol in hand. The weapon is loaded because the slaves from the castle will be embarked, and he takes no chances. His crew is ready: his boys stand with cutlasses and cleavers at the side ladders by the waist railing, and on the quarterdeck and forecastle, swivel guns are mounted—small-caliber cannons loaded with scrap and nails, rotating on an iron pivot, and from now on, they will be manned day and night.

With its narrow upper decks, the pear-shaped flute ship is not really suited for transporting slaves. On many ships, the gun deck is used to accommodate them, but Burghoutsz prefers to let his sailors keep their own sleeping quarters. That's also better in case of emergency when all hands need to be called. The male slaves are, therefore, placed on the orlop deck at night, which is low—you can't stand up in it—but it's long and wide. On the aft deck, under the quarterdeck, there is enough space for the women and children.

The waist is divided into two sections, separated by a sturdy wooden partition with a gate that can be closed. The decks are clear; he hasn't had cabins built, only a frame over which a sail can be stretched in case of rain or harsh sunlight. Outside the ship, just below the railing, old boarding nets have been attached to prevent any escape attempts.

He makes another round. Just to be sure. He peers toward Elmina Castle, where the quay on the riverside is lit by flickering torches. Dozens of canoes crowd the area, black natives stand on the gunwales, gesturing and shouting at each other: the asafo Assamfoe, the company of the fishermen and canoe operators, has made its appearance, as it is they who traditionally transport the slaves to the Dutch ships. Tonight, they control the bay. On the beach farther away, large fires have been lit. The sound of drums echoes heavily across the water's surface.

The skipper nervously clenches his jaw. The pistol in his right-hand feels damp; he would have much preferred to bring the slaves on board himself. "Everything ready?" he asks boatswain Graauw for the umpteenth time.

"All ready."

"Prepare for trouble."

"On your command, skipper."

"Good," he finally decides. "Let them come."

During the evening, the slaves were taken from their dungeons in the castle, chained together in pairs and bound in groups of ten with ropes. Men, women and children separated from each other.

The company's chirurgeon conducted one last inspection in the courtyard, right in front of the old Papist church, under the watchful eye of a representative of the Chamber of Assurance and Damage. The representative asked critical questions, as his responsibility is significant; once the slaves are approved for embarkation, liability transfers to the insurer. He checked for gray hair (reducing the value by a third), missing toes or fingers (reducing the value by a sixth), spots on the body (reducing the value by three-quarters), signs of ringworm (reducing the value by a sixth), as well as old age, poor vision, hearing loss, wounds, broken bones, hernias, scurvy, dysentery, and so on.

The chief chirurgeon answered patiently but did not let himself be pushed around. He knows his people well: if there was anything to be noticed, he had already seen it. "No losses," he concluded with satisfaction.

The representative reluctantly agreed. He, the senior merchant of Elmina, Burghoutsz and the chirurgeon then jointly signed the insurance policy and the market certificate.

Bomba Jan stands in the castle courtyard, overseeing his group of slaves. They stand silently, two by two, in groups of ten. These are fine slaves, Bomba Jan thinks. There are none better. No filthy Calabaris or Bantus, but beautiful, healthy, intelligent and hard-working blacks like himself. "Listen carefully," he says loudly so they can all hear him clearly. Over the past few days, he's gathered information: where are they from? What dialect do they speak? He isn't such a good bomba for nothing. A good bomba always has work. "Listen carefully," he repeats, speaking in Akim, Kyerepon, Ewe, Ga, and, for good measure, in Twi as well. "I am Bomba Jan. From now on, I am your master. You will listen to me, and you will obey me. I am bomba because I am fair and just and will treat you well. I am bomba because the whites trust me. The whites said: take care of our blacks, Bomba Jan, make sure they don't get sick, don't cause trouble, and obey us."

As he speaks, he walks down the rows like a general, looking them in the eye, playing with the coiled whip in his large hands; the nine strands make a snapping sound against his palm. "There are old women who spread rumours," he continues. "They say the whites want to eat you. That on the ship, you'll be slaughtered and cut into pieces, stuffed into barrels of brine and sold as meat in the white harbours on the other side of the world." Bomba Jan laughs scornfully. "It's lies. Children's stories! Even the whites know very well that all blacks taste like shit. They'd rather eat each other. No one wants to eat you. It's nonsense and babbling, and from now on, no more talk about it. The ship will take you across the great water. There is land there. There is work. That's why you're going. The whites have no use for dead, sick or injured blacks. They need strong men and women who can work hard and bring in the harvest. If you obey, nothing will happen to you."

He points to the gate. "Behind that gate lies the ship. The ship will be your home. The ship belongs to the white *aene*. The *aene* is God, and on his ship, his will is the law. There is nothing he cannot do. Never look the *aene* in the eye and never speak to him unless you are spoken to. Even the white men on the ship are under his command. You will obey all the whites. Always, immediately and unconditionally. Is that clear?"

They stare at him, no one speaks.

"You are now going onto the ship. The asafo Assamfoe will take you there in their canoes. Follow the instructions when you reach the boat. It is dark, and the whites are nervous and have no patience. Do what they say. If you don't do what they say, you'll face the whip or the stick. Don't talk back to them. Don't insult them. Don't raise your hand. Don't refuse anything. If you do wrong, you'll be tied to the mast. You don't want to be tied to the mast. *Terrible* things happen at the mast. Trust Bomba Jan!"

He doesn't know if they believe him. They look at him, but their eyes are dull. Their minds are shut. They're not listening. They are like fish pulled above the water with a net; they gasp for air with open eyes and empty gazes. That's not good, he thinks. If they ever needed good advice, it's now. "Once you're on the ship, go straight below deck. The men's quarters are low and dark, and it will be cramped. But it's only temporary. In good weather, you'll be allowed outside during the day to breathe fresh air and feel the sun. Accept your fate. There's no point in complaining. If you need to ask for something, come to me. If you need *anything*, come to me. I am the bomba. I will take care of you."

He nods, satisfied with himself. He has been clear. If they make mistakes, if they fail, that's on them. He will punish them. He's learned many ways to do that by now. But it's better to be punished by Bomba Jan than by the whites. The uncles are too harsh. They are beaten too. And the boatswain is a devil.

The guards stare at him. He's standing idle. He's talking to himself. Bomba Jan flashes a guilty grin. "Let's go," he says, laughing.

Bomba Jan goes with the first group. He stands in the canoe, paddling through the night toward the *Griffin*, which shines like a beacon on the dark gray sea ahead of him. He's glad it isn't raining. Rain makes the wood of quays, the side ladders and the decks slippery, leading to accidents during embarkation. That would be a very bad omen.

The air is almost cool here, he thinks. And at sea, there are no mosquitoes, no black flies, or *tumbu* that lay their eggs in your skin and whose larvae eat your flesh. Bomba Jan is glad to be heading back to the sea. He does enjoy his new women, but after a few months, their nagging and bickering begin to wear on him.

He looks at the nine prisoners, sitting silently on the thwarts, their hands between their knees. These are the men he was ordered by the skipper to mark. In the torchlight, the rough smears of pitch on their backs are clearly visible. He knows the paint sticks for a long time, it's a nasty substance.

Bomba Jan turns to them, making a gesture that grabs their attention. He speaks softly, almost in a whisper. "You are the leaders. I've seen that. That's why you've been marked. You are my mouth, my ears and my eyes. If I say or command something, you will pass it on to your brothers and sisters."

One of the slaves looks at him with a dark gaze. Bomba Jan sees that he bears a fresh brand. The wound is slightly infected. He is the pawn of Quassie Patoe, for whom Bomba Jan was expected to risk his life.

"Why should we do that?" asks the slave, who doesn't yet realize he is a slave. His tone doesn't sit well with Bomba Jan—too bold. A sign of trouble. Bomba Jan leans in a little so the slave can hear him better. "You're a troublemaker," he whispers, his voice cool, almost businesslike. "That's why I marked you with paint. You can cause trouble so that others, perhaps innocent brothers, perhaps women or children, are punished. I don't like that."

"I didn't do anything."

"No, nothing," Bomba Jan admits. He presses the handle of his whip firmly against the infected brand. The slave jerks and lets out a cry of pain. His eyes are filled with shock.

"I see you," Bomba Jan says quietly, continuing to press. "Be careful. If you make mistakes, you'll be punished. For the first few days, you'll stay in your cage. You're not allowed outside, like the others. You shall lie in your own filth until I decide you can come out."

"I'm not a slave," the slave pants. "I am Quameno Ewussi of the Enyampa. I am a free man."

Bomba Jan shrugs. He thinks some men will never see an elephant, even if it's standing right in front of their nose. "Slaves have no name," he says. "You are number nine, orlop deck, first quadrant." He stands up and looks at the ship, now close by. The lights shimmer in the water. He sees the white sailors, pistols and cutlasses in their hands. Bomba Jan smiles. He waves. Yes, he thinks, it's going to be a long journey. It's good to be heading back to the sea.

35 *Back: Bomba Jan Michielsz*

As a child, he is already big and broad-shouldered. Large hands and feet. A round head with a flat nose. Yet he doesn't inspire fear; his gaze is friendly, and he smiles often. Because his front teeth are missing, he has a lisp, which sometimes makes people think he's slow. But don't awaken his anger; it takes four or five grown men to stop him when he's enraged.

⚓

Lying in the tall grass, the sun on your skin, your black skin. Hot sun. Bright light. Insects buzzing before your eyes, swallows darting through the air. Trees. Coconut palms. If you're lucky, you might see a lion. Every boy wants to see a lion.

Black people. Brown people. A richly varied landscape of shades, strictly divided by rank and class: nobles, Akanists, caboceers, grandes, warriors, serfs, pawns, mulattoes and slaves. But while he can go where he pleases, others are in chains.
    Onyame, why are they different?

There is an early, fundamental lesson he learns: a Dutch surname is an advantage. Then you can say: I am a tapoeijer, *my lineage is white.*
    Onyame, am I white?

An old man stands in the way, an iron shackle around his neck. He is skin and bones. "Move aside," says Bomba Jan proudly (he is eight). The old man hesitates for a moment but then steps aside. Bomba Jan grins and feels big, bigger than the old man. The old man is cattle. Black cattle.
    Onyame, I am a Hollander.

"When I'm old, I'll become head clerk too," he declares confidently (now he's ten), pointing his large, childlike hands at the group of slaves in the castle courtyard. "I'll buy many slaves make a lot of profit."
    The white clerk sits at his folding table and laughs heartily at him. "Head clerk?" He playfully taps Bomba Jan on the head. "Stupid negro. Bring me a jug of beer."
    Onyame, am I black?

The Company is everything. The Company is God. Gold. Chika. Guilders. Spanish dollars. Pieces of eight. Bomba Jan, fourteen years old, travels with the white merchants through the interior, passing through small kingdoms and tribal groups, searching for trade goods. He is a porter, messenger and jack of all trades. Along the way, an endless stream of languages, dialects and accents pass by. He picks them up quickly; he has a knack for languages, much to the amazement of the whites.

The merchant says: "You're not stupid, tapoeijer. Tell that black bastard we're not going higher than ten thousand bushels."

"He says you're cheating him, boss."

"Is that so? What a bastard. Tell him it's take it or leave it, boy. If he doesn't back down, we'll go somewhere else."

The Denkyira chief looks at him sceptically, puffing on his Dutch gouwenaar (three pipes for a stiver). "I've heard you have a white ancestor, negro. Is it true?"

"Dutch grandfather." Bomba Jan, seventeen years old, pokes the fire with a stick. He finds these kinds of conversations uncomfortable. He pulls his head down between his imposing shoulders.

"You look like an Akim."

"My mother was Akim."

"Hm." The chief spits disdainfully on the ground. "White pigs and black whores. Your ancestors weep with shame, negro. With us, you'd be a slave."

Bomba Jan straightens up. His chest is already broad, his muscles rippling under his skin. "Your world is no bigger than your miserable field," he says proudly, "Jan Compan will destroy you. Nothing is mightier than the white God."

But at night, in the dying glow of the campfire, he doubts his own words. Silently, he prays to the heavens: Onyame, forgive me.

In the hinterland, clever swindlers produce fake gold; one guilder of good chika is worth eight guilders of counterfeit. Bomba Jan teaches the whites to be cautious. "This is filthy junk, boss, look." He places the nuggets on a flat stone and hits them with a hammer. The stuff crumbles into gritty grains. "Mixed with dirt and coral and copper."

The Dutch assistant chuckles and gives the Denkyira vendor a hard kick in the backside. "Go sell that to the English at Cape Coast Castle, you filthy black Hamite." He gestures to the soldiers in his escort. "Get rid of those counterfeiters."

The soldiers laugh and eagerly start beating them.

Bomba Jan concludes that it's apparently acceptable to swindle the English whites.

The antelope stands with pricked, trembling ears in the field just below him. Moist eyes look in his direction, but the wind blows toward him, and he lies flat behind the red rock. The antelope neither sees nor smells him.

"God almighty," pants the white merchant excitedly next to him.

Bomba Jan shakes his head. It was a tough trek, tracking and traversing the savannah—the whites aren't very good at it. They tire quickly and understand nothing about the land or the animals. He raises his hand. "Better to wait, boss."

"Wait?" The white man growls. "Give me the musket."

"The light isn't good, boss."

"Goddamn, you black bastard, don't contradict me."

The shot rings out, and the bullet tears a hole in the antelope's hindquarters. The animal disappears into the sun, into the bushes, blending into the African sky.

"Damn it! Go find her, *tapoeijer*."

"There's nothing to find, boss, she's gone."

Never tell the truth to whites.

Onyame, why do they beat me?

Awakening. In the mulatto quarter, those without skills fall into poverty, whose fathers have left for Holland, leaving them behind with nothing. The mulatto fund is meagre. How do you get ahead?

Slaves are in demand, and good bombas are scarce. He gazes at the ships in the bay, trying to understand them. Where do they come from? Where are they going? What is life like there?

Determined, he takes the plunge and tries to speak with the white skippers in the taverns next to the castle. Hat in hand. Eyes on the ground. "I speak all the languages, boss. I can talk to them." His hand gesture spans the inland as far as he can see. "Saboe, Twifo, Fetu. Kumasi. I've been everywhere."

The Dutchman eats boiled pork. The fat drips into his beard. "You're a cheeky monkey, just showing up here like this."

He's a hard man, Bomba Jan knows. The white sailors are all heartless. He replies humbly: "Yes, boss, but boss Coenraad said I should speak to you."

Bright blue eyes size him up. "Are you a troublemaker?" The tone is threatening.

"No, boss, I want to work hard. I'll take good care of your slaves."

The scrutinizing gaze lingers. The Dutchman bites into his pork. Chews. "Name *of Michielsz, huh?" Speaking with his mouth full. He chuckles. Thinks. Finally, he says:* "If you call me 'boss' one more time, I'll have you flogged. I'm a skipper, not some landlubber."

He knows the word. "No, aene."

"Have you ever sailed on a boat?"

He shakes his head.

The Dutchman grins maliciously and spits out a piece of rind. "Seasickness will knock you down a peg, you black bastard. But you've got balls, I'll give you that. Get in that sloop and go aboard. And if you're worthless, I'll sell you across the ocean, along with your kind."

That doesn't happen. He has found his destiny.

Onyame, I am Bomba Jan.

36 Duisterbloem Banishes the Devil

"But if that slave says in his heart: My master is taking a long time, and he begins to beat the men slaves and maid slaves, and to eat and drink and get drunk, then the master of that slave will come on a day he does not expect, and at an hour he does not know, and he will punish him and assign him a place with the unfaithful."

From: The Bible, Luke 12:45-46

⚓

Never in his boldest dreams had Reverend Duisterbloem expected that Satan would torment him with desire for a black woman, a slave no less. Helpless and unable to speak to anyone about his temptations, he withdraws more and more from the outside world, praying, reading his Bible, searching for answers or explanations. Every morning, he faithfully leads his church service in the castle, provides comfort to the sick at Coenraadsburg, buries the dead and fulfils all the duties assigned to him, but still, he is distracted—that much he can admit. The devil is gaining ground, he knows, but he is powerless to stop it. Of course, he could have asked for a different maid, but he lacks the courage or the will to do so.

God looks down on him. God waits. God wants to see what he will do, so he must be strong and resist, but Satan makes him weak, leaving him sleepless at night, lying in bed, sweating and yearning for the filthiest, most outrageous sexual acts he can imagine. For nights on end, he has lain there—hands clasped on his mattress—staring at his throbbing, stiff phallus, resisting the urge to satisfy himself. It's starting to show: his already gaunt face has become even more hollow, with pale, tightly drawn skin, protruding cheekbones and dark circles under his eyes.

Tonight, however, he has mustered his courage. He has waited, kneeling by his bed, praying until darkness fell. The time has come. He has gathered his strength. He will confront Satan. With God's help, he must succeed. God anointed Jesus and clothed him with power, and Jesus went through the land doing good and healing all who were under the power of the devil, for God was with Him.

With hunched shoulders, he creeps across the floor, dressed only in his worn, stained nightshirt, and presses his ear to the door, listening for sounds on the other side.

Silence.

That's a good sign.

He crouches down, sweating from the tension, and carefully opens the door. His house, which stands on the edge of the village and is rented by the Classis of Amsterdam, is made of wood and has two floors. Behind the door is a rough staircase leading to the lower floor, where the kitchen is located, along with the maid's sleeping quarters. It's not a large house. In Midwout, his parsonage was at least three times as big, with multiple rooms and separate spaces for the servants. You could already see civilization there despite all those filthy Indians. That's not the case here. We are pioneers, he thinks, preachers of God's word in a black wilderness.

He sneaks barefoot downstairs. The stairs creak. When he reaches the bottom, he almost trips over a large rat. The creature squeaks and slips between his legs into the darkness. Duisterbloem slaps a hand over his mouth, barely managing to stifle a scream. He mutters, "The Lord is my strength, He is my protector, the Lord came to my aid. He is my God, Him I will honour, the God of my father, Him I praise and exalt."

Around his neck hangs a simple iron cross. He grabs it with his left hand, holding it straight out in front of him as if it were a weapon as if he could banish all the evil in the world with it. Then he storms into the kitchen, where he gives the sleeping maid the fright of her life. She jumps up with a scream from her reed sleeping mat, her back slamming hard against the stove, causing pots, pans, meat forks and a fire poker to clatter to the floor.

Duisterbloem, with wild eyes, thrusts the cross at her.

"Go away, Satan!" he shrieks, quoting from Matthew as he hobbles toward her with bent legs. "Worship the Lord your God and serve Him only!"

The maid has nowhere to go. She's trapped between him and the stove, but she frantically tries to stay as far away from him as possible. Her body stretches backward, causing her simple nightgown to suddenly reveal large patches of naked skin: a thigh, a breast, a nipple. Duisterbloem can't avoid it; his eyes are drawn to them like flies to honey. He sees those dark temptations, that black satin skin, he sees everything that has kept him awake for nights on end. His self-control is gone. That nipple seems to stare back at him, mocking him. He sees everything in that nipple, all his desires, his cravings, his lust. The images flood back: the filth, that terrible, delightful, pleasure-filled, lustful filth! He stands there with the iron cross in his hand, visibly becoming erect; his cock juts like a weapon through the fabric of his nightshirt. And something in his head snaps. He grabs under his shirt with his free hand and begins to masturbate with wild, uncontrolled motions, all the while screaming: "You are cursed, vanish from my sight into the eternal fire prepared for the devil and his angels!"

The maid stares for several long, slow-motion seconds at this nightmare she will never forget: a half-naked, pale white man hysterically pleasuring himself, still brandishing the cross menacingly, while shouting incoherent words, his eyes rolling back, and thick globs of saliva flying through the air.

"And the Lord... commanded... the angel! ... to sheath! ... his sword!"

It doesn't take long. Duisterbloem lets out a drawn-out cry, his eyes bulging as he jerks and spasms, climaxing as his seed shoots across the kitchen. He immediately collapses, exhausted, onto his bony knees.

But by then the maid has already fled outside, screaming into the night, away from the evil spirits that have taken possession of the house and bewitched its occupant.

37 Sweerts, Abena Gyan and Quassie Patoe

"Our warehouse inventory now includes 8,717 snaphaunces. Despite your encouragement, you know my hesitation to sell them to the natives. What if our own weapons are turned against us? But I must admit: the English, the Danes and the privateers have no such doubts; the Royal African Company is said to have already traded more than 10,000 firearms this year. It is whispered that even the Ashanti prefer to offer their slaves at Cape Coast Castle in exchange for English snaphaunces. If I set aside my concerns, I am still short by 3,000 pieces."

From: letters of Director-General Nicholaas Sweerts to the Gentlemen Ten of the West India Company, December 1687

⚓

"Quassie Patoe," greets director-general Sweerts. "Defender of Anomansa. Leader of the Enyampa." He leans back in his chair, a cold smile on his lips. Behind him, beyond the castle battlements, the sun sinks into the ocean. "Thank you for accepting my invitation so late in the evening." He lifts his glass of *genièvre*, a juniper-flavoured gin that has quickly become immensely popular. "And forgive the presence of Abena Gyan." He gestures toward her, sitting on a few cushions on the stone floor before him, her back resting against his legs. "But the private quarters in the castle are stuffy and hot. Here on the parapet is some wind."

Quassie Patoe inclines his head slightly. He has nothing against Abena Gyan. Quite the opposite. Her glistening skin is very pleasing to him. And the comfortable kaftan she wears is made of fine, expensive fabric, concealing a body he personally wouldn't mind possessing. He himself is dressed impeccably, in his lion's mantle and high snakeskin hat. In his right hand, he holds an ivory staff, intricately carved with curls and animal figures. "The first lady is never too much," he lisps exaggeratedly, his eyes roaming over her long legs. "I am your servant, Your Excellency Sweerts. What can I do for you?"

Sweerts looks at him without much warmth. "Nothing formal," he says. "It's about that Puteijn."

"Puteijn?"

"The corporal."

"The one who was executed?"

"Indeed."

Quassie Patoe straightens in surprise. "What about him?"

"Corporal Puteijn turned out to possess more than his rank would suggest. I wondered if you might know something about that."

"What sort of possessions?"

"*Chika.*"

Even more surprise. Quassie Patoe is now all ears.

"You are aware of many things that happen outside the castle. Perhaps you've heard something."

"Was it stolen?"

"No, no, nothing has been stolen," Sweerts gestures dismissively. "But the origin is unexplained, and it's over four hundred guilders—that's a lot, far too much for a nobody like Puteijn."

"I... didn't know him," says Quassie Patoe, frowning. He remembers Puteijn as a clumsy, unremarkable white wretch.

Sweerts studies his face. "I do believe," he continues, "that these boys earn a bit on the side here and there. The Company has explicitly forbidden it, but as long as it's not too much, we turn a blind eye. This, however, falls under excessive abuse. And if an ordinary corporal is walking away with sums like this, then there are higher-ups somewhere who are cheating the Company out of large amounts of money."

"Large amounts, indeed," Quassie Patoe repeats thoughtfully, feeling a surge of doubt. Why doesn't he know anything about this? Who bypassed him? He hesitates for a moment, then makes a grand gesture with his ivory staff. "The world is vast. Soldiers come and go. I can't see everything."

"That disappoints me," says Sweerts dryly. "The ensign of the asafo Enyampa knows a lot, has a finger in every pie. Hardly anything changes hands here without his involvement."

Quassie Patoe doesn't flinch. "White soldiers follow white orders," he says calmly.

"Anyone trading slaves clandestinely has a long way to go to reach the coast. In the interior, in Wassa, every turn threatens with ambush. For a mark of gold, they'll slit your throat. That requires adequate protection. But not from villagers or warriors with assegais—no, sir, you leave that to trained soldiers with guns." Sweerts drums his fingers. "The white man murdered by Puteijn was a former merchant from Vlissingen," he continues. "And the two black caboceers were Denkyira: they are currently doing everything they can to get their hands on

European weapons. They have to, because the Ashanti are threatening their borders."

"The king has made a treaty with the Dutch," Quassie Patoe protests. "He can't risk trading outside the Company. He'd lose the last friend he has."

Sweerts shakes his head. "If the Ashanti defeat him, he'll lose more than his last friend. It'll cost him his friggin' head. He knows very well that I don't have the men or the resources to support him inland. In case of war, he has nothing to gain from the Dutch."

Quassie Patoe remains silent, looking toward the horizon: the top edge of the sun is sinking into the ocean. There is something else he's heard. "It is rumoured," he says, "that the blacks in Luanda are dying from a white plague. People are covered in bumps and spots."

Sweerts stares at him. "Smallpox?"

"I don't know the name of the white man's disease."

"Good God! That means the Portuguese slave source is drying up."

Quassie Patoe squints. "If the brown whites can't get slaves anymore, they'll come here. Where else?"

"Of course, they have no alternative, although it's against the law." Sweerts empties his glass as a black servant brings a storm lantern. "Gold has been found in Brazil. The Portuguese are flush with money; they can deliver weapons in abundance in exchange for slaves. Slaves that are meant to be sold to *us*. So is the king cheating on us? Is the temptation too great?"

"The Denkyira are filthy whore-hyenas," Abena Gyan agrees, stretching shamelessly and grinning at Quassie Patoe, her teeth gleaming in the lamp's light.

Sweerts stands up and walks to one of the heavy forty-two pounders along the parapet. He peers along the iron barrel. The bay has turned into a grey blur. "Perhaps that Vlissingen merchant organized clandestine slave transports to the coast," he continues, "and hired Dutch soldiers for protection. Maybe he didn't pay Puteijn enough. Or not fast enough. Puteijn was drunk. The man lost his mind and stabbed them all." He turns and looks sternly at Quassie Patoe. "No one is allowed to trade outside the Company, Quassie Patoe. It has to stop."

Quassie Patoe pulls a disgruntled face. "I don't know anything," he insists.

"You knew that Vlissingen merchant?"

"A shady character. He came by from time to time."

"You didn't do business with him?"

"He supplied. He bought. Always small amounts."

"Such as?"

Quassie Patoe shrugs. "Takoelah wood. Grains. Limes. Chickens. He scoured the coast in a canoe. Traded with the English at Cabo Corso."

Sweerts growls. "The king demanded compensation for his two murdered caboceers. I paid it. My God, while he was swindling me!" He raises his fist. "I want to know who else is involved. Someone will pay."

"And quickly," says Abena Gyan. She stretches her leg—it's a very beautiful leg, dark and gleaming in the lamplight—and waves a slender hand haughtily at Quassie Patoe. "Off you go, Quassie Patoe, go catch those scoundrels."

He shoots her a withering look.

Outside the castle, he gathers his lieutenants. It's pitch dark by now, but his eyes are blazing with fury and humiliation. Quassie Patoe kicks at a chicken that scurries in front of him. Feathers scatter in the black night. He looks toward the village, *his* village, the huts, the taverns, the brothels, the asafo companies, the people. Something has slipped past him. Someone has bypassed him. When he closes his eyes, he sees Abena Gyan. Her mockery. Her body. Am I a dog, damn it? God, he would take her until she begged for mercy. Whore of Eguafo. Daughter of a slimy eel. Goddamn it. Who is responsible? The white ensign? The ensign is dead. The white sergeant? The sergeant is dead. The corporal? Also dead. He turns around and sees the castle looming like a massive black mountain against the dark sky. All dead. Yes. What does that mean?

He starts walking. The air is heavy and oppressive. No rain tonight. The young warriors cluster around him.

A vacuum, that's what it means.

He stops.

"I want a woman," he says abruptly. "Now."

He stares thoughtfully at the ivory staff in his hand. Who knows the way? Who can fill the vacuum?

Me.

He looks at his lieutenants. I can also supply the Portuguese. I'm the only one left. I have weapons and warriors. He slaps one of his boys on the shoulder. "*Eééh*," he grins, completely wrapped up in his own thoughts. "The Dutch don't need to know anything."

They look up at him with adoration. He will surely become the *tufohen*, the father of them all. They will do anything for him. Anything.

Yes, he thinks, the Denkyira need me. No one moves without Quassie Patoe.

Oh, how I will fuck tonight.

38 Vogel's Distrust

"(...) We hear rumours regarding a notorious French pirate with more than three hundred men aboard, who is said to be sailing upwind near Axim. He has taken a Brandenburg ship and engaged in battle with Capt. Thomas Towers, whose ship is heavily damaged and many of whose men have been killed. (...)"

From: The Local Correspondence of the Royal African Company of England, by James Walker, 1687

⚓

The next morning, the *Griffin* is finally freed from her anchors. Riding the waves, she leaves Elmina behind, with reefed sails into the wind and the coast to starboard.

Skipper Burghoutsz peers at the pennant, the small flag atop the main mast, which points stiffly to the northeast. Two points abaft the port beam. He nods in satisfaction to his first mate, who stands by the binnacle house. His boys have just logged the speed.

"Seven knots, skipper!"

"Good." Seven knots is fine. With his hands behind his back, he walks to the halfdeck's companionway and observes a group of male slaves in the cordoned-off section of the waist. Buckets of seawater are being scooped, and the blacks wash themselves as best they can. The Dutch sailors walk watchfully around them, cats in hand, ready for the slightest hint of insubordination, but today the atmosphere is relaxed. The weather is beautiful, the sun is shining, there's no hunger or thirst, and so far, there are no sick or injured.

"All well, boss!" shouts Bomba Jan. He stands like a king by the freshwater barrel near the mainmast, doling out ladles of water, which are greedily drunk. He has divided the slaves into four more or less equal quarters (except for the group of leaders, who are always kept separate). The first group consists of young boys, no older than sixteen, responsible for various practical tasks on board, from untying and retying the slaves, cleaning the decks, to distributing food and drink. Bomba Jan runs a tight ship. With a firm hand, he leads the work crew, giving instructions, explaining patiently, cracking jokes, and occasionally handing out a cuff to the head.

The skipper nods approvingly, but that doesn't diminish his vigilance: on the foredeck and halfdeck, the sailors stand ready at the swivel guns.

He turns and looks down through the hatch of the quarterdeck. Below him, on the aft deck, the women and young children are settled. The *Griffin* has just exited the bay, so there are barely any cases of seasickness yet, although they will soon increase now that they've caught the full swell of the ocean. As a precaution, his chirurgeon has prescribed wet cloths and *poleponze*—a thick drink made of brandy, sugar, nutmeg and lime juice. For now, the women have been put to work as a distraction. They scrub the floors with pumice stone, clean the gutters and sprinkle all the wooden surfaces with vinegar.

"There she is," says Burghoutsz, peering through his spyglass. At first light, the lookout had shouted, "Ship to port!" An hour later, it can be seen from the deck as well: a white speck on the horizon. "Right on time." He gestures to the first mate: "Now we'll see if he keeps his word."

The mate pulls a sceptical face. "That man's never done anything decent," he grumbles. "Ten to one he'll try to enter us."

Afternoon. The sun blazes, the ocean sparkles. Bomba Jan peers over the railing at the *Meyboom*, about four hundred feet away. Both ships are sailing close to the wind, running parallel to each other. The *Meyboom* has opened its gun ports, and the cannons are run out, their muzzles pointing outward. He can see the crew on deck. They're armed with sabres and snaphaunces. The metal gleams brightly in the sunlight.

Bomba Jan shudders. He has locked the slaves below deck, chained as if it were night, even the women and children. It's too dangerous now. The waist is empty, the hatches are closed and secured, the latrine tubs removed, and even the wooden barrier has been temporarily taken down. There's nothing to betray the presence of slaves.

He glances over his shoulder. On the quarterdeck stand the skipper, the first and second mates, and the Company's chief chirurgeon. The skipper is armed with a pistol. His lips are a thin line. Everyone is staring at the *Meyboom*.

"Stay calm!" bellows boatswain Graauw for the hundredth time. His heavy clogs thump across the waist deck. "No one move a muscle!"

The sailors are armed, hanging in the rigging or crouched behind the deck rails. Below them, on the gun deck, the batteries are fully manned. Pumps, fire hoses, plugs and buckets are ready.

Bomba Jan checks his old musket again. The flint is new, the barrel oiled. It's a good musket, though he would have preferred a snaphaunce.

"Take in the tops!" comes the sudden order.

The sailors scramble across the ratlines, and the *Griffin* lowers its topsails. Bomba Jan immediately feels the ship steady on the water. On the other side, to leeward, the same is being done; both ships seem to be tethered together. He can make out the Zeeland skipper, a man in a red waistcoat and a broad-brimmed hat with an ostrich feather.

"Back the sheets!"

The foresail and mainsail are backed. Now the wind spills out, and the *Griffin* immediately comes to a halt. Bomba Jan hears the water lapping against the hull. He sees eddies at the bow.

"Lay aloft for top and tackle!" shouts Graauw.

The sailors balance on the footropes beneath the yards. The canvas is secured with reef lines. The swell picks them up, and the ship begins to sway helplessly. Screeching and tumbling, a flock of seagulls darts between the two ships.

The crew holds its breath; if there's going to be any shooting, it will be now. But the clock ticks on. The guns remain silent.

"Slooooop!" comes the shout from the other ship.

They hear the tackle creak.

Sighs of relief. Bomba Jan relaxes and Gillis Graauw taps the deck with his half-pike.

"No fighting today, lads. Muster on the forecastle."

Skipper Vogel climbs aboard. With smooth, almost lazy movements, he swings his long, booted legs over the railing, and the ostrich feather on his hat bobs merrily along. His pale eyes take in the waist, the men on the forecastle and quarterdeck, the weapons and the swivel guns. For a brief moment, his eyes meet Bomba Jan's. His eyes gleam. Bomba Jan feels a shiver run down his spine. He doesn't know this white man, but he senses he has the evil eye. Instinctively, he pulls his head in.

They are about the same height, but Vogel is slimmer than Burghoutsz. His posture has a lazy, feline quality, like a panther lounging on a long, broad branch, paws hanging down, basking in the sun, purring like a house cat. But there's nothing weak in his eyes.

"Nice little ship you've got here," he says. "And I see a negro with a firearm.

On a white man's ship."

He sniffs deeply. A heavy, tarred sail is stretched over the main hatch in the waist. "And I smell even more blacks. Hundreds, if you ask me."

Burghoutsz doesn't respond. He looks to port, where the *Meyboom* is bobbing on the water. Her keel's underbody is clearly visible. "You're riding high," he says.

"What?"

"You've got no cargo aboard."

"No." Vogel grins. He taps his nose with his finger. "I'm not stupid."

"What are we doing here if you don't have any cargo?"

"I do have cargo. Just not here."

"That's not the deal. We're here to transfer slaves."

"Yes, but since I never trust a Hollander, especially not when they're with the Company, I tweaked the plan a bit."

Burghoutsz sighs, annoyed. "I have no intention of breaking any deals. I just want my slaves, and then I want to get out of here as fast as possible."

"Yes, but maybe Sweerts has other ideas, doesn't he?" Vogel walks over to the port railing and gestures eastward with both hands. "I bet that Company cruiser of yours is just behind the horizon, lying in wait. I bet it's patiently waiting until my slaves are transferred, and then—*flash!*—there she is, with full sail and eight knots on the log, outpacing me and boarding my ship. Ship gone and skipper Vogel ends up in the hold. Money gone. Everything gone. And maybe the noose, because your boss is a bastard."

"I know nothing about that," says Burghoutsz coolly. "The *Westsouborgh* was anchored when we left."

"I don't blame you, sir, by God, no. Every bird sings as it's beaked." He laughs and shakes his head at the same time. "Slaves on board aren't for me. It stinks like monkeys. Shit and piss everywhere. My boys got moody because of it."

He peers at the main mast. It sways with the swell. Up and down. Up and down. "I bet there are already about thirty of them puking down below, now that we're lying still. And the rest will follow soon enough. I can smell it, lad, that sour stench—I'll never forget it. It seeps into the wood and if you're not careful it never comes out again. I scrubbed my whole ship clean. I made them scour and scrub with stones, swabs and mops until their hands were raw, then I had the decks hosed down. And after that, I sent them all ashore."

"Where?"

"A nice little spot on the coast. Don't worry, they're safe and healthy, and no one knows they're there. I'll tell you the plan: I'll take you to them, you can inspect the whole lot, pay me, and I'm gone. After that, you can get them all on board."

"What's in it for you?"

"Time. At low tide, that cruiser can't follow me—my unloaded pinnace rides too high—and by the time she can hail me, I'll be riding the wind, far too fast. Here, I'm vulnerable. There, I'm not."

They look at each other.

Burghoutsz shrugs. He says, "Have it your way."

Bomba Jan opens the hatch to the aft deck, where the women and children have been locked up since early morning. A sour, pungent stench greets him—vomit. It fills his nostrils and makes him retch immediately. He lifts his head slightly backward, fills his lungs with fresh air and holds his breath. The sailors assist him. Together, they force open the hatches. On the quarterdeck, a ventilator is set up—an upright canvas column hoisted by ropes, extending into the quarterdeck hatch, designed to catch the sea breeze.

Bomba Jan steps into the darkness. He hears groaning and whimpering. Dark silhouettes sway back and forth as if in a trance, but most lie still on the wooden floor or in the bunks, too sick to move, curled up into shivering, miserable heaps, soaked in that sticky, sour mess, which sloshes with the ship's movements, splashing against the bunks and walls, seeping into cracks and crevices, so that everything is saturated.

Bomba Jan drops to his knees. He can't hold his breath any longer. His lungs burn. He exhales. He breathes in again. The air is hot and thick, utterly foul, and his body violently protests. He burps bile, his mouth wide open, gasping for oxygen. "Out," he gasps, weakly waving his arms.

On the orlop deck, where the male slaves are kept, it's even worse. The low, claustrophobic space allows no fresh air, and many of the prisoners are unconscious. The heat is so suffocating that the sailors first douse themselves with buckets of seawater before going in. They've tied wet cloths over their faces and carry burning juniper branches for some relief. With hunched backs, they struggle between the bunks, dragging slaves in pairs or small groups toward the hatch, where they are hoisted up by ropes. No one speaks. They only hear each other's panting and throat sounds. Sweat streams down their flushed, red faces. Slaves who can walk are made to help, and there's no patience—any hesitation is met with a sharp lash from the cat. They work for hours, until they're exhausted and gasping for breath, lying in the waist by the railings, black and white side by side, while the *Griffin* exuberantly rides the waves.

39 *Back: Aldemar Burghoutsz (4)*

After a year at sea, the calluses on your hands are so thick you can pick up a pan of boiling water with your bare fingers.

⚓

Amsterdam, 1664
The ferry approaches the Texel quay, and Anna is standing on the pier, he already recognized her when the small boat passed the Schreierstoren.

She smiles. Dimples in her cheeks, a sparkle in her eyes. He holds her close, wrapping both arms around her, burying his nose in her hair, and he smells the scent of the bakery. Cinnamon and sugar. Behind him, the masts of over a hundred ships rise up. Amsterdam hasn't changed, but he has; he's become a part of it, a cog in that giant Dutch trading machine. He stands a little straighter, a little firmer: a confident Dutch sailor.

"I bet you didn't miss me at all," she teases.

He doesn't know what to say. His heart is bouncing in his chest. "Naahh."

He's rougher now. His hands have turned into fists. The boy she once knew is gone. That makes her a little sad, though she's glad he's come back safe and sound.

Aldemar laughs. He's proud of the steel in his arm muscles. He tells her about his adventures. About cold nights atop the mizzenmast. About Gillis Graauw and Red Rick.

Shipowner Gijsen lives in a massive merchant's house on Hogendijk in Zaandam. He is a tall, stern man with interests in timber, paper, oil, mills and ships, and he prides himself on knowing all his servants and labourers by name.

The weather is beautiful. Blue skies, white clouds. Behind the house lies a garden, bordered by pollard willows, poplars and a privet hedge. Through the leaves, the Zaan River glistens. Carts rattle back and forth along the dike.

In a stylish, open gazebo in the middle of the garden, tea is being served. Shipowner Gijsen and Skipper Rijkjan sit on upright chairs, and Aldemar stands awkwardly by, holding his woollen cap in his hand.

"Tea, Burghoutsz?"

"Gladly, sir."

This presents a problem: the delicate porcelain cup is small and the handle is tiny, and he also has to hold the saucer. Sweat breaks out on his forehead. His cap goes under his arm. With great effort, his shoulders hunched, he sips a very small bit of hot tea. The cup trembles in his hand, making a faint clinking sound against the saucer.

Shipowner Gijsen pretends not to notice. He smokes his pipe and blows out thick clouds of smoke. But his grey eyes gleam. "Skipper Rijkjan is pleased with you."

"Yes, sir."

"He says you have potential."

"Potential, sir?"

"Possibilities."

"Yes, sir."

"He suggests you could become a helmsman."

Silence.

"Do you want to become a helmsman, Burghoutsz?"

"Absolutely, sir."

"I need capable men, loyal people. Do you understand what I mean?"

"Yes, sir, loyal."

"If you work hard and study diligently, there's a future for you. Good craftsmen are well-paid. I like to keep my people satisfied. There's plenty of work and a lot of competition."

Aldemar nods. He steals a glance at the skipper, who sits there like a stone statue.

"Skipper Rijkjan wants you to serve as the third mate abaft the mast. That's a big responsibility, but I always agree with my officers' recommendations. They're rarely wrong. But don't betray that trust, boy. Mark my words: I'm a pretty good friend, but a very bad enemy."

Shipowner Gijsen looks at him for a long time. He drinks his tea. He smokes his pipe. When Aldemar leaves the garden, he has the appointment in his pocket. Third mate: helmsman-in-training. Twenty-four guilders a month.

The *Purmer* is a workhorse, relentlessly driven across the northern seas, heavily laden with timber, wine, even more timber, and anything else they can get their hands on. From the Baltic, she sails back to Texel, Vlieland, the IJ, and the Zaan. And so it goes, in an almost monotonous rhythm tied to the seasons. Only in winter, when the Baltic Sea mostly freezes over, do the men stay home.

Aldemar learns responsibility behind the mast; his decisions have an impact on the lives of the crew. He has power over them. The mate on duty sets the course and the position of the sails. In all weathers and at any time of day or night, he makes them brace the yards, haul in the sheets, and furl the sails, even when they're exhausted or sick. This inevitably creates distance. Aldemar is no longer part of the old group and he feels their resistance. Sidelong glances. Unspoken words. Whispering behind his back. It doesn't take long for the dislike to become mutual. One day, when Red Rick is sentenced to ten lashes with the rope again, Aldemar can barely suppress a feeling of satisfaction. He feels guilty about it for days.

Only Gillis stays loyal to him. Gillis is different. Gillis has a deep, elusive intelligence that far surpasses the calculating pragmatism of his peers. Gillis doesn't talk much. Gillis observes the world as if he's looking out through a window, and if you get too close, he just locks the shutter. He can sit for hours, unmoving, on the mizzen top, crouched, arms hanging between his legs, gazing out over the sea.

"What do you see, Gillis?"

"Nothin'."

But when Aldemar is on the quarterdeck, bent over his books, Gillis clambers down and sits beside him.

"What's that?"

"It's called *The Great Treasury of Seamanship*."

"What's it about?"

"It's a book about sailing."

Gillis's short, stubby fingers slide carefully over the cover.

"Can you read, Gillis?"

Gillis stares out at the sea. He shakes his head, irritated. "Nah."

"Don't you want to learn?"

For a brief moment, there's a spark in his eyes. Longing? Ambition? But it fades just as quickly. Gillis locks his shutter fast. "Stupid stuff," he mutters. He leaps into the rigging, climbing effortlessly over the shrouds, past the topmast, disappearing from sight.

Third mate. Second mate. First mate. Aldemar Burghoutsz is climbing the ranks. By the time he's twenty, he knows the northern waters like the back of his hand. But times have changed and they need to stay vigilant; England and Holland are at each other's throats, and the English are eager for quick spoils, their frigates prowling the North Sea like wolves, hunting for prey. The merchantmen seek the company of Dutch admiralty ships. Sailing in convoy to the Sound.

But sometimes they're on their own.

"Sail ahead!" calls the lookout from the topgallant yard of the foremast.

Skipper Rijkjan peers through his spyglass. In the dusk, a white triangle is visible on the western horizon. He waits for the Purmer to crest a wave. Now he can see better. "A full-rigged ship," he concludes.

"Three-master!" confirms the lookout.

Rijkjan's expression turns worried. "Hard to windward," he orders.

Aldemar is at the whipstaff. He calls to the boatswain on deck: "Bring her around! Get your men to work."

The Purmer heels over, swinging toward the Danish coast, which suddenly feels a lot farther away. Skipper Rijkjan places his hands on his hips. He looks out to port and says, "If they follow our course change, we're in trouble."

"She's changing course!" the lookout immediately calls out.

"Goddamn it!" He strides out onto the quarterdeck, feeling the wind. Broad reach*. The sky to the west is glowing orange. An Englishman?

"We've got to stay ahead of her until it's dark," he mutters to himself. "Then we might have a chance." Set more sail? Risky, with this wind. He glances to port again. The ship is noticeably gaining on them. "Set the topgallants," he orders the boatswain.

The boatswain frowns.

The Purmer is heavily loaded. Despite extra sail, she barely picks up speed, and the strain on her masts and yards is immense, too much; she groans and creaks. Skipper Rijkjan gazes anxiously upward. He signals to Gillis Graauw, who is hanging in the yard above him. "If the topgallant mast snaps, we're done for, Gillis! Keep an eye on it!" Gillis quickly climbs higher, bracing his feet against the vertical mast.

The crew shake their heads. "This won't end well, skipper. We're top-heavy."

"It's an Englishman!" the lookout shouts.

"There's no point, skipper," says the first mate. "They're far too fast. Why drive her into the ground?"

He's right. The skipper hesitates. His hand touches the vibrating, singing windward backstay of the mainmast, which is spraying fine droplets of water. How much longer until dark? Too long. He listens to his ship. The Purmer is protesting, in pain. The mainmast bears the full force of the mains, topsails and topgallant sails, all reefs shaken out. The wood pulls and strains, close to breaking.

And then?

---

* Broad reach = the wind is coming from behind the beam but not directly from the stern.

What then?

Go down with the ship?

He surrenders. "Back the sails," he says.

The English officer is on board. He wears a black tricorne hat, a blue coat and immaculately white trousers with stockings. In his right hand, a cutlass. His soldiers stomp across the deck, muskets loaded, barking at the crew.

"Don't resist!" warns Rijkjan. "Line up along the starboard side."

The officer eyes him curiously. He has a clean-shaven, not unpleasant face. "Wood?" he asks in Dutch, though it comes out sounding like "hood," pointing to the large hatch in the waist.

The skipper nods. "Wood, yes. From Riga."

"Splendid." Two soldiers are sent below. The officer strolls forward, leisurely inspecting the lined-up crew. When he reaches Red Rick, he stops, frowning, and studies him closely. "Are you English?"

"No," replies Red Rick, standing stiffly at attention.

The officer smiles. "Deserted?"

"No."

"What's your name?"

"Rick."

"Your father's name?"

"Uh... Jans."

"From?"

"Franekeh."

That last unspoken "r" gives him away*. The officer tilts his head. He turns to Skipper Rijkjan. "Is this man Dutch?"

"He is," Rijkjan answers.

"I think you're lying."

The skipper's face tightens, and he presses his lips together.

"It's not difficult," says the officer. He taps the skipper on the chest. "Say Franekeh."

"What?"

"Say: Franekeh."

---

* In Dutch, the pronunciation of the letter 'r' is often a distinctive rolling sound, particularly noticeable in the final position of words. Red Rick's failure to properly pronounce the 'r' in "Franeker" (a Dutch city) reveals him as non-Dutch.

"Franeker?"

The officer nods.

To Red Rick: "Say it again: Franekeh."

Red Rick starts sweating. "Franekehhw."

The officer narrows his eyes to slits. He turns to Cross-eyed Jan: "Say: Franekeh."

"Fra – Franeker."

He goes down the line, and they all say "Franeker."

The officer has heard enough. He signals to his soldiers and points to Red Rick. "Put him in irons. We'll find out who he really is back home. No doubt a deserter from a line ship; we know exactly how to deal with those." He glares menacingly upwards. "You'll swing from the highest yardarm, sir!"

Red Rick looks around wildly. He forgets his Dutch: "Boss..."

Skipper Rijkjan is helpless. His face is as red as a beet. "I can't do anything, Red Rick."

A pistol is shoved against Red Rick's head.

The officer lets them into the longboat. There they sit, fifteen heads minus one. The sea swells. It's getting dark. In the east, the Danish coast is still faintly visible. But they all look the other way, where their own ship slowly drifts away from them, confiscated by the English.

"Goddamn it," curses Janus the Crow, shaking his fist.

But they're more sad than angry. It's as if they're saying goodbye to an old lover. The ship's bell clangs. Ting. Ting. A lantern glows on the quarterdeck. It's an old ship, an old lady. And now strange voices echo aboard.

"She'll never survive," whispers Dikkie the cook, tears in his eyes.

Aldemar sits at the back of the boat. He looks at the English frigate and thinks of Red Rick. "What now, skipper?"

The skipper sighs resignedly. "Row. To the shore. What else?"

40 The *Meyboom* Escapes

"Arnout, you no I cant write meself but cousin Wilfred offerd to make this letter so I can let you no that I miss you and that its all good here but that your father had a strook and now hes paralized on the right side and can't do nuthin no more and I had to manage the hous all by meself with only your wage. But I got a job cuz of the Adelaer family in the kitchen, aunt Alda made sure of that and Wilfred helps lots too so I can pay the rent. I took Stijn outa school, he helps master Steen in the workroom and learns a trade, so hopefully he can bring in a stiver too, and Martha can already walk. You shuld see her in her litle clogs outside in the sun, you'd be proud of her, me luv. Monday I got to taste coffie in the kitchen and I dont get why they make such a fuss over it cuz its awful nasty and bitter, even with sugar. I hope your doin good and you stay healty and the howly God help you over there with them savages. Thanx again for the doll for Klaartje."

From: letter to an assistant clerk in Elmina, winter 1687

⚓

Skipper Burghoutsz wades ankle-deep through the water, followed by Bomba Jan, the Company's chief chirurgeon and a few stout, square-shouldered crewmen. He scans the crescent-shaped beach where the slaves have been gathered. Armed guards stand around them in small groups, glaring grimly, muskets and pistols at the ready. A swivel gun is mounted on a fallen tree trunk that lies stretched out on the sand, its barrel pointed directly at him and his small party.

The beach is surrounded on three sides by trees, with dense underbrush and here and there rocky outcrops; an almost impenetrable wall cutting it off from the inland.

Burghoutsz nods in understanding. The spot is well-chosen, there will be no intervention from the land side.

He glances over his shoulder, where the *Griffin* sits anchored beyond the breakers. Further along, but closer to shore, nestled in a channel between a few long sandbanks, the *Meyboom* lies with its sails backed, ready to flee at the slightest sign of trouble.

The sand gleams so brightly it nearly hurts the eyes.

"I don't like this," mutters the chirurgeon. He carries his bag in hand, sweat dripping from his nose and chin. "I don't trust those fellows one bit."

They walk up the beach. Burghoutsz positions the crewmen in a half-circle behind him. "Keep your eyes peeled, lads," he mumbles. His pistol points toward the armed men on the beach. "We're not getting tricked here."

The standoff lingers for a moment. Both sides eye each other warily.

Finally, a broad, square-built man strides toward them. He's wearing a straw hat and a bleached, threadbare vest, but the bandolier across his chest is well-oiled and stocked with powder pouches. Calm eyes meet theirs, which reassures Burghoutsz; this man has his nerves under control.

"I'm bosun Brok," the man says in a thick Zeelandic accent. "You can inspect the slaves if you like."

"Where's Vogel?"

"Skipper Vogel stays on the *Meyboom*."

The chirurgeon does his work. With an expert eye, he walks past the groups of bound slaves, his hands behind his back. The slaves don't look up. Their heads are bowed. Some have their eyes closed. They are tired and disoriented. That's understandable, the chirurgeon thinks. A long journey. Hardship. Fear. Every human has a breaking point. Even blacks. But fatigue isn't the worst thing and they're well-fed, there's no sign of neglect.

After a general inspection, he approaches a group of women. He sets his bag down in the sand and places his hands on his hips. "It's damn hot today," he says kindly, in Dutch.

The women look up. Their eyes give nothing away. He's just another white man: an old, stout fellow with a balding head and sagging skin.

"Yes," he repeats. "Damn hot." From a distance, he examines their hands and feet. Palms and soles: scratched and scraped from the journey. That's normal. No wounds. No blisters. No infections. Good.

They're tied together with ropes, with loops around their necks and wrists. Not too tight. Not too loose. He approves of that too. He grabs one of the women by the upper arm. She flinches and pulls back. That won't do. They need to keep things moving, or they'll be here all day. And the first one always sets the example.

"Come on, girl," he says, giving her a light slap on the cheek with the back of his hand. Now he has her attention. "Hurry up."

He pulls her forward, makes a scissor-like gesture with his fingers near his mouth. "Open up."

No reaction.

Another slap. A bit harder this time. *Whack*!

"Open your mouth."

She opens her mouth. But as his fingers go in, she lets out a cry and jerks her head back.

"Calm down."

Whack!

Her eyes are wide open now.

"You'll learn," says the chirurgeon. He glances sideways at the others. Their eyes are watching. Their minds are working. It's all quite simple if you think about it. Basic psychology. Like teaching a dog to sit.

His fingers are in her mouth. He feels her gums, the inside of her cheek. No ulcers. No sores. No warts. Her mouth is clean. Strong teeth.

He smiles. "Nothing wrong."

His fingers glide down her neck. No deformities. Good muscle tone. The pulse in her neck beats rapidly. Agitated. Hmm. Careful, lady. Collarbone. Unbroken. Sternum. Thorax. All fine. Long muscles in her upper arms. Triceps. Biceps. Strong hands. Beautiful, slender fingers. Long nails. Clean. Couldn't be better. Firm breasts. Feel good. She's childless. Excellent. Flat stomach. Pubic hair. Mons pubis. Vulva.

When he touches her vagina, she pulls back again.

Whack!

He looks at her more sternly now. Holding the rope with one hand, he says, "What must be done, must be done."

Again. She submits this time. His finger slides inside. Another resistance.

Whack!

Moist. No mutilations, as some donka women often have for religious reasons. They cut off the clitoris. Unwise. Leads to infections, often death. Undesirable.

He turns her around.

Spine is straight. Stable. Firm buttocks. Anus is clean. No protrusions or swelling. Good. Turn her around again.

"Look at me." He takes a step back and bends his knees, as if to test their strength. "Now you."

She stares at him, speechless.

"You understand." He bends his knees again and gestures toward her. "Come on."

She mechanically mimics the motion, bending her knees into a curtsy. Her eyes never leave his. Disbelief. Shock. He recognizes that too. These are stages of the human mind. He knows: now he could make her do anything. The further you push, the stronger the effect. Submission. Instinct. If he were to say, "Jump off a cliff," she would obey. But he's not a monster. His credo: use as little violence as possible.

He nods at her. His expression is impersonal. He wouldn't recognize her if he saw her again. There are too many. All those faces, all those bodies. "Next."

He knows the next one will be more obedient. By the fourth, he won't need to strike anymore. These are natural laws. It's predictable.

Skipper Vogel dangles – casually, like a seasoned acrobat – halfway up the starboard mizzen shrouds of the *Meyboom*, a spyglass in one hand, a tankard of brandy in the other. His pinnace sways lazily in the current of the channel, with only a few fathoms between keel and bottom. She has no cargo, just a few rows of water casks and brick ballast in the hold. That makes her dangerously light – he has to be careful when setting sail – but the weather is fair, and the wind is light, and she sits so high in the water now that he dares to manoeuvre her like a dinghy between the sandbanks. Still, he regularly peers through his spyglass toward the ocean, searching for the three masts of the *Westsouborgh*, certain that they'll appear.

He takes a sip of his brandy.

On the main deck, his men are dismantling the last remains of the makeshift slave quarters. Get rid of it. The wood creaks as it's carelessly tossed into the water; he doesn't want that stinking mess on board any longer.

On the beach, more than half a mile away, his slaves are being inspected. From that distance, the people on the sand look like tiny little puppets. It's going slowly. Far too slowly for his liking. But it looks calm. No trouble. Sailors are sailors, he thinks. And business is business.

He glances to port. The sandbank is nearly dry. He sees the bulky shapes of sea turtles struggling through the shallow water toward the shore. The creatures want to come ashore to lay eggs. If there were time, he'd send his men out to catch them; fresh turtle meat is delicious.

He takes another sip. The brandy simmers in his throat, the sun sparkles on the crystal-clear water. He chuckles. If you didn't know better, you'd say life was good.

There is one reject. A man. The chirurgeon is adamant. "This black has a deformity in his spinal cord," he says. "Unfit to work on the plantation. He can barely walk."

Bosun Brok furrows his brow. He stares darkly at the slave, who stands apart, shoulders slumped and head bowed. "You have to take him," he protests. "Orders from the skipper. What are we supposed to do with him?"

"That's not my concern. I inspect slaves, and that's what I'm doing. This one is unfit. The underwriter will never accept him."

"This morning, there was nothing wrong with him."

"Are you an expert? Then you can take it up with the Company yourself."

The bosun bites his lip uncertainly. Skipper Vogel never leaves room for negotiation, that much is clear: he wants no more slaves on board. "Take him for free, then," Brok suggests.

"No, no, absolutely not. We'd have to feed him and care for him. It's a non-starter."

"I can't just leave him here, can I?"

The chirurgeon shrugs. "Do what you want."

Bosun Brok walks over to the slave. "What's wrong with your back?" he asks harshly, in Dutch, as he doesn't know the coastal cant.

The slave stares at him, uncomprehending.

No use. Of course not. And that chirurgeon won't budge. Brok wipes his sweaty forehead. "Goddammit." This is supposed to stay secret, he thinks. Nobody is supposed to see these slaves, especially not the locals. He doesn't understand much about politics, but he knows his skipper's temper all too well. If he leaves the slave behind or lets him go, and there's trouble, he'll be the one to suffer, and a furious skipper is the last thing he wants to deal with.

He chews his cheek. Sighs deeply. Then makes a decision.

His pistol is tucked behind his belt. It's loaded.

"He can't be left behind," he says, with a vague tone of apology to the chirurgeon.

The pistol feels heavy in his hand. He points the barrel at the slave's head. The slave's eyes widen. Fear strikes him as he suddenly realizes what's about to happen. But it's too late. The boatswain pulls back the hammer. As he squeezes the trigger, the flint strikes the frizzen. A spark ignites the powder. There's a bang. Smoke. The recoil snaps his arm upward. The bullet hits the slave's forehead, who makes a small jump and then collapses backward, lifeless.

"Good God!" Brok exclaims.

Skipper Vogel watches as the sloop pushes off from the shore. His men are in the boat, rowing toward him, five men on each side, their strokes synchronized and smooth. His bosun stands at the bow, waving his straw hat—a signal that everything has gone according to plan. Vogel waves back. He's seen it all. He heard the shot. He's guessed what happened, and bosun Brok acted well; he left no witnesses behind.

He nods in relief. It's done. The slaves are no longer his concern. He's kept to the deal, and his payment is in the boat. *Chika*. He looks back. The ocean glistens. On the horizon, sails appear, and immediately his expression darkens. He curses violently. Three masts: the *Westsouborgh*.

Bosun Brok sees it too. It's still far away. They have time. But not much. He looks down at the chest of money at his feet and angrily stomps on a stray crab scuttling between the floorboards of the boat. There's a crunch. Yellowish blood smears the wood of the planking.

We're not giving this away, he thinks grimly. "Row!" he roars at the men on the oars. "Pull, goddammit!"

Burghoutsz peers through his spyglass. The *Westsouborgh* is now fully visible and closing in fast. The wind blows strong from the east, offshore. The Dutch flags are stretched taut. "She's going to cut him off," he says.

Between the sloop and the *Meyboom* lies a sandbank, a long stretch of flat land with perhaps a foot of water covering it, and in some places even completely dry. Nowhere is there enough depth for the boat. Bosun Brok hesitates. The tide is coming in, but he can't wait for that. Navigate through the gullies? He roughly calculates the distance. No time. It would take too long. He looks again at the *Westsouborgh*. She's sailing full and by. Seven or eight knots in this wind, he thinks. Bloody traitors. The skipper was right; you can never trust those Hollanders.

"Out!" he yells. "Over the sandbank!"

The crew rows the boat onto the sand.

"Take your weapons! Leave everything else behind." He kicks off his clogs, grabs the chest of money, and hoists it onto his shoulder. It's heavy. Let's hope the lock holds, he thinks. Then he leaps out of the boat. Warm water splashes around his feet. "Run!"

Eleven men splash through the water. The sand is alternately hard and soft, with patches of dark, mucky mud where they sink deep. Stumbling and cursing, they struggle to stay upright. In the heat, they're soon out of breath. Their rifles and pistols get wet, there's nothing they can do. They pass turtles, unbothered, plodding in the opposite direction, heavy, pocked flippers dragging them along.

Bosun Brok pants like a workhorse. The chest digs into his shoulder and weighs him down. Pain in his side. His heart pounds. The hot air burns his lungs. Keep going, he thinks.

Vogel sees his men approaching. He grins.

Damn Brok! Leaving behind a perfectly good sloop like that.

He signals to the crew on deck, on the yards and in the tops. "Ready the sheets!" he orders. "Prepare to brace hard!"

The *Meyboom* pulls at the anchor like a horse straining at the reins. The anchor line is taut. The hull trembles from the tension. A few burly crewmen stand by the capstan, ready to turn. The rising water in the channel swirls. Incoming tide. He feels the current growing stronger. Schools of fish dart beneath the ship like dark shadows, waiting for the sandbanks to submerge. To the east, clouds are forming. The wind will pick up soon and rain will come with the evening.

He pats the mizzenmast. "Easy now, girl. You'll be off soon." He roars to the waist, "Lower the dinghy!"

The *Westsouborgh* cuts through the water. The wind picks up as the afternoon progresses. It sails parallel to the coast, with just a few miles left to the sandbanks. In front of and beside the bow, the grey backs of dolphins are visible. They leap and dance ahead of the ship, effortlessly, curious and playful. But the crew pays them no mind. The quartermasters drive the sailors on. They hang from the braces and sheets, and down on the gun decks, the cannons are being run out.

The eleven men reach the edge of the sandbank. Panting and coughing, they collapse onto their knees in the water. Bosun Brok staggers under the weight of the chest. Blood runs down his left shoulder. He looks up at the *Meyboom*, bobbing on the water of the channel, just a stone's throw away, with its starboard side facing him. The skipper stands high above him on the quarterdeck railing. "Do you have the gold?" he calls down.

Bosun Brok nods. He can't speak yet. His breath wheezes. His lungs burn. He points at the chest, raising his thumb in the air.

The skipper nods. "Well done, Brok! The dinghy will pick you up. Hurry."

A small rowboat comes across the channel toward them. The lone rower looks sceptical. "You can't all fit in. No fuckin' around or we'll capsize."

Bosun Brok struggles to his feet. "Take the chest," he rasps.

The chest is loaded into the boat. "Alright, four men in. The rest hang over the side."

The men look anxious. None of them can swim. But they have no choice, and bosun Brok sets the example. He grips the gunwale and lets himself into the water. The sea is cool. Pleasant. It washes the blood away and soothes the pain in his shoulder.

"Finally," says Vogel. He rubs his hands together, not even waiting for all the men to be fully aboard; they're still clinging to the side ladder ropes as he orders the anchor to be raised. The cat block is hooked and the anchor is hoisted under the crane.

"There's a stiff breeze, skipper," says bosun Brok calmly, his face twisted in pain as he steps barefoot and upright onto the quarterdeck. The chest of money is back on his shoulder. His nose tests the wind. "Aye, a good strong breeze." He sets the chest down on the deck, right at the skipper's feet. "Here you go," he groans. "With compliments from the West India Company. Your money."

Vogel looks at the chest. He looks at his bosun. Then at the approaching cruiser. The fire behind his eyes burns bright. "Goddamn, Brok, well done." Then he winks, slaps Brok jovially on the back, and nonchalantly kicks the chest with his right foot against the mizzenmast. "I suggest we get the hell out of here. Crack the whip, man!"

The bosun nods, pressing his lips together. He plants his feet wide on the quarterdeck, surveying the deck and rigging. He massages his shoulder. The crew stare at him. He raises his head, a sudden grin stretching from ear to ear. "Loosen the seizings, make sail, you mongrels!" he roars. "Faster, by God! Move it!"

They shoot up the shrouds. They climb the yards. They balance on the footropes. The mainsail flaps for a moment. They brace hard to the wind, pulling on sheets, halyards and braces. The blocks squeal. The ship comes alive as one sail after another is set. The wind takes hold, though it's not much, but the acceleration is unmistakable. The pinnace is agile and responsive. She's as light as a feather.

Vogel and Brok glance simultaneously over the port side. The *Westsouborgh* steadily closes in: a massive, threatening bulk. She's adjusted course, sailing with the wind two points abaft the beam. They see the double row of open gun ports on her starboard side.

"There we go, skipper! By God."

The channel cuts diagonally through the sandbanks, dead west, toward the open ocean. And from the ocean, a straight, invisible line stretches from the *Westsouborgh* to the mouth of the channel. The point where both lines converge is just over a mile ahead. That's the finish line—they must reach it first, because if the cruiser cuts them off, they're done for.

"It's going to be tight," says Vogel, his hand on the trembling, taut backstay, the main cable of the topmast. His eyes gleam. "But if I have to, I'll sail straight through his course."

Every inch of sail is set now, even the sprit topsail way up at the bowsprit. The *Meyboom* heels over slightly. She's so light she's threatening to tip. The sails are taut. The ropes are singing. She's making hardly any bow wave. But the sea foams and rushes by. Fast. Faster. The channel grows wider and deeper. The invisible lines converge.

Skipper Vogel grins wickedly. The dragons on his forearms writhe.

"He's not going to make it," mutters Burghoutsz from the beach. The spyglass seems fused to his eye. From his vantage point, the *Westsouborgh* seems to be ahead. She's sailing deep and steady in a perfectly straight line. The *Meyboom* will catch the full sea wind only after clearing the sandbank.

"We're making too much leeway," mutters bosun Brok. He peers at his skipper and the first mate. The *Meyboom* is now heeling so far over to port that her shroud cleats are dragging through the water. He can barely keep his footing, gripping the railing with one hand. The channel is as wide as a river now, the last bits of sandbank barely visible, submerged by the rising tide.

"Haul tight on them bowlines!" roars Vogel.

Bosun Brok echoes the orders. The crew works frantically. Everyone knows it's do or die.

Vogel looks to port. There she comes. He can make out all the details: the Dutch flag, the letters of the Company. There are men on the gallion. They're holding snaphaunces, and the gun ports on the battery decks are open. As long as we stay ahead of those eighteen-pounder chasers, he thinks. As long as she doesn't pull alongside …

Then they hit the surf. And—suddenly—the wind picks up; an easterly breeze, unimpeded from the sea. The *Meyboom* gets a shove. The topmasts above bend under the strain. A wave rolls beneath her, lifting her up, and she pitches forward, the bow momentarily plunging dangerously into the water. The impact is immense. Foam sprays over the forecastle. The masts sway to port as the shroud cleats once again skim the water's surface. The crew in the rigging cling on, holding their breath in fear.

"*Braaaace!*" bellows bosun Brok.

The crew braces hard. They shout. They call out. They haul. They slacken. The masts swing back. The ship rights itself. She regains her balance, and the bow rises again. It almost feels as though she's sprouting wings, as if the ship is lifting off the sea. And then, suddenly, she surges forward, with the wind full in the sails, with mainsail, mizzen and topsails all set, with upright masts and level yards. The crew cheers. Skipper Vogel howls. He leaps into the mizzen shrouds and shakes his fist at the *Westsouborgh*. "Let's see you catch us now, you cowhumpers! Come and get us if you can!"

He jumps back onto the deck. The second mate is carrying a snaphaunce. Vogel snatches the weapon from his hands, cocks it, and runs to the port railing. He aims the long barrel at the *Westsouborgh*.

It's a futile gesture. The ship is out of range. The bullet disappears into the void, but the shot symbolizes his victory. He clears his throat and spits a thick glob of phlegm contemptuously into the ocean. "Miserable cheeseheads!"

Bomba Jan crouches by the body of the shot slave. He gazes at it, thoughtful, almost sorrowful. He has seen enough corpses in his life, but this death feels like a waste. It makes him sick. He touches the body. It's still warm, but the skin has already taken on a greyish hue. The first flies are coming to check things out. The swarms will soon follow.

A human being is just meat, thinks Bomba Jan. The black man didn't have to die. There was no need. A free man can become a slave, that's just the way it is, it's the law, but if he's unfit as a slave, then he should be able to return to his old life. Why not? Who would that harm? They could have asked him in advance if something was wrong with him. Why didn't they see it? They're supposed to be the experts, aren't they?

He looks at the white sorcerer, the Company's chirurgeon, standing a little further away with the skipper. The chirurgeon sees everything, thinks Bomba Jan. Why didn't he stop the white pirate? It was within his power. He could have done it.

His fingers clasp a small stick. With the stick, he pokes the corpse's left side, almost as if he expects the dead man to wake up. He sighs. He gazes out at the sea.

In the distance, on the horizon, he can just make out the escaped ship: tiny, yellow specks of sail.

The slaves have to be brought on board the *Griffin*.

The longboat is stripped, the thole pins are ripped out. It's hard work. Back and forth they go. One crew of rowers per trip. Through the surf, landing on the beach. Ten slaves in the boat. No more can fit; the waves are too strong. Ten men on the oars. And back again. Once more, through the resisting sea, but going back is harder; if they misjudge the waves, the longboat fills with water. Or they end up broadside, allowing the water to crash in over the stern. The ocean mocks them, and the slaves don't help. They get in the way. They distribute their weight poorly. The sailors curse and swear.

One time, the boat capsizes. Black and white tumble into the water. Luckily, it's not deep, but the current pulls, knocking them down. Everyone staggers back to the shore. The longboat is dragged onto the sand.

On board. Again.

'Pull, you bastards!'

The sailors row with all their might. Their faces are flushed. Blows are struck. 'Goddamn nigger, sit down!'

It goes on until dusk falls.

41 The Ambush

"God, the Most Merciful, the Most Compassionate, the King, the Holy, the Peace, the Believer, the Protector, the Almighty, the Powerful, the Possessor of Greatness, the Creator, the Developer, the Shaper, the Infinite Forgiver of Sins, the Subduer, the Giver, the Sustainer, the Opener, the All-Knowing, the Constrictor, the Expander, the Humiliator, the Exalter, the Bestower of Honour, the Dishonourer, the All-Hearing, the All-Seeing, the Judge, the Just, the Subtle, the Aware, the Tolerant, the Great, the Forgiving, the Appreciative, the Most High, the Possessor of Greatness, the Protector, the Maintainer, the Reckoner, the Sublime, the Generous, the Watchful, the Answerer, the All-Encompassing, the Wise, the Loving, the Glorious, the Resurrector of the Dead, the Witness, the Truth, the Trustee, the Strong, the Firm, the Protecting Friend, the Praiseworthy, the Recorder, the Originator, the Restorer, the Giver of Life, the Taker of Life, the Ever-Living, the Self-Sustaining, the Finder, the Noble, the Unique, the Independent, the Mighty, the Most Powerful, the One who Promotes, the Delayer, the First, the Last, the Manifest, the Hidden, the Ruler, the Most Exalted, the Just, the Acceptor of Repentance, the Avenger, the Bestower of Forgiveness, the Kind, the King of Kings, the Lord of Glory and Honour, the Equitable, the Gatherer, the Self-Sufficient, the Enricher, the Preventer, the Bringer of Distress, the Benefactor, the Light, the Guide, the Everlasting, the Eternal, the Inheritor, the Guide to the Right Path, the Patient One."

From: Islam, the 99 beautiful names of God

⚓

Mussulman Ali rubs the left thigh of his small, grey, scruffy horse. He is worried. His fingers glide over the long, taut tendons. The animal occasionally twitches its leg, and it would be a shame if he had to part with it. That would mean a journey to the insignificant kingdom of Tropassa, the only place on the West African coast where horses are bred. Horses are not made for this climate. Mussulman Ali presses his cheek against the warm, caked fur. The animal turns its head and looks at him with dark, moist eyes that seem to understand what he is thinking.

"We've been together a long time, little donkey," says Mussulman Ali softly. He looks over the horse's back at the forest path winding over the hills. In a distant bend, he can see the figures of three of his men. They trudge under the burden of heavy packs on a nearly three-hundred-mile journey northward along the old caravan route toward Salaga, where his home, three wives and fourteen children await.

The men are alone, without any escort. Splitting up is better, Mussulman Ali has decided. He can't take any chances; too much is at stake. He has killed spies and left no witnesses, but he knows he is still being watched. His three men look ragged. They are unknown, anonymous travellers who draw no attention. And he trusts them, they are family.

But he remains uneasy. Their responsibility is great, and their fate is no longer in his hands. Just like the burden they carry: it is the money he received for the hundred and ten slaves. It is his future.

The horse snorts.

"Yes, yes, I know," says Mussulman Ali, turning away. He begins to massage the cramped tendons. He can be gentle when needed. Meanwhile, he whispers the ninety-nine names of God. *Asma' Allah al Husna.*

The path through the jungle is muddy from the heavy rains. The horses keep slipping, risking broken legs, so the men are forced to dismount and continue at a slow pace, dragging the unwilling animals behind them.

Mussulman Ali walks at the front. He's no longer young, and the struggle through the thick muck weighs heavily on him. Panting, he clings to the reins of his horse, overwhelmed by fatigue, hoping his men don't notice his weakness. Under the trees, the air is hot and thin, often leaving him light-headed staggering like a drunk. It makes him angry and a little sad because, not so long ago, none of this seemed to matter. He could keep going when others gave up, and sometimes he'd crack the whip—just because—to spur the others on. But every leader is eventually defeated, he knows. It's just a matter of time.

And maybe now, his time has come. Perhaps God has new plans for him, *audhu billah*.

Ah, it's been raining for so long. It seems like more water falls every year. He sighs, runs a muddy hand through his beard and glances back. His men follow in silence, shoulders slumped, their eyes fixed on the ground. That's a mistake—no one is paying attention, no one is watching the path or the surroundings. Suddenly, Mussulman Ali catches movement in front of him—behind the trees, around a sharp bend in the path. He curses himself in shame and anger.

But it's already too late. When he looks ahead, he sees the warriors, the muskets and the spears pointed at them. A very tall, very thin Wassa warrior stands in the middle of the path, legs wide, his left arm outstretched, palm forward. His skin is jet black, gleaming with rain, and like Mussulman Ali, he wears an Arab kaftan, tattered and colourless from the dirt. His eyes glimmer in the grey-green dusk.

"Hu! That's far enough!" he commands almost kindly, but Mussulman Ali hears a deep, threatening tone beneath it, so dark that a shiver runs down his spine.

The Wassa chief is surrounded by at least thirty men, and some of them have quickly and silently spread out on both sides of the path. Some of them are crawling through the vegetation. He can see the barrels of their muskets through the bushes. Mussulman Ali remains perfectly still, stretches out his arms and spreads them wide, palms facing upward. He does this more to warn his own men than to show that he means no harm himself because if anyone loses control now, he knows from experience there will be a lot of deaths on both sides.

"Mussulman Ali," calls the Wassa chief. "We heard you coming from afar. Though, of course, we already knew you'd be traveling this road north."

Mussulman Ali nods. That doesn't surprise him at all. But he remains silent and shows no emotion. He's already put on his Mask of Stone. Smiling won't help here. In the chief's right hand, he sees an old flintlock pistol pointed in his direction. He's absolutely certain he'll be dead the moment he makes a wrong move.

"Backroads, huh? Always taking the backroads and shortcuts, that's Mussulman Ali. Heading to Kumasi and maybe even farther, all the way to Salaga, where women and children wait. *Eééh?*" The Wassa chief laughs, but there's no mockery in his voice. "The people in the villages said: Mussulman

Ali has done good business with smugglers. He's stolen slaves from the Denkyira and sold them quietly along the coast. On hidden beaches and in secret coves. Sneaky Mussulman Ali. That's what they said." He's coming closer now. His legs are impossibly long and thin. As he walks, it seems like a strange, awkward dance—first bending deep, then rising tall, his upper body stiff like a wooden puppet, his enormous bare feet dragging in the mud. "The king of the Denkyira asked: brother Wassa, have you heard of the treachery of the Mussulman, our old ally? That can't be true, can it? And Asare, the king of Wassa, said: the king of Denkyira suspects that the Mussulman is doing business with the white rogues along the coast. That he's violating the treaties and stealing slaves. That can't be true, can it?" The Wassa chief rolls his eyes and makes clicking sounds with his tongue. "What will the Company whites think if the king turns a blind eye while his subjects deceive him? What would happen to the old treaty that grants the king of Denkyira the rent payments from Elmina Castle, a right passed from the Komenda to him?"

Mussulman Ali doesn't respond. He stands and listens to that voice, which cannot deceive him, for blood, poison and black smoke flow from it. This black devil seems to serve a far higher, far darker power than—say—the white *djinn* he's done business with.

"Brother Wassa, they said, go to the coast and seek out the mussulman, but don't take the trade routes, no, follow the secret paths through the jungle, the paths of panthers and elephants, and when you find him, ask him if what they say about him is true." He is now standing right in front of Mussulman Ali, towering over him by two heads, so much so that he has to press his chin against his chest to look down at him. He leans forward, and now that head comes dangerously close—large yellow teeth fill Mussulman Ali's vision, suffocating him with the stench of rotting flesh and foul breath.

"So I ask," continues the Wassa chief, "is it true?"

Mussulman Ali struggles to hold on to his Mask of Stone. It must stay in place or he's done for. He stares into bloodshot eyes and suppresses the urge to flee. "No," he finally says, his voice hoarse and distant, as if coming from far away. "No, it's not true."

The head jerks back. The Wassa chief stares at him for a moment, seemingly surprised by the response. The pistol in his hand spins circles in the air. He looks past Mussulman Ali's shoulder, aims the barrel at the first of his men and without so much as blinking, pulls the trigger. The shot is deafening. Mussulman Ali flinches, and when he looks up, one of his men is gone, replaced by a corpse in the yellow mud with only half a head left. Around it, like a halo, lies a fan of blood and fragments of skull.

The horses, startled, have broken loose and are standing some distance away, nervously snorting and pawing the ground. Valuable cargo—saddlebags, tent cloths, cooking utensils and provisions—has fallen to the ground in the commotion, trampled and unrecognizable in the muck. The rest of his men stare in disbelief at their fallen comrade.

"Watch out for Mussulman Ali," says the Wassa chief, handing the now-unloaded pistol to one of his warriors and receiving an Arab scimitar in return. He looks at it briefly, examines the blade, and then makes a few stiff hacking motions through the thick air. His wet skin sprays droplets. "He's cunning and slippery as an eel. And above all, he's dangerous, for he kills without hesitation anyone who stands in his way."

Mussulman Ali grinds his teeth. His mind races, desperately searching for a way out. He thinks: I've been betrayed by the same baboon who sold me the slaves. But I can only blame myself—I've been too greedy, blinded by the *chika*. He looks at the murderer, who chatters on, unfazed.

"... the Wassa don't like traitors, especially not boastful blacks who think they've invented everything and run the show. The *bebiny* who sold you the Denkyira people took a long time to die; now he lies under the earth with his own prick in his mouth, so he can be pleased with himself for all eternity." His teeth glint, his laugh echoes down the path, but Mussulman Ali can see that even his own men fear him.

The curved sword suddenly points in his direction. "Where is the gold?"

"Gold?"

The Wassa chief pulls a face as if in pain. "Oh, Mussulman Ali shouldn't insult us by pretending we're fools. That leads nowhere. He got a lot of *chika* for his slaves. Gold from the white man's ship."

Mussulman Ali smiles sadly, knowing there's no point in keeping up the act. This devil knows everything; he is also a creature of God, so it's God's will that he sees right through him. Yes, now he's sure: this is a turning point. God truly has other plans for him. *Allahu Akbar*. He thinks of the three anonymous men he sent on their journey north. "The gold isn't here," he says meekly. "Of course not. I knew the danger. I knew I was being watched. So, the gold is traveling a different path, unnoticed, under the care of others. Everyone watches Mussulman Ali, but no one watches the gold." He lowers his head and waits. Somewhere deep inside him, his father says, "*If you show your true face, Ali bin Fahrad Al-Fulan, there will be consequences. They'll devour you, body and soul."*

Mussulman Ali nods. God and his father are right. A shadow falls over him. It all happens quickly, but he's not surprised. A blow follows an explosion in his head. The jungle spins. Mussulman Ali falls, and the world disappears from his sight.

42 Slaves on Board

"(...) The Dutch envoy in Offra requested last year to establish a second post at Fida or Popo, in addition to the factory there, in order to gain more control over production on the Slave Coast and to strengthen our competitive position against the English and French. I refused, as my resources are limited, and I had to swiftly deal with the Brandenburgers in Pocquesoe and those same French and English in Commanie. The first has been successful, the second still needs to be definitively accomplished.

Although the envoy has excellently fulfilled his duty—Offra did, after all, supply reasonable numbers of slaves this year—he is now once again asking for assistance; the chief of Offra has risen up against the king of Allada, and the latter is now blocking the trade routes, causing the supply to completely cease.

However, I cannot afford any diversions. No soldier can be spared, my frigates are blockading Fort Frederiksburg, and my cruiser secures the coast from Axim to Mouree. The envoy will have to wait until next year. My decision is final."

From: Letters of Director-General Nicholaas Sweerts to the Gentlemen Ten of the Dutch West India Company, winter 1687

⚓

The *Griffin* sails heavily laden along the coast, her holds full. It is customary, before departure to the West, to visit the Dutch factories one last time. Perhaps there is still a pledgeable slave for sale here or a caught thief there. Every slave counts. It also gives the crew a chance to make any necessary improvements onboard, fix malfunctions and solve problems.

Logbook of the *Griffin*, Sunday, December 14:
"At the roadstead of Sekondi, fort bearing west-northwest, 4°56'N, 18°8'W.

Sails clewed up, anchored with three fathoms of water beneath the keel. Hailed by bumboats offering provisions, but all trade refused. Dined ashore with the fort's merchant, eating an antelope which he claimed to have shot himself. He was pleased with a small cask of Schiedam corn brandy I had brought for him. No slaves for sale. The surroundings struck me as very impoverished."

Bomba Jan's days are full. From early morning until late at night, he's busy with the cargo. There's always something going on. The slaves are needy; they are hungry or thirsty, and there is always someone sick.

"I'm in pain, master."

"Where does it hurt, child?"

"My foot."

Bomba Jan squats down. The child's foot is swollen. "Did you fall?"

"Yes, master."

Bomba Jan smiles. He gazes absently toward the starboard. In the distance, he sees a large flock of gannets diving straight into the sea. Must be a school of sardines, he thinks and nods to the child. "Alright, go to the chirurgeon."

In the morning, the slaves must gather in groups. The men stand naked—row after row, tied together with ropes—in the waist. They are counted. Has anyone stayed below deck? Are there any sick? Does anyone have the runs? That is feared, for regular diarrhoea can turn into a bloody flux. And boatswain Graauw demands a report. He stands like an admiral on the quarterdeck, legs apart, hands behind his back.

Bomba Jan runs back and forth. "All heads present, boss."

He receives nothing more than a grim nod. Boatswain Graauw is a man of few words. His grey eyes scrutinize Bomba Jan with unwavering suspicion, and the scar on his cheek is a thick white line on sun-browned leather.

Bomba Jan runs back to the waist. "Wash!" he bellows.

Buckets of seawater are hauled up on ropes. The naked bodies, soiled during the stifling night on the orlop deck, are quickly cleaned. The salty water heals small wounds and rashes. Every slave must rinse their mouth with vinegar. Nails must be short and clean. Bomba Jan checks carefully. He tolerates no sloppiness, for the boatswain is watching. Always.

Meanwhile, the cleaning crews of the day descend the stairs to the night quarters. Cleanliness is paramount, there is always at least one crew both above and below deck scrubbing. To mask the stench, a heated cannonball is placed in a pot of pitch. It hisses and steams.

Anyone who doesn't do their job properly gets a beating. "That barrel isn't clean." Bomba Jan looks into a black, sweaty, apathetic face. "Have you lost your tongue?"

"No, bomba."

"Ten lashes with the rod."

After the roll call, fresh water mixed with tamarind is distributed to prevent scurvy. Breakfast consists of barley porridge served in wooden bowls. The male slaves receive a little tobacco every other day, as smoking is considered good for the constitution. Drums and hollow wooden percussion instruments are handed out.

"Sing," orders Bomba Jan. "Dance."

The male slaves sing their songs—deep, low voices echoing over the water. They dance lazily to the rhythm, keeping time with their chains. This keeps them moving; healthy slaves fetch a good price, so anyone who doesn't join in is punished. Bomba Jan strikes before the white crew can lash out, for his rod is merely a reinforced, flexible twig, while the white man's whip leaves long, bloody welts on the skin. "Sing," he urges. "Sing, or you'll be tied to the mast." He makes a show of beating, with a lot of noise, for boatswain Graauw's eyes are always watching from the quarterdeck. He quickly shouts, "They're dancing, boss! Everyone's dancing!"

On the quarterdeck, stoves have been built. The female slaves cook millet in large pots and prepare fufu from yams or plantains. As long as they are busy, there's no time to daydream. But the mothers rock their children and stare at the nearby, yet unreachable, coast. They, too, sing. Soft voices. Sad melodies.

Logbook of the *Griffin*, Wednesday, December 17:

"Southern breeze. Ten miles southwest of Boutry. Sailors working on the ship. Traded with a few fishermen: dorado, large sea bass and cassava. Mild flogging of a male slave at the rack for insubordination. In the afternoon,

tacking against the wind, we reached the Boutry roadstead. Sighted Fort Batenstein, 4°49'N, 18°9'W. The local merchant has no slaves for sale. The factory is in deplorable condition and infested with vermin. Three barrels of palm oil purchased."

Bomba Jan stares at the disappearing beach of Boutry, one of the finest spots on the Gold Coast. There, on the white sand between the trees, he once spent many lazy hours in his youth, lying on his back, making funny faces at the swinging monkeys in the treetops and picking oysters from the roots in the river. A sweet memory.

"Boss?"

He turns around, a smile on his face, and looks at the three slave boys standing shoulder to shoulder before him. Between them lie eight large, white-furred rats. "Mill rats," Bomba Jan says in surprise. "They nest in the flour." He nudges one with his foot. "Fat little beasts. Good meat."

The black boys look proud. In the pitch dark, they've been hunting in the hold, wriggling between the bales and barrels. In their youth, they're unbeatable, the heat and stench don't bother them. They're not afraid of the dark, by now they know the ship like the back of their hands.

"Did they bite you?" Bomba Jan asks.

"No, boss."

He checks their fingers, just to be sure. Rat bites are dangerous, he knows, those creatures are nasty pests. But the meat tastes fine, much better than the salted beef from the Dutch barrels. Bomba Jan laughs, sticking his tongue into the gap between his canines. "You'll each get a leg later. Now, off you go."

In the night, there are always hidden places, even on a crowded ship. Everyone is asleep—the crew in their hammocks on the gun deck, the officers in their stuffy cabins above the quarterdeck. Bomba Jan makes his rounds. At the aft part of the lower deck, beyond the women's quarters, there is utter darkness. Space is scarce. He squeezes past crates and chests, steps over coils of rope and folded canvas. His storm lantern casts shadows that move with his steps, and he knows exactly what's going on when he suddenly hears noises: quickened breathing, muffled moans. In a dark corner, he vaguely sees movement. He stops, stands still, waiting for the knife. Behind him, he hears stealthy footsteps, and cool steel grazes his neck.

"There ain't nothin' here for ya, Bomba Jan," whispers a white voice he recognizes but immediately forgets.

"No," Bomba Jan replies hoarsely. The glow from his lantern briefly illuminates the dark corner. He sees one of the crewmen, his canvas trousers around his ankles, behind a bound slave woman. She lies naked, face down on a coil of rope, her mouth gagged with a dirty rag. The sailor doesn't look at Bomba Jan. He waits, staring straight ahead, pretending he doesn't see him. Bomba Jan quickly moves his hand and with it the lantern. The scene disappears, darkness returns. Now there is nothing.

The knife scrapes against his unshaven skin. A voice close to his ear: "No one talks, Bomba Jan."

Bomba Jan shakes his head.

"Maybe you shouldn't be here tonight."

The pressure of the knife fades. Silence. Bomba Jan turns silently and makes his way back. He has seen nothing, heard nothing.

The group of nine male slaves stands on the waist deck, illuminated by the light of an almost full moon. The ocean shimmers and sparkles. Along the coast, about two miles to port, flickering lights are visible: beach fires.

The slaves who were marked by Bomba Jan in Elmina gaze meekly ahead. Considered potential troublemakers, they are only allowed on deck at night, by the skipper's orders, while everyone else sleeps. The watch on duty keeps an eye on them, with two crewmen standing alert at the swivel guns on the forecastle deck.

Bomba Jan seems to never rest, he is on deck even now, handing out water, pipes and tobacco.

"The slave who has slaves under him is as cruel as his master," Quameno Ewussi says mockingly, blowing out thick clouds of smoke. He rubs his brand, which is still infected. "What if I jump overboard?"

Bomba Jan ignores the remark and smiles. The slave can't escape, he personally checked the rope tying him. "Why would you?"

"Or I could kill myself."

"How?"

"If I attack you, those white dogs up there will shoot me to pieces."

"What would you gain from that?"

"At least they wouldn't profit from me." Quameno Ewussi shivers. He has a slight fever. His wound burns. It oozes pus.

Bomba Jan sighs. Some people refuse to give in. But he needs to do something about the infection. "You mustn't touch it," he says.

"What?"

"If you keep scratching it, it won't heal."

"I don't want it to heal."

In the morning, the ship's chirurgeon arrives. "Lay him on the deck," he orders.

Two sailors and Bomba Jan force Quameno Ewussi onto his back. Quameno Ewussi resists. "Let me go!"

One of the sailors slaps him on the head.

The chirurgeon inspects the wound. "He's scratching it open on purpose," he observes.

Bomba Jan nods. "He's got no sense. I warned him."

"Hold him down tight." The chirurgeon grabs a knife.

Quameno Ewussi starts to scream and gets another slap. The chirurgeon calmly cuts away the red, infected flesh around the wounds. He casually tosses the pieces overboard. "Gunpowder."

With one hand, Bomba Jan pulls out a small pouch of gunpowder while holding the slave down on the deck with the other.

The chirurgeon takes the paper pouch, opens it with his teeth, and carefully pours the powder into the wound. With his tinderbox, he swiftly strikes a spark. The spark ignites the powder, causing a bright, white-hot flash. Quameno Ewussi screams in agony.

"Tie his arms behind his back," orders the chirurgeon. "By God, we'll see who's got the stronger will here."

43 Quassie Patoe among the Ahante

"(...) I tell you: Wealth, health and happiness are only available in limited measure. If they were equally distributed, every person could live with dignity. Once, it was so. But the world has changed; there are rich and poor. Whoever is richer could only have achieved this at the expense of others. How? Through witchcraft and dealings with the whites. (...)"

From: Traditions of an akomfo, sorcerer of the Akim

⚓

At sunrise, Quassie Patoe departs in a twelve-meter-long canoe, accompanied by ten native oarsmen and a helmsman at the tiller. His crew is skilled: they quickly navigate past the rocks of Elmina, set a single, triangular sail and proceed rowing and sailing westward, just beyond the reach of the surf, with the coast to starboard.

Maintaining an average speed of five knots, they reach the bay of Chama just before noon. There, amidst an expansive, nearly impenetrable jungle, lies the Pra River. The river mouth has a wide watercourse, shielded by sprawling sandbanks.

Quassie Patoe sits at the back of the boat. His felt hat shields him from the sun, but the heat is oppressive. He gazes toward the river. On a sandbar near the shore, he spots a few crocodiles lying with their jaws wide open, flanked by large groups of white pelicans. "Reef the sail," he calmly orders.

The rowing ceases, and the canoe comes to a stop, bobbing on the waves. The oarsmen drink eagerly from leather water sacks and share pieces of coconut and guavas. Then, they begin guiding the boat through the gullies in the sandplates, chattering and debating, under the critical direction of a cursing helmsman. When the bottom scrapes against sand and mud, they leap overboard and pull the boat into the deeper water of the river.

Steep banks rise up: green, impenetrable walls of overhanging plants and trees. The sound of birds is deafening: parrots, herons, ibises and weaver birds, mingled with the howling of monkeys. The canoe glides through smooth, deep green water, which has now turned fresh. Silver fish dart beneath them. The river remains wide, perhaps three hundred feet, but the jungle closes in and the trees grow taller, until the sky is nothing more than a narrow blue line above their heads. No wind. The heat shimmers. Right beside them, a long, brown shape cuts through the water's surface, follows the canoe for a dozen yards, and then silently disappears into the depths. An iguana? A fish? No one knows.

The oarsmen remain silent. This mysterious world weighs heavily on their spirits. The oars dip cautiously into the water.

After about an hour and a half, they spot a rock in the middle of the river, surrounded by a muddy shallows thick with aquatic plants. Quassie Patoe clicks his tongue in warning, and the helmsman nods. He steers the canoe wide to port, along the greenery. As they pass, they see motionless crocodiles lying among the plants, waiting for prey. Quassie Patoe puffs out his cheeks. Sweat streams from his chin.

Another hour passes. Fully grown, towering kapok trees rise above everything else, some reaching heights of over a hundred feet. The river splits in two, and in the middle an island appears, with a muddy beach and a jetty made of crisia wood at its farthest point, facing them.

They've already been spotted. Five black men stand on the jetty, armed with sabres, spears and muskets.

The boat scrapes up onto the shore.

The village lies in a clearing on the island, hidden from view by the river: a cluster of small, round huts and a long, rectangular communal house surrounding a square of packed earth. Far above, the intertwined crowns of the kapok trees close off the sky like the roof of a cathedral, with trunks like buttresses and branches forming vaulted arches. The foliage softens the harsh sunlight into a diffuse, greenish twilight.

Quassie Patoe stops by a crackling fire. Next to it stands a sorcerer, hunched and gray. Around him, four stretchers have been placed on the hard clay. On them lie black men with terrible wounds. Quassie Patoe stares at them in astonishment. "What happened?" he asks.

"These are the warriors who attacked the white fort in the west," croaks the sorcerer.

"In Poquesoe? Fort Frederiksburg?"

"Flying iron tore their flesh apart," explains the sorcerer. He doesn't know the word canister shot—there is no word for it in Twi or any of the other languages. "There is nothing I can do," he says apologetically to the Ahante warriors who brought the wounded. "They have become spirits."

"You can try, *akomfo*," protest the warriors. "These are our men. Perhaps you can call upon the ancestors and ask them for guidance."

The sorcerer shakes his head sorrowfully. He touches one of the wounded, who looks as though he's been pelted with sharp stones. His body is covered in long, deep wounds—bones visible in places. "Sometimes, it's better to die," he says resignedly. His leathery face is creased around his eyes, and his irises glimmer in the firelight. "Come back when you're ready. I will show them the way."

A little later, Quassie Patoe sits cross-legged on the floor of the communal house, picking at the fabric of his loincloth. Across the rectangular room sits a group of grim, black men.

"Why am I here?" he asks, though he knows very well why: a secret messenger had been sent, who had respectfully asked him— the presumed *tufohen*— to come here, deep in the forest, where a large group of Ahante were hiding. That pleased him. They need him, that much is certain. With suppressed triumph, he reaches beside him, pulls out a pipe and begins filling the bowl with Brazilian tobacco.

One of the warriors on the other side of the floor is very young, but his face is serious, with dark, brooding eyes. "The white corporal, the one who was hanged, was one of the many soldiers who worked for us," he explains, his voice carrying a condescending tone. "They guarded the transports through Wassa territory to the coast. Those new muskets they call snaphaunces are very accurate. I've seen it. They load and fire quickly and almost never jam. We want snaphaunces too. The muskets we have are worthless. I asked the white merchant for them."

"The white merchant organized the transports?"

The young man nods. "The white man knew the grandes of the Denkyira. He boasted about his friendships. He said the king knew about it. He paid well. We shared in the profit. But we prefer snaphaunces to old muskets. With snaphaunces, we can fight the Dutch."

Quassie Patoe furrows his brow. Expertly, he strikes a spark with his tinderbox and lights his pipe. He asks, "Why would you want to fight the Dutch? They've been here for years and years, as long as we can remember. It's not wrong to hate them—they are unclean barbarians who don't wash, and if you're not careful, they'll touch you with their left hand—but they are also powerful merchants."

"We don't hate them. They do what they do. They pit us against each other and walk away with the profit. Anyone who opposes them is destroyed. We understand that; every lion fights for its own pride." The young man leans forward and picks up a wooden bowl of palm wine with both hands. Before drinking, he says, "But the Brandenburgers offer more. They want to work with us."

Quassie Patoe shakes his head, snorting. "The Brandenburgers are no different from other white men. Pigs eat everything, always and everywhere."

"Yes, but for now, as I see it, the Ahante can rise in power through them. The Brandenburgers have no problem selling slaves to the Portuguese. Why would we do business with the Dutch when the Portuguese pay much more?"

Quassie Patoe furrows his brow. *Eééh*, he thinks, this is an ambitious negro. And dangerous, if there's one thing the Dutch and English don't want, it's the return of the Portuguese. "There are dead warriors here," he says, pointing to the four stretchers outside. He glances for a moment at the old, dancing sorcerer. "Canister shot, fireballs, blunderbusses. White men's weapons are powerful." Leaning back, he takes a puff from his pipe, blowing thick clouds of smoke, listening to the sounds around the house—the movements of dozens, maybe even hundreds of warriors. A rebellion? A grab for power? The rise of a new generation? Apparently, new forces have emerged, he concludes. "And the Denkyira?"

The young man shrugs. "The king wants weapons, we want our share. He brings slaves from the interior. As long as he does that, we are friends. If it stops, we will do business with another king. With Obiri Yeboa of the Ashanti, for example."

Quassie Patoe chuckles. "The Denkyira don't like competition."

The young man's eyes gleam. "We do what we want."

"That's not what I see. Maybe you need some help."

The young man swears. He wants to rise angrily, but the men beside him calm his temper.

"Don't worry," says Quassie Patoe confidently. "I see what I see too: a young lion wanting to establish his own pride. I like that." A future king? Perhaps. The Denkyira see themselves as rulers of the hinterland—everyone owes them tribute—but kingdoms rise and fall and a good businessman must think ahead. No, he decides, this young cub is not foolish. He suggests, "The Ahante have an interest in both the Dutch and the Denkyira."

The young man spits into the coal fire that sputters on a bed of hardened clay. "The Dutch attacked Fort Frederiksburg," he says with contempt in his voice. "And they failed. The fort still stands and the Brandenburgers remain. So they are not all-powerful. No one is all-powerful. We cannot rely on them."

"The Dutch frigates block the sea. That's power enough."

"That cannot last. The coast is long. The white ships will be needed elsewhere." For the first time, there's a smile. "The white merchant is dead. We need someone to replace him, a man who knows the Denkyira, someone who can organize the transports and provide protection from the Wassa and Ashanti raiding bands." He looks Quassie Patoe squarely in the eye. "The Portuguese want more slaves. Luanda has dried up due to the white disease. They will trust you. You are the leader of the asafo companies."

Quassie Patoe nods gravely, though that claim isn't true, at least not yet, but he feels like a father. He thinks: A true leader moulds the clay. "You're making a good choice," he agrees. "I'm indignant I wasn't approached sooner."

The young man lowers his eyes, staring sullenly into the fire. The orange light flickers over his skin. "There's no turning back," he says quietly.

In the square, the old sorcerer addresses the wounded: "You are lost, the fathers do not accept you." His hands make sweeping gestures, his fingers pointing toward the sky. "This was not a battle between men. There are devils at play. The whites have weapons that blacks would never create." He ponders whether the whites are even human. Perhaps Onyame is not the god of the whites. *Their God seems to be a terrible one.*

He listens. The spirits are angry because the whites disrupt the balance. Perhaps they must be resisted with the same weapons and the same destruction, and then everything will change. He calls upon God: "*Odomankoma Nana Nyankopon.* Let the warriors die. Their role is finished. Fathers, take them in, they have been brave and suffered enough. *Nyame mu Enyame.*"

As he looks around, the trees seem to move, and in the darkness between the leaves, he sees shadows. The old man shudders. When the Ahante warriors return, with Quassie Patoe in their wake, the men on the stretchers are dead.

44 The Suffering of Mussulman Ali

"When the merchant saw that the spirit was about to behead him, he gave a great cry and said: 'Stop! Just one more word, please; be kind enough to grant me a reprieve; give me time to bid farewell to my wife and children and to divide my goods among them by writing a will that I have not yet made, so that they may not be left in dispute after my death. Once that is done, I shall immediately return to this place to submit myself to whatever you please to demand of me.'
'But,' said the spirit, 'if I grant you the delay you ask for, I fear you will not return.'
'If you will take me at my word,' the merchant replied, 'I swear by the God of heaven and earth that I will return to you without fail.'"

From: One Thousand and One Nights, the story of "The Merchant and the Spirit"

The sun burns on his head as Mussulman Ali regains consciousness. He feels a slow, pounding headache that makes him nauseous. His vision is blurry, with black spots drifting from left to right. His hands and feet are bound. His joints ache. But the worst is the thirst, his mouth is parched. Mussulman Ali groans. He feels sand beneath him. Stones. Twigs digging into his back. Above him, the rustling of coconut palms.

Wind. Coast. The sea, he absently concludes.

His right arm is numb, and he tries to shift his position as he feels a hand on his shoulder. The fingers tap encouragingly on his skin. A familiar voice sends a shiver down his spine: "They said, 'He'll be dead; he's already an old man.' But I refused to believe it. Mussulman Ali is as tough as an old goat and as stubborn as a donkey."

The hand grabs him by the neck. Mussulman Ali is roughly pulled upright and set against the trunk of a palm tree. The spots dance before his eyes. For a few seconds, he thinks he'll lose consciousness again. His stomach churns, but there's nothing to vomit, only a green trickle of bile escapes the corner of his mouth.

"Perhaps," the voice says, "now there's time to talk."

Mussulman Ali rests his chin on his chest and shakes his head. He can't speak at all. He makes stammering, incoherent noises.

A bag is pushed against his mouth. A moment later, he feels warm water in his throat. He gags, and his own bile tastes bitter.

"Take it easy, old man," the voice says.

The water slides down his throat. He looks up and sees the stretched face of the Wassa chief, the man with the black breath. His large yellow teeth grin at him. "Small sips, never too much."

Mussulman Ali swallows, against his will. He has no defence. After a few seconds, he vomits everything back up. The pain is intense.

"Black bile. Yellow bile. Get it all out." The Wassa chief doesn't give up. Only when a significant amount of water stays down is he satisfied. Mussulman Ali feels the moisture seeping into his body. His headache pounds. He can barely breathe. With crossed eyes, he looks up. "*Ggh*," he manages to say.

The other nods understandingly. He sits next to Mussulman Ali like a brother beside a brother. Mussulman Ali can now see the sea. Blue and green. And the sky. Clear, with grey clouds in the east. The wind brushes over his taut, dry face. It's pleasant, like the caressing fingers of his eldest wife. Memories flow through him. The house in Salaga is whitewashed in Arabic style, with a staircase and a rooftop terrace, with plants, herbs and a pergola. All the rooms open onto the courtyard and there's even a shaded colonnade. In the garden, there's an old, fully grown fig tree next to his own well. He recalls the evenings, when the sun sets in that uniquely African way, sitting together with his sons and the Arab traders from the city, and in the background the *muezzin* calling for prayer.

Those are good memories, he thinks.

His exhausted body is now completely limp. Even if he wanted to, he couldn't escape.

The Wassa chief says casually, "I slaughtered and ate your horse."

Mussulman Ali gazes absently at the ocean, and his eyes produce tears. That surprises him. Such a dumb beast, he thinks. Why? In the distance, on the horizon, he sees the faint outline of a ship's masts. Dutch? English? The tears are salty on his lips. It was a tough little creature, that horse. Didn't deserve to be eaten. Not at all. I hope this dog's intestines rot and he dies a slow, miserable death. Yes. He'll burn in hell.

"And after that, I killed your men, one by one."

Mussulman Ali closes his eyes. He's very tired now. But there's no respite.

"I've thought long and hard. What to do now? The *chika* is gone. Your three fugitives have too much of a head start. And I have no power with the Ashanti." The Wassa chief chuckles. "They'd slice me to pieces and feed me to Pataku. Or to Awendade, the lion." He puts an arm around Mussulman Ali's shoulder. To a casual passerby, they would truly seem like friends. "That's what you'd want, huh? But we're not fools. We don't chase after ghosts." Now he laughs like Pataku himself, a cackling, giggling, insane laugh. "So, after I had my fun with your men, I slept off my haze. My ancestors are strong and alive. In my dream, they said: take him to King Boa Amponsem of the Denkyira. He will reward you. Brother Wassa, the king will say, I sent you on a mission and you've returned, not just with the answer, but with the very object of my wrath. Thank you. A thousand thanks. Here, take a golden robe and thirty virgins and a hundred lion hides, and from now on you may move freely in all Denkyira lands, trade at will, and claim any women you desire. *Eééh?*"

He's laughing so hard now that his long, spindly body bends forward, and tears stream down his cheeks. His flat hand slaps Mussulman Ali's shoulder with full force. "Yes, that's what we'll do."

Mussulman Ali doesn't hear it. He feels the wind on his face again. His cracked, swollen lips part. He still sees that tough, unsightly little horse in his mind: its gray skin, crusted with mud. He thinks: it's a filthy creature, always has been. How many times did I say: horse, don't wallow in the mud. You're not a pig, are you? Or a dog? And the dumb beast would snort as if it understood the joke.

A soft, moist, velvet-like nose seems to touch his skin for a moment.

Now time has disappeared. Perhaps there is still a rhythm of light and darkness, but it is only faintly perceptible, something that happens far outside of him, barely registered by a distant part of his consciousness. Everything is mist, you could say—a limbo without beginning or end, without shapes, without dimensions, and he is alone with his thoughts. And, of course, with Pain, his faithful companion.

Fortunately, he still has his memories. And God, *Allahu Akbar*. His mind prays: I seek protection in Allah and in His power, against the evil I face.

Yet he feels alone. God does not show Himself or make Himself heard. Perhaps Pain is God. That could well be, he's thought about it. It's not such an unlikely idea. But if Pain is connected to torment or penance, then he hopes that God will explain *why* he is being punished.

The surah says: And they who believe in the revelation to you, O Mohammed, and in that which was revealed before you, in their hearts, they have the certainty of the Hereafter.

He believes, so where is that certainty now? Of course, he expected to be judged—that's what he's always been taught—but he thinks he has been a good Muslim, a worthy brother, so this state of being is surprising. It's not what he hoped for. The suffering is too severe, and the relentlessness of Pain drains him. Is this the bridge over the fire to paradise? Were his sins so great that the bridge is as narrow as a hair and as sharp as a sword? He tries to look below him, but there is no below. There is only mist.

He is starting to feel a little afraid now. *Jahannam*, the hellfire, is eternal. He has used violence. He has killed: whites, blacks, slaves.

But never Muslims. Never!

Yet—should he feel regret?

Was it wrong? Had he been too greedy? Did he want too much?

God has His own reasons. God has seen everything.

From far away, a voice suddenly calls out. "Where are you, Mussulman Ali?"

Is that God? No, he recognizes that voice. That... is the devil. He vaguely remembers being taken on a long journey, powerless and half-conscious, along dark paths and through pouring rain. At that time, he might have still hoped for an opportunity to talk, to save his skin. But that was, of course, futile. All humanity was meaningless. The devil is only focused on delivering evil, other motives do not matter, never have. The Wassa chieftain was put on his path and that was that.

And then?

Yes, then the journey ended. Then there were nights, so black, that he has erased the memory. He only remembers that Pain entered his life. Pain crouched beside him and touched him, and from that moment there was no turning back. That's when he fled: in his own twilight world, where he could hide from the dark devil, who did things to his body that he can't even imagine anymore, things he doesn't want to know. Whatever happens out there, here it is safe.

There's that voice again: "Are you still alive, Mussulman Ali?" Laughter follows. A long, malicious laugh.

He shudders. Keeps quiet. His mind shrinks like a slave before a punishing master.

Footsteps. Heavy, echoing, approaching footsteps.

A giant enters his world.

Pain has grown again. Now, it's so tall that in the real world—the world outside—it would tower above the treetops.

The formless, massive figure walks straight through him, through his soul, through the ends of his nerves. It drives out all thoughts. They are one now, Pain and him. Together, like blood brothers, they flow through the mist, like smoke, finding every opening in his dying body, every weakness, and tearing it apart, raw flesh and bone and entrails and blood. It lasts long. It lasts an eternity. He screams, but no sound comes. He cries, but no one hears him.

45 Fetching Water in Chama

"Article VIII: The skipper is obliged to air out his ship once or twice a week below deck with some wet gunpowder, to provide the slaves once a week with a little brandy on one day, half a biscuit on another, and on yet another day, a little tobacco, in order to keep them in good spirits. He shall also, at times, have them dance in the flatfoot, and give each of them suffering from scurvy a capful of lime juice in the morning. (...)

Article XXXI: For the sick slaves, the skipper shall make every effort and provide all necessary means required for their treatment, as well as show the sick all possible care and compassion, and immediately separate them from the healthy slaves to prevent further infections and discomfort. (...)

Article XXXVII: The skipper shall, under penalty of severe fines, forbid the sailors and crew from molesting the negresses. (...)"

From: **Standard Instructions for Skippers to Elmina and Angola, by the Directors of the Dutch West India Company**

Logbook of the *Griffin*, Friday, December 19th:

"*Topgallant sail wind, turning north-northeast. By midday, sighted Accada, Fort Dorothea, 4°45'N, 19°6'W. No slaves for sale, only a small stock of mediocre-quality ivory, which I declined. Laundry day for the crew. No sick men. Spirits reasonably high, but the heat is affecting us.*"

Fresh drinking water is scarce; in most places, it is milky and quickly spoils, but in Chama, water of good quality can be drawn. The nearby Fort San Sebastian is a large white structure on a green hill, surrounded by houses and huts, with the beach directly at its foot. The distinctive, wide-spanning staircase leading to the main entrance is recognizable from afar.

The *Griffin* cautiously navigates through the shallows and sandbanks. Crew members on the fore shrouds measure the depth with lead and lines. The first mate stands in the binnacle house, giving instructions to the boatswain, who directs the team at the mizzen sail.

"Eleven fathoms," call out the crew.

"Shorten the sails," orders the mate.

Burghoutsz peers through his spyglass. To the left of the fort, a few barges and a Dutch hooker float. The other side is protected by cliffs. They have already been seen: the flag at the fort is lowered and raised once in greeting. But he takes no chances. The slaves are below deck, the hatches secured and covered with canvas. He has given the crew extra weapons, opened the gunports and manned the guns.

"Drop anchor," he orders. "And let out forty fathoms of chain." He gazes at the sky and senses the wind, which has been blowing dry and hot from the north for a week now; the time of the *Harmattan*, the desert wind, is near. Inland, a blanket of dust hangs over the hills.

"No one comes aboard," he commands. "Lower the longboat."

San Sebastian is manned by a merchant, a squad of soldiers and a few carpenters. In Chama, there's a large sawmill where the wood for the Dutch trading posts gets churned out. The racket from the huge saws, worked by slaves, echoes over the water.

When Burghoutsz reaches the shore, he is met by the Company's merchant, a large, sweaty fellow with sand-coloured hair and a wild beard. "Good to see a Christian face, skipper. By God, those black mugs wear on you after a while. You here for water?"

"I need sixty barrels."

"Slaves on board? I smelled you the moment you dropped anchor. No mistaking that stench." The merchant nods. He scratches his belly. "We got plenty water."

They walk up the path toward the fort. Huts belonging to the natives stand on either side. Under a long, thatched shelter on poles, a small group of Africans is carving a canoe. With chisels, they patiently gouge out the excess wood from a single tree trunk.

The merchant and the skipper reach the steps leading to the fort. Mosquitoes buzz around their heads.

"Damn rotten bugs," grumbles the merchant, his face covered in red welts. "Mosquitoes. Centipedes. Tarantulas. Everything bites and stings. Pus. Abscesses. Sores. No salve'll fix it. Lost two soldiers just last month. Polish lads." He starts up the steep, winding steps. "Didn't speak a lick of Dutch. Catholic as the Pope, the pair of 'em. Now they're in the ground, dead before they were twenty years old." He pauses, staring blankly at the endless green wall of jungle stretching out behind the fort. "I can't even remember their names."

The main entrance is triangular, leading into a gatehouse. Two sentries sit on benches, looking far from battle-ready without their cuirasses, belts or bandoliers. You'd have to be out of your mind to stand guard in full kit in this heat. They're lazily leaning on their muskets, barrels pointed skyward. A jug of beer sits in the shade of the stairwell.

"The wizard's here," one of them announces, barely glancing up.

The merchant's face darkens. He wipes the sweat off his brow, his jacket stained white with salt. "Damned sorcerers," he mutters to the skipper. "Untrustworthy bunch."

It's a big fort, built by the Portuguese long ago, and far too spacious for the few Dutchmen stationed here. There's a first ring of walls, and through a second entrance, they reach the courtyard, surrounded by whitewashed two story buildings. Here, there's some shade. The white stones are cool, and the merchant lets out a relieved sigh. He gestures toward a group of black women—Company slaves—squatting beside a huge pile of worn Dutch bedsheets, sorting the fabric by size and colour.

"Delivered by that hooker out there," he says, nodding toward the ship. "Sixteen thousand sheets. They love 'em in the hinterland. I trade 'em for anything—dye wood, redwood, ironwood, pepper, gum, you name it." He picks up a piece of cloth and holds it up. "From Jan and Marie in Overschie," he jokes, giving the skipper a greasy wink. "Probably conceived all eleven of their kids on this." He makes a face, tosses the sheet back onto the pile, and moves on. "Look, there's our witch doctor."

In the middle of the courtyard stand three natives: an old gray-haired man, a younger one bound with a rope, and a third holding the rope.

The merchant raises his hand jovially and strides toward the old man. "*Ackie, akomfo*, you dirty old scoundrel."

The old man nods silently, his shifty eyes darting from the merchant to the skipper. "You from the slave ship?" he asks, toothless.

Burghoutsz doesn't answer. He looks at the bound negro, whose legs are covered in scratches and bumps. The paths leading to the fort run over treacherous cliffs and rocks, he knows. The locals say: you must put your eyes in your hands to keep from losing your feet. He asks, "Is this man for sale?"

"He's a pawn," the *akomfo* confirms. "For the right price, you can have him."

"Why is he a pawn?" asks the merchant.

The shifty eyes flick back. "He owes us money, that's why. He can't pay."

The merchant nods. It's a common situation. He turns to the prisoner. "What do you owe them?"

"Cowrie shells, goats, tobacco."

"Why?"

"I borrowed."

"You can't pay it back?"

"I can pay it back."

The old man shakes his head in frustration. "You shouldn't talk to him. I'm here to ensure he's been treated fairly. He was warned three times, as is the custom. He borrowed and can't repay." He points to the third man. "This is his neighbour and creditor. The village has decided he can sell him as a slave."

"Hm." The merchant nods, but he doesn't believe a word of it. He turns to Burghoutsz and whispers, "They probably set him up. Happens all the time. But pickings are slim, not many slaves are offered, especially in Chama." He runs his hand through his greasy beard and addresses the creditor: "You understand, if you're selling him unjustly and it comes out, you'll have to compensate him. You'll owe seven times the price. Got that?"

"Yes."

"If you owe him seven times the price and you don't have it, then you'll be the one going on the boat. Do you understand that?"

"Yes."

"I'm required to tell you." He sighs, picks at his nose a bit, then says to the skipper, "I'll be damned if I miss out on commission just because I don't trust it. If these charcoal monkeys want to screw each other over, that's their business." He sizes up the prisoner, who is of average height, well-built, and healthy. No scars. No sores. "Had smallpox?"

"No."

"Syphilis?"

The creditor shakes his head in irritation. "I've known him my whole life."

"How old is he?"

"In white years: twenty."

The merchant laughs mockingly. "You're a fool, I bet you don't even know your own age. If he's twenty, then I'm the Emir of Turkey. But I'll admit you lot are a crafty bunch of swindlers. Doesn't he have a wife and kids?"

"One wife, but she's staying in the village. I took her from him."

"Why? Don't you have your own wives?"

"Yes, but she's a good wife. I wanted her for myself."

"For yourself? Aren't you a horny devil? Don't you want to make money? No *chika*?" He raises his head and turns to the skipper, speaking in Dutch. "Are you interested? Maybe you'd like to make some money for yourself. We'll split the profit."

Burghoutsz nods. He's allowed to deliver a few slaves as private property. "Fine by me."

The merchant says to the sorcerer, "For a prime woman, I'll pay eight thousand cowrie shells."

The creditor furrows his brow. "Eight thousand?" he asks hesitantly.

The merchant grins, thinking, Gotcha, sucker. He walks into the deep shadow under the outer wall. His men have stretched a canvas there against the rain, and underneath is a barrel that's replenished daily with fresh water from the river the locals call Bossum-Pra. He scoops some out with a wooden ladle, picks out the inevitable insects with two fingers, and drinks greedily. "Listen," he says, water dripping from his chin, "nine for the man, eight for the woman. That's a good deal, you can't deny it. You'd be a very rich Ahante."

The sorcerer resists. "Not long ago, we got eleven thousand for a healthy male."

"Yeah, but that was for an eighteen-year-old boy."

"Ten thousand then."

"Only if you throw in the woman too." He looks at the creditor. "Have you slept with her yet?"

"*Eééh?*"

"Screwed!"

"Ah." The man looks surprised, then nods.

"And was it so good that you're willing to give up eight thousand cowries for her?"

Understanding dawns slowly. "No, no, of course not."

"Well then, go fetch her, you damned *bebiny*."

In the late afternoon, with the orange sun just above the horizon, Burghoutsz and the merchant sit on a wooden platform by the outer wall, gazing out over the bay. Far below, the water boat, loaded with barrels, is being rowed toward the *Griffin* by twenty black oarsmen.

"Judging by all that water, you've got more slaves than I thought," the merchant says slyly. He grabs the carafe of corn brandy from the rickety table between them and fills two glasses. "I was under the impression the prison house in Elmina was only half-full."

"We had a stroke of luck."

"Hmm. I heard an Arab trader was kidnapped for stealing blacks from the Denkyira." He downs his glass and gestures toward the *Griffin*. "And I bet my month's wages they are sitting in your hold."

Burghoutsz looks at him, surprised. "Kidnapped by whom?"

"By those Wassa rats. Dragged off to Abankeseso, deep inland. Word is the king's holding court there for the time being." The merchant leans back in his chair, which groans dangerously under the strain. His forearms show old white scars from yaws. "There'll be trouble, I guarantee you."

Burghoutsz stares thoughtfully at the water boat, which has now reached the *Griffin*. "Well, if everything comes to light, we'll be long gone," he says. "Sweerts will talk his way out of it."

"Maybe, but the balance is tipped. Ashanti. Fante. Ahante. Who knows which one's going to come out on top? One way or another, the Denkyira will have to fight."

In the distance, the first water barrel is being hoisted aboard. "Hóóó!" shout the sailors. The sound echoes over the water.

"There's always someone to fill the vacuum," says Burghoutsz, swatting at the mosquitoes with one hand. "And the king will keep doing business with us."

"Maybe so, but I dare say he's found new customers."

"Zeelanders?"

"Portuguese, for God's sake. And let me tell you something else: French ships have been spotted. Word is Du Casse is on his way to the Gold Coast." The merchant leans closer to Burghoutsz and raises a warning finger. "You'd best be on your guard, skipper. Du Casse is out for Dutchmen, and if he finds 'em, he'll eat 'em alive."

46 Back: Aldemar Burghoutsz (5)

"At war!"

⚓

June 1665

The trade on the Baltic Sea has nearly come to a halt. Dutch merchant ships hardly dare to set sail anymore. In the cities, hunger is widespread. Civilian ships are requisitioned by order of the Admiralty and used in military operations. To make matters worse, Amsterdam is suffering under the yoke of the plague for yet another year. The damage is immense. Efforts are made to isolate the sick—the victims are transported to the hospital outside the city walls as quickly as possible—but the plague continues to spread. People are afraid.

Shipowner Gijsen must surrender two of his East Countrymen, including the brand-new *Purmer II*, under the command of skipper Rijkjan. Aldemar serves as second mate; their own little crew remains largely intact—minus Red Rick—but the number of sailors is increased to over a hundred, supplemented by three squads of soldiers. An overcrowded ship.

Skipper Rijkjan surveys the apparent chaos on his decks: they are strewn with weapons and cannonballs of all kinds and sizes. The soldiers are in the way and the extra sailors are landlubbers, recruited from taverns and brothels. Scum. The dregs of society.

"Crack the whip," growls the skipper. "By God, order will reign on this ship."

In the Oude Kerk, they eat white bread. It is late May, Aldemar's last day in Amsterdam.

"Where to?" Anna asks, worried.

Aldemar shrugs. He is silent and surly. The fleet will soon set sail. "No one knows." But he can guess: the English are lying in wait with more than a hundred warships off Lowestoft, just across the water.

Anna looks at him, but he avoids her gaze. All of Holland holds its breath. Fathers and sons are going to war. You can feel the fear in the air.

"Be careful, Aldemar."

Empty words.

The Dutch fleet consists of seven squadrons. The Purmer II is assigned to the fourth, under the command of the young Lieutenant-Admiral Stellingwerf on the frigate Zevenwolden. In formation, the two fleets approach each other, more than two hundred warships in an eight-mile-long line. The sea is packed.

"God help us," whispers skipper Rijkjan, as the full scale of the two fleets sinks in. He looks at his flags: the wind is northwest and the Dutch have the lee, sailing northward toward the English ships.

Cannons roar. Aldemar watches as the gun barrels spit thick, greasy smoke over the water. The signal flags on the *Zevenwolden* cheerfully send their orders. Thirty-six-pounders spray their cannonballs and the air is filled with the screech of steel.

"Hold steady!" shouts the skipper. "Stay in formation!"

Aldemar throws his full weight onto the whipstaff, and below deck, the gun crews labour. The gun deck is stripped of all partitions and fitted with eight gun ports on each side. The cruiser ahead of them begins to fire. To starboard, the English three-deckers sail in the opposite direction. The blasts are deafening.

"Fire!"

The *Purmer II* shakes in all its joints as the starboard battery guns fire one by one. The recoil tips her dangerously to port, and the sea below churns and foams. Gunpowder smoke hangs like mist above the water. The response is swift: from behind the clouds of smoke, the English guns thunder back. The sound of hitting shrapnel: sharp knocks on the wood of the masts and hull. Splinters fly, dislodged blocks bounce across the deck. A strip of sail from the foremast tears vertically, and Aldemar feels the resistance in the whipstaff; the ship bucks and trembles as if it wants to bolt. He sees Gillis Graauw and several deckhands rushing along the shrouds with new sailcloth.

"Hurry up!" the boatswain yells, kicking and beating the inexperienced sailors on deck, who are tugging far too weakly on the sheets.

The *Zevenwolden* takes a full broadside: three, four English cruisers focus all their fire on the flagship. A chain shot sweeps her quarterdeck clean. From the *Purmer II*, they watch in horror as the officers are swept off the deck in an instant—vanishing as if into thin air. Lieutenant-Admiral Stellingwerf is like a puppet suddenly split in two. Chaos everywhere. Through the smoke, no one can read the signal flags anymore.

The rising screams paralyze the crew. Thinking becomes impossible. Aldemar cowers in the binnacle house. There's nothing worse than a howling thirty-six pounder invisibly hurtling toward you and crashing in with an enormous impact. The spars seem to explode. The scorching ball unleashes its energy in a chaotic, mowing motion across the gun deck, spreading death and destruction, sweeping away everything in its path, and then bursts out the other side. In a split second, the men below decks are smashed to pulp, crushed by wood and steel, and the survivors scream helplessly. Aldemar Burghoutsz grips his whipstaff, shattered.

The English fleet is better trained; they sail in perfect keel formation along the Dutch line. The wind shifts to the southwest and part of the Dutch fleet tacks while the others do not, breaking the line and allowing the English to break through. Ship fights against ship. The flagship Eendragt takes a direct hit to the powder magazine and blows up, taking Commander-in-Chief Van Wassenaer with it. The fleet fights desperately, but there's no saving it; by evening, the retreat is sounded. They limp back to Texel, leaving behind eight sunken and nine captured ships, more than a thousand dead and two thousand prisoners of war.

Holland mourns.

"Pregnant?" he asks. He looks at her belly, which is just her belly, with nothing remarkable about it. He can hardly believe that inside—somewhere, very small—his child could be growing. He shakes his head, a little embarrassed by his own ignorance. "Are you sure?"

Anna smiles. Now they have to marry. Quickly. Before the minister becomes suspicious. Or her father.

He nods, trying to smile back. But it's difficult; since the sea battle, the images of dead, torn-apart sailors have haunted him. Sometimes he wakes up in the middle of the night, drenched in sweat and thrashing his arms.

47 Quassie Patoe and the Portuguese

"(...) Those who cross the ocean are tamed by being made to eat salt: salted fish and pickled meat, because salt numbs, makes one submissive and heavy. Yes, by consuming a lot of salt, the African's natural ability to fly is suppressed. The whites know this. They say: to keep them calm, you must give them salt. Salted negroes don't flee, but become sick and get scurvy, they become paralyzed, their gums bleed, and their skin turns grey. They become as unclean as the whites; they are leeches and vampires. It's no coincidence that Africans refer to the disappearance of a family member by saying: 'He went to get salt,' because it essentially means that he has been taken away into slavery."

From: Traditions of an akomfo, sorcerer of the Akim

Heavy rains batter the jungle. The canopy bends and sways under the force of the water. Deep and unrelenting, the thunder rumbles, punctuated by sharp flashes of lightning and sudden, violent crashes.

Quassie Patoe follows the hidden path to Simpo, a small village not far from Commanie. Under the canopy, it feels as though he's beneath a leaking vault; water pours down in heavy streams through gaps and cracks, splashing onto the path. In the dark green twilight, he trudges westward through the forest, sometimes ankle-deep in mud, until a palisade blocks his way.

He halts and waits.

A few villagers emerge from behind the wooden wall. They size him up, studying his face, illuminated by a flickering storm lamp.

Quassie Patoe isn't afraid. Everyone knows him.

Behind the wall, the jungle abruptly ends: an open savanna, where the rain pours down unimpeded. Hunched over, he runs after the villagers through gently rising terrain. Mature bombax trees stand on small mounds around them, indifferent to the rain, like gnarled, twisted, ancient sentinels. Here and there, termite mounds tower in wet terracotta hues, some as tall as a grown man. Lightning streaks across the sky with horizontal branches. In the open space, the men are vulnerable, so they quicken their pace, racing through the wet, knee-high grass.

A mile. Then the land dips again. The jungle wall on the other side of the meadow is thick and dark, but the path winds inward, and they are swallowed up once more. Relieved, they enter the warm twilight world. As the rain eases a bit, the soaked ground steams, wisps of mist hanging between the trees.

A quarter mile further, a few miserable huts loom into view. Simpo.

They are met by a large group of heavily armed Ahante. Among them, Quassie Patoe catches the gleam of metal cuirasses. Iron helmets. Spears and swords. Stern, bearded faces look in his direction. His heart skips a beat.

Portuguese.

Night falls quickly. The green twilight gives way to darkness, and the rain continues to pour down relentlessly on the thatched roofs of the huts. There is no fire, except for some smouldering charcoal on the clay floor. The men huddle together in the stifling space of the communal house, the Portuguese on one side, the Ahante with Quassie Patoe on the other. Between them stand eight large, stacked, elongated wooden crates.

The Portuguese lieutenant looks at them disdainfully. He has a thin face with a straight, narrow nose. Long black hair clings wetly to his head. "Where's the Zeelander?" he asks.

Quassie Patoe shrugs. "Dead."

The lieutenant furrows his brow. "You work for the Dutch Company," he says softly. "How can I trust you? You're deceiving your own people."

Quassie Patoe takes a deep breath, hiding his irritation. "The Dutch are not my people. I am Enyampa."

"A wise dog doesn't bite the hand that feeds him."

"I am my own master. The Portuguese gave their word not to trade in Dutch territory. The lieutenant breaks that promise. He deceives the Dutch. What does Quassie Patoe do? He looks after himself."

This causes a stir. The Portuguese soldiers murmur in discontent. But the lieutenant silences them with a simple gesture. He smiles. "Extraordinary circumstances sometimes require an alternative approach," he concedes coolly. "But its nature is temporary."

"Of course."

"God has His own plans," the lieutenant continues. "Do you know the Bible? It is written: 'You have delivered us to lawless enemies, to detestable apostates.'" He crouches down, the leather of his boots creaking. His cuirass shows traces of rust. With a halberd, he pries open the lid of one of the crates.

Quassie Patoe peers inside. Between folds of cotton, he sees brand-new snaphaunces.

"Twenty per crate," the lieutenant states. "As a down payment."

Quassie Patoe grunts approvingly. He leans forward, his fingertips gliding admiringly over the smooth, greased barrels. "And the rest?" he asks.

"Upon delivery of the slaves."

"The lieutenant has travelled a long way, overland."

"Frederiksburg is unreachable. The Dutch have been alerted and are looking for us. We don't dare bring our ships to the coast, but with a small yacht, we sailed, guided by the Ahante, to a place called Pompondee three nights ago —a hellish spot with foul pools and poisonous fumes that the Dutch avoid like the plague. After that, we trekked inland with the help of porters." He sighs wearily. The dark circles under his eyes are deep. "It was a hard journey."

The other crates are opened. In addition to rifles, they contain paper bags of gunpowder, bullet pouches, bandoliers, powder grinders, greasy cloths and tin flasks of oil. The items are passed from hand to hand. Everything is inspected carefully and the Ahante warriors murmur with satisfaction; the Portuguese snaphaunces are of excellent quality.

"We can't use the white soldiers anymore," Quassie Patoe warns. "The Dutch director-general is a cunning old wolf. He's sensed trouble. It's too dangerous."

"You don't need the whites anymore," the lieutenant says confidently. "With these guns, you'll protect your own shipments. Even the Wassa can't withstand this." He steps forward, placing a hand on Quassie Patoe's shoulder. "You need to go to the king as soon as possible," he urges, in a tone suggesting friendship. "We'll buy every slave the Denkyira can provide."

Quassie Patoe grimaces. He doesn't like being touched by whites; they do with their right hand what they should with their left. He asks, "Are there no more slaves in Luanda?"

"Luanda is doomed. We can't wait."

"The king will demand many weapons."

"We'll supply all the weapons he wants."

Quassie Patoe nods, his gaze fixed on the gleaming new rifles. "My services aren't cheap," he boasts. "I'm an important man. I know everyone. Everyone knows me." He exaggerates a little more: "If I wish it, the Dutch will look the other way."

A chest reinforced with iron plates is slid across the floor toward him. When the lid is lifted, he sees glittering yellow metal, filled to the brim. His heart begins to race.

"Gold has been found in Brazil," the lieutenant says softly. "There is enough for everyone. Even for the future *tufohen* of São Jorge da Mina."

48 Duisterbloem's Decision

"What fodder, a stick, and burdens are to a donkey,
that is what bread, discipline, and work are to a slave.
Put him to work under strict rule, and you will have peace,
but if you give him nothing to do, he will seek freedom.
A yoke and a halter bend the neck,
for a wicked slave, there are corporal punishments and tortures.
Make him work hard, or he will become lazy,
and from laziness, he will learn all sorts of evil."

From: The Bible, Deuterocanonical Books, Wisdom of Jesus Sirach, 33:24-27

After his daily visit to the sick in Fort Coenraadsburg, Reverend Duisterbloem enjoys taking a walk. From the simple wooden bridge over the Benja River, a path runs along Krabbenberg and the Dutch cemetery toward a few small fields where the Dutch grow fruit and vegetables. The path is unpaved, but it's old and lined with trees with wide canopies. In the shade beneath, it's relatively cool, and the reverend pauses for a moment, wiping the sweat from his face with a handkerchief. Mosquitoes and other insects buzz around him. Bright yellow weaver birds with black heads chatter in the branches. Reverend Duisterbloem watches their restless activity; the little birds never seem to find peace, and their nests hang like small, intricately woven baskets between the leaves.

He shakes his head. Less than an hour ago, he had been present as a slave boy took his last breath. The boy had been sick for a long time, the chirurgeon had said. He had tried everything, even mercury, but to no avail. The slave only grew sicker, his skin looking like burnt paper. And then: the quiet death, an almost imperceptible passing, without final words. It was the dreadful death of a heathen, for this slave had not been converted, let alone baptized, and was therefore doomed to hell, everlasting and eternal.

The weaver birds chatter as the reverend walks on, hands behind his back. He wonders: if God uses slavery to bring the blacks into contact with the gospel, why did He allow this life to be lost? What is the meaning of it? Why didn't He first call the boy to Him, so there might have been a chance for eternal life in the presence of Jesus Christ? Didn't the slave have a right to redemption?

He slumps his shoulders, his gaze lowered to the ground. His bloodshot eyes glance around furtively. To his left, a few old black men sit on felled tree trunks, playing a native board game called *oware*. The clicking of the game pieces ceases as they recognize him; the news that he had assaulted his female house slave in a fit of rage, possessed by evil spirits, has spread far into the interior. They stare at him with suspicion. Their gazes pierce his back.

Are they mocking him? And when he feels shame before them, and before that black slave woman, does he then see them as equals? That's a horrifying thought, he believes, just as horrifying as his desire for black women. They are a criminal race, he thinks fiercely. Forsaken by God, doomed, despised, and excluded from the ranks of nations!

He reaches the gardens. With a critical eye, he peers at a small field to his right, where the abromenades have grown tall. The plants look spindly, the leaves at the top are thin, limp and brown in colour. On the other side of the field, a few hundred feet away, a group of Company slaves is clearing a new plot of land. With hoes and spades, they remove weeds and bushes. Two overseers sit on chairs in the shade of a solitary tree, drinking beer.

Reverend Duisterbloem comes to a stop. He too is thirsty. From a pocket in his overcoat, he pulls out a flask of gin. The intoxication keeps him calm, though he drinks more than is probably good for him. He takes his first sip upon waking and continues throughout the day.

He sighs and thinks back to his time at the theological faculty. Innovators tried to sow confusion by claiming that the New Testament rejects slavery. It made him furious. He would shout at them: "Read the letter to Philemon: when the slave Onesimus had run away from him, the Apostle Paul sent him back to his master!"

He sees one of the overseers suddenly stand up and begin yelling at a slave. The sound is distant, and the reverend can't make out the words. The overseer points to the ground and slaps the slave on the head. The slave doesn't react. He continues hacking furiously. The overseer shakes his head and places his hands on his hips. He points to a spot further away. The slave walks over and begins hacking there.

The scene irritates him. The slave does as he is told, he thinks, without any sense of the purpose behind his actions. He doesn't want to be punished, he just wants to stay alive. There is no goal, no soul. "Slaves must be converted," he mutters to himself. "Without conversion, they remain heathens, little better than animals."

He scratches under his inflamed armpits. The itch is almost unbearable. He thinks: we have a duty to convert them to the true faith so they can find salvation. Corinthians says: Where the Spirit of the Lord is, there is freedom. But the slave is not converted because it doesn't suit the merchants. It's too much trouble, it gets in the way of profit. And thus, he concludes, the life of that sick slave boy was lost. It is *our* fault, a sin before God. For every soul counts.

In the evening, the spirits come, but he wards them off with gin. He sits alone at the table in his austere dwelling, with a flickering oil lamp in front of him and nothing but darkness beyond. Silently, he drinks, scraping away at the sharp edges of his consciousness.

It's this godforsaken continent, he thinks. In New York, despite everything, he could feel at home. There, the seasons change, just like in Holland, and there is a community of true Protestants, Dutch and English side by side. People marry, families are formed, white children are born and they have roots in the soil.

The drink slides down his throat. Hot. Burning. Sweat beads on his forehead. "Isolation," he mutters. "Lawlessness." Here, in Africa, there is nothing. There are no white women or children. There is no community. Whites live on islands in a sea of black savages. No wonder a man is tempted.

"A man has needs," he mumbles to the darkness. The spirits shuffle around the table, just beyond the reach of the flickering light. He sees their movements, swipes his hand through the warm air. "Go away!"

A voice, maybe in his head: "Unnatural, sinful relations with black women, vile acts that produce bastards!"

"Yes," he whispers. "Like that bomba, that Bomba Jan." He nods. Swallows. "More drink. More brandy." He stares ahead. His gaunt, hollow-eyed face is grim. His role here, he concludes, is finished. There are only lies here. Africa has defeated him.

"I want to leave," he says the next morning to a surprised director-general.

Sweerts furrows his brow. He leans back in his chair. "Leave?"

"Back to Holland."

"What? You've only just arrived!"

The reverend sets his face stubbornly. "It's enough. God has spoken to me."

Sweerts eyes him sceptically. "I've heard," he says, "that you chased your maid out of the house."

"That has nothing to do with it."

"I must tell you, Reverend, that while they may be slaves, if the Company provides them, it expects that you handle them with care."

"It's not what you think."

"If you have special—uh—desires, there are plenty of options. In the villages, you'll find native women more than willing to fulfil any wish."

Reverend Duisterbloem flushes. "You're mocking me, sir. The maid had a delusion. There's nothing I want from her."

"She seems to think otherwise."

"It's a misunderstanding."

Sweerts examines the red-rimmed eyes and the gaunt face. Only now does he notice the reverend's springy hair seems thinner. His shoulders sag, with long, drooping arms, as if he's carrying something unbearably heavy, something beyond his control. He's heard that people avoid him and that the man behaves like an outcast, an apostate. "Are you ill?"

"Ill is not the right word. My soul is disturbed." The reverend searches for words. "God is testing me. What was straight has become crooked."

"You're rambling, sir. Explain yourself."

The reverend glares at him, his eye sockets dark like the hollows of a skull. In that darkness, feverish eyes gleam. "I owe you no explanation. I am not in the Company's service."

Sweerts sighs. "You're not well-liked. Now I see why."

A mocking laugh follows. "I'm here to spread God's word, not to lick boots."

"Nevertheless, you show great dedication when it comes to caring for our sick."

That seems to unsettle him. His angry expression fades for a moment. He says, "For the Lord your God is a God of love. He will not forsake you or cast you into ruin." He looks at the director-general with a strange, almost pleading expression. "I am merely His instrument. I do what I can."

"Yes, so it seems. But what will happen to them when you leave?"

"We have comforters of the sick. No one is indispensable. The classis will send another minister."

"Hm. They will accuse you of breaking your contract. In Amsterdam, you will have to atone." Sweerts stands up. He walks around the reverend, catching the scent of his body. Sour. Sweat. And something else beneath it. Something darker. Coppery. Blood? He's heard of fanatics who flagellate themselves. It wouldn't surprise him. "Africa is a strange continent," he says kindly. "It affects the white man's mind. Perhaps you should rest."

The reverend snorts indignantly. The angry look is back. He waves a long, bony finger. "Each person is tempted when they are dragged away by their own desire and enticed."

"Is that from the Bible? What do you mean by that?"

"Why do you deliver slaves to Curaçao? An accursed place, sir. You sell blacks to Spaniards. To papists! The Pope is the antichrist, and you hand them over to the devil."

"Aha."

"A merchant must, if there are no Protestant buyers, prefer to take a loss rather than trade with Roman Catholics."

Now Sweerts is beginning to get annoyed. "Perhaps you believe you're speaking to an illiterate," he says coolly. "This debate is old and worn. But I am indeed a merchant, not a preacher."

"Christ has freed us from slavery."

"You're preaching in the wrong church."

"It is God's church." Emotions flicker across the reverend's face. Suddenly, he seems overcome by doubt. "I admit that Christ has freed us from the bondage of sin and the devil, but not from physical slavery."

Sweerts impatiently waves his hand, clearly having had enough. "If you wish to argue, then do so in Amsterdam."

"That's exactly what I want. That's why I'm here."

"Then I won't stand in your way. But if you preach *against* us, I will take action, rest assured. I won't tolerate insubordination, not even from the pulpit."

"I've heard that the *Griffin* doesn't have a preacher on board."

Sweerts looks up in surprise. "You want to board a slave ship?"

"It's the quickest way to leave this place."

The director-general shakes his head. "Skipper Burghoutsz already has a lay preacher. He's been working with a fixed, very tight-knit crew for years."

"The skipper holds no authority in this. A minister is preferred. The Company is clear on that."

Good God, Sweerts thinks, what an insufferable man. "You don't need to explain the Company's rules to me."

"You could give the order. You have the power. I could sail to the West and return to Amsterdam from there."

Sweerts feels the irritation like a knot in his stomach. He'd love nothing more than to kick this scarecrow out of his office. "You're a stubborn one, sir. My patience is being tested." He looks at the reverend with disdain, drumming his fingers. Burghoutsz will be furious, he muses, but let him deal with this fool, and I'll be rid of him. "Fine. You'll get your way. I'll amend the ship's orders."

49 The Shark

"A slave who has a believing master should not show him disrespect because they are brothers. On the contrary, he should serve him even better, because those who benefit from his service are believers, and beloved."

From: The Bible, 1 Timothy 6:2

⚓

Logbook of the *Griffin*, Wednesday, December 24:
"*Wind north-northeast. After heaving anchor, set course towards Elmina to prepare for the passage west. The two additional slaves are a meagre gain after several weeks of cruising along the coast; a waste of provisions, four to five stivers per day. By noon, the breeze diminished somewhat. Topgallant sails hoisted, bow to port. Two cases of dysentery, which were immediately placed in quarantine. Also, a number of black women are chronically seasick.*"

Sunday is a day of rest, and this is strictly observed, after the morning service, the crew has time for themselves.

"Permission to fish, sir?"

Boatswain Graauw sizes up the trio of young hands. They're inexperienced lads. Wearing nothing but their sailcloth trousers, rolled up to their knees, their bare, scrawny torsos deeply tanned. "Have the cages been stowed in the bulwark netting?"

"Yes, sir."

"What are you aiming to catch?"

"Tuna!"

A curt nod, and they're off. Leeward, behind the forecastle, they attach an iron hook to one end of a coil of rope. One of the boys had already secured a piece of pork rind earlier. That goes on the hook.

"Overboard with it," says the tallest of the group, a lanky lad with freckles and a button nose.

The hook splashes into the sea, the rope unspooling quickly due to the ship's speed.

"Tie it off."

The line is wrapped around a cleat under the starboard railing and expertly secured with four knots.

Now it's a waiting game. They crouch together, muttering and whispering. Every now and then, they sneak glances at the boatswain, as if they can't quite believe he's letting them go about their business.

Time passes slowly.

A group of blacks crawls out of the hatch. "Drink, boss?" they ask.

The white guard nods and the lid is taken off the water barrel beside the main mast. On the quarterdeck, the second mate stands with his hands behind his back. To port, just faintly and low on the horizon, a thin strip of coastline is visible.

Zzing! Goes the line.

The boys leap up, clambering onto the railing, their hands gripping the fore shrouds.

"Where?"

They squint. Eager hands grab hold of the rope, ready for the fight, but the line goes slack. They stare, disappointed. "Did the hook come off?"

Then, the excited, cracking voice of the lookout rings out from high up in the main mast: "You've got a shark on the line! A bloody sháááárk!"

That gets things going. A few of the older hands scramble up the rigging.

"There!" shouts one. To leeward, half a cable's length from the ship, they spot a dark fin cutting through the water. Suddenly, the line pulls tight again, whipping over the side. The boys brace themselves, their faces flushed with excitement. They pull as if their lives depend on it, but the rope won't budge. In the distance, a tail slaps the water.

"It's no good!" yells the lanky one with the button nose, sweat beading on his forehead, smeared with grime.

"He's at least nine feet!" shouts the lookout.

"Nine feet?" repeats one of the hands. "You'll never get that bastard on board."

The fin darts the other way now, opposite the ship's course. The rope groans. If it wasn't tied to the cleat, they'd have had to let go.

The older sailors jump in to help, leaning over the side, climbing onto the foremast stay, and many hands grab the line.

"Haul together, lads," one shouts.

They grin with joy; the monotony's been broken. With combined effort, they pull, finding the rhythm, and someone naturally breaks into a hauling song:

"In the brig, they'll lock him tight,
Day and night so cold,
They'll give him naught to eat,
But water and hardtack bold!"

Hand over hand. Steadily, they move back from the railing, using the open space. Now, there are sixteen of them, moving in rhythm, working hard: leaning forward, gripping, bracing, pulling, leaning back. And again. They're all singing now. The rope scrapes over the railing, and slowly, a coil begins to form on the deck.

The fish doesn't stand a chance. It makes one more stubborn leap, closer this time, and they all see it: a flash of bluish-white, a gleaming mass with a black tail. Water splashes wildly.

Again. Bit by bit, the line comes inboard. A wet smear forms on the edge of the railing. The men sweat and sing.

After half an hour, the resistance suddenly increases. The sea splashes and churns under the ship.

"There it is!"

The shark's snout appears. The hook is driven clean through its head. In one last attempt, it summons all its strength: its tail thrashes the water, its pectoral fins slam against the hull.

"Hold fast! Don't haul! Don't let the line snap!" roars boatswain Graauw from the quarterdeck, leaning far over the railing.

The sailors stand firm and unmoving, braced on bent legs, leaning back on the rope, teeth clenched, waiting for the beast's fury below to fade.

The minutes tick by. The ship's bell rings: six bells in the forenoon watch.

Then ... relative silence.

Graauw says, "It's had enough. Get its gills above water."

They haul, watching the boatswain, who spurs them on by spinning his arm in circles. The line stretches over the wood of the railing and creaks ominously.

The shark's head rises and crawls like a snail up the vertical hull. They can see its mouth, its teeth, rows of teeth. Where the hook sticks out of the snout, a faint trickle of blood flows into the sea. The rope is now so tight that with every movement, it sends out the finest droplets of water, almost like mist.

"That's far enough!" shouts Graauw. His hand makes a stopping gesture. "That line's about to snap. If that beast goes wild now, you'll lose him." He signals to another group of young sailors. "Use the longboat to tie a rope around its tail."

They don't need telling twice. Excited, they run through the waist to the stern, climb up, disappear into the hatch, stumble into the gunner's cabin, crawl through the stern ports, and pull the longboat, which the ship is towing, up to the rudder and jump in. With the help of cables and ropes, they carefully manoeuvre along the starboard side, bouncing on the bow wave.

There's the shark right in front of them. Bigger than they thought. The tail sways like a scythe, moving with the current.

"What a beast."

"It's a mako."

"No, it's the devil."

"Is it dead?"

"No."

They hook the boat onto the foreshroud cleats. A one-inch rope is tossed down to them, and they can already hear the creaking and groaning of the tackle.

"Careful, boys," warns Graauw, leaning overboard more than twenty feet above them. "One slap of that tail, and you're done for."

But nothing happens. The rope is quickly and expertly tied just in front of the tail fin. The shark doesn't move; it's over before they know it, leaving them almost disappointed.

"Skipper on deck!" calls the watch.

Immediately, silence falls.

Burghoutsz descends into the waist. The shark hangs upside down, its snout three feet above the deck. Around it, in a half-circle, stands the crew, the three young lads at the front, faces proud, backs straight, with the lanky boy and his button nose leading the way. His face beams. He makes a grand gesture that encompasses the entire fish from top to bottom: "Our catch, skipper, caught ourselves. Nine feet. Nine!"

Burghoutsz nods silently. His eyes take in the shark: an enormous fish, huge, with a torpedo-like body, but lifeless, unmoving. He reaches out with his fingers, feels the skin, which looks smooth but is rough as sand; he could cut his hand on it.

"Don't touch it, skipper, please," begs an old sailor as he crosses himself. "This beast isn't from God."

"Nonsense," mutters the lanky boy, his face full of offended annoyance.

The skipper's fingers slide downward, following the contours of the snout. His hand nears the corner of the mouth. There's some blood there. And behind it, glinting, are rows of jagged, triangular blades. His index finger inches closer but hesitates as he suddenly notices the left eye, right on the edge of that flat, grey-blue head. A black, soulless void stares back at him. For a moment, he's frozen. The jaws snap shut with a loud crack, a sickening hinge-like motion of the upper and lower jaws. He jumps back barely in time, his fingers safe, trailing behind him.

50 *Back: Aldemar Burghoutsz (6)*

"By God, I believe the devil shits Dutchmen!"

⚓

Second Anglo-Dutch War, 1665-1667

The *Purmer II* lies in the dock at the Zaan River. Workers and craftsmen swarm around her, repairing and reinforcing the battery deck. Shipowner Gijsen stands nearby, looking displeased. He says to the Admiralty's agent, "What can a little ship like that do? Better to confiscate a few East Indiamen instead."

"Every bit helps," the agent replies impassively. He's used to these kinds of conversations; they all complain—shipowners, captains and merchants alike. "It's war, after all."

"Damn English," mutters Gijsen.

Aldemar stands a bit farther away. He visits daily, taking the ferry from Amsterdam. Once the ship is ready, they'll sail straight to Zeeland. Holland has significantly expanded its fleet, building sixteen massive ships of the line. Everyone is waiting for the go-ahead from Admiral De Ruyter, who has promised to deal the English a decisive blow.

Yes, Aldemar thinks, we must marry quickly, or it won't happen this spring, and when it is obvious that Anna is pregnant there will be trouble. Moreover, he's acutely aware of his own vulnerability. One direct hit, he realizes, and a person is reduced to blood and pulp. He's seen it: the sailors, unrecognizable, sliding across the deck like heaps of raw meat, moving with the ship's motion. Four-fingered Gisbert had been there; only his head was identifiable, rolling about like a ball. Gisbert had a wife and four children. No, Anna cannot be left behind unmarried. He has to take care of her. He has money, he's saved. He'll sort everything out today. He sighs and puts his hands in his pockets. It's all become very complicated, he thinks.

The wedding is simple and brief. Family and friends gather in the square in front of the Oude Kerk. Dad and mum have come from Enkhuizen, dad wearing a new smock and mum looking beautiful in her dark dress. Baker Govers has been grinning all morning. Skipper Rijkjan is there, along with the *Purmer II*'s first mate and Gillis Grauw, silent as always.

The wedding procession moves among the churchgoers. The minister stands on the stone floor and can barely make himself heard. But it goes as it should and Anna beams in her light-green gown. Aldemar solemnly says, "I give you this ring as a symbol of my love."

In the courtyard of the bakery on the Oudekennissteeg, there is a modest celebration. Due to the war and the plague, the mood remains subdued. Street musicians come in to play, but the guests need to be encouraged to dance. There's bread, herring, corn brandy and grog, but because of the English naval blockade, the fish isn't very fresh, the grain is scarce and the bread is expensive.

As darkness falls, Skipper Rijkjan gives an apologetic look and waves his ship's orders. "I'm sorry, Anna, but we have to go."

Aldemar looks at his new wife. "I must leave."

"Yes," she says.

The guests sing a song and raise their glasses. Aldemar embraces Anna. He wants to hold her, but his mates pull him away. "Let go, lad. The ferry is waiting."

He cries. Her fingers slip from his hand.

The sea battle off the Flemish coast lasts for four full days. Death reigns on the ships. Dark clouds of smoke, smelling of tar and cordite, block the view, while below deck,

unseen and unknown men toil at the cannons, in gunpowder smoke and unbearable heat. The English have a new weapon: their hollow, fuel-filled shells explode and spontaneously set the decks on fire. The wood is blackened, sails charred. The dull, echoing thuds of the batteries continue day and night. Here and there, the sea burns. People float in the water, most of them dead and burned, some still half-alive, exhausted, clinging to debris, but no one helps; they are neither seen nor heard.

The *Purmer II* shakes and shudders. The yard of the mainmast is shot half away. The wood is splintered and scarred by bullets and shrapnel. Frayed rope flutters uselessly in the wind. The crew struggles in the rigging to keep the ship steerable and moving while bullets whistle past their ears. In the waist, marines from the Admiralty gather, firing their muskets and swivel guns at the enemy ships. Aldemar does not know how the battle is progressing, who is winning or losing. By now, it no longer matters, he just wants to go home, back to Anna and the baby in her belly. He cringes as the shells explode.

Boarding hooks slam into the wood of the starboard railing. The English ship grinds and scrapes alongside, hull to hull. There are cheers. English cheers. Redcoats leap aboard, met by the Dutch marines. A few more shots are fired with pistols and muskets, but soon it's man to man. Cutlasses. Short swords. Knives and pikes. A tangle of men, panting, groaning and cursing. The crew strikes with clubs, hooks and cleavers. Even Dikkie the cook joins the fight, swinging an axe he swiped from the forecastle.

Below on the gun deck, the gunners have managed to reload their batteries in record time. They shout their triumph as the fuses are lit. The cannons blast at close range and splintered wood flies in all directions. The explosions scorch the hull of the English frigate, and flames lick upwards. The English powder catches fire. A dull thud echoes from deep below the waterline.

The great yards of the two ships nearly touch. Like a devil from a box, Gillis Graauw appears. With a long knife in each hand, he leaps onto the enemy's main yard and climbs up the shrouds, rigging and lines, with the enraged English sailors in hot pursuit.

Skipper Rijkjan watches him go. "Goddamn daredevil!"

Gillis deftly dodges a few grabbing hands and swings himself onto the English mainsail. Without hesitation, he plunges his knives forward into the canvas. A loud tearing sound follows. Using his own weight, he slides down, making two long slashes. The mainsail flaps uselessly in the wind.

Gillis swings downward. Feet first, he crashes into two English sailors, and the whole lot tumbles over each other. Knives flash. The sailors swear and curse, but Gillis is already gone, sprinting across the slippery deck and diving headfirst to the other side, right into the starboard shrouds of his own ship, where he is greeted with loud cheers. The crew hauls him aboard and slaps him on the back.

"Jesus Christ," mutters skipper Rijkjan. He runs over to Gillis, who sits on the deck, panting, still clutching his knives. "You madman!"

Gillis stoically endures a hug. His soot-blackened face shows no emotion, but his eyes gleam. He stares at the ruined English mainsail while the Dutch marines empty their swivel guns onto the enemy deck.

Anna looks at him, brushing a lock of hair from his eyes. His gaze is distant, his thoughts far away. He doesn't even seem to notice her. She rubs her belly, which is already starting to swell, but her joy is dampened. Sometimes, she sees him sitting, crouched in the courtyard of the bakery, staring into his own world.

"Wake up, Aldemar."

He finally responds. He looks at her with surprise, as if he hadn't expected her. "Where's Gillis?" he asks, and she hears panic in his voice.

The baby lies in the crib, wrapped in cloths. Her tiny hands wave in the air. She blows softly and makes little throat sounds. Aldemar looks at her in amazement. A daughter. His child. He could never have imagined that it would be so small. So fragile. She looks like a doll.

He glances at Anna, who is lying in bed. Her eyes are closed. There is still a bit of sweat glistening on her forehead. Her face looks tired, with dark circles and lines around her mouth, but thankfully, she's sleeping. Finally. The birth hadn't been easy.

"Eh," his daughter coos.

He looks again. His index finger touches one of her little hands. The tiny fingers close around his. The grip is surprisingly strong for such a small being. And her energy is palpable. That's good. She's warm. And she drives away the images of war. He thinks: the war was death and here is new life. For the first time in months, his mind feels a little lighter.

The flute ship is brand new and lies at the Zaan River. The oak planks gleam in the sun. The wood is still light in colour. No stains. No cracks. Masts, yards, rigging, ropes, stays, blocks and cleats: everything looks new and unused. On the sprit before the gallion, a fearsome figurehead stands with the body of a lion and the head of an *eagle. The creature spreads two small wings, and its forked tail curls around the sprit.*

Onshore stands shipowner Gijsen, surrounded by the officers of the Purmer II.

"It's a fine ship," says skipper Rijkjan.

"Yes. Master craftsmanship," replies Gijsen. He's proud of his ships. "Commissioned by the West India Company. She's bound for Africa."

He looks at his men one by one, seeing the lingering pain in their eyes; the war hasn't spared them. You can recognize sailors these days by their vacant stare — they're the men who lived through Lowestoft or the Four Days' Battle of '66. These boys have had their share, he thinks, and the group has thinned out considerably. God knows what horrors they've seen. And the Purmer II is heavily damaged, laid up on land. What should they do? Wait? Sit at home? Twiddle their thumbs? No, he decides. They're good lads. I've got work. There's always work.

"Listen," he says. "Even at the West India Company, sailors aren't easy to come by. Officers are scarce. This ship's not yet ready for the tropics."

Skipper Rijkjan nods in understanding. "She's got to fetch salt."

"Exactly, from Bonaire. Bricks there, unrefined salt back. The salt will preserve the ship. It'll resist tropical rot for a long time. The Company's asked if I can arrange a crew for her first voyage, on consignment. It pays well. What do you think?"

They glance at each other. A flicker of light appears in their eyes.

"What's her name?" asks Aldemar.

Shipowner Gijsen smiles: "The Griffin."

Little Emma lies on his chest, her tiny fingers pinching his lips and nose. Aldemar grimaces. Their little room is small but cozy, and even in winter it's pleasantly warm. From below comes the smell of freshly baked bread; father Govers has opened the ovens. They hear the muffled sounds of the workers: voices, laughter, the scraping of the bread shovels.

"How long will you be away?" Anna asks. She lies beside him, resting her chin on her hand.

"Hm. Ninety days there, ninety days back, if we're lucky. Plus the time needed for loading."

She makes a face. He's been home for weeks, aimlessly wandering around the docks. Reluctantly, he occasionally helps with odd jobs for the baker, more in the way than useful. But now the absence in his eyes has faded a little, and last night he didn't wake up sweating and screaming for once.

Bonaire, she thinks, she's repeated that name in her head a hundred times.

Bonaire. Curaçao. The other side of the ocean. She has no concept of distance, remembers only the stories of privateers and pirates, of natives and exotic animals.

"It's always warm there," he continues with a smile, as he tickles his daughter under the chin. "And the sea is clear as glass, and there are palm trees."

"Maybe you'll be home by Christmas?"

"Maybe." He sighs, closes his eyes. For a moment, he hears the echo of the English cannons again. Gillis Graauw climbing over the yardarm, knives in his hands. Blood flowing over the decks. But it's just a glimpse, nothing more than that. "Yes," he says with relief. "By Christmas. That would be nice."

"Look, Emma, the sea!" He holds her in his arms and lifts her high above him. Emma laughs in the wind. Fine water droplets in the air as the waves crash against the pier. Maybe she tastes the salt. A tiny hand grips a lock of his hair, pulling. Surprising pain. "Ouch!" He bursts out laughing. "Little monkey!"

There's the IJ. Further off, the Zuiderzee. Green water, a grey sky and white caps on the waves. "The sea, Emma, the sea!" he cheers, dancing with her in his arms.

Anna makes plans for the future. He could become a skipper for the West India Company: sailing to the Gold and Grain Coasts and back, six months away from home. Forty-five guilders a month, and a clever skipper saves on his living expenses—he gets seven stivers a day for provisions and uses five—plus a bonus for a safe return. And maybe, later, a little house on Texel or Vlieland, where so many sailors live. Skippers like to be close to their ships, they say, their first love on the water and their second on land.

He sleeps. She sees his eyes move. Dark dreams behind his eyelids. When he leaves, Anna thinks, he'll be all alone. Who will wake him when the monsters disturb his sleep? She places her palm on his forehead. The heat radiates through his skin and she can almost feel the images beneath. He has never spoken of the war at sea, but sometimes, she passes a stranger in the street—just some man with the same look in his eyes—and now and then, she catches a glimpse: a story, a sentence, a word.

God, make him whole again. She leans over him and smells his skin, his breath. Now he'll do what he's always wanted. But she hopes he still knows that himself.

With Gijsen's barge to the Roadstead. Farewell at the Texel quay. It's drizzling. The sky is leaden, and the water dark and threatening. The boat departs and he watches them, shoulders slumped. There they stand, on the pier, among all the other people:

his wife, his daughter. Anna holds Emma. Her little hand waves, but only because her mother makes her do it.

When I return, he thinks, *she'll wave on her own.* For the first time, he's aware of the time, how long he'll be away from home. The world beckons, but they stay behind. He sighs. The barge foams through the IJ and the figures left behind grow smaller and smaller.

51 Dinner in Elmina

"(...) We are unable to establish a steady supply of good quality cattle in Elmina. In Axim, the animals have fairly grassy meadows and grow fat, as they do in Accra and with the Brandenburgers in Pocquesoe, but here they remain lean and scrawny, and the milk they produce is so poor that even twenty to thirty animals cannot sufficiently supply the table of the director-general. They are small and light, and it would be a very good cow if it reached a weight of forty stone at full maturity. The meat, too, is spongy, tough, and unpleasant in taste. Nonetheless, people are still bold enough to ask a hundred guilders or more for fully grown animals.
The locals themselves prefer dog meat. Many of them maintain breeding farms and sell the pups at very high prices, as they are considered a delicacy at feast meals."

From: Correspondence of Chief Chirurgeon Zacharias Augustijns to the Collegium Medicum of Amsterdam, October 1687

In the castle, the large table in the governor's room is elegantly set, as it is every evening: with white linens, silver cutlery and Delft faience crockery. Company slaves in livery serve the dinner. Large platters carry salted fish, pickled herring and bacon.

Director-General Sweerts sits at the head of the table, casting a critical eye over what is being served. Small jugs of dripping pork. Dried sausage. The smell of warm apple syrup teases his nostrils. He snaps his fingers, irritably pointing to a stain on his napkin. The frown on his forehead is enough to strike fear into the black waiter.

"In essence," he hears the chief chirurgeon say from the other side of the table, "the black constitution is not significantly different from our own. I can assure you, no one has ever been able to demonstrate any physical difference beneath the skin. The root of segregation lies in the mind, in the spirit."

Sweerts glances at him absently, his mind elsewhere. That afternoon, in the topmost section of the fort on Jago Hill, he had ordered the room of the deceased ensign Vermeulen to be cleared out. He had been present himself when a heavy leather sack was found under the bed.

"I must disagree," the chief merchant politely interjects, a man with hollow cheeks and dark circles under his eyes. "Invisible does not mean absent."

Sweerts had immediately suspected what he would find in that sack. Gold. Of course. And this time, the amount was far more than four hundred guilders. The ensign, who had appeared to be a decent man, who had sat at this very table night after night, with whom he had shared bread—by God, he must have been at the top of a corrupt pyramid. More than two thousand guilders! Sweerts bites his lip, fiddling again with the tropical sore that now runs as a moist, deep line from the corner of his mouth to his cheek. This whole affair, he concludes, has become a festering wound, just like that damn sore that refuses to heal.

"I believe you yourself have observed," the chief merchant continues, "that blacks can eat *pement*, a green pepper, without harm, whereas it can be fatal to whites." He stabs at his pickled herring with a knife. "That must surely suggest a physical difference?"

"Perhaps Van Leeuwenhoek's wondrous new instrument can shed more light on the matter?" suggests the quartermaster, eager to appear erudite.

"It's the humours," adds one of the head clerks beside him, mouth full. "Too much black bile."

Sweerts eyes the quartermaster, who is accountable only to him. A pale man. Competent enough for his role, a typical pen-pusher. Pious. Not very imaginative. Is he involved in this swindle too? Is *everyone* conspiring against the Company? He scoops a lump of duff onto his plate while the chirurgeon across from him shakes his head in irritation.

"You speak beyond your expertise, sir. There is nothing to suggest that the fundamental fluids of the human body are unequally present. I have performed autopsies on many bodies, both white and black, and have never observed any difference in the amount of phlegm, blood, or bile." He turns to the quartermaster. "And by the way, with all due respect, Van Leeuwenhoek is no physician. He is like a child with a new toy. This year he published a study on the coffee bean. The coffee bean!"

"Utter waste of time and money," nods the quartermaster, watching dispassionately as a grain worm crawls out of his biscuit. "You'd think such a learned fellow would have better things to do."

No, Sweerts concludes silently, the quartermaster lacks the guts.

"What sort of instrument are you talking about?" asks the chief merchant, not the least bit rattled.

"A very strong magnifying glass," explains the chirurgeon smugly. "Would you care for some saltfish?"

"You cannot perceive the divine," grumbles Reverend Duisterbloem, seated at the far end of the table, nibbling sparingly on a piece of bread. He looks at them darkly. "The divine is given to Europeans. We are the sons of Japheth, Noah's favoured. The chirurgeon is right: the difference lies in the soul."

Perhaps the problem has solved itself, considers Sweerts. They have all disappeared: the ensign, the sergeant and the corporal. If you cut off the head, the whole beast dies. He glares maliciously at Duisterbloem, the only one at the table over whom he has no authority. "Surely this debate hardly holds your interest, Reverend?" he asks sarcastically. "Perhaps not everyone is aware of your desire to leave us?" The fierce look in the reverend's eyes pleases him.

"But it doesn't add up," the senior merchant says stubbornly. "If it's a divinely granted superiority, then there was initially no difference? Wouldn't that mean blacks and whites were equal before that divine intervention?"

Reverend Duisterbloem raises his head in anger; the senior merchant has more or less voiced his own thoughts. But he can't admit that here. "Watch yourself, sir," he warns. "I will not tolerate godless ramblings at this table."

"It's just logic," the senior merchant protests.

"Heresy," the quartermaster accuses, pointing his spoon with his mouth full. "That's what it is."

Sweerts takes a bite of his duff and thinks about the gold he confiscated in the name of the Company. Should he posthumously disgrace the ensign? Tarnish his good name publicly? The idea is tempting; it suggests justice, but in that case, he'd have to report the gold. He turns aggressively toward the quartermaster, who irritates him endlessly. "Perhaps it has escaped your notice," he snaps, "but didn't Reverend Hondius from Hoorn write that reformed believers who trade in slaves are sinful, because they are people of the same nature as we are?"

The others at the table stare at him in astonishment.

"God Almighty," the chief chirurgeon grins. "That sounds like blasphemy in your own church, Your Excellency."

Only half a mile further, Quassie Patoe sits cross-legged on the beach, with the fishermen of the asafo Apendjafoe in front of him. The day's catch is spread out on woven mats: grey mullet from the river, mackerel and sardines from the sea. A four-foot-long barracuda. He points to a pile of squid. "That one, and that one and that one," he orders. He selects the fattest specimens for himself and has them set aside. The smaller, scrawnier fish go into the barrel for the Dutch; every tenth fish is for them, no matter how much is caught. The rest is for sale.

Technically, a Dutch commissary is supposed to inspect the catch, but Quassie Patoe made arrangements against that a long time ago. The Dutch commissary has a taste for little black boys and Quassie Patoe could satisfy him in exchange for a bit of independence. It makes life much simpler, he thinks. He doesn't like interference. The whites only eat salted fish anyway. He shudders with disgust.

Meanwhile, he half-listens to the fishermen's heated negotiations. On Mondays, they're all agitated because no fishing is traditionally done on Tuesdays—it's considered bad luck—so every sardine is precious. When, after much haggling, the catch is finally divided, he gives a sigh of relief and—in the name of the Company—grants permission for them to sell their share. "Thank God," he says haughtily as he stands. "*Aseda Nka Enyame.*"

The fishermen beckon to the women, who have been waiting in groups with their buckets in the background. They will sell the fish at the market.

Quassie Patoe turns his back to them and looks toward the village, where the first fires are being lit. Darkness is creeping closer from the hills. Tonight, he will quietly set off toward Abankeseso, on his way to his first smuggling transport. But he is troubled. Rumours about Mussulman Ali have reached him. Was he killed? Captured? He doesn't care much for the Moors, but he has a lot of respect for Mussulman Ali. They've known each other for a long time. Old father, *aggia aqada*, he calls him. That means something. Once—during long evenings in the forests of Abramoe and Tjefel, by the light of the moon and the fire—Mussulman Ali told him the stories of Mohammed, a warlord with countless heroic deeds to his name. Mohammed is a much more compelling figure than the white man's Jesus, who preaches nonviolence, which nobody believes anyway, because Quassie Patoe has never met a white man who turned the other cheek.

Above his head, bats flutter: vague, elusive shadows in the air. His stomach tightens. Yes, he is worried. Something is wrong.

52 Bomba Jan's dream

"The Negroes are all idolaters by nature; yet there is no country or village, nor almost any family among them, that does not differ in faith and religion. Some of them imagine that mankind was created by a great spider, which they call Anansié; others believe that God, whom they call Jan Compaan, created both black and white people at the same time; that the blacks were given the gift and possession of gold, and the whites the gift of art and science: therefore, the former must serve the latter for all eternity."

From: Description of Guiana, by Jan Jacob Hartsinck, 1770

Bomba Jan is dreaming. The sun shines in a white sky, and he seems to float like a feather on the wind, with the green haze of the jungle far below him. He sees the shadow of Akrampa, the vulture, soaring through the air on mighty wings. The wings make a deep, whistling sound.

"Are you here again, Bomba Jan?" Akrampa caws. "Why do you keep coming back? Haven't I given you answers?"

Bomba Jan calls out: "It's about the white man's God, Akrampa, He is elusive. He is fierce. He knows no mercy. Is He an evil spirit?"

"There is no difference, Bomba Jan."

"Is the white man's God the same as Onyame, He who created Himself?" He thinks again of the crow-like figure of the reverend, that sorcerer of the whites, who—without the consent of the people—teaches black children strange beliefs and alienates them from the old traditions. "Is Onyame God?"

Akrampa the vulture glides through the air. He laughs, but his answer is lost in the wind. His wings make powerful strokes, and his speed is dizzying. Bomba Jan flutters helplessly, uncontrollably, in the white light. Soon Akrampa is nothing more than a speck. The sun sets. Darkness approaches, and an icy wind rushes over his skin.

Bomba Jan shivers in his sleep.

53 The Temptation of Quassie Patoe

"Oh mati, we sailed on the same ship. It doesn't matter whether you are Tio or Zombo, or Bobangi, whom everyone calls 'Ko,' or speak Bantu, come from Nsundi or Mbata, or are Teke, related to the Mondongo, which means 'foreigners,' because they come from even farther away, or if you grew up along the Ubangi or Congo River, in the Kwango Valley, Ambaka, Ovimbundu, or Mbundu. The ship makes us kin. We are brothers, and our bond is written in blood."

From: Testimonies of a Slave, Windall Plantation, Comowini Stream, Sukika Creek, Suriname, 1689

⚓

"Tell me," says the old king Boa Amponsem, leaning stiffly forward on his portable ivory throne. "What do you see?" His hand gestures broadly across the square. In the square stand his court, his bodyguards, his commanders, a handful of warriors, his wives, his children and grandchildren—more than a hundred and fifty in total—and behind them, his people, rows deep, jostling for space, eager for spectacle.

Quassie Patoe looks around dutifully. He is tired, very tired. He has trudged through the jungle for five days on his way to Abankeseso, deep in the Denkyira kingdom. He is sweating, thirsty and stands directly under the midday sun. What am I supposed to see, he wonders, what's the point?

"Power," says the king, whose throne is shaded by a massive, wide-spreading ironwood tree in the centre of the square. He purses his lips. He wears a golden crown on his head. "I choose, and I decide. Not the Dutch, or the Portuguese or the English, or any white man."

Whatever you say, thinks Quassie Patoe. "Of course," he says impatiently. "The king stands above everyone."

Boa Amponsem stares at him for a long time, playing with his solid gold bracelets. He seems dissatisfied with the response. "The people on the coast are blind," he finally says. "They see only stone walls and cannons. And large, white ships." He snorts. "In the jungle, large, white ships are not so useful. Does anyone see a ship here?"

His court laughs dutifully, shaking their heads, feeling very important.

They're like puppets, thinks Quassie Patoe. Cows. Livestock. "No, no ships here," he agrees.

The king doesn't laugh. It wasn't a joke. He makes an irritated gesture toward his people and the laughter abruptly stops. He says: "The Dutch run things on the beach. How wide is that beach? Not very wide, but they pay tribute for it. To *me*. All the land belongs to the Denkyira. We are the mightiest of all the Akan tribes. We are the *Adawu Dawu Denkyira*, the devourers of elephants. So, I am the most powerful king. I am Boa Amponsem Dakabere, and I am known as the king who eats *chika*. I use everything made of gold only once, that's how rich I am. For every occasion, I have new golden ornaments made. I use gold the way other people use coconut shells. I do what I want, and everyone around me does what I want. Do you know what happens to people who don't do what I want?"

Quassie Patoe remains silent. This king is full of hot air and his farts go in all directions, he thinks. The Denkyira treat all other blacks as slaves. All other blacks hate the Denkyira. That will come back to bite them one day. He glances over his shoulder. Behind him stands the group of Ahante warriors. They look serious, their lips tightly pressed together.

"Everyone wants to be as powerful as I am," the king continues. He taps a wrinkled, gold-covered finger on the armrest of his ivory throne. "The Ashanti king would love to sit in this chair. And the pigs who call themselves Fante. The Wassa and the Encasse pay me tribute. I deliver gold from Axim to Zacondé." He points to his commanders. They are tall, broad-shouldered men with assegais on their backs. "I have united the villages and brought their warriors together. I now have a great army. If the Ashanti make the mistake of thinking they can defeat us, we'll teach them a lesson." He leans back. His hands rest on his bare knees. He drums impatiently with his gold-ringed fingers. "Are you a Dutchman?"

"Of course not," Quassie Patoe replies.

"An Ashanti, a Fante?"

"No."

"An Arab, then?"

He looks up in surprise. "No."

"That's good to hear," says Boa Amponsem in a cynical tone. "Because Arabs have proven to be very untrustworthy."

Now he's alarmed. Quassie Patoe struggles to keep his face composed. They stare at each other.

The king smiles for the first time. He brushes some imaginary dust off his shoulder cloak. "I cannot rely on the Dutch," he continues calmly. "I have to do business with whoever can help us get firearms. But who can I trust anymore? The white trader is dead and I've lost two important caboceers. Do you know that the Arab they call Mussulman Ali has stolen slaves from us?"

"No," says Quassie Patoe immediately. His mouth is now bone-dry.

"Someone who operates as an intermediary between us and the arms suppliers could become a very influential man. Such a person could earn a lot of gold and respect." His gaze shifts to the Ahante warriors. "The question is: can I count on him? Can I trust him?"

"I can assure you..." Quassie Patoe begins, but the king cuts off his words with a decisive gesture that rings like a bell.

"Your words come too quickly," he says irritably. "Like vomit. Perhaps you are working with the Arab." He snaps his fingers.

The Wassa chief had kept himself hidden. Now he leaps forward into the sunlight, with every intention of striking fear. He succeeds. The Denkyira people murmur in disgust and amazement, for his stretched face and yellow grin immediately make it clear that he possesses the evil eye, and they all know very well that's not something to joke about. "This," declares the king, "is a brother of the Wassa, who has been hunting for us."

Quassie Patoe waits. He stares with growing bewilderment at the harlequin-like figure, who dances across the square with a swaying torso, waving both hands, stomping with long, wide feet.

"Yes, hunting," the figure agrees, and his voice is deep and heavy. "People underestimate Pataku the hyena. They say he eats carrion and is a coward, but Pataku is smarter than Awendade the lion. When you see him, you think: what a monstrosity, how could such a filthy beast be a hunter?" He approaches Quassie Patoe, who can now smell that rotten breath as well. "But when Pataku starts trotting," he continues, "he moves effortlessly forward. And Awendade, the king of the wilderness, knows all too well that when he's old and tired, he'll eventually end up in Pataku's belly." The Wassa chief taps a finger against his forehead. He looks Quassie Patoe directly in the eyes, as if searching for something there. "Everyone fears him, *that*'s why they laugh at him."

He steps back and points to a piece of sailcloth lying in the middle of the square. There's something underneath it, the cloth bulges in the centre. "It's important," he says, "that we know who is friend and who is foe. Uncertainty leads nowhere. The king says: the friends of my friends are my friends, and the enemies of my friends are *my* enemies. So the question is, Quassie *tufohen*, highest servant of the whites: are you a friend or a foe?"

Quassie Patoe remains silent. His unease grows. What does this ridiculous spectre want? Have they set a trap for him?

The Wassa chief walks over to the sailcloth and grabs a corner, pausing for effect, and then, with a sweeping motion, pulls it away.

A blood-covered head becomes visible, a face without ears, nose, lips or eyelids.

Quassie Patoe stares at it, transfixed. The head is upright on the red, caked clay of the square. Behind all that sun-baked blood is the hint of dark skin, but the head isn't that of a negro, for he can see black-grey, straight hair.

It takes a moment, but then something clicks in his mind as he recognizes the head of Mussulman Ali. He struggles to suppress a rising, squeaking gulp of air in his throat.

"The Arab," says the king impassively from his throne, "is a traitor and a thief. The Wassa brother captured him and brought him to us."

"Yes," agrees the Wassa chief, crouching beside the head. His right hand taps gently, almost kindly, against the matted hair. "We talked, Mussulman Ali and I." He looks at Quassie Patoe. "Do you know Mussulman Ali?"

"Everyone knows Mussulman Ali," Quassie Patoe whispers hoarsely.

"Did you know of his theft?"

"No."

"Did you know about the slaves he delivered to the coast?"

"No."

"The slaves were sold to a white pirate. A lot of gold was paid. Do you know where that gold is?"

"No."

"They say the white pirate will sell the slaves to the plantations across the great water, but the king doesn't believe that. The white pirate is known as a gold smuggler, not a slave trader. The king believes the Dutch bought the slaves from him. Is that true?"

"I don't know."

"You know everything about the Dutch."

"The Dutch do whatever they want."

"You lie easily, Quassie Patoe. Why do you deny everything?"

"I'm not lying." Quassie Patoe sweats in the sun, but under his skin, he feels cold. He would like to skin that black devil slowly.

The Wassa chief smiles kindly. He stands up, bends down, grabs the head with both hands under the chin, and begins to pull.

"Argh!" Mussulman Ali groans.

The effect is dramatic. The people of the Denkyira, the king's court, his wives, his children and grandchildren, his warriors and commanders, even the Ahante, all let out a simultaneous cry of astonishment.

"There's more of him," giggles the Wassa chief, who seems very pleased with himself. He points to the ground, making digging gestures. "Down there."

Quassie Patoe steps back. "Why?" he asks. "You could have killed him."

"Why?" laughs the Wassa chief. "Why does Pataku the hyena do what he does? Because he was made that way." His toes tap the head, which is now mercilessly exposed to the sun. Mussulman Ali makes a faint, gurgling sound. "He can't speak anymore," the Wassa chief says regretfully. "Lost his tongue, I fear. The Mussulman is deep within himself, far away from here. Maybe he still hears us. Faintly. Like the rustling of the wind."

Anger and hatred surge through Quassie Patoe. He stares helplessly at the ruined eyes of his old friend while the Wassa chief reaches under his belt and pulls out a pistol. "Are you his accomplice?"

"No."

"Here, take this gun. If you're his accomplice, show mercy and end his suffering." He offers Quassie Patoe the pistol. "Take it. It's loaded. Use it."

Quassie Patoe hesitates. His gaze shifts to the pistol. If he accepts, he's lost.

But Mussulman Ali needs his help.

"If you're his friend," says the king calmly, "then you're a thief, just like him. And we deal swiftly with thieves."

"If you're his friend," repeats the Wassa chief, now pressing the pistol almost against Quassie Patoe's face, "I'll do to you what I've done to him. But if you don't kill him, I'll let him rot in the sun. Who knows how long he'll last. His pain must be unbearable. No man should suffer so much pain. But what do you care? You're not his friend. Or are you?"

Quassie Patoe closes his eyes. The blood pounds fiercely in his throat and temples, and the mix of anger and doubt makes him nauseous. He's already dead, a voice in his head says. What's the point? Once, long ago, when he—Quassie Patoe—was still a boy, Mussulman Ali had pulled him out of the water. The water had been deep and black and had closed over his head. "It's foolish," Mussulman Ali had later said reproachfully, "to jump into water if you can't swim."

He opens his eyes and sees Mussulman Ali's head trembling slightly. "He's not my friend," he says hoarsely. Black spots dance before his eyes. "Do what you want. I can't help him." He turns and walks away, while the humiliation scorches his soul.

54 Departure

"And Raguel stood up, and gave him Sara his wife, and half of his goods, slaves, and beasts, and money."

From: The Bible, Tobias (Tobit) 10:11

The *Griffin* is back in Elmina. In the middle of the bay, she lies with furled sails at her mooring anchor, surrounded by boat traders who, as always, persistently hover around. The sailors are buying items for personal use: cages full of chickens and ducks, a piglet and a goat, coconuts, palm oil, spices, pots and trinkets. The goods are carefully stored in corners and crevices, out of sight of boatswain Graauw, who unceremoniously throws anything that gets in his way back overboard.

There's a nervous atmosphere, as everyone feels the departure is near. The ship's holds are loaded with provisions, the water barrels are full and the slave cargo is complete. There's no longer any reason to delay.

In the afternoon, there's a commotion when Reverend Duisterbloem climbs aboard. He stands on the waist deck with slumped shoulders, a duffel bag at his feet, and looks around with a dark expression. "I assume my arrival was announced," he says to the skipper, who stands above him on the quarterdeck.

Burghoutsz, flanked by his officers, nods, though his tone is devoid of any warmth: "The director-general informed us."

"I'll make myself useful, skipper."

"I doubt that."

The reverend presses his lips together and surveys the length of the ship. He knows very well that in this confined, isolated world, the skipper is all-powerful—even the church can't change that—but he can still accomplish much: the black slaves are heathens and the sailors are superstitious. He will spread God's word. "You'll come to appreciate me," he adds.

There's no reply; when he looks up again, everyone is gone. Resigned, he shrugs his shoulders.

In the binnacle house, Burghoutsz and the first mate bend over the sea charts on the log table.

"Raise the anchor," orders the skipper. His fingers impatiently glide over the paper, tracing the contours of the West African coast. "Factor the Guinea Current into your reckoning and account for a daily drift of about thirty miles." He taps the map. "We should be able to pick up the trade winds at that position."

Pensively, he stares through the open window. The ocean gleams like metal under a low, veiled sun, and the air is hazy and bone-dry. The *harmattan* extends its influence, as it does every year. Dust is everywhere on the ship. Desert sand. It gets into clothes, seams and cracks. It's even in his nose and throat. "By God," he grumbles, "I'll be glad when we reach the open ocean." Then, to the mate: "Keep the slaves below deck until we're underway."

The first mate nods and steps outside. On the quarterdeck stands the motionless, square figure of boatswain Graauw. They exchange a glance. Graauw's eyes flicker briefly, like small dots in the twilight. No words are needed. The half-pike thuds on the planks, the boatswain's mates whistle and the deckhands scramble up the rigging. Fifty fathoms of anchor rope are hauled in. Moments later, the *Griffin* swings around and points her bow to the southeast. Song fills the air as halyards and lifts are run through the blocks.

The middle passage has begun.

55 *Back: Aldemar Burghoutsz (7)*

A tanned, weathered face from the sun, lines around his eyes, and a distant, often absent look. Dark hair, tied in a long ponytail down his back. Anyone who sees him will say: look, a sailor.

Amsterdam, Spring 1669

The journey took longer than expected. There were setbacks: storms, calms, hunger. The first mate didn't make it. Scurvy. Aldemar has taken his place, and spring is already approaching; a light green haze covers the trees.

Today it's raining. A harsh wind stings their faces. They're no longer used to it; the cold bites through their coats.

Aldemar and Gillis Graauw stand in the barge. Their shoulders touch. Gillis in his dark blue overcoat. His boyish face is gone. Instead, a hard, angular face, with a blond stubble beard and a tight mouth, almost without lips. The scar on his face is a brownish-red streak. Gillis has become the boatswain, chief commander before the mast. His brawny, square figure commands respect among the crew. Or maybe it's his eyes: pale gray, piercing searchlights that see everything.

Aldemar hunches against the rain and wind. He grins as he endures the cold. It's strange to be back, he thinks. Everything looks the same, yet also different, as if I'm no longer a part of it. The people have continued their lives while I was on the other side of the world. They don't know what I've seen or who I've become. He savors the tingling feeling in his stomach, that nervous yearning for home, and buries his hands even deeper into his pockets. His fingers are red and numb.

Amsterdam's Schreierstoren comes into view, hazy and shrouded by the rain. They look at it as if they're seeing it for the first time.

As he walks down the Texel quay, he is alone. There is no one to welcome him. That amuses him; he imagines how he will suddenly appear in front of their faces in a few minutes. "You'll be surprised," he chuckles to himself. He strides on, his bulging duffel bag slung over his shoulder. The rain sweeps through the streets and the cobblestones are slick under his worn clogs. There's the Zeedijk. Overhanging shop fronts drip with water, small waterfalls crashing onto the street, people taking shelter under awnings, beneath vendors' stalls. He doesn't see them. He darts right onto the Korte Niezel. Boats lie side by side in the canal. A horse stands in front of a shop, steaming as if it's on fire. Left onto the Oudezijds Achterburgwal. The nervous, fluttering feeling in his stomach intensifies. He's soaked now. Despite his clogs, he runs, half stumbling, into the Oudekennissteeg. There's the bakery. Around back to the outhouse and courtyard.

There's not much left of baker Govers: a ghost with a pale, translucent skin and jutting cheekbones. Except for a few tufts, his hair is gone, and his apron is so filthy it looks like he works at the fish market. He stares at Aldemar with hollow, uncomprehending eyes.

Aldemar looks around. The bakery is nearly empty, neglected, dirt lies beneath the ovens, and the lanterns hang sadly crooked. Where are the apprentices? The bread? He grabs the baker by his shoulders. "What's happened, baker? Where's Anna? Where's Emma?"

"Anna?"

"Goddammit! Answer me!"

The baker shakes his head. "Buitengasthuis*."

---

* The Buitengasthuis ('Outer hospital') was situated outside the city gates.

"What?"

"The plague house."

Aldemar's eyes bore into the baker's. They stand there, motionless, like two dolls, for almost a minute. Slowly, something starts to sink in.

He asks, with a hoarse voice: "The plague house?"

He sits against the wall, his hands limp by his sides. Suddenly, Baker Govers speaks, but Aldemar doesn't hear everything, it's as if a wasp is buzzing through his head.

"They thought it was over," mumbles the baker. "But it's never really gone, said the chirurgeon. They both got it. Black spots on their skin. A cart came with two armed constables and they were taken away. It's the rules, they said. All plague victims are isolated. First to the nuns in the city hospital, then by boat to the Buitengasthuis, past the Leidse Gate. We weren't allowed to go with them. It was over in a few days. Emma was already dead. No one has seen them since. They were buried quietly in the cemetery behind the plague house. The housemother told us." Baker Govers cries. He shakes his head, as if he still can't believe it. "Why not me?" he asks. "Why them?"

Aldemar nods. His eyes are dry. He feels the rage like a red-hot iron in his chest. Blame bubbles up inside him. "Yes, why not you, by God? You were her father. You're a coward. No man hands over his daughter and granddaughter. You should have fought the constables. You should have fled. You could have taken them with you, filthy cowardly rat. You don't give up what's yours!"

Baker Govers is an old man. He bows his head. His thin shoulders slump even further. "You don't know what you're saying," he whispers.

Numb, Aldemar walks over the bridge by the Leidse Gate. It's not raining anymore, but thick grey clouds race across the sky, dark shadows sliding over the city. The water in the canal is high and choppy, but he doesn't see it. The world has become a blur.

Beyond the bridge, the road stretches out, and a little further on, the Buitengasthuis looms—an imposing building, like a monastery, surrounded by water and trees. The ditch lies deserted and the iron gate to the entrance is closed. He wanders aimlessly around the building. The water reeks like a cesspool, as the house dumps its waste directly into the canal.

To the west lies the cemetery. Tall poplars bow their crowns to the wind. The unpaved path to the graveyard has turned to mud. His clogs sink deep into it. Behind a stone wall, he sees long rows of wooden crosses. There are hundreds, haphazardly *placed, seemingly without any order, thrust into the earth. He looks around, confused: mud, rough mounds and furrows, bordered by puddles and sprouting weeds. The crosses sway in the wind. There are no names, just rough, ragged planks nailed together.*

Where are you? Where?

He walks along the graves, searching for something—anything—that might give him solace. But there is nothing. The crosses seem to mock him. The trees groan with derision. At the end of the central path stands a handcart. In its bed lies a heap of soaked, coarse linen sacks. Body bags. He stares at them in disbelief for minutes. Then he covers his mouth, sinks to his knees, and finally understands.

Time flows slowly, cruelly, through him. Rain showers. Swiftly moving cloud banks. Light and shadow. He sits motionless on his knees as the cold seeps up through his bones. He has no thoughts, just that crushing weight on his chest, around his heart.

A shadow approaches. Two muddied shoes slide into his field of vision. He doesn't look up but feels a hand on his shoulder.

"Go home, boy." A woman's voice. "Jesus takes care of the dead."

He shakes his head. The sky is empty. There is no heaven. "Thrown away," he whispers. The rain lashes his skin. His fingers grasp the fabric of her skirt, pulling her toward him. His cheeks press against the cold, wet cloth, but somewhere beneath, he feels the warmth of her body. He buries his face there. Tears. At last. Uncontrollable. The woman stands still, letting him be. Just a person. Just compassion.

He looks without anger at the old, gaunt man who was once baker Govers. He thinks, if the wind catches him, he'll blow away.

"I'm going now," he says.

The old man nods. He seems distant; his eyes keep drifting upward, his head slightly tilted, as if listening to voices.

"To the sea," Aldemar adds for clarity, thinking the old man might not have understood.

"Yes, yes, to the sea."

Aldemar hesitates. He craves the gin and the rush that will follow, that will numb the pain and cloud his thoughts, but the old man looks so helpless. There's a glisten of saliva in the corners of his mouth. He says, "I'll be gone a long time, baker. Maybe a year."

"Yes." The old man nods again. Now he seems impatient, as if Aldemar is wasting his time. His eyes drift upward again. "Yes, of course. It's fine. Go now."

Aldemar shrugs and turns away. There's nothing left that ties them together. "I'll be back," he says, but he knows it's a lie.

Part 2
Du Casse
January 1688

"Despair not, show no mercy to your enemies,
nothing in the world can harm us,
for God is with us."

Jan Pieterszoon Coen (1587 – 1629)

56 Coastal Survey

"(...) Commanie is increasingly becoming a problem. I cannot emphasize enough that the infiltration of the English and their attempts to sow discord continue to undermine our position. We have had a treaty with the King of Eguafo for decades, stipulating that trade may only be conducted with the Company, yet they continue to allow this rule to be violated, as the English claim they too — since the time of the Royal Adventurers — hold ancient rights.

Granted, the English trading post burned down last year, their fort never materialized, and this year they were driven back into the sea by the natives upon their return (in which — I freely admit — I had a hand), but their captains and merchants conduct business offshore with the Twifo tribe and inland traders. Frankly, I trust the Twifo more than I do the loyalty of the King of Eguafo, for he is an unreliable character, despite his solemn promises and assurances."

From: letters of Director-General Nicholaas Sweerts to the Gentlemen Ten of the West India Company, January 1688

⚓

"*Zut!*" Lieutenant Jean Baptiste Du Casse is irritated, as he so often is. He is an impatient man. Everyone on board knows that. He lounges in his chair in the great cabin, legs spread wide, his right arm over the armrest, a cup of wine in his left hand. He squints at the skipper of a Dutch yacht he has just captured. That is what he enjoys: seizing Dutch ships. However, a yacht is just a small boat, hardly worth a prize, and it was no match for his massive two-deck war frigate. The yacht's skipper stands in front of him, bewildered, barely comprehending that he is suddenly a prisoner. He had been hauled aboard amidst curses and threats, and now, for good measure, he is being guarded by a French sergeant with a rapier in his hand.

"Your boat doesn't interest me," snaps the lieutenant. "If you behave, maybe you'll get it back. Tell me instead what's going on in Commanie, *huh?*"

The French sergeant translates, but his Dutch isn't very good, and he has to repeat his sentences several times before the yacht skipper understands him. This grates on the lieutenant's nerves. "If you cooperate, you can go back to your ship. If you refuse, I'll hang you. And your crew with you."

The yacht skipper looks distressed. Sweat beads on his forehead. Du Casse has a notoriously bad reputation and he seems to have it in for the Dutch in particular. "The English factory has burned down," he says hesitantly, unsure of what the other man wants to hear.

"Arson?"

"By the natives, sir."

"There's no longer an English presence?"

"No, they've all fled."

"And the Dutch?"

"Their factory is still there, but there's barely any trade. All exports are controlled by local traders. I've heard the West India Company plans to build a fort to regain control."

"Hm." The lieutenant frowns and drains his cup of wine. That's bad news, he thinks. Without the presence of the English, those Batavians* will feel increasingly powerful. He scratches his head. "I assume the *Anglais* won't accept the status quo?"

"You mean?"

"That they'll want to return as soon as possible to rebuild their factory."

"Perhaps, sir, but you'd have to ask them yourself."

Yes, he thinks, but when it comes to the French presence on the Gold Coast, the Dutch and the English can suddenly become very united. Like Protestants sticking together, you might say. He grimaces at the thought: his own parents were Huguenots, and that's a painful memory, which is why there was no place for him in the French Navy until last year. But he has renounced Calvinism and is now married to a good Catholic woman. He asks, "How many Dutch?"

The yacht skipper shrugs. "A merchant, a few craftsmen and a few soldiers. It's not much. The factory is a ruin."

A ruin is good, the lieutenant thinks. That means they're careless. Or have no money. There are rumours that the Dutch Company has attacked the Brandenburgers. That's a violation of the treaty with King Frederick William and yet another sign that the Batavians can't be trusted. Never. They're swindlers and opportunists. Honestly, the world would be a better place without the Dutch.

He sizes up the yacht skipper, who stands embarrassed like a schoolboy before him. "Do you work for the Company?"

---

* The term 'Batavian' refers to the earliest history of the Dutch. In the seventeenth century, they liked to identify themselves with this Germanic tribe, which rebelled against the Roman occupation in the first century AD.

"Yes, sir."

"Where were you headed?"

"Batenstein."

"Batenstein." The lieutenant snorts. "Let me tell you something, *capitaine*. You're not going to Batenstein. You're going to Commanie, with me on board. We'll sail along the coast and get the lay of the land. Your Dutch yacht won't raise suspicion."

"No, sir," the yacht skipper says obediently.

The lieutenant chuckles. He's just a country bumpkin, he thinks, a cockroach, *un cafard*. "If you don't cooperate, I'll put you at the mast, and believe me, it'll be my pleasure."

A little later, he stands on deck, his face in the wind, the *Tempeste* beneath his feet. It's a fine ship. The French ships are a bit broader than the Dutch, have less draft, but sail higher and faster into the wind and are more lightly armed along the broadsides. To port lies a second frigate, almost identical to his own: a sister ship.

We're coming for you, he thinks grimly. I've always captured and seized Dutch ships. I took the island of Arguin from them, and Gorée. Senegal belongs to France. And now I will establish factories and forts in Commanie. Then I'll have a foothold on the Gold Coast, and after that, it's Elmina's turn. Elmina will become French, *mon Dieu*, I swear it.

He walks to the starboard railing and looks down. There bobs the captured Dutch yacht, lashed to the *Tempeste* with grappling hooks and rope. On the rowing deck stand ten black oarsmen, shoulders hunched, heads bowed. Rowing slaves. He chuckles. They're mine now, he thinks. Damn Batavians. Rabble. Let them go back to their dikes and polders. If we want enemies, we've got enough with the English and the Spaniards. That's how it's always been. Those Dutch don't even know what they really are: herring fishermen in the North Sea. Cod catchers. But I am their scourge, and I will drive them out. There is no greater country than France.

His cabin is a mess. Clothes and shoes are scattered everywhere. Sabers. Pistols. His desk is covered with papers, books and scrolls. He has no peace, no patience. He always wants to move forward, always in a hurry. In his hand, he holds the articles of association from the Compagnie Française de Guinée, of which he is co-founder, owner and director. He sighs, because things are not going well. French slave production has been inadequate for years. They need two thousand heads annually, in the Caribbean and in Guyana, but they never reach more than a few hundred. The plantations complain bitterly and are on his back. His company is suffering losses. Again. It's enough to drive a man mad.

He points to the man standing before him. "Slaves, frère François, slaves, slaves, and more slaves."

Brother François nods. He is a Dominican monk with a narrow face and sunken cheeks. His black habit hangs around him like a sack. "Of course, Lieutenant," he says in a soft, hoarse voice.

"We did good business in Issiny," the lieutenant continues. "You built your mission post and perhaps we've gained a foothold there. Souls, slaves and ivory. *Voilà*. I intend to achieve the same in Commanie."

Brother François bows his head. He doesn't want to be conceited, that is a sin, but he has held a holy mass in Issiny, among the natives, and left a fellow brother behind to win souls. Yes, he thinks, God's word will be spread.

"In Commanie, we will build a church," the lieutenant presses.

"With God's will."

"Yes, with God's will and my sword." The lieutenant looks with disgust at the habit, which is full of stains. The monk gives off a horrible, sour odor. Where is it written, he wonders, that all men of God must stink? Is that also God's will? He himself uses an abundance of scented water, sprinkled on a lace handkerchief. He continues: "In Commanie, I want a factory and a fort. And a native settlement along the river."

"That is our duty," brother François agrees mildly. "We are the shepherds' dogs, the dogs of God."

"And I want Christianized slaves. No heathens are to board French ships, like the English and the Batavians allow."

Brother François briefly raises his eyebrows. He has always learned: when someone shouts this loudly, he is drowning out his conscience. Does the lieutenant ever think about his parents, whom he rejected in exchange for the king's favour? What would God think of that? But he remains silent. He doesn't want to rub the lieutenant the wrong way. He says, "We will baptize them, willingly or by force."

The lieutenant chuckles. "Willingly is better." But to him, it makes no difference.

He wakes the ship early, the sun has barely risen. An hour earlier, he had already carefully dressed in an inconspicuous grey outfit—knee-breeches and overcoat, with white lace cuffs and black riding boots. His moustache is curled, his fashionable goatee freshly trimmed. "Let's go," he says, rubbing his hands together.

His crew stands in the waist and on the forecastle deck, and from the hold beneath the deck, he sees the upturned faces of the French musketeers. "A little more patience," he says to them, as if speaking to small children. "When we go ashore, you'll get to fight." He grins. He has a broad, charming smile that quickly wins friends. "But first, I'm going to scout the coast. And while I'm gone, polish your muskets and sabres, make sure your bandoliers are full and your powder is dry. And then we'll finally drive out those Batavians."

The musketeers nod eagerly. They've been stuck on the ship for far too long. They would do anything to get ashore.

The lieutenant nimbly climbs down the side ladder, jumps aboard the yacht, and stomps his boots on the Dutch deck. On his command, the black rowers are chained to the benches. "You've changed owners," he snarls contentedly at them, though he knows full well they don't understand French. He beckons brother François aboard, along with three musketeers and the Dutch yacht skipper, who has spent a sleepless night in the hold and looks dishevelled. "*Alors*. Let's go," he says, scanning for a still-invisible coastline.

The yacht detaches from the *Tempeste* as a scorching hot wind blows from the east. There are no clouds, no rain in sight. The yacht's skipper adjusts the triangular sail and the boat tilts slightly, cutting through the sea like a knife.

The lieutenant, brother François and the three musketeers sit huddled in the back, on a slightly raised aft deck where a couple of built-in benches run along the sides. A canvas sunshade is stretched over the aft deck, shielding them from view.

After two hours of sailing, the coast emerges, and the lieutenant springs to his feet. "Put the rowers to work," he signals to the yacht skipper. He wants to be agile and fast; from this point on, they could run into the Dutch. He glances back, where the Dutch flag flutters above the golden scrollwork of the transom[*]. *Bon*, he thinks. He gestures to his musketeers: "Stay under the sail. They mustn't recognize us. We're just an innocent yacht with harmless Batavians on board. But keep your muskets ready."

The rowers hook their oars to the tholes. At a signal from the yacht skipper,

---

[*] Transom = the often elaborately decorated rear of a 17th-century ship

they begin rowing. Their deep voices sing a song while they rhythmically bend and stretch their black backs. Assisted by the sail and a following sea, the yacht races swiftly toward the coast.

Commanie is a haphazard cluster of villages, intersected by a narrow river. From the sea, the Dutch trading post lies on the left bank, and on the right side, the charred remains of the English settlement are visible: blackened posts and beams pointing toward the sky. Rolling hills follow the river inland, the banks lined with beautiful ironwood trees.

The lieutenant peers through his spyglass, studying the trading post: it's a simple wooden structure with a rotting fence around it. No artillery, he notes, no defences. A faded Dutch flag flutters on the roof.

He chuckles, and glances with amusement at brother François, who is sweating on the bench beside him. The sun beats down on the sail and brother François looks uncomfortable. His smile is pained.

The yacht turns, and the wind is now more forward than abeam; the sail no longer gives much speed. The trading post drifts slowly by. In the garden stands a white man in a dark coat. A Dutchman. He waves at the yacht.

The lieutenant cheerfully waves back, only his arm visible from beneath the sunshade.

A little farther on, when the English ruins are also out of sight, the jungle presses right up to the shore. They are alone again, but the lieutenant remains on guard; there is a well-worn path along the coast leading to Elmina Castle, just ten miles away.

By midday, past the fishing village of Ampinnie, a small, barely visible inlet appears.

"Yes, this is it," he mutters, peering intently through his spyglass. He knows this place; two years ago, he came here and established the first contacts inland.

"We'll return tonight," he announces. "And then we'll land here."

57 A Landing at Night

"For we were all baptized by one Spirit so as to form one body—whether Jews or Gentiles, slave or free—and we were all given the one Spirit to drink."

From: The Bible, 1 Corinthians 12:13

In the fishing village of Ampinnie, Quassie Patoe, ensign of the asafo Enyampa, lies naked on his sleeping mat that night. It is cool in the hut, which is spacious and clean. Quassie Patoe enjoys coming here, as Ampinnie is an oasis of peace; hardly any whites or traders visit, and the villagers keep to themselves.

Since his adventure in Abankeseso, he has avoided company as much as possible. The image of Mussulman Ali, Mussulman Ali's *head*, continues to haunt him. Sometimes it feels as if the Arab is calling him, as if he is walking behind him. He has even caught himself glancing suspiciously over his shoulder from time to time. He finds that far from reassuring.

But no one knows about this, of course, as it might be considered a weakness. "I am Quassie Patoe," he whispers under his breath. His right hand searches to the side and finds the warm thigh of his concubine, who is very young, extraordinarily beautiful, and, moreover, his property. She sleeps. He can hear her deep, regular breathing. That reassures him somewhat.

Two days ago, he delivered his first shipment of slaves to the Portuguese. To everyone's satisfaction and without any problems. The reward was great. Gold. Weapons. If he can manage this a few more times, he will be a wealthy man. But he can't summon a sense of satisfaction.

He curses to himself, staring blankly at the palm leaf roof above him.

Sexual intercourse. He had thought *that* would cheer him up. This woman is good, and willing too. He turns his head and stares at her profile, still able to smell the scent of their sex. Yes, a fine concubine. And she's young enough to sell at a profit later when he tires of her. But the act hasn't satisfied him. He saw Mussulman Ali squatting in the corner of the hut, with a cheek full of qat. Mussulman Ali asked, "Am I not *aggia aqada*, your old father?"

That had put an end to his lust.

Quassie Patoe taps his fingers softly on his chest, irritated with himself.

The hut is a little isolated from the village, on a small hill shaded by a few ironwood trees, with a view over the beach and the ocean, and he had the entrance placed so that the sea breeze would usually blow in.

But sleep is out of the question now.

He stands up, stretches, and walks outside. The village is quiet. On the beach, he sees a dog rummaging among the fishermen's canoes, searching for food. Fishing nets hang on lines between the trees, slowly swaying in the wind. With half-closed eyes, he urinates against the trunk of a coconut palm. He listens to the surf. The waves glow faintly in the night, and on the water, he sees two massive, moving shadows. Pitch-black masts, sharply silhouetted against the dark grey sky. It takes a few seconds for it to sink in.

"*Eééh?*"

Ships.

Three-masters? Englishmen? He doesn't know much about white men's ships, but he instantly realizes that something isn't right. The shapes are heading straight for the coast, maybe a mile east of the village. Sails are being reefed. He hears the whistling of rope. No running lights, no lanterns. An attack?

He turns around, darts into the hut and hastily gathers his things. His concubine wakes up and sits up halfway, staring at him in confusion.

"Stay quiet," he warns. "Don't leave the hut, no matter what."

Then he's gone, into the darkness.

The jungle is dangerous at night, especially when you're alone. He moves cautiously along the path, wary of snakes or wild dogs. His assegai hangs over his shoulder and in his hands he holds the long, unloaded snaphaunce ready in front of him. On either side, a wall of dense foliage rises: ironwood trees, guava bushes, palms. The heat hangs still and oppressive above the path.

After about a mile, he silently creeps through the bushes toward the beach, balancing on the balls of his feet. A small inlet is bathed in moonlight. Two frigates lie motionless and dark in the water, their anchors dropped. Rowboats drift back and forth, packed with men. *White* soldiers. He can see their muskets and pikes. They are gathering on the beach. Orders are whispered. Along the shoreline, a trio of cannons stand, complete with gun carriages. He sees crates. Cannonballs. Barrels. Quassie Patoe squints. In the pale light, he makes out a standard-bearer with an enormous flag. On the flag are lilies.

Frenchmen.

Goddammit, he thinks in Dutch as a rush of excitement surges through him.

He looks to the left and can see the path that runs parallel to the coast toward Elmina. Ten miles. Yes. He needs to hurry. He must warn the director-general, the asafo warriors and the soldiers at the castle; if he's fast, he might just be able to prevent a disaster.

He crouches down and crawls out of the bushes. Cautiously, he creeps along the beach, seeking cover behind shrubs and rocks. After only a few dozen meters, the palms grow almost to the water's edge, and the shadows deepen. The sounds from the beach fade away. Relieved, he pauses for a moment and wipes the sweat from his forehead. Adrenaline pounds in his temples. He doesn't exactly know what a Frenchman is, but from the way the Dutch talk about them—in the castle, on the fort—they must be a dangerous white breed. It's truly astonishing how many types of white people there are. Ah, it would be good to spring into action, to fight, to kill and to collect skulls; after all, that's what he exists for. He looks at the path, which winds off into the distance. Quassie Patoe will be the saviour of the Company, he thinks. The Dutch will reward him richly, and he will finally be the *tufohen*, the leader of all the asafo companies.

He glances around once more, half-expecting Mussulman Ali, the *spirit* of Mussulman Ali, to suddenly appear. But there is nothing, only the sounds of the nocturnal jungle—and the ocean in the background.

Finally, he picks up the pace, running with the smooth agility that comes naturally to him, his snaphaunce in his left hand and his assegai in his right.

Hardly two hours later, he watches with a hint of jealousy as Abena Gyan, the concubine of Director-General Sweerts and daughter of the king of Eguafo, sits in a European dress, sipping from a cup of tea. The European dress irritates him. As does the tea, for that matter. An Akim woman, especially one of noble birth, shouldn't be dressing up like a monkey, he thinks. Such a woman should show her body; there's nothing shameful about that. Vague, sensual fantasies flutter through his mind. With difficulty, he turns his attention to Sweerts, who is furiously banging on his desk and repeatedly shouting, "Goddamn French!"

Quassie Patoe nods along in agreement. He covered the ten miles from Ampinnie in record time, but he's hardly tired. His body is hardened. If necessary, he could immediately run back at the same pace. He just wants the director-general to give the signal so he can mobilize the asafo. He can't wait to lead them. Fight. Spill blood. But he waits, seemingly patient, because the director-general has to go through the obligatory stages: surprise, disgust, anger. It's all very predictable.

He glances again at Abena Gyan. She's clearly upset. Her teacup trembles as she brings it to her lips. He wonders: why? Is she upset because the Dutch trading post is under threat? Unlikely. Did she know about the landing of the French ships? That would be surprising. Nevertheless, she's the daughter of the king, and the king is known as a calculating man. Could he be conspiring with the French? Quassie Patoe can barely suppress a grin. If that's true and it comes to light, Abena Gyan won't be the director-general's concubine for much longer. The French will lose. He's certain of that. Then the director-general will chase her out of his bed. And after that, she'll have to leave the castle and the village, *if* she's not booted out first. An outcast princess.

Eééh. That's an enticing prospect. And a chance for revenge. He'd punish her arrogance and, at the same time, teach her not to wear European clothes. With a firm hand, no doubt about that. He sets his snaphaunce in front of him, the stock on the ground and the barrel across his lap. Before, he thinks, they notice that my member is standing upright.

"How *many* French?" asks the director-general in a gruff voice.

Quassie Patoe purses his lips and tilts his head back and forth. A little exaggeration can't hurt, he decides. "Five hundred, maybe six."

"Did you see any locals? Villagers collaborating with them? From Eguafo? Komenda? Twifo?"

"Locals? Yes, blacks, Your Excellency Sweerts, plenty of blacks. Those French, they've got it all figured out. Cannons and blacks. Goddamn."

Sweerts furrows his brow. He glances sideways at Abena Gyan with a dark look. "Did you hear anything?" he asks. "Is the king planning something?"

She shrugs her shoulders and shakes her head. Her eyes focus critically on Quassie Patoe. "From Eguafo?" she asks. "Did you see them?"

Quassie Patoe notices a layer of sweat under her nose. She knows nothing, he realizes. She acts as if she's a queen herself, but she's scared. The king wouldn't tell her anything; she's just a woman, only useful because she shares the bed with the white boss. He chuckles to himself. "It was dark," he says calmly. "I'm not sure. Twifo. Komenda. Eguafo. What's the difference?"

Her eyes narrow. Her gaze reveals that she caught the disrespect in his tone. "The king is loyal to the Company," she says. "He will help us."

Sweerts growls. "How did they know the *Westsouborgh* isn't stationed at Elmina? That it sailed off with the *Griffin* toward Benin? That they had free rein, by God?"

"Ships can't go ashore." Quassie Patoe shrugs, but his eyes remain fixed on Abena Gyan. "We don't need anyone. Quassie Patoe commands the asafos. He will throw the French pirates back into the sea."

58 Du Casse Digs In

"(...) Du Casse is a troublemaker and a murderer. Even Louis XIV only admitted him to the French navy after long hesitation and not before Du Casse had offered him half of his pirate loot. He is determined to penetrate the highest circles. His ambitions know no bounds. He has promised his king slaves, despite the lack of French trading posts on the African coast, because what he doesn't have, he will take by force. His Company is a front, a weapon of war in the guise of a trading house. In Arguin, he caused such devastation that the natives fled the island, fearing his cruelties and impulsive actions. He has shipped free natives to the West as slaves, never keeps his word, and only does what serves his own interests, for though he presents himself as a true French patriot, he owns the richest plantation in Martinique, with 2,600 slaves in his service, and he is always in need of fresh forces.

Two years ago, we already apprehended him once when he tried to set up a clandestine trade in Commanie with chiefs, merchants, and anyone who would listen to him. He promises them everything, even French citizenship. He has even sent black envoys to Paris with the empty promise that they would get an audience with the Sun King.

Indeed, I tell you: I am ready to work with the English to permanently drive this French scoundrel from the coast."

From: Letters of Director-General Nicholaas Sweerts to the Gentlemen Ten of the West India Company, January 1688

⚓

The King of Eguafo extends his hand with a smile, almost kindly, his fingers pointing forward. "*Bonjour, monseigneur, je vous salue*," he says in carefully memorized French. "You are a famous man."

Lieutenant Du Casse lightly touches the outstretched fingers. "More infamous, I fear," he says apologetically. "Some seem to think I am a bad man. *Un criminel*."

"The Dutch have indeed made considerable efforts to tarnish your reputation." The king stands upright between his commanders, each of whom is a head taller than he is, but that doesn't seem to bother him. In his right hand, he holds a lion's tail, its tuft swishing back and forth. Behind him, the outline of the Dutch trading post is visible. The pale moonlight illuminates a deserted courtyard. Bats flit noiselessly through the night.

The lieutenant furrows his brow. The King of Eguafo is not known for his loyalty. Du Casse knows he is allied with the Dutch Company and has even married off his daughter to the director-general. Imagine that. Does he now believe the French are winning? Does he think the time is ripe to switch sides? The lieutenant studies the king's somewhat puffed-up face, his cunning eyes, and his gray-white frizzy hair.

"*Oui*," he agrees. "Very unfair, but rumours are persistent. I hope I will be given the chance here to prove my sincerity."

"I came right away," the king says with a quick nod. "It is important for friends to support each other. *Nous sommes amis, n'est-ce pas?*"

"Of course. *Bien sûr.*" The lieutenant flashes his most charming smile. The French invasion force, consisting of a few hundred soldiers and musketeers, wasted no time. Before dawn, they overran Commanie and seized the Dutch trading post. No force was needed; the Dutch were asleep, completely surprised, and the Dutch merchant offered no resistance. It wasn't a grand victory, not at all, but sometimes the smallest gains suffice. Commanie is cut off from the outside world, as is the fishing village of Ampinnie to the east. Now, the French can begin building fortifications. And Du Casse himself will ensure alliances are made—with Eguafo, Komenda, Twifo and anyone else who comes forward. He has plenty of funds.

"But," he adds sympathetically, "I worry about your daughter, Your Excellency."

The king shakes his head and raises a dismissive finger. "No need," he says softly, almost whispering. "The Dutch don't need to suspect anything. I will continue to support them openly. My daughter is an excellent informant." He chuckles. "Director-General Sweerts is very fond of her."

The lieutenant bows his head in appreciation. Very convenient, he thinks. The whore.

"*Non*'," the king confirms proudly, swinging his lion's tail. "No one knows I'm here."

"*Mais*, it's all very complicated," he says a little later after making himself comfortable in the now-abandoned Dutch trading house. He's had mats and rugs brought in and spread out on the floor. Now they sit there, he and his commanders, in the main hall of the building, the king on a small ivory throne surrounded by his two shields and seven enormous elephant tusk horns, his men seated cross-legged around him with their weapons laid out in front: muskets, machetes and assegais. In the cellar, they found a good supply of corn brandy. The jugs have been opened and the glasses brought in. They're enjoying it.

"Who can make sense of it all?" he asks gravely. "The Denkyira and the Ashanti are watching each other closely. If one gains the upper hand, Eguafo will also be in danger. The Twifo threaten our borders. The Ahante are rebellious. In the east, the Fante are advancing. And in the meantime, the whites are at each other's throats."

The lieutenant sits on a wooden chair opposite him, surrounded by brother François and a few of his officers. "There must be stability," he suggests.

"Exactly. But as long as the English and the Dutch keep bashing each other's heads in, there will never be peace. They pit the tribes against each other. The Ahante tried to do business with the Brandenburgers, but the latter aren't strong enough. And the Portuguese have been driven out."

"France is the most powerful country on earth."

"France only has influence in Fida. That's far from here. We've done much to become friends with the French king. Two years ago, we sent ambassadors to La Rochelle. Since then, nothing has changed."

"We're here now," says the lieutenant impatiently. "A company has been established. We want to commit. The French plantations need many slaves."

The king purses his lips. He says, "We can supply slaves, as many prisoners of war as you want, but only if we are strong enough to wage war against the Denkyira, the Twifo and the Ashanti."

"France will help you. We have ships and weapons."

"Big words." The king leans forward, his face showing scepticism. "We are living in the unfortunate days, *monsigneur*. I'll tell you what will happen: the Dutch will come. They don't give up. They'll ask me to support them, and I will agree to their request, but I will not send warriors. In troubled times, we never march into battle, nor do we raise our weapons. I will wait, make empty promises, come up with excuses, and sit on my backside. I promise the French this: if the fortunate days return and you defeat your enemies, we will become allies. If not, we will count our blessings and continue doing business with the Dutch."

The lieutenant leans back in his chair. He drinks from his brandy and smiles reassuringly at the king, but beneath the pretence of camaraderie, his anger burns. The tip of a knife isn't sharp enough for you, he thinks, you cowardly black bastard, now you finally have the chance to break free from the Batavians and what do you do? You crawl back into your hole and let me pull the chestnuts out of the fire. Silently, he promises himself revenge: if I win, I'll make sure you disappear from the stage, I'll kick you into the jungle and into oblivion, take your riches and your horns, and my men will rape your women. That thought calms him a little. "*Bon*," he says, still smiling. "Whatever you wish."

The following morning, he is everywhere at once—having barely slept an hour—stationing guards, directing his men, checking the defensive line. He is anxious. Onboard, with the holds full of French soldiers and musketeers, his attacking force had seemed competent enough, but on land, and without the desired reinforcements, it is merely a paltry little army. From the nearby villages and lands—from Saboe, Acanni, and Cabes-Terra—he has managed to round up loose groups of locals: disgruntled blacks with worn-out muskets, assegais, bows or clubs. A rabble of low rank. Idlers. Thieves. He had to persuade them with promises, gold, goods and endless talk. He's tired of talking.

Now he looks east, where the first light is colouring the sky. Did he act too quickly? No, he decides, how could he have known that the king of Eguafo would abandon him? He had briefly considered launching a swift surprise attack, moving in one fell swoop toward Elmina and taking the castle by surprise, but—upon reflection—he realized it was better to dig in; defending is easier than attacking. They will come, those Batavians, that's for sure. He peers down the deserted path leading to Elmina. He has had a wall of woven branches constructed. It runs from the edge of the forest to the beach, with his men lying behind it, the barrels of their flintlocks poking through the weaving. In the underbrush to the left, a few hundred natives lie in ambush. Three cannons are positioned a bit further on. And beyond the surf lies the *Tempeste*, with her gunports open. Seeing his ship gives him courage. Let them come, he thinks grimly. I'm here to stay.

"God is in heaven and watches over us," says brother François to the group of curious children as he points to the sky. They don't understand him. That's not a problem, he thinks. He observes them. They look poor, not very healthy either. Two of them have yaws: clusters of bumps on their dark skin. He says, "God is good, and Jesus is His son. *Voila.* I will build a church here for Jesus." His hand makes a sweeping gesture, encompassing the flat, grassy hill behind the beach and the river that flows below, winding through ironwood trees and low shrubs. "You will soon come to know Him." He smiles at them kindly and declares, "Jesus is love."

In his mind, he has already built the church—a beautiful white building made of white-plastered stone, with a single tower and a steep roof. A church with a view of the ocean. He imagines the same black children in school uniforms, with healthy, glowing faces. A school, yes. And a hospital. It's an exciting prospect, but only possible if Du Casse can keep the Dutch at bay.

He sighs. Sometimes he thinks the lieutenant is too ambitious. "But God is with us," he says to the group, only to reassure himself. "He will help us, our faith is unshakable." He nods. Yes, he thinks, everything is a test, but God and the Dominicans know the truth. He will teach it to them—the children, the blacks, the slaves. *Contemplari et contemplare aliis tradere.*

He turns his head and surveys the military preparations on the other side of the hill. The musketeers are taking their positions. There will be fighting, he knows, and there will be deaths. He mutters a prayer, concerned for them all, while the children watch him. To praise, to bless, and to proclaim, he thinks, that is my calling. I do not fear the enemy.

59 Battle for Commanie

"(...) If the asafo companies do not assist and support us in the event of an attack by a hostile power or by inland natives, the salaried troops of the Noble Company would not be able to protect us; therefore, it is of the utmost importance to live in harmony with them and cooperate, so that in times of need, we may call upon them for help."

From: letters of Director-General Nicholaas Sweerts to the Councils of the West India Company, January 1688

Director-general Sweerts stands somewhat awkwardly in the square next to Elmina Castle. He is in full regalia, complete with cuirass and helmet, and it feels uncomfortable. He is no soldier, not at all, although, over the years, he has trained in fencing and knows how a snaphaunce works. But he believes it is better to stand here, out in the open, so that everyone can see him because without an ensign, he is militarily decapitated, and everything now depends on him. Moreover, leading the troops can only enhance his reputation.

He smiles, seemingly full of confidence, and looks around. Behind him stand eight squads of white soldiers, led by his sergeants (minus one) and corporals (also minus one) and a small group of mulattoes, together forming five sections—about a hundred men. It's not much, but it's all he can spare, as the rest are needed to man the cannons of the castle and Fort Coenraadsburg. But surrounding them are six full asafo companies, more than three thousand warriors from the native ranks: the Enyampa, the Asamfoe, the Allade, Ancobia, Akim, and Denkyira. Their flags flutter in the wind, their battle cries fill the air. With spears, they strike their leather-covered shields in rhythm with the drums and rattles. He spots Quassie Patoe, standing like a field commander before his men, his snaphaunce raised high. He challenges them, spurs them on, making them sing, roar and stomp, and his long, black body glistens with oil. Sorcerers weave between the rows, holding the skulls of defeated enemies high, visible to all those excited young men who grow increasingly aggressive.

Sweerts lifts his head and feels the warmth of the rising sun. He chuckles and can't entirely suppress a feeling of pride. With a gloved finger, he taps the scab near his mouth. The sore seems to finally be healing. Those Frenchmen, he concludes cheerfully, are going to get a good beating today.

Lieutenant Du Casse hears the singing long before he sees the flags. The path to Elmina seems empty, but the air is filled with a low, persistent hum coming from the east. He quickly glances at the faces of his men. Worried looks are exchanged. They've heard it too.

"Stay calm!" he urges. But the sound isn't what he had expected. This is much larger. It's swelling. And now he can faintly hear rhythmic drumming. Nervously, he walks behind the rows of musketeers. His eyes inspect snaphaunces, pistols and sabres. The men are dead silent now. Their faces are grim, some anxious. The wall of branches across the path suddenly seems very thin and far too low.

"I see something!" someone shouts.

The lieutenant squints, narrowing his eyes. Yes. Now he sees it too. Movement. The sun is shining and the air shimmers. Still far off, swaying up and down, the tops of hundreds of flags and banners appear. And the singing fills his ears. *Zut.* He curses silently and gestures to his officers. "Get ready. Do not fire until I give the order."

Quassie Patoe feels agile and strong. It's as if he has gained extra senses. He sees, smells and feels everything with a precision and clarity he has never experienced before. He isn't tired, even though he hasn't slept all night. If feathers had appeared on his arms, he would have barely been surprised, and he would have flown upwards with ease.

He almost dances along the path under his crocodile-skin cap, right in front of his troops, his feet hardly feel the sharp stones on the road. There's still about a mile to go, plenty of time to revel in the sight of the winding column of warriors behind him. From where he stands, the land slopes down slightly, and he can see far, as far as the road stretches, and there isn't a single spot unoccupied. There they come, the lions of Elmina, warriors like him, because he shaped them himself. He, Quassie Patoe. "Enyampa!" he bellows once more, excited as he is.

"Enyampa!" the vanguard replies. They grin at him. Their faces are eager. Their eyes gleam.

Sweat and blood, Quassie Patoe thinks, and he almost shudders with pleasure.

About half a mile before Ampinnie, the column halts. The singing fades away. The long snake of warriors coils up, the front ranks fanning out into a wide wall of men from the shoreline to the jungle. Sweerts gives measured orders and the sergeants and corporals organize their sections, with the Dutch soldiers at the front and the asafo units forming wing formations on the left and right. Silently, they stand in formation, restless like racehorses waiting for the starting gun.

Sweerts surveys the ranks. He holds his saber in his left hand and his snaphaunce in his right. The sun bakes on his helmet and sweat trickles down his neck. How many enemy soldiers are there? He doesn't know. It doesn't matter. There will never be enough, because the asafo warriors are unstoppable. "Forward," he says grimly. "Let's crush their skulls."

When the enemy's singing stops, the lieutenant knows the battle is near. He listens to the silence, which isn't really silence: he can hear the chatter of weaverbirds, the buzzing of bees and the ocean in the background. The road ahead is still empty, but he can feel them approaching. The tension among his musketeers is palpable. All guns are aimed. Then, slowly but surely, the sound of hundreds, thousands of approaching footsteps begins, accompanied by the clatter of gear and metal striking metal.

"Here they come," he says, gripping his sabre, bracing himself.

The asafo Enyampa takes the far left side of the attack line, with their feet in the sand. Quassie Patoe keeps the line in check: it must stay closed, just a little longer. But they are moving faster and faster. His legs carry him effortlessly. He runs ahead of them, jogging through the sand between the coconut palms. He sees the wall of branches and the barrels of the muskets. Faster and faster he runs. His feet do their work, the sand kicking up behind him, and his men follow. He sees the first puffs of smoke: gunshots. Muskets. Dull bangs. A roar escapes his throat. There's no turning back now. His warriors roar with him. In the front line, the first casualties fall, struck by musket balls. Quassie Patoe doesn't notice. He's at full speed now and the world flies by in a blur. The wall of branches is chest high. It doesn't faze him. He leaps up and clears the obstacle with ease. Like a wild lion, he lands among the enemy, followed by his warriors.

"*Feu!*" roars the lieutenant.

The French gunners light their fuses. The three cannons fire one by one: massive thunderclaps that shake the ground. Aimed at the centre of the attack line, the grapeshot crashes down among the white soldiers. Earth and sand, splinters of wood and palm leaves explode into the air, along with the arms and legs of men. Screams and cries fill the air. A group of black weapon-bearers vanishes in an instant.

But it's futile; the asafo warriors overwhelm the defence. The cannons become useless after one shot—there's no time to reload. The musketeers fire their guns, volley after volley, row after row, but as the enemy draws closer, leaping over the wall of branches, it becomes hand-to-hand combat. There are too many. They slash, strike and cut down everything in their path. They roar and scream. The lieutenant fights back. His sword flashes. But in his mind, he already knows he has lost.

Quassie Patoe is tireless. He has discarded his snaphaunce. They attack him with sabres and swords, with pikes and the butts of muskets, but he dodges them almost effortlessly. His assegai stabs and slices. Blood sprays and spurts. White men bleed too. That pleases him. He sees their pain and their fear, their anger and their death. Each death flows into him. Ferociously, he strikes all around him. His ancestors are there. All of them. And they are content.

Now Sweerts finds himself in the thick of the melee. Frantically, he tries to swing his cutlass left and right, but there is barely any space, and he's struggling just to keep from losing the weapon, just like his snaphaunce, which lies useless somewhere behind him. The press of bodies shoves him forward and back, helpless like a puppet, all he can do is duck away from a sabre, a pike, a knife. No one seems to really notice him. It's as if everyone is fighting with each other, but not with him. It irritates him.

Damn it.

He wriggles between two of his men. For a moment, he can move. He peers ahead and sees a blur of colours, arms and flashing steel. Sweating, his face red, he wrests his cutlass free and thrusts it blindly forward. Resistance. Someone screams. From under the rim of his helmet, he looks up and sees a stunned face.

"*Quoi?*"

A battle-hardened musketeer clutches his belly. Sweerts pulls the cutlass back. To his own surprise, there's blood on the blade. The musketeer collapses to his knees, but Sweerts has no time to think—he's pulled along again by the throng of fighters. A dull blow lands on his helmet, knocking it halfway over his eyes. No time. A French bastard swings an axe at him. Parry. *Dzéng*! The impact is so strong he loses feeling in his right arm. God! His weakened fingers claw at the hilt, but the cutlass slips from his hand. He stumbles back, his breath ragged. He's lucky, because, somehow, there's a bit of space. The axe swishes past him, missing him by a hair. The French bastard disappears, pushed away by other bodies. The sound of panting, straining men. The smell of sweat. Blood. Filth. His legs stumble over a corpse. He falls. Legs everywhere. Feet. Red sand. This is it. They're going to skewer me now. I should have...

Something lifts him up. A strong, black arm.

"Stand up, Your Excellency."

With two arms wrapped around his head, he glances sideways and sees the grinning, blood-splattered face of Quassie Patoe.

"*Sauve-que-peut!*" the French scream. "Every man for himself!" They flee to the waiting longboats, in groups or alone, retreating and fighting. There, they can catch some breath; the sailors, taking cover in the boats, lay down suppression fire and shoot at the pursuing warriors. Chaos ensues. Most of the asafo warriors have thrown away their guns and are now armed only with melee weapons, making them easy targets. Panicked, the musketeers push the boats out to sea.

The lieutenant stumbles through knee-deep water, gasping for breath. With both hands, he pulls at the longboat, helped by about thirty musketeers and sailors. The oars are quickly fitted into the oarlocks.

The boat breaks free from the bottom, bobbing wildly on the water. Men climb aboard, jostling each other, cursing and shouting. Others hold onto the sides, letting themselves be dragged along. The oars splash into the water.

The lieutenant sees a group of black warriors with raised machetes charging towards them. He has no weapons and is defenceless. "Faster, faster, for God's sake!" he shouts.

The French row like madmen. Pistol shots ring out from the boat, and one of the asafo warriors falls face-first into the water. The lieutenant clings to the side with both hands, being dragged along, his legs trailing behind him. The sea grows deeper, waves rolling under the boat. The warriors fall behind, their disappointed howls a relief. But there is no triumph. He watches them, defeated and humiliated. In barely half an hour, his invasion has been utterly crushed.

Sweerts stands on the beach. With a weary gesture, he tosses his helmet to the ground and runs a hand through his hair. It itches. Sweat drips down his nose and chin. His clothes are soaked. Like a true soldier, he feels over his own body, searching for injuries.

Nothing. A miracle.

"Thank God."

The sun bakes the beach, and around him, he sees the battered bodies of the French musketeers—there are more than two hundred. Here and there, a few black men lie on blood-soaked sand. And an arm. A leg. Abandoned weapons. Vultures circle high in the sky. He sighs and stretches his fingers, stiff and aching. From gripping his sabre so tightly, blisters have formed on his palm.

He nods encouragingly to the Dutch merchant standing dejectedly before him.

"I couldn't do anything, sir," the merchant says. "There were too many of them."

"Don't worry," says Sweerts shortly. "We took care of it." His eyes scan the sea. Far off, at the edge of the horizon, he sees the French sails disappearing. Their escape bothers him, but he no longer has any frigates available. God damn it, I would've loved to get my hands on that French bastard. "Go back to your trading post," he grumbles to the merchant. "Perhaps those local traders will tone down their arrogance now."

He turns and looks down the beach. The black warriors are chopping off the heads of fallen enemies, egged on by their sorcerers. The skulls will be kept, as every slain enemy feeds the asafo's sense of invincibility. It's an old custom, very un-Christian, and not something to boast about, but Sweerts has learned to let them have their way after a battle; their bloodlust is not easily sated. Let them blow off steam, he muses, in the end, the palm wine will do its job.

Exhausted, he sits on a wooden beam, still dazed from the fight.

A little further on, his own white soldiers flock together. They smoke pipes, drink brandy, and look indifferently at the asafo warriors, who laugh as they toss around French heads.

Maybe I should be satisfied, he thinks. I'm healthy. I've got money.

And I've got Quassie Patoe.

Across the narrow river, near the remains of the burned-out trading post, stands a small group of Englishmen: a captain, a corporal and a squad of musketeers.

Sweerts isn't surprised; the English may have suffered a minor loss when their trading post went up in flames, but that doesn't mean they've given up on Commanie. On the contrary, you can never get rid of them, he thinks, they're as stubborn as we are, though you'd think they'd have other concerns with all the turmoil in their own country—it's rumoured that William of Orange is preparing an invasion. Yet, despite years of war, despite the skirmishes and countless incidents, he doesn't dislike them. They're competitors, but not ideological enemies like those papists from France or Portugal. You could even say, he smirks, that we've unintentionally done them a favour by driving the French off the coast.

He waves them over with an arm gesture, but only the captain descends the bank and wades through the shallow water to the Dutch side. He's a tall, stiff man in a spotless uniform. Pointed moustache. Square chin. When he reaches Sweerts, he nods politely, his blue eyes darting around, taking everything in. "You've wreaked havoc here, sir," he says in English.

Sweerts nods. "We outnumbered them."

"Damn bold of those French."

"It's not the first time."

"No." The captain stands with his hands behind his back. With his boot, he traces lines in the sand. "There's talk they want to set up missions in Takorari, Commanie and Benin."

"There's nothing here to gain for either Brandenburgers or French."

The Englishman furrows his brow. They avoid each other's gaze, both staring out at the sea. The French ships have now disappeared beyond the horizon.

"Was it Du Casse?" asks the captain.

Sweerts purses his lips. "Perhaps."

"Hm."

A long silence. They stand awkwardly side by side, shoulder to shoulder. The captain draws more lines in the sand with his boot.

"Bloody Frogs," he says.

Sweerts coughs politely. He rubs the blisters on his palm and feels uneasy.

Silently, they watch the asafo warriors as they light their fires, clapping and singing as they perform their rituals. The heads of the French musketeers are laid out in long, straight rows. "Savages," mutters the captain disapprovingly.

Sweerts nods, but reluctantly. Maybe they are savages, he thinks, but there are a lot of them, and they're *mine.*

60 The Storm

"(...) When the sailors see no hope, when their ship is adrift in the storm, when there is nothing more they can do but wait, they say they are drifting 'on mercy,' and in that dark hour, they sing Psalm 107:

Those who go down to the sea in ships, who do business in great waters; they see the works of the Lord, and His wonders in the deep. For He commands and raises the stormy wind, which lifts up the waves thereof. They mount up to the heaven, they go down again to the depths; their soul is melted because of trouble. But when they cry unto the Lord in their trouble, He brings them out of their distresses.

I sang with them, with my heart in my throat. For Satan danced on the waves."

From: a letter by Reverend Duisterbloem to the Deputati Ad Res Exteras Commission of the Classis Amsterdam, Spring 1688

⚓

An unruly sea torments the Bight of Benin. Whitecaps appear on the waves. The *Griffin* struggles against the countercurrent; despite a favourable wind from the southwest, the short waves break her speed and make her roll heavily.

Burghoutsz stands in the binnacle house. He has had the shutters closed and secured with battens, the slaves will remain below deck, as it's too dangerous above. With a worried glance, he checks the weather glass, which shows a spectacularly rapid drop in air pressure. He scans the sky. A flock of shearwaters hurries eastward. Behind them, a solitary brown booby. A fiery red sun sinks into the ocean. They are far from the coast now. Around them, there is nothing but water. "We're in for a storm, maybe a cyclone," he mutters to the helmsman. "Keep her as close to the wind as possible."

Dusk falls, and as he steps onto the quarterdeck, he sees electricity flicker through the water. The sea shivers. He doesn't like it. The mainsail and foresail are reefed. The ship's bell rings three double strokes. He warns the men on the dog watch: "Keep your eyes peeled."

He can't sleep. Throughout the night, he regularly appears on deck. The pressure in the weather glass continues to drop. Boatswain Graauw is now present as well, and both men observe the dark, clear sky. A waning moon shows a faint, misty glow, but the sea itself seems to radiate light, as if a green fire is burning beneath the waves.

"Take down the topgallant masts," Burghoutsz orders. "And rig a preventer stay just in case."

Graauw nods. As a precaution, he has the men of the morning watch bring extra tools from the hold to the forecastle: axes, hatchets and boathooks. Buckets. And rope and canvas. He has already had the longboat lashed tightly to the railing. Tilting his head, he listens to the sea. She moans and groans. She's preparing, of that he's certain.

By morning, the wind shifts. Dark grey, threatening masses of clouds roll in from the east. The sails begin to flap and the *Griffin* lurches on long, rolling waves.

"Aloft!" shouts Graauw, who hasn't been to his bunk all night. "Secure that mainsail before it tears to shreds!"

The crew climbs up. With combined effort, the mainsail is bundled around the yard and fastened with gaskets and seizings.

The wind picks up, coming in from the northeast, blowing the crests of the waves apart. The rigging hums, with notes rising higher and higher. Graauw stares aloft, where the double-reefed sails bear the first slamming gusts. The cloud cover is so thick and dark that the rising sun barely sheds any light.

"Set the storm jib," orders Burghoutsz, gripping the main stay tightly. His eyes scan the deck for the thousandth time, checking everything secured, everything that must be fastened. "Rig lifelines across the waist, I don't want anyone swept overboard."

In the binnacle house, three helmsmen are leaning their full weight on the whipstaff, struggling to keep the ship's bow into the wind. Heavy swells are rolling in from the east and the *Griffin* begins to pitch. Foam sprays white, thick and frothy over the forecastle.

Bomba Jan is bent over in the aft hold, where the enslaved women and children are locked up. It's pitch dark, save for a single lantern he's placed beside him— the *aene* has expressly forbidden any other light. Bomba Jan knows what awaits them. He can feel the fear and tension from the women and children around him. He's warned them, but they don't understand what he means—they've never been at sea.

"Stay in your cages," he shouts once more, as the rolling and pitching grow more violent, making it nearly impossible to stand upright. Bomba Jan grips a beam tightly while holding the lantern steady with one hand.

The ship creaks and groans. The sea pounds against the hull outside, surging, gurgling and foaming, but all the hatches are tightly closed and the gun ports have been caulked as much as possible throughout the night.

He hears the first whimpering. "Nothing's wrong," he calls out to reassure them. But he thinks: this is nothing yet. It's only just begun.

Burghoutsz stands with one foot in the binnacle house and the other on deck, holding onto the lifeline, his eyes darting between the rigging above and the sea beside them. "Hold her steady before the wind, lads!" he says again and again, each time the *Griffin* resists, drifting off course, stubborn, wanting to do her own thing. In the troughs of the waves, she nearly falters, her sails hang limp for a few anxious moments, and that's where the greatest danger lies—she could lose control of the rudder. Once the following sea almost caught them off guard, but luck was on their side, and they managed to turn her bow just in time, right before the green, churning wave could strike them amidships.

"Two feet of water in the bilge, sir," reports the carpenter, and Burghoutsz sets more men to the pumps. Everyone is working, even the exhausted men of the free watch who had been toiling all night, and water sprays in streams from the scuppers.

There they go again. Over the crest of the wave, sliding down the long, transparent side faster and faster, waiting for the calm in the wind, a surreal moment of stillness as if time has stopped, everyone holding their breath, then the next wave picks them up a point abaft the beam, surging beneath, lifting them higher and higher, until they must cling to the lines and the back wall of the binnacle house seems to become the floor. Finally, relief comes as the double-reefed topsails snap full, the howling storm assailing their ears once more, the shock of the surging hull beneath them as the ship picks up speed and listens to the rudder again.

The swirling masses of clouds are black and charged with electricity; it crackles and flashes in horizontal and vertical branches. The wind howls and shrieks, tugging with all its might at ropes and blocks, at stays and sails. Massive ground swells rise up like walls before them. Water washes over the decks, sweeping away anything not tied down.

High above in the rigging, the crew toils. They balance precariously on the shrouds, gripping whatever they can hold, swaying helplessly with the masts. They gather on the tops, where it's relatively safe, until Graauw yells them back up, onward to a new task.

Then comes the rain: without warning, the clouds burst open and the wind drives the water in fierce, lashing sheets almost horizontally across the ship. Lightning flashes. Thunderclaps boom in the sky. Visibility is nearly gone. The sailors mutter prayers under their breath.

Now there is panic. In the darkness of the lower deck, Bomba Jan hears them crying and screaming. With his lantern, he tries to shed some light, tries to be their beacon. "I am here!" he bellows. "Everything is fine!"

But the ship bucks and plunges as if God Himself is shaking it violently in His hands. In the dark, he hears the women helplessly sliding from side to side, moving with the ship's motions across the slick, wet planks, damp with water and piss. He can smell the sharp scent of vomit. They set each other off. But there is no respite. They must endure it. He stumbles toward one of the bunks and grabs at a few random arms and legs. "Goddammit! Hold on!"

A massive crash silences everything for a moment. The ship slams onto the water, and in the darkness, it feels as though they are falling into an endless abyss. The walls tremble and groan. A woman starts screaming. Then the hull rights itself again and shoots almost straight upward. Bodies tumble backward. Screams. Shouts. The children are crying.

But Bomba Jan stays on his feet. As he stumbles and trips along the bunks, holding the lantern in front of him, he sees them appear and disappear in the flickering light, body after body, all faces turned toward him, with frightened expressions and wide-open eyes. He pats heads and shoulders encouragingly, strokes the cheek of a terrified child here and there. "Hold on tight!" he shouts. "Hold on to anything you can grab!" He coughs, overwhelmed by the stench and the lack of fresh air. The darkness moves. The space sways. What is up, what is down?

The wind picks up even more. All sound is drowned out by the howling, roaring storm. *Snap!* Goes the cross-sail. The loose canvas flaps wildly on the crossjack and topsail yard, threatening to tear the rigging apart. Boatswain Graauw shouts and curses, stomping his half-pike on the deck. "All hands! All hands!" He kicks off his clogs and scrambles up the rigging himself. Everyone is clinging to the yards; the wind cuts like a knife and the rain feels like biting sand. The remnants of the sail are gathered and secured, but the ship is nearly uncontrollable now. It pitches and rolls so violently that the sailors hang helplessly from the wood and rigging, fearing for their lives. The *Griffin* shudders from keel to masthead, threatening to broach. The helmsmen deploy the sea anchor, a canvas drag that floats behind the ship to keep its bow into the wind.

Graauw bellows and curses. He climbs the rigging like a monkey, driving the men with hard slaps toward the topsail yard. That cross-sail must be raised again, no matter the cost.

Reverend Duisterbloem is too frightened to be seasick. In the stern cabin, far at the back of the ship, he lies all alone in pitch darkness on his straw mattress, helplessly at the mercy of the storm's fury. He can only remain in place by clinging desperately to the beams of the ceiling. There is no candle, and since he can see nothing, his imagination runs wild: he envisions himself inside the belly of a wild, monstrous creature. A sickening feeling shoots from his stomach to his throat each time the beast dives, throwing itself nearly vertically downward, only to rise again and climb the next mountain of water, with flapping wings. It wails and shrieks, a sound that cuts through to the bone. Occasionally, his trembling fingers reach below him, where his Bible lies under his bony hips, a fleeting sense of reassurance, before he immediately grabs onto the beams above his head again.

Let it stop, he prays, dear God, let it stop.

But the monster growls and snarls. It mocks his fear. Once more, it dives, dragging him into the black depths. He calls upon Jonah, reciting the words by heart, and he bellows: "In my distress I called to the Lord, and He answered me. From deep in the realm of the dead I called for help!"

Halfway through the night, the foremast snaps. It sounds like a gunshot. Wood splinters and is sucked away by the storm. Spars, sheets, braces and halyards break loose, the shrouds snap like threads, and the foresail disappears with one sweeping motion into the sea. The screams of four sailors swept overboard are drowned out by the roar of the wind. They vanish into the water, never to be seen again. The forecastle deck tears apart, the forward windlass breaks off and blocks on cables swing like deadly projectiles across the deck.

Far behind, Graauw and a few sailors cling to the mizzenmast. Helplessly, with resigned eyes, they watch the skewed, vague outline of the foremast, leaning over to starboard.

"What now?" shouts one of the sailors, clinging to the topsail yard with arms and legs. His voice is barely audible, and Graauw's face is just a blur in the driving rain. His square shoulders stand dark against the rising walls of water behind him. His bloodied, wrinkled fingers grip the canvas. High in the air, in darkness, rain and wind, they have, in a few hours, cobbled together a new cross-sail as best they could.

Graauw shakes his head. He does what he can. But sometimes it's too much. His whole body trembles—whether from exhaustion, worry, or maybe fear. He doesn't answer, he must gather new strength.

Bomba Jan is exhausted too. He lies on his stomach, clutching the bars of a bunk while children cling to his arms and legs. His candle is out and gone. There is nothing but darkness, there is nothing more he can do. He is insignificant. His arms ache. His fingers cramp. His face is scraped, and he is bruised and battered all over. The children whimper and moan, but their resistance has ceased, they are as tired as he is, enduring the violence of the storm, half-conscious and beaten into submission. The ship dives and climbs, pitches, crashes and tumbles. Water slams against the sides, washes across the floor, streams over their faces and along their limp bodies. Bomba Jan listens to the ship. But he does not despair; pain is life, and he still hears her heartbeat.

With ropes, the crew tied themselves together in groups. The last man in each row is fastened to a cleat, so if someone is swept away, the rest will hold him back. It's the only safety they have. Now they struggle on the forecastle and the gallion as the waves crash towards them, with foam-topped crests between breaking cross-seas. They chop at the tangle of rigging, ropes and wood with axes and cutlasses. The foremast hangs at an impossible angle over the starboard side, dragging the foretopmast and torn sails through the water. The wind strikes from the side. The ocean pulls and tugs, determined to crush them, but the crew refuse to give in. With grim faces, they try to clear the ship, standing knee-deep in the swirling, glowing water.

61 Confrontation at Sea

"Masters, give your slaves what is just and fair, knowing that you also have a Master in heaven."

From: The Bible, Colossians 4:1

⚓

Days Later.

The *Tempeste* only suffered the tail end of the storm. By the time she reached the Bight of Benin, the worst had passed. Together with her sister ship, she had ridden the heavy swell, rolling and pitching with her bow into the wind, but she was never truly in danger. Now, the sun shines again, and the wind has calmed to a cooling breeze.

Yet the mood is bleak.

The lieutenant has locked himself in his cabin. No one is allowed to see him. Shame and rage vie for dominance. He slouches in his chair, unshaven and dishevelled, battling his emotions and drinking wine from morning till night. The humiliation is unbearable. He concocts scenarios for revenge, imagining himself punishing, killing or crushing the king of Eguafo in every conceivable way, not to mention the Dutch, and especially those damned Elmina negro bands he had so severely underestimated. Deep down, he knows it's his own fault; he was too complacent, too sure of himself, too arrogant. By God. He would give anything, *anything*, to turn back time and start over.

In his desperation, on the 19th of January, he fired his guns indiscriminately at the Dutch occupiers in Taccorary, but without any plan. The settlement was nothing more than a ruin and there was nothing to gain there. The few Batavians fired back half-heartedly with poorly aimed twenty-four pounders. A waste of time and ammunition.

Where to go? Fida? Offra? Issiny? No. They would mock him behind his back. It is better to reflect. Until then, he will continue sailing, perhaps aimlessly, but far from the coast, hidden from French eyes.

Helpless, he searches for something to hold on to, something that can give him new purpose, something that can save him from disgrace at home in France or the West Indies. That need must be fulfilled; no man can live with such a stain on his name. The lieutenant curses. That haughty, noble clique! But it will not happen again. By God. Honour is everything.

He steadily drinks his wine, glass after glass, and in the loneliness of the night, he sees the dead musketeers—*his* musketeers—on the shore, in the waves, among the trees, beheaded, stripped of all dignity, slaughtered like pigs.

By midday, he is jolted out of his lethargy by a loud knock on the cabin door. It makes him instantly furious. "*Casse-toi*! I don't want to be disturbed!"

A muffled, hesitant voice responds from behind the door. He recognizes his first mate. "A ship, lieutenant, what are your orders?"

"What kind of ship?"

"A full-rigged ship. Possibly a Dutchman with heavy damage, likely from the storm."

"Eh?"

The lieutenant awakens.

"She's down to two masts," he observes, peering through his spyglass. "Her fore is gone." His own voice sounds hollow in his ears. He has emerged from the cabin with his head bowed, carefully avoiding the gazes of his men. In the waist, along the bulwarks, wounded musketeers lie out in the open. They bear gunshot and stab wounds, sprained and broken limbs, bruises, welts and bumps. He feels their eyes on him. What are they thinking? Are they mocking him? No one speaks, the silence is oppressive.

On the quarterdeck, he only has to endure the presence of his officers, and with the wind in his face, he feels slightly better; it clears away the fog of alcohol. "Is it truly a Dutchman?" he asks again and again. He can't make out the flag, the ship is still too far away.

"*Une flûte*[*]!" calls the lookout from the masthead.

The helmsman looks at him triumphantly. "*Voila*, a Batavian," he says confidently.

He orders more sail to be set and the yards to be braced fully. The French ships pick up speed, the wind is favourable, and they heel slightly to starboard, moving in perfect unison with the long, slow swell from the southwest. Through his spyglass, he watches the Dutch ship struggle: she carries topsails and topgallants on her two remaining masts, but the mainsail hangs awkwardly, there are provisional clamps around the topmasts, and she's flying a makeshift triangular foresail, stretching from the bowsprit to the main topsail yard. Unstable, slow, and sitting too deep in the water. Yes, the storm has beaten her up badly, he concludes. That feels good. His anger now grows stronger, overpowering his shame. There, in the distance, he might have found something on which to vent his frustration. A Dutchman in distress. By God. His hands itch.

"She's taking on water," notes his helmsman, who has sharp eyes.

The lieutenant nods. And that draft—damn it, he'd bet his life it's a slave ship. Could fortune be turning? Could he finally catch a break? A full load of blacks could never erase his defeat, but still—it would give him something to show for it, at least some value.

"Prepare to board," he commands, his voice sounding stronger now. "And open the gun ports."

Now he can meet his men's eyes. He descends the steps into the waist and walks past the mattresses. The musketeers lie side by side, their heads resting against the bulwark. They stare at him with empty gazes; they are like him—humiliated and defeated. The lieutenant crouches beside a soldier with a thick, bloodied bandage wrapped around his head. "How are you holding up, *garçon*?"

No sound. The musketeer shakes his head. He can't speak.

---

[*] A typically Dutch fluteship.

The lieutenant nods, understanding. He feels he must say something, something reassuring, but it's difficult to find the right words. "Those damned *noirs* got the better of us, didn't they?" His fingers awkwardly pat the soldier's arm. The musketeer reeks of sour sweat and vomit. I forgot my handkerchief, he thinks, holding a hand to his nose. "You'll be fine, lad. *Courage*." He peers over the bulwark. The distance between them and the Dutch ship has significantly shortened. He can see the flag: red, white, blue. "We're going to board that Batavian," he continues, trying to sound upbeat. "An easy target. Big prize. Maybe it wasn't all in vain."

The musketeer still doesn't respond. He lies limp on his mattress, his hands by his sides. His eyes are closed, which the lieutenant finds disappointing. He likes making friends, pretending camaraderie with the common soldiers, but in the presence of sickness and death, all his charm evaporates.

As he stands, he sees brother François approaching. That doesn't sit well with him either. But he hesitantly raises his hand.

Brother François has a strange, wild look in his eyes. In Commanie, he barely escaped with his life, so terrified that he soiled himself as he scrambled into the longboat, fighting for a spot like everyone else, driven by primitive instincts. He lowers his head. "We have been punished," he mutters shakily. "God is not with us."

"It had nothing to do with God," the lieutenant replies firmly. "It was an overwhelming force, that's all."

Brother François looks at him blankly, his hands trembling. He points toward the Dutch ship. "Are you going to attack them again? Isn't it enough? How many more French deaths will weigh on your conscience?"

"I don't think that..."

"You promised us a church!"

"*Zut*! The dead will be avenged, frère François. Direct your anger at the Batavians." The lieutenant feels embarrassed; the musketeers around them are listening. What is that monk thinking? Damn it. He doesn't have to justify himself. "They'll pay," he says tersely. "By God."

He strides away from all the misery, from the naysayers and doom-mongers, from the cowards and quitters, the wounded and the dead, from everyone who doesn't share his ambitions. No wonder we were defeated, he thinks angrily. They weigh you down like a stone, stopping you from moving forward. It's been like this his whole life: swimming against the current. "Get the wounded below deck," he shouts. "This is a warship, *au nom de Dieu*!"

In the cabin of the *Griffin*, a dim light prevails, as three of the stern windows have been shattered in the storm and replaced with wooden boards. On the large table, candles flicker, casting a faint glow. The air smells stale and musty. The table is strewn with maps.

Skipper Burghoutsz sits gloomily at the head. His eyes, lacking much sympathy, study the representative of the Chamber of Assurance and Damage. The representative hasn't been invited to sit. He stands on the other side of the large table, a small, scrawny man with a greasy drooping moustache, clearly uncomfortable aboard. He sways nervously and fidgets with his mouth. "The French," he says, "will attack us. They want the slaves."

Burghoutsz nods. For what feels like the hundredth time, he glances at the cargo manifest in front of him. Four hundred and fourteen slaves. Insured. And during the storm, they had done everything to save them. He asks, "What happens if I hand them over to that Frenchman?"

The representative shakes his head. "That's not covered. You'd be surrendering voluntarily."

"It is voluntarily while I'm under threat?"

"You could put up resistance, even if only briefly." His voice trembles slightly, just like the hairs of his moustache. "I tell you this because I have to. It's in the terms."

Burghoutsz leans back. "You could adjust your report."

"And commit fraud?" The representative wags a disapproving finger. "With all these witnesses? Even if your men were to lie for you, every single one of them—an unlikely scenario—those Frenchmen would boast about it openly. They'd make sure the world knows, and sooner or later word would reach the Company. In that case, an inquiry would follow, along with liability and ultimately punishment—I guarantee you."

"If we fight, we're done for. That includes you. They're too many, and my ship is hardly seaworthy anymore."

The representative sighs in frustration. "Resistance is a flexible term," he suggests. "You don't have to sacrifice everyone."

They look at each other, Burghoutsz with a contemptuous curl at the corner of his mouth.

"You mean," he finally says, "that I can surrender with a clear conscience after ten or fifteen of my men are dead. Is that what you're saying?"

"I didn't make the rules, skipper."

Burghoutsz waves his hand in disgust. "Thank you for your insight, sir. I've heard enough."

The two French frigates break formation: the *Tempeste* turns on her heel, the yards swing around, but she keeps the windward side and sails behind the Dutch ship, crossing her wake, while the sister ship takes the other side, lagging slightly, a point or two, to avoid getting caught in the lee. It's not a difficult manoeuvre; the *Griffin* is easily overtaken.

The lieutenant stands on his quarterdeck, inspecting the enemy ship. Up close, it's worse: a heavily damaged forecastle, the anchor windlass gone, but the bowsprit reinforced with extra stays and shrouds, with a double stay on the main mast, allowing it to carry both sprit and jib sails. Well done. Smart thinking. He sees sailors scurrying around the mizzen rigging like little puppets. "They're reeving new lines," he mutters to himself. Well, he thinks, you have to give those Batavians *some* credit; they know how to sail a ship. He sees the boatswain on the half-deck, the helmsmen in the binnacle house, and the skipper on the quarterdeck. No uniform. Bareheaded. Hm. A captain should be properly dressed, he thinks, even if his ship is falling apart. He himself wears a light blue coat with puffed breeches, brown boots and a wide-brimmed hat; clothes make the man. He gestures curtly to his first mate. "Take the wind out of her sails."

The *Tempeste* carefully closes in, positioning herself one point aft to port, less than a quarter of a cable's length from the Dutch ship, immediately stealing her wind. The *Griffin* comes to a halt, her sails suddenly hanging limp.

"Reef!" the lieutenant shouts triumphantly. He has her trapped. He wants to keep her within range. Both ships now lie almost perfectly broadside. A silence falls. The sea splashes beneath the bow. To starboard, the threatening French sister ship waits, her double row of gunports open, ready to enfilade. French and Dutch sailors stare at each other.

The lieutenant beckons his interpreter, who holds a brass speaking trumpet. "Translate my words," he says.

On the other side, skipper Burghoutsz listens to the voice, which reaches him hollow but loud and clear. "Surrender," it says. "If you do what I say, nothing will happen to you. Your ship is damaged. There's nothing you can do. Give me your cargo and you're free to go."

He doesn't move a muscle. He observes the man in the light blue coat, studying him closely. The Frenchman is tense, full of impatience. He thinks: how far are you willing to go? Are you Du Casse? His gaze shifts to the sky. The air is blue, the wind is dying down even further, barely noticeable now, the waves are smooth and the swell feels like silk. You may have the windward side, but how quickly can you get out of my range with this dwindling breeze? Are you willing to fight yourself?

As soon as they had spotted the French that morning, he had the bulkheads on the gun deck removed. Now, below deck stretches a single open space, with wet duffel blankets between the cannons and tubs of slow-burning match cord down the central passage. A thick layer of sand covers the deck floor. "Open the gunports," he orders decisively. "I'll sell my skin dearly."

Boatswain Graauw doesn't hesitate for a second. "Broadside to port!" he shouts.

The lieutenant furrows his brow as the Dutchman's gunports open. Twelve cannon barrels reveal their muzzles, and from this close, he can see the shadows of the crew moving behind them. What's this? Is that Batavian insane? Does he want to fight? Damn, they've rigged splinter nets and reinforced their yards with lashings and leg irons.

They stare at each other, from quarterdeck to quarterdeck.

"What's your cargo?" he has his interpreter ask.

The skipper on the other side now holds a speaking trumpet to his mouth as well. "Slaves," he answers truthfully.

"How many?"

"Enough."

"I want them."

"Come and get them."

"*Zut.*" The lieutenant bites his lip. He hesitates. If he opens fire, he'll lose his prize. If he boards, he risks the lives of his remaining musketeers. In a fit of anger, he snatches the speaking trumpet from his interpreter's hands. He thinks: I'll be damned if that Batavian doesn't know a few words of French. "*Imbécile*! I'll blast you to God!" he shouts furiously through the horn.

The signaller in the main mast top flags to the sister ship. Immediately, she sets more sail and slowly but surely positions herself on the starboard side of the *Griffin*, one cable length away. The midship gunport on the second deck suddenly spews fire and smoke. The sound follows a moment later: a muffled boom. Just behind the Dutch ship, the sea explodes. Water shoots up and then falls back down, in a shower of thick droplets over the stern, the gilded ornaments and the quarterdeck.

"The next one will hit!" the lieutenant bellows. "I'm not letting you go!"

Skipper Burghoutsz stands rigidly upright. The droplets fall over him, soaking his shirt. The Frenchman shouts through the speaking trumpet, but Burghoutsz doesn't understand. He doesn't care.

"He's determined, skipper," says Graauw from the quarterdeck. "We're caught in the vice."

The skipper lifts his head. Squinting, he looks at the *Tempeste*. He says, "Give her one back."

"What?"

"Eight-pounder. Midship. Full force."

Now Graauw hesitates. He glances at the binnacle house, where the helmsmen stand. Their faces show concern, but no one says a word.

"They're going to finish us off, skipper."

"Do as I say."

The blast of the eight-pounder is not as loud, and the force isn't enough to pierce the *Tempeste's* timbers, but even so, the lieutenant is stunned. The shot hits his frigate right at the broadside, between the two gundecks, almost midship, and the impact makes him flinch. Shrapnel tears into the frames, ripping away chunks of planking, and flies like bullets through the gunports. Dazed, the crew lets the French ship drift slightly away, backing off from that mad Dutchman.

The lieutenant peers at Burghoutsz, who stands like a statue on his deck, hands behind his back. Stubborn fool, he thinks, *salaud*, you're betting that I won't tear you to pieces, that I know the value of your slaves. But, by God, I'll get you. "Bring the musketeers on deck," he orders calmly. "Let's see if he can fight."

Burghoutsz watches as the soldiers appear. They fill the French waist deck, and there are more of them than he expected. He himself has no more than seventy men, and though they are tough, they are not soldiers.

"It's over, skipper," the first mate behind him says almost with relief. "A man-to-man fight is pointless, they'll bash our heads in. We have nowhere to go."

Burghoutsz doesn't respond. He looks at the insurance representative, standing pale as a ghost at the back of the quarterdeck. He listens to the ocean. The wind has died down further, there's hardly any swell. The three ships move sluggishly with the waves. He lifts the speaking trumpet to his mouth. In French: "If you come any closer, I'll fire my twenty-four-pounders!"

He turns to boatswain Graauw again. "Fetch Bomba Jan."

62 The Fall of Bomba Jan

"And cast the worthless slave into the outer darkness. In that place there will be weeping and gnashing of teeth."

From: The Bible, Matthew 25:30

⚓

Bomba Jan sits gloomily by the companionway to the orlop deck, his back against a coil of rope. He is tired; in the past few days, he has barely slept, and he's beginning to wonder if this journey is cursed. The storm was bad enough, but now another disaster looms, and it feels too much like a bad omen. Are the ancestors angry? Is it Onyame? Or the white man's God? He sighs. Below him, he hears the male slaves, their chains, their voices. They're scared, just like he is. Will the Frenchman take the slaves? Will he himself end up a slave, too? He has no illusions: a black man is a black man. All blacks at sea are saltwater slaves.

He hears shuffling above him. The main hatch slides open a little. Daylight breaks through the darkness and a face becomes visible. "Bomba Jan, the skipper wants to see you."

The *aene's* face has a strange expression, Bomba Jan thinks. Tight. Jaw clenched. And his eyes have a peculiar gleam. Almost feverish. He studies Bomba Jan long and hard. The *aene* says, "They want to steal our slaves, Bomba Jan. We can't let that happen."

"No, *aene*."

"Remember those men you marked with paint at the castle? The troublemakers?"

"The nine?"

"Exactly, yes, the nine. Bring them up, Bomba Jan."

Bomba Jan climbs back down. Through the hatch. Down the stairs to the orlop deck. Darkness and foul air reign there. With a lantern, he crawls on his hands and knees past the benches. There is a palpable, nervous tension.

"What's happening, Bomba Jan?"

"Are they going to fight?"

"Free us, bomba, save us."

Bomba Jan doesn't answer.

The nine are in the back, separated from the rest, laid head to foot, foot to head. They look at him, their eyes glittering in the orange light of the lantern.

"You need to go up," he says.

They don't like that. "Why?" one of them asks.

Bomba Jan shakes his head. He doesn't know. Does the skipper plan to hand them over to the French? As a bribe? Maybe. Could be. Yes, the *aene* looked strange. Angry. Furious even. But it's useless to speculate. He fiddles with the locks, pulls the chain through the slot. "Get out, hurry up," he says brusquely.

Up the stairs to the deck. The nine, stiff-limbed, slowly stand up on the gun deck. They try to adjust to the light filtering through the hatch above. Bomba Jan ties them together with ropes, leaving a little slack between each man. Two shipmates stand a little way off, their long knives drawn, their faces serious. Not a word is spoken.

Bomba Jan looks at Quameno Ewussi. For the first time, there is a look of uncertainty in the slave's eyes.

Through the hatch onto the main deck. Light. Warmth. Blue sky. The ocean sparkles, the water is almost smooth. Bomba Jan holds the rope, the nine hesitantly following behind him. He looks to the right, where the crew has gathered, waiting for what's to come. Then he looks to the left and up, towards the boatswain on the quarterdeck. Beyond that, one level higher, stands the skipper. The skipper seems not to have moved the whole time. Bomba Jan addresses the boatswain. The sun shines directly into his eyes, forcing him to raise his hand to shield his face. "Ready, boss. Here they are."

The lieutenant closely watches the events on the Dutch ship. He senses something is about to happen. On the waist deck, he sees ten black men appear: nine naked slaves and one bomba. He thinks, *merde*, those men look good. Those are Guinean slaves. His greed grows. What are they going to do? Are they going to use them as shields? He looks up, where his sailors stand by the yards, ready to set sail. But there's almost no wind left, damn it, barely a breeze, and to port he can see completely flat patches of sea. What if that Dutchman fires his guns? There are dozens of wounded men on the battery deck. Do I sacrifice them? Do I even care? On his own deck, the musketeers crowd together. They look over the rail at the other side, eager to take action, to get revenge. The humiliation runs deep with them too.

He makes a decision, raises his hand. "Set all sails," he growls. "We'll catch whatever wind is left. And if that's not enough, we'll row her with our bare hands if we have to—but he *will* yield."

Skipper Burghoutsz watches as the *Tempeste* sets her mainsails, topsails and topgallants. They fall from the yards, buntlines and sheets are pulled tight. What little wind there is lightly fills the canvas, and the ship groans into slow motion, turning its bow toward the *Griffin*, about three hundred feet away, pushing the seemingly oily sea ahead of it.

"They're coming," mutters the first mate. "God help us."

All the crew now stand on deck, armed with muskets and pistols, cutlasses and swords, knives, blunderbusses and anything else they could find: clubs, boat hooks, machetes and axes. Someone begins to pray and the voice echoes over the ship. It's Reverend Duisterbloem, who has appeared on the quarterdeck, holding his Bible. "We have sinned against the Lord; we shall rise and fight as the Lord our God has commanded us!"

The crew hears the words. Some nod or call out "Amen," determined to sell their lives dearly.

Burghoutsz surveys the decks and slowly shakes his head. His jaw is clenched so tightly that his mouth is just a thin, straight line. A vein visibly throbs in his neck. He beckons to Bomba Jan, standing apart from the crew. "No Frenchman will take our slaves, Bomba Jan!" He points to the nine slaves that the bomba holds by a rope. "Throw them overboard."

Bomba Jan stares at his captain with a look of disbelief, the rope hanging loosely in his hands. He thinks maybe he didn't hear the *aene* correctly. The words grind through his mind. Overboard? How overboard? Into the water? And then? What if they can't swim? How can they swim with those shackles on? It's impossible. They'll sink—the ocean is deep. He looks at the nine men, one by one. They stand there lost, with confused expressions. They can't speak Dutch, but they sense that something's wrong, and they pull back, tugging at the rope.

Bomba Jan pulls back too. He wraps the end of the rope around a cleat and ties a knot in it. "Wait here," he says, unnecessarily. He runs across the main deck to the stairs leading to the quarterdeck. The boatswain is there. "I didn't hear it right, boss," he calls out, desperate. "Can you say it again?"

Boatswain Graauw nods, looking just as uncertain. He turns around and addresses the skipper, standing above them at the rail of the poop deck. "The bomba doesn't understand, skipper," he says. "And neither do I."

Burghoutsz stands with his back to the sun. His face is in shadow. "You heard me," he says with restrained anger. "Overboard with them."

"You mean ... into the water?"

"Into the water, boatswain."

"Permission to come up, skipper?"

"Permission denied."

Graauw stands motionless, indecisive, staring up. His eyes search the skipper's face. He stammers, "I don't believe that..."

The skipper suddenly moves. With a curse, he rushes to the stairs, swinging down, striding across the quarterdeck and leaping into the waist. He grabs Bomba Jan by the shirt and drags him toward the nine waiting men. "What's unclear, Bomba Jan?" he hisses, slapping Bomba Jan on the back of the head. "Have you forgotten all your languages? Do I need to repeat it, in Akan or in Twi? By God, will you obey my orders?"

Bomba Jan cringes. He wants to obey, but how can he throw healthy, strong men into the water? "It's wrong, *aene*," he cries out.

The skipper curses again. He kicks Bomba Jan. "Wrong?" he shouts. "Since when does a wretched *nigger* dare to defy the will of his skipper?" He shoves him aside in anger, grabs the rope, and yanks the knot loose. "No one steals our slaves!" he roars at the crew, who silently watch. "*You don't give up what's yours!*" Backing up, he drags the bound prisoners across the deck.

Quameno Ewussi watches the commotion with growing unease. He despises Bomba Jan, whom he sees as nothing more than a filthy, black-painted white, but he can also sense that, somehow, Bomba Jan is standing up for him. Quameno Ewussi knows that the *aene* is untouchable, higher in rank than God Himself, you could say, so if even a grovelling pig like Bomba Jan is objecting, then something has to be very wrong. He can see that the *aene* is furious—he has never heard him raise his voice before, much less seen him strike someone. He feels the nervousness and fear of the Dutch sailors. Quameno Ewussi thinks that the white men on the other ships are coming to get him. Slaves are valuable. He knows that well. But the *aene* refuses to back down. So what is he planning? The Dutch ship is damaged, and they are outnumbered two to one. What does a trapped animal do? It's dangerous. The *aene* will do anything to survive. That thought makes him nervous. Quameno Ewussi has a very bad feeling.

The *aene* tugs on the rope. The nine follow, shuffling their feet, and Quameno Ewussi is the last in line. He sees Bomba Jan sitting on the deck, his dignity gone, like a dog that has been beaten. Their eyes meet for a moment, and Bomba Jan quickly looks away. Quameno Ewussi is shocked. If Bomba Jan can't even meet his eyes, what is about to happen? Why aren't we resisting?

Then he notices the portside rail of the ship. In the middle is a hinged section that is now open, like a little gate, for people to board and disembark. That is where the *aene* is heading. Does he want to go off-board? Is he going to put them on the other ship?

The *aene* keeps pulling the rope, but the first man in line stops just short of the gate. He resists by planting his feet wide apart. He is a large, very strong man, and the *aene* can pull all he wants, but he isn't budging. The first man turns his head, his eyes wide with fear, his face twisted in terror. Sweat beads on his forehead as he shouts in Akan, "The white man wants to throw us into the water!"

Quameno Ewussi feels a stab of fear. He looks around and sees nothing but hostile, white faces. The *aene* shouts at the sailors, and suddenly, there are hands, countless hands, and angry shouts, and Quameno Ewussi is half-lifted and pushed forward. It's now impossible to brace himself. He's powerless, being dragged along, and there's the open gate, and he sees the man in front of him stumble and slide across the deck towards the gap in the railing, sideways, with his legs trailing behind.

And now Quameno Ewussi falls too—he curses and cries for help, but no one listens. His hands find the railing, and his fingers grip the edge of the wood, but only for a moment, the force is too great, the sailors push him forward while the slaves tied to the rope in front of him pull him toward the edge. His fingers slip, and now he can see the sea below him, dark green and smooth, and there he goes, falling down after the others. The sudden slap of the water (surprisingly cold) hits him. He tastes salt in his mouth and hears a deep, bubbling sound. He tries to scream, but the water closes over him, and his throat only makes a weak, groaning noise. Above him, the sun glitters in beams through the green water, with the ship looming like a massive, shadowy block in the centre of his vision and schools of small fish darting through the light. He moves his arms, but the shackles prevent him from swimming. There's no air. His lungs ache. And his shock slowly gives way to understanding. The rope tugs at his waist and the chains are heavy; he sinks, spiralling downward into a dark abyss. And there, just below him, he sees a line of eight men, connected by the rope, their faces in mute comprehension, slowly vanishing into the void.

63 On Board with the Devil

"By whom a person is overcome, by him he is also brought into bondage."
From: The Bible, 2 Peter 2:19

The *Tempeste* fires her guns, unexpectedly and ruthlessly, two shots from the forecastle. The cannons blast over the water, and thick, dirty white clouds of gunpowder billow to leeward towards the Dutch ship. The *Griffin* is struck aft: heavy, solid balls smash hot and searing against her hull, piercing through beams and ribs, causing chaos in the chief gunner's room just below the cabin. The defenceless ship lurches oddly. Already crippled, she now takes another pounding. The sea churns and swells beneath the heaving. The gunpowder smoke drifts slowly across the ship, hanging like a yellowish haze over the decks. A fire breaks out. But no one notices.

Madness descends.

Reverend Duisterbloem watches as a sudden thick mist rises, covering the ship and rendering it almost invisible. There is the smell of saltpetre and sulphur, and he hears the explosions and feels the trembling and shaking of the wood so that he has to hold on to the railing of the quarterdeck. Right before him, in the waist, the embodiment of Evil reveals itself, a vision of inhumanity that takes his breath away. Led by the skipper, the sailors swarm across the decks, with contorted, furious faces, in pairs and groups, and together they violently drag the slaves from the orlop deck, pulling them across the gangway through the main hatch, dragging them to the portside railing and hurling them into the sea. There is no justice, no reflection, no mercy. The blacks beg and resist, they fight and struggle, they scream, cry and moan, but they are hindered by their shackles, and those who resist too much are mercilessly beaten down. He sees how the young boys, who not so long ago had treated him to roasted millers, are thrown overboard with combined force. The people in the water grab onto each other, dragging each other down, buried by new bodies that land with great force on the surface of the water.

The reverend trembles with disgust and fear: he is now certain that he has ended up in hell. Yes, he thinks, the storm has indeed dragged us into the depths. We are under the world. He clutches his Bible tightly, his knuckles and fingers white, and mutters incomprehensible prayers. There are so many impressions that he can no longer take in the individual images; only chaos, a tangle of people, a struggle of bodies, a hum of sound, and he could swear he sees Satan himself, high above him on the yards and in the rigging: a scrambling, dancing and jumping devil with red skin, curved horns and a forked tail. The creature laughs and shrieks, it cheers with every splash into the water, and it points at him and screams: "That's what you get, Duisterbloem! With your pale prick in a lustful black whore! I will punish you!"

Duisterbloem falls to his knees and stretches out his right arm. His Bible held high. "No!" he whispers, and with closed eyes, he recites the incantatory, threatening words from Ezekiel: "Now the end has come upon you, for I will send My fury against you, and I will bring upon you all your abominations, and I will not spare you!"

Bomba Jan weeps. Snot drips from his chin. With his back against the railing and his buttocks on the deck, he is nothing more than a spectator now, ignored by everyone and everything. There is nothing he can do. The little authority he had is gone; he is not even deemed worthy of being thrown into the sea.

When he looks up at the sky, he sees the sun. The light blinds him, and prisms shift in his tears in all the colours of the rainbow. It hurts, it stings, and it burns, but Bomba Jan prefers blindness to the sights on the deck. He wants to see nothing more.

The devil grins at Reverend Duisterbloem. 'I'm not done yet,' he says. 'Believe me, it can always get worse.'

A sharp, triangular dorsal fin cuts through the water. The crew freezes in their tracks, staring down. From the deck, the creature is clearly visible: a gray, nine-foot-long back glides past, followed by a slowly swaying, scythe-shaped tail. It seems to be sizing up the blacks fighting for their lives on the surface, circling cautiously. Large, expressionless eyes dart back and forth. The drowning men begin to wail and frantically splash at the water. The shark doesn't react. For a moment, it seems to hover still, then swims in fluid, zigzagging movements downward into the depths, disappearing into the blue-green darkness.

The crew stretches their necks, their faces filled with superstition; they all remember the devilfish they hauled out of the water just over a week ago.

"By God, it's back," one of them says.

"There it comes again!" shouts another.

A dark shadow rockets upward like a bullet. Suddenly, one of the slaves seems to leap from the sea with superhuman strength, his arms stretched out in front of him. Beneath him, the shark twists around its own axis, breaking the surface, with its tail higher than its head, its white belly gleaming, and two long, dangling sex organs in plain sight. The crew stares in disbelief: for a split second, the man and shark perform a silent, macabre aerial dance together. Then they fall back, and the water begins to churn and foam. There's blood. The sudden scent acts like a signal. No one knows where they come from. Hundreds of fins.

And the sea turns red.

The lieutenant can't believe his eyes. Stunned, he watches the chaos aboard the Dutch ship and the massacre in the water. He raises his hand makes a cutting gesture to his helmsmen, who—just like him—are staring open-mouthed to starboard. There's no point in boarding, he thinks. What is there to do? Fight over dead blacks? How many are already in the water? Two hundred?

He sees his musketeers crowding the railing. Should he sacrifice them just to stop a mad Batavian?

He shakes his head.

Non.

Black fins dart through the water. The scent of blood is so strong that the sharks are driven into a feeding frenzy. They attack everything, even biting at the hull of the ship. They snap at each other, devouring one another. The water is dark red. Seagulls fill the air with their screeching.

"What a filthy mess," the lieutenant sighs, turning his face away in disgust.

64 Ruination

"Shall be put to death: he who speaks strongly and forcefully against slavery."

Confucius, Hun Tsu: Tso Yu

"I do not know what happened. I saw him off, and all was well. There are no witnesses. But I never trusted him. He was a tormented man."

From: Testimony of Director-General Nicholaas Sweerts to the Council of the Dutch West India Company, Winter 1688

⚓

Below decks, Gillis Graauw stands like a bodyguard before the entrance to the women's quarters, his legs slightly apart, holding a half-pike in his left hand and cat-o'-nine-tails in his right. He knows they will come. Once they're done with the men, they'll want the women and children. He clenches his teeth and shakes his head firmly. No, even if they are blacks, heathens or slaves. He knows he can't hold them off for long, there are too many of them, and they've all gone mad. Damn bastards. He plants his feet a little wider.

The first group descends the stairs noisily. In the dim light of the lower deck, he can only see their silhouettes. The clattering of clogs and shoes, the waving of knives and clubs. Gillis spreads his arms, and when they see him, silence suddenly falls. "You're not getting past me," he growls.

They hesitate, looking at each other. "Orders from the skipper," one of the sailors mutters.

"Don't care." Gillis angrily thumps the deck with the half-pike. He stares the sailor down. "You going to tell me what to do, by God?"

They remain silent. The respect for the boatswain is strong. But more men keep coming down the stairs. They fill the deck, spreading out until he faces a wall of men.

One of the quartermasters steps forward. He's a tall, blond fellow in canvas trousers and an outworn vest. "We have the right, bosun," he says. "They're going overboard. All of 'em. They're just niggers."

"You talk too much," Gillis growls. He spits on the floor to show his disdain. "The skipper's in charge."

"The skipper's lost his mind." He lunges forward, striking out with the cat-o'-

nine-tails. The quartermaster turns his head, but the iron points tear his cheek open. He screams in pain. A second strike. A third. Gillis shows no mercy. Never. He lashes with all the strength he has. Flaps of skin fly, and the quartermaster staggers back, his arms raised to shield his face.

Gillis kicks him once more for good measure. Fury sparkles in his grey eyes. He glares around the deck defiantly. "Who's next, goddammit?'"

The fire in the aft section is devouring beams and planks. In the master gunner's room, the tiller, the beam that connects the whipstaff to the rudder, is burning. The *Griffin* is now completely without steering. Flames are licking at the floor. Below that lies the powder magazine.

When Burghoutsz steps onto the deck, the wall of men parts respectfully.

Gillis stands waiting for him, legs apart, glaring from beneath his eyebrows. The cat-o'-nine-tails writhe and lashes in his fist.

"You're in the way," Burghoutsz says calmly. He stops a yard away from Gillis, his right hand behind his back. "You'd better step aside."

Gillis stubbornly shakes his head. "There will be no murdering of women and children here. Not on my ship."

"*Your* ship? By God. I am the law."

They size each other up. Neither man looks away.

Burghoutsz says, "If you refuse, it's mutiny."

"Then I'll hang."

"There's no time for that."

Burghoutsz steps back and reveals the pistol in his right hand. "You follow my orders or I'll blow your head off." He extends his arm, pointing the barrel.

Gillis lifts his head defiantly. He looks at the other with pity. Perhaps they both remember the old days: the voyages on the *Purmer*, the Baltic, trading in Riga. Perhaps they think of Red Rick or Dikkie the cook.

"Step aside, Gillis."

"Never."

Burghoutsz curls his finger.

At that moment, the powder magazine explodes.

The fireball shoots out from all sides of the stern, taking wood, fittings and the transom with it. The Mizzenmast rockets upward and crashes back down with thunderous force. The bow lifts briefly, and the ship seems to leap. Sails and rigging whirl about, and yards snap off. And among it all: people, whole people, pieces of people, white and black, tumbling through the air. In three or four seconds, it's over. The stern is engulfed in flames. The fire burns yellow, red, and sometimes even purple.

From a distance, the lieutenant takes it all in, peering through his brass spyglass. He points toward the main deck and the forecastle, where tiny, unrecognizable figures are scurrying back and forth, fleeing the fire. Shaking his head, he turns to brother François, who stands beside him with a horrified expression. "Look," he gestures, "they're trying to lower the longboats." But he feels no pity. Drown for all I care, he thinks grimly, the sharks are still there—let them clean up the mess.

One of the boats comes loose, swinging wildly from the tackle. There are men inside. The ropes are hacked apart, but in the panic, it's done out of sync and the bow swings down first. The figures fall out, into the water, into that red soup of flesh, blood and fish. He can hear their screams. Then the other side drops. He hears the splash as it hits the water, but with the thick smoke, he can barely see anything—the boat is just a faint shadow in the brown haze. Are there still people inside? Are they still alive?

It happens quickly now: the midship passage burns, then the orlop deck and finally the forecastle. The *Griffin* tilts backward, the quarterdeck sinks into the water, and the figurehead points upward, with the bowsprit like a reproachful finger in the air.

"There she goes," he says.

Hissing and steaming. Smoke and fire. The stench of burning flesh.

The lieutenant shivers. He looks up at the sky. The wind seems to pick up. "We're leaving," he orders. "May God have mercy on them."

Epilogue

"We acknowledge to the descendants of the enslaved that we have caused much suffering."

Dutch Council of Churches (2013)

"I tell you: we are sinners, and we feel no remorse. But our conscience will catch up with us. A day of reckoning will come.
God said: I have listened and heard, but what they say is not right; no one repents of their wickedness and says: What have I done?
Yes, God will judge us.
God, and history."

From: a letter by Reverend Duisterbloem to the Deputati Ad Res Exteras Commission of the Classis Amsterdam, Autumn 1688

Amsterdam. The stately room in the West India House exudes calm and authority, with oak paneling, gold-framed portraits on the walls and to the left, an enormous standing clock, its ticking emphasizing the silence.

Reverend Duisterbloem sits uneasily on a wooden bench in the centre of the room, looking up at the members of the Chamber, who observe him sternly from behind their massive desks. They wear white collars and sombre black vests.

"Why do you think he did it?" asks the man in the middle, the chairman and highest in rank, who has a rosy, round face and wavy white hair.

Reverend Duisterbloem shrugs. He doesn't remember much. As far as he's concerned, they were all possessed by the devil, but he can't say that here, not in this bastion of capitalism and greed, where all faith has been banished and only profit and dividends are worshipped. "I didn't know him," he answers neutrally. "I only saw him occasionally, when he was on deck with his officers, and in the mornings during prayer, but he never spoke to me."

"Did you find that the skipper behaved oddly beforehand?"

The reverend rubs his beard, marred by patches of scar tissue. As his fingertips touch the skin, he feels the unnatural smoothness. Burns. Blue and red. It looks horrible, people on the streets avoid him because of his scars. "They all behaved like madmen," he says quietly. "It was so long ago."

"And the insurance man?"

"The insurance man?"

"The representative of the Chamber of Assurance and Damage? Was he present when the skipper made his ... uh ... decision? Did he take part in the discussions?"

"There were no discussions, as far as I know." All those questions barely register. Reverend Duisterbloem sighs. He stares at his fingers, which are crooked. The pinky and ring finger on his right hand are missing. *Fft*. Gone. When he grabs something, he sometimes drops it without realizing. No strength. No feeling. "I don't know any representative," he says flatly. "Never saw him." That's the truth, he thinks. I didn't go outside much during that time. I was wrestling with God and the devil, and the cabin on the ship was dark and safe, and I was just grateful to get away from that cursed land. He sees images of the storm and that long night in the dark, himself trapped like Jonah in the belly of the whale. He shivers for a moment, tries to clear his mind, focusing on the steady ticking of the clock. Tick. Tock. Tick. Tock.

"How did you escape yourself, Reverend?"

That question startles him, and he almost guiltily sits up straight. The final act is unclear to him, vague shadows somewhere at the back of his mind. He sees himself running across a sloping deck, with an overcoat on fire, slipping and struggling between bodies and body parts. Then a fleeting image of him desperately grabbing onto the gunwale of the launch boat. That must be when he lost those fingers, he figures, though he has no clear memory of it. Voices. Screams. Pain. Yes, that too. "*Éééh*," he stammers helplessly, searching for words.

The chairman of the Chamber strokes his chin thoughtfully, leaning back. The men behind the tall desks whisper to each other, occasionally casting glances at him.

He endures it passively. Go ahead and stare, he thinks stubbornly. I'm not crazy. And I have nothing to do with you. You are lazy and arrogant. What do you know of suffering in a faraway land? He shakes his head. The boat fell into the water. There were only five of them left: himself, the second mate and three sailors. One of the men had a broken leg. And the water was red. He gazes at the row of windows on the opposite wall, far above the Council members' heads. Stained glass, with small square panes. The light streaming in is soft and honey-coloured. That calms him a little. Tick, tock, says the clock. "God helped me escape," he mumbles.

"Of course," says the chairman politely.

"I remember the fear," he continues tonelessly, sticking his hands between his knees. "Those fish were monstrously large. The boat kept bumping into them, swaying back and forth. We thought we would be thrown overboard. That would have meant certain death."

"Naturally, but—"

"There were only two oars left. We used them carefully to row away. There were no survivors, not a single one. Everyone in the water was torn apart by those terrible jaws. We could see it, we saw it, we tried not to look..." His eyes fill with tears, but he angrily waves a hand. "What does it matter to you?" he suddenly shouts. "You only care about the insurance money."

The chairman makes a distressed face. He points with a finger. "A lot of damage has been incurred, sir. It's no small matter."

"Yes, a lot of damage," the preacher repeats scornfully. "Do you happen to know there was theft, too?"

"Theft?" The chairman leans forward. "By whom?"

This draws a mocking laugh from him, through his tears. "You know nothing, sir. They all steal. Gold. Slaves. Whatever they can. They're all scoundrels, from top to bottom, both black and white, they're all the same."

He looks at the clock. The counterweights are made of heavy copper. Tick. Tock. Time moves on. Yes, he thinks. That's it. He stands up, wipes his eyes with his sleeve, and glares rebelliously at the men in black, those high-ranking merchants who inhabit the canals, who control the ships, manage the flow of money and play people like puppets. But they don't know God. They haven't smelled the shattered corpses down in the dungeons of Fort Coenraadsburg, in the damp and darkness, under the wings of bats. "I have nothing more to say," he declares. "They're dead. All of them. To hell with your insurances."

Reverend Duisterbloem leaves the chamber without permission.

"That you are sprung from two races
(Cham and Japheth) in your seed;
One as servile should be counted,
The other shows of freedom's deed;
That you, too have come descending
From heathens, (spiritually) blind;
That you've now been reaccepted,
Indeed, as a Christian child."

Jacob Steendam, The goldfinch (Den distelvink, 1649)

Notes

This book is a novel, with fictional characters and events. However, the general outline is historical, and the (political/social/military) context is portrayed as accurately as possible. The attacks on the Brandenburg forts Dorothea, Frederiksburg, and the settlement in Taccorary all took place at the end of 1687. The Frenchman Du Casse did indeed attempt to capture Commanie in early 1688. For the sake of the story, however, some liberties have been taken with the chronology. The settings, landscapes, forts and settlements are authentic and based on old travel accounts.

I chose a period in which, at least for the Dutch Republic, it was more or less business as usual so that attention to the events would not be diverted by major wars or conflicts but would remain focused on trade and the pursuit of profit, the struggles it entailed and the price that was paid for it. 1687 and 1688 were years during a period when the slave trade was becoming increasingly important, but the supply to the West (Curaçao, Berbice, Suriname and Spanish America) remained a challenging operation for all parties.

Several characters are historical:

Nicholaas Sweerts was director-general of the Dutch West India Company from 1684 to 1690. Little is known about him—no more than a likely mention of him in the chapter of Oudmunster in Utrecht—he purchased a prebend (a share of income from church property) in 1690 and is mentioned as a testator in a proxy dated March 13, 1705 (source: the Utrecht Archives). His background in the story is fictional.

The German Johann Niemann was governor of the Brandenburg fortifications on the Gold Coast from 1686 to 1691.

King Boa Amponsem I ruled the Denkyira kingdom from 1637 to 1695.

Abraham de Graaf indeed managed his maritime school in Amsterdam during those years and was an examiner for the Dutch East India Company (VOC).

Jean Baptiste Du Casse (1646-1715) was a notorious privateer and, from 1686, a French naval officer. In 1687, he was still a naval lieutenant but eventually rose to the rank of lieutenant-general and governor of San Domingo. In 1689, he unsuccessfully attempted to capture Berbice and Suriname from the Dutch.

The Dominican friar Fra Gonzalez François is mentioned in the sources about Du Casse.

Sometimes, it's just fun to tie things together:

There was a skipper named Jasper van de Vogel who, in 1687, commanded a smuggling ship called the Meyboom sailing along the Gold Coast.

Bomba Jan Michielsz, born in Elmina, does appear on the crew list of a Dutch slave ship (the Beekesteijn), but not until 1731.

The Gijsen shipowner family from Zaandam is historical.

As early as 1850, there was a bakery named Govers located on the Oude-Kennissteeg in Amsterdam.

In addition:

Regarding the use of old (nautical) terms: ships in the seventeenth century were complex, sophisticated "machines" and very modern for their time, but navigation at sea was a major problem (it was only around 1800 that longitude could be calculated with reasonable accuracy). For the sake of authenticity, historical accuracy and particularly atmosphere, extensive use has been made of the original terminology. However, readers are certainly not expected to understand every term literally. Enthusiasts can make use of the glossary.

The original Dutch title of this book is *Kroesvee* (as a designation for a cargo of black slaves), a term that links curly black hair with livestock and is (in Dutch) even more derogatory than the English translation *Black Cattle*. The term appears in the cargo lists of the Middelburgsche Commercie Compagnie from Zeeland (1720-1888), a later competitor of the West India Company.

Dutch Protestants were, up until the early 17th century, staunchly opposed to slavery. However, when the plantations in the Brazilian colonies (captured from the Portuguese) required large numbers of cheap laborers, they quickly capitulated, and a justification was soon found in the Bible. By 1687, the trade in Africans was entirely commonplace.

The justification is found in Genesis 9:18-29, where Noah curses his son Ham and condemns his descendants to slavery. The interpretation by the Coevorden minister Picardt can be regarded as typical (see p. 5).

In 1687, the Second Chartered West India Company (the WIC)—founded in 1675—held the state monopoly on trade and shipping in West Africa south of the Tropic of

Cancer, in the Americas, as well as on all islands between Newfoundland and the Strait of Magellan. The company had a working capital of more than 6 million guilders. The directors (the Gentlemen Ten) met in the West India House in Amsterdam.

In 1687, the WIC was by far the largest transporter of slaves, closely followed by Portugal and England. Spanish America was the largest customer, for Spain itself could not export slaves from Africa due to the Treaty of Tordesillas (1494), in which Spain and Portugal, the dominant maritime nations at the time, divided the world outside Europe between themselves by means of a demarcation line. The Dutch mainly transported their slaves to Curaçao, where they were sold to the Spanish.

The original Portuguese name of Elmina was São Jorge da Mina (Mina means 'mine'—as in: gold mine). The castle was established in 1482 and was captured by the Dutch in 1637.

The indigenous name of the village near Elmina is Anomansa, meaning "inexhaustible water source."

Due to the increasing pressure from privateers and smugglers, the WIC deployed a cruiser on the African coast in November 1687 for the first time in a long period: the Westsouborgh. The ship is portrayed in the story as more imposing than it actually was: a frigate with no more than fourteen guns.

'Guinean' words: In 1602, P. de Marees compiled a small dictionary as an appendix to his description of the Gold Coast, giving the impression that a single language was spoken throughout this vast region. In reality, the linguistic landscape consisted of various languages and dialects, including Akan, Akim, Kyerepon, Ewe, Ga, and Twi. However, where indigenous terms are used in the book, they have been drawn as much as possible from this glossary, summarized as ' Guinean'.

A 'tapoeijer' was a child of an African mother and a white (Dutch) father. These mulattoes or half-bloods had a separate status in Elmina and lived in their own quarter in the village, known as the Akrampafo. Akrampa (from Akan = vulture) is a nickname for the supreme god Onyame in his role as creator.

The first name Quameno (or Kwame) means 'Saturday,' and Quassie (or Kwasi) means 'Sunday.' The descendants of the Akan still bear a first name that corresponds to the name of the weekday on which they were born.

Slaves were bought and sold in a specific unit: the pieza de India. This stood for a healthy, well-built man or woman between 15 and 36 years old. Persons aged 8 to 14 were counted as two-thirds of a pieza, and those 7 years and younger as half a pieza. Infants (children up to two years old) were sold along with their mother.

Therefore, the actual number of slaves on a ship did not necessarily correspond to the number of pieza de India registered in the cargo list.

The position of the *bomba* on a slave ship was exclusive to the Dutch slave trade. There is no exact translation for the word, but the term "black overseer" comes closest to describing the role and duties. The bomba was active both on the African coast and on ships of the WIC and the MCC (Middelburgsche Commercie Compagnie from Zeeland). Those who worked as bombas were free Africans. For Dutch slave traders, their presence on the slave ships was of great importance, as they served as intermediaries between the crew and the slaves. The bomba spoke both Dutch and the common African languages. Bombas were paid for their work. No evidence has been found that bombas, as free individuals, worked on ships of non-Dutch slave traders.

The Second Anglo-Dutch War lasted from 1665 to 1667 and took place entirely at sea. Peace was signed after the famous Raid on the Medway, during which the Dutch captured the English flagship HMS Royal Charles.

As early as 1724, Elmina had seven so-called asafo companies (militias of indigenous warriors affiliated with the WIC). For the year 1687, I have assumed six, though there were probably fewer.

Longitudes: the Dutch used the Ferro prime meridian, which roughly differs by 18° from the Greenwich prime meridian.

The story of Du Casse has been greatly simplified: in reality, he arrived with four ships in Commanie and, supported by local tribes, established a small trading post, but was forcibly expelled by the Dutch a few months later.

The political situation in Commanie has been downplayed and simplified for readability; in reality, the English and Dutch were so fiercely at odds that it led to the so-called Komenda Wars (1688-1700). For experts: the influential merchant John Cabess has been deliberately left out.

The events in the final chapters are fictional. Such extreme abuses, however, have been documented on other ships (for example, during the voyage of the English slave ship Zong in 1781); they were sometimes employed to collect insurance money.

Explanation of the quotes and pieces of correspondence at the beginning of each chapter:

Bible and Quran texts are authentic, but Bible texts never from more recent translations, because in those versions words related to slavery were replaced with more neutral terms such as servant, helper, service, and forced labor.

The references to *Nauwkeurige Beschrijving van de Guinese Goud-, Tand- en Slavekust* ("Accurate Description of the Gold, Ivory, and Slave Coast of Guinea") by Willem Bosman (chief merchant in Elmina until 1702) are authentic, but have been edited or shortened in places.

The description of "land sickness" in Chapter 8 is, shortened and in fragments, an almost literal translation from *Berigt van de in de Tweede Helft der Maand Mei en in het Begin van de Maand Junij 1861 te St. George D'Elmina Waargenomen Ziektegevallen onder de Europesche Bevolking* ("Report of the Cases of Illness Observed Among the European Population at St. George D'Elmina in the Second Half of May and Early June 1861") by Dr. C. F. Lucke.

On the inevitability of the slave trade in Chapter 13: the mentioned source is authentic, *Reizen op en beschrijving van de goudkust van Guinea – Volume 1* ("Travels on and Description of the Gold Coast of Guinea - Volume 1") by J.A. de Marée.

Chapter 14: A literal quote from *Korte beschryvinge van eenige vergetene en verborgene antiquiteten der provintien en landen gelegen tusschen de Noord-Zee, de Yssel, Emse en Lippe* ("Brief Description of Some Forgotten and Hidden Antiquities of the Provinces and Lands Situated Between the North Sea, the IJssel, the Ems, and the Lippe") by Reverend Johan Picardt.

Chapter 22: The status of vultures on the West African coast: from *Beschryvinghe ende historische verhael van het Gout koninckrijck van Gunea anders de Gout-Custe de Mina genaemt liggende in het deel van Africa* ("Description and Historical Account of the Gold Kingdom of Guinea, Otherwise Called the Gold Coast de Mina, Situated in the Part of Africa") by P. de Marees.

The description of the "cruelty of the Negroes" in Chapter 23 is an adaptation of the text in *Reizen op en beschrijving van de goudkust van Guinea – Volume 1* ("Travels on and Description of the Gold Coast of Guinea - Volume 1") by J.A. de Marée.

On the morning routine on a sailing ship in Chapter 26: adaptation from *Two Years Before the Mast: Adventures on a Sea Voyage to the Northwest Coast of America* by Richard Henry Dana Jr.

Chapter 31: An old formula; the result determines the angle between the sun and the horizon, calculated with a cross-staff.

Chapter 34: On the nature of the white slave trader based on excerpts from *Liberated Central Africans in Nineteenth-Century Guyana* by Monica Schuler.

Chapter 37: The English also feared Du Casse; the text is almost verbatim from *The Local Correspondence of the Royal African Company of England* by James Walker.

The whites caused the differences between rich and poor: Chapter 43, from *Liberated Central Africans in Nineteenth-Century Guyana* by Monica Schuler.

Chapter 44: Excerpt from *One Thousand and One Nights*, the story of The Merchant and the Genie (based on the French edition by Antoine Galland from 1704).

The instructions concerning the treatment of slaves on board the ships in Chapter 45 are a translation from *Instructions for Skipper Andries Graan on the Company Ship Leusden, December 25, 1732*.

Chapter 47: On the effect of salt on slaves, from *Liberated Central Africans in Nineteenth-Century Guyana* by Monica Schuler.

Chapter 50: The statement is from Sir W. Batten, dated July 19, 1667, following the Dutch victory at Chatham.

The Negroes are all idol worshipers in Chapter 52: a literal text by Jan Jacob Hartsinck.

Chapter 59: The text about Dutch dependence on the asafo companies is based on *the Resolution of the Director-General and Council*, October 19, 1716.

In the Epilogue: Pastor Duisterbloem quotes from the Bible: Jeremiah 8:6. The Deputati Ad Res Exteras of the Classis Amsterdam was a four-person committee that, since 1636, managed the interests of the overseas (Protestant) churches.

In the main text, quotes, adaptations of quotes, references or historical facts from various sources are regularly used. For example:

Chapter 6: Sweerts refers to three Dutch skippers, each of whom had four slave voyages to their name during that period: Jan van Arrel, Jan Balck, and Huijbert Janszoon. It was not until the 18th century that this number was surpassed. The Dutch all-time record is held by a certain Jacob Visser with seven voyages.

Chapter 7: *Febris biliosa putrida*, known in English as seasoning. Almost every European had to endure this dangerous illness upon arriving in the tropics. The Latin term is used in various 18th- and 19th-century sources.

Chapter 13: In a passing phrase, Mussulman Ali quotes the Quran: Al-Maidah 60 and 63.

Chapter 15: The catechism booklet that Aldemar reads was written by Marnix van Sint Aldegonde and dates back to the late 16th century; the questions and answers are authentic.

Chapter 15: On the Fate of Negroes, Jews and Whites: a quote from the Reverend Johan Picardt (1660).

Chapter 16: Sweerts refers to the Treaty of Boutry, one of the oldest agreements between a European state and an African tribal coalition. The Ahante and the WIC agreed on close cooperation in trade in 1656. The treaty would last for 213 years.

Chapter 18: Sweerts' alphabet lesson comes from the educational booklet by Jacob Borstius, and here, too, the questions and answers are authentic.

Chapter 24: When Mussulman Ali describes his three wives as pure daughters of Aminah bint Wahab, he is referring to the mother of the Prophet Muhammad.

Infections with dracunculus (a parasitic worm) were particularly common around Elmina. The symptoms described in Chapter 26 are authentic.

Chapter 27: The two verses of the shanty come from Het Bittere Zeemanslied (or The Bitter Sea Shanty). It probably dates back to the clipper era (19th century); very few Dutch shanties from the 17th century have been preserved.

Chapter 29: Soldier 2 is infected by the sand flea (tungiasis).

The value of slaves was influenced by their physical health; there were guidelines for this. The enumeration in Chapter 34 comes from *Africans in Bondage: Studies in Slavery and the Slave Trade* by Paul E. Lovejoy (1986).

Chapter 42: The (highly simplified) text of Quameno Ewussi comes from J.A. de Marée: "For the slave who has slaves under him will be just as domineering towards his own serfs as he is subordinate to his master."

In Chapter 44, Quassie Patoe meets a young Ahante warrior. This could be an early version of the folk hero John Conni, who in 1708 captured the Brandenburg fort Dorothea and successfully defended it against the Dutch for years. He is still honoured every year, both in Ghana and in the Caribbean.

Chapter 48: The phrase "They are a criminal race! Forsaken by God, doomed and despised" is from the poem *De Slavenhandel* ("The Slave Trade") by Cornelis Loots (1816).

Chapter 49: The crew sings *Een Nieuw Liedeken ter Eeren de Boots-Gesellen ende andere Jonge Maets, die de Zee beminnen* ("A New Song in Honor of the Boatswain's Mates and Other Young Sailors Who Love the Sea"). From *Matroosen vreught* ("Sailors' Delight") (1696).

Chapter 58: Brother François quotes Thomas Aquinas: *Contemplari et contemplare aliis tradere* ("to contemplate and to pass on to others what is contemplated").

Chapter 60: Jargon and descriptions concerning maneuvers on a sailing ship in a heavy storm are based on *Two Years Before the Mast: Adventures on a Sea Voyage to the Northwest Coast of America* by Richard Henry Dana Jr. (1842).

Chapter 63: The reverend quotes fragments from Ezekiel 3:9.

Finally: I have tried to be as thorough as possible with the source citations. Should the reader unexpectedly discover an omission, please report it via **info@johnmeilink.com**.

John Meilink,
Rosmalen, the Netherlands, October 2013-December 2025

* The original Dutch version *Kroesvee* is included in the literature list of the new Historical Canon of the Netherlands (June 2020), section 'VOC and WIC.'

Literature

? - *Matroosen vreught, vol van de nieuwste ende hedendaaghsche liedekens, aldermeest gebruyckelijck onder de zeevarende luyden* ("Sailors' Delight, Full of the Newest and Most Current Songs, Mostly Used Among Seafaring People") (1696);

Aderinto, Saheed - *African Kingdoms: An Encyclopedia of Empires and Civilizations* (2017);

Austen, R.A. - *The Trans-Saharan Slave Trade: A Tentative Census* (1979);

Bailey, Anne Caroline - *African Voices of the Atlantic Slave Trade: Beyond the Silence and the Shame* (2005);

Bakker, Theo - *Beurtvaarders, trekschuiten en overzetveren* ("Regular Boats, Tow Barges, and Ferries") (2011);

Balai, L.W. - *Het Slavenschip Leusden* ("The Slave Ship Leusden") (2011);

Bathurst, C., et al. - *The Modern Part of an Universal History, from the Earliest Accounts to the Present Time, Volume 13* (1781);

Beliën, H.M., et al. - *Gestalten van de Gouden Eeuw: een Hollands Groepsportret* ("Figures of the Golden Age: A Dutch Group Portrait") (1995);

Bezemer, Dirk, et al. - *Slavery, Statehood and Economic Development in Sub-Saharan Africa* (2012);

Boekholt, P.Th.F.M. and Booy, E.P. de - *Geschiedenis van de school in Nederland* ("History of Schools in the Netherlands") (1987);

Bosman, Willem - *Nauwkeurige Beschrijving van de Guinese Goud-, Tand- en Slavekust* ("Accurate Description of the Gold, Ivory, and Slave Coast of Guinea") (1704);

Boucher, Philip P. - *France and the American Tropics to 1700: Tropics of Discontent?* (2010);

Bredius, A., et al. - *Amsterdam in de Zeventiende Eeuw* ("Amsterdam in the Seventeenth Century") (1897);

Briggs, Philip - *Ghana - Bradt Travel Guides* (2010);

Bruijn, J.R. - *Commanders of Dutch East India Ships in the Eighteenth Century* (2011);

Bruijn, Jaap R. - *Het Zeevarend Kader van de Marine en de VOC in de Achttiende Eeuw* ("The Maritime Officers of the Navy and the VOC in the Eighteenth Century") (2001);

Casse, Jean Baptiste du - *Relation de voyage de Guynée fait en 1687 sur la frégate La Tempeste* ("Travel Account of Guinea Made in 1687 on the Frigate La Tempeste") (1935);

Casse, Le Baron Robert du - *L'Amiral Du Casse, Chevalier De La Toison d'Or* ("Admiral Du Casse, Knight of the Golden Fleece") (1876);

Clark, Nancy L. and Alpers, Edward A. - *Africa and the West: From the Slave Trade to Conquest, 1441-1905* (2010);

Commelin, Caspar - *Beschryvinge van Amsterdam* ("Description of Amsterdam") (1726);

Damme, Andries van - *Beschryvinge van Amsterdam: zynde een naukeurige verhandelinge van desselfs eerste oorspronk* ("Description of Amsterdam: Being an Accurate Treatise of Its First Origin") (1726);

Dana, Richard Henry Jr. - *Two Years Before the Mast: Adventures on a Sea Voyage to the Northwest Coast of America* - M. Ballot Edition (1842);

Davids, C.A. - *Het zeevaartkundig onderwijs in de Republiek gedurende de zeventiende eeuw* ("Maritime Education in the Republic During the Seventeenth Century") (1991);

Davies, K.G. - *The Royal African Company, Volume 5* (1999);

Delepeleire, Yves - *Nederlands Elmina, een socio-economische analyse van de Tweede West-Indische Compagnie in West-Afrika in 1715* ("Dutch Elmina, a Socio-Economic Analysis of the Second West India Company in West Africa in 1715") (2004);

Dinther, Nico van - *Het Fregat Prins Willem de Vijfde* ("The Frigate Prince William the Fifth") (2018);

Emmer, P.C. - *De Nederlandse Slavenhandel 1500-1850* ("The Dutch Slave Trade 1500-1850") (2011);

Emmer, P.C. - *Geschiedenis van de Nederlandse slavenhandel* ("History of the Dutch Slave Trade") (2019);

Engelen, Marcel van - *Het kasteel van Elmina* ("The Castle of Elmina") (2013);

Enthoven, Victor, et al. - *Geweld in de West: een militaire geschiedenis van de Nederlandse Atlantische wereld, 1600-1800* ("Violence in the West: A Military History of the Dutch Atlantic World, 1600-1800") (2013);

Feinberg, Harvey M. - *Africans and Europeans in West Africa: Elminans and Dutchmen on the Gold Coast During the Eighteenth Century* (1989);

Den Heijer, Henk - *Het Slavenschip* ("The Slave Ship") (2011);

Den Heijer, Henk - *Naar de koning van Dahomey* ("To the King of Dahomey") (2000);

Den Heijer, Henk - *Expeditie naar de Goudkust* ("Expedition to the Gold Coast") (2006);

Den Heijer, Henk - *Goud, ivoor en slaven* ("Gold, Ivory, and Slaves") (1997);

Heyden, Ulrich van der - *Rote Adler an Afrikas Küste* ("Red Eagles on Africa's Coast") (2001);

Hondt, Pieter de - *Historische beschryving der reizen* ("Historical Description of Voyages") (1748);

Hrodej, Philippe - *L'amiral Du Casse: de la marchandise à la Toison d'Or* ("Admiral Du Casse: From Merchandise to the Golden Fleece") (1997);

Jong, M.A.G. de - *Staat van oorlog* ("State of War") (2005);

Jonge, Mr J.C. de - *Geschiedenis van het Nederlandsche zeewezen* ("History of the Dutch Navy") (1837, 1841);

Joosse, L.J. - *Geloof in de Nieuwe Wereld* ("Faith in the New World") (2008);

Koene, Bert - *De Caeskopers* ("The Cheese Buyers") (2011);

L'Espine, Jacques le Moine de - *De Koophandel van Amsterdam naar alle gewesten der wereld* ("The Trade of Amsterdam to All Parts of the World") (1801);

Law, Robin - *Ouidah: The Social History of a West African Slaving 'Port', 1727-1892* (2004);

Law, Robin - *The English in West Africa, 1685-1688* (2001);

Lennep, Jacob van - *Zeemans-woordenboek* ("Sailor's Dictionary") (1856);

Lindeboom, Gerrit Arie - *Circa Tiliam: Studia Historiae Medicinae* (1974);

Lovejoy, Paul - *Transformations of Slavery: A History of Slavery in Africa* (2000);

Lovejoy, Paul E. - *Africans in Bondage: Studies in Slavery and the Slave Trade* (1986);

Marée, J. A. de - *Reizen op en beschrijving van de goudkust van Guinea* ("Travels on and Description of the Gold Coast of Guinea") (1817);

Marees, P. de - *Beschryvinghe ende historische verhael van het Gout koninckrijck van Gunea* ("Description and Historical Account of the Gold Kingdom of Guinea") (1602);

Meillassoux, Claude - *The Anthropology of Slavery: The Womb of Iron and Gold* (1991);

Meuwese, Mark - *Brothers in Arms, Partners in Trade* (2011);

N´Diaye, Tidiane - *Der verschleierte Völkermord* ("The Veiled Genocide") (2010);

Onnekink, David and Bruin, Renger Evert - *De Vrede van Utrecht* ("The Peace Treaty of Utrecht") (2013);

Paasman, A. N. and Paasman, Bert - *Reinhart: Nederlandse literatuur en slavernij ten tijde van de Verlichting* ("Reinhart: Dutch Literature and Slavery During the Enlightenment") (1984);

Paesie, Ruud - *Lorrendrayen op Africa* ("Smuggling in Africa") (2008);

Perbi, Akosua Adoma - *A History of Indigenous Slavery in Ghana from the 15th to the 19th Century* (2004);

Postma, Johannes - *The Dutch in the Atlantic Slave Trade* (2008);

Raedt, Georgius de - *Bedenckingen over den Guineeschen slaef-handel der gereformeerde met de papisten* ("Reflections on the Guinea Slave Trade of the Reformed with the Papists") (1665);

Rawley, James A. and Behrendt, Stephen D. - *The Transatlantic Slave Trade: A History* (2005);

Rodney, Walter - *African Slavery and Other Forms of Social Oppression on the Upper Guinea Coast* (1966);

Roper, Louis H. and Ruymbeke, Bertrand Van - *Constructing Early Modern Empires* (2007);

Salverda, Eelco - *Theorieën over het Verband tussen de Akan en het Oude Ghana* ("Theories About the Connection Between the Akan and Ancient Ghana") (1993);

Schalekamp, M. - *Hedendaagsche historie* ("Contemporary History") (1785);

Schuler, Monica - *Liberated Central Africans in Nineteenth-Century Guyana* (2000);

Segal, Ronald - *Islam's Black Slaves* (2001);

Snelders, Stephen - *Vrijbuiters van de heelkunde* ("Pirates of Surgery") (2012);

Spooner, Frank C. - *Risks at Sea* (2002);

Tindal, G.A. and Swart, Jacob - *Verhandelingen en berigten betrekkelijk het zeewezen en de zeevaartkunde* ("Treatises and Reports Concerning Maritime Affairs and Navigation") (1841);

Vos, Ron de - *Nederlandse schoeners en brikken* ("Dutch Schooners and Brigs") (2009);

Windrow, Martin - *Warriors: Fighting Men and Their Uniforms* (2015);

Winschooten, W. - *Seeman* ("Sailor") (1681);

Witsen, Nicolaas - *Aaloude en hedendaagsche scheeps-bouw en -bestier* ("Ancient and Modern Shipbuilding and Management") (1690).

Illustration credits

Title page: Monogram of the Chartered West India Company;

Title page Part 1: digitally edited fragment of *The Cannon Shot* (c. 1680), oil painting by Willem van de Velde the Younger (1633-1707);

Chapter 1: *Hunter on the Watch*, digitally edited photograph from c. 1895, by Ramseyer, Friedrich August Louis (1840-1914);

Chapter 3: Elmina Castle, Ghana, digitally edited photo merged with composite created by ChatGPT 4.0 AI (DALL-E 3);

Chapter 8: Statenvlag (Dutch States' flag), a digitally edited fragment of *The Surrender of the Royal Prince* (1670), an oil painting by Willem van de Velde the Younger;

Chapter 9: hooker ship, a digitally edited fragment of *Hooker Ship Setting Out Its Drift-Net with a Fresh Sail* (c. 1786), copper engraving by Gerrit Groenewegen (1754-1824);

Chapter 13: digitally edited fragment from *The Smokers* (c. 1630), oil painting by Adriaen Brouwer (1605-1638);

Chapter 20: digitally edited fragment of *The Battle of Texel* (1673), oil painting by Willem van de Velde the Younger;

Chapter 25: Fort Coenraadsburg (Jago Hill), Ghana;

Chapter 30: Entrance door to Elmina slave dungeon, Ghana;

Chapter 34: digitally edited fragment of *The Captive Slave* (1827), oil painting by John Philip Simpson (1782-1847);

Chapter 45: Fort Saint Sebastian, Chama;

Chapter 47: digitally edited fragment from the film *The Battle of Grolle* by Eva Roemaat (2019);

Title page Part 2: digitally edited fragment of *View of Dordrecht* (1660), oil painting by Albert Cuyp (1620-1691);

Chapter 56: digitally edited photo by Fotografia H. Le Lieure, Rome (c. 1890);

Glossary

Abiessa – 'Guinean': three
Abromenade – cassava
Accaba – 'Guinean': slave
Ackie – 'Guinean': good day
Admiralty – the governing body of the war fleet. Predecessor of the navy (until 1795). The Dutch Republic effectively had five admiralty boards at that time
Aene – 'Guinean': skipper/captain
Aguane – 'Guinean': fugitive
Ahl al-Fatrah – Arabic: ignorant, unbeliever
Akan – both the language and the ethnic group in Ghana and eastern Ivory Coast. The Ashanti, Fante, Denkyira, Ahante, and Wassa tribes all share the same origin.
Akkra – Accra (Ghana)
Akomfo – from Akan: witch doctor, sorcerer
Akrampa – from Akan: vulture
Akrampafo – the mulatto quarter of Elmina
Alhamdulillah – Arabic: "All praise is for God"
Allah-i-takabel – Arabic: "May Allah accept my prayer"
Allahoe Akbar – Arabic: "God is the greatest"
Allahumma – Arabic: "Oh, God"
Anomansa – indigenous name of the village next to Elmina Castle. Means "inexhaustible water source."
Aoro deie – 'Guinean': "My lord, how are you?"
Asafo – militia of African warriors affiliated with the WIC
Assegai – indigenous throwing spear
Astagfiroellah – Arabic: "I seek forgiveness from God"
Audhu billah – Arabic: "I seek refuge with God"
Barge – flat-bottomed boat used mainly for the transport of goods and people
Batakari – warrior tunic (originally Ashanti)
Batten – a strip used to stretch tarred canvas over deck hatches to prevent water ingress
Beam wind – a wind at right angles to a vessel's course (wind blowing at the ship's side)
Bebiny – 'Guinean': negro
Benin cloth – blue and white striped cloth produced in Benin for the WIC, resold on the Gold and Slave Coast

Binnacle house – the enclosed space on a ship where the whipstaff (a long steering stick) was located and where no metal objects were allowed to prevent interference with the compass.

Bismi'llah ir-Rahman ir-Rahiem – Arabic: "In the name of God, the Most Gracious, the Most Merciful."

Blunderbuss – firearm with a short, large caliber barrel that is commonly flared at the muzzle to help aid in the loading of shot and other projectiles of relevant quantity or caliber. The blunderbuss is commonly considered to be an early predecessor of the modern shotgun

Boarding net – rope net stretched over the deck to prevent enemy boarding

Boatswain – also: bosun. Highest-ranking petty officer in charge of sailors

Bomba – typically a non-white overseer of slaves on Dutch ships

Borodee – plantain

Bosun – slang: boatswain

Bowline – rope to keep a square sail from flapping

Bracing – using ropes attached to the ends of the yards to adjust the sails to the wind. When bracing full, the sails are set to catch the most wind. When bracing back, the wind strikes from the front, causing the ship to stop

Breeching – heavy rope used to absorb the recoil of a ship's cannon

Brine – salted water

Broadside – all artillery on one side of a ship

Bumboat trader – waterborne vendor, floating shop

Caboceer – indigenous black (slave) trader. Derived from the Portuguese word "cabociero," meaning chief or authority

Calabaris – inhabitants from the coastal regions north of the Gulf of Bonny in present-day Nigeria

Calomel – mineral of mercuric chloride used to treat mucous membrane inflammations and worms

Canister shot – metal projectile filled with shrapnel and balls

Canvas – "Dutch canvas": sailcloth made from hemp fiber

Capitaine-de-vaisseau – French: captain at sea

Careening barge – a heavy flat-bottomed vessel used to careen ships (tilting them sideways so work can be done on the keel and hull)

Cartridge – paper bag/pouch filled with gunpowder

Cat-o'-nine-tails – a flogging whip with ends of rope or leather, sometimes weighted with iron points

Chika – 'Guinean': gold dust or gold in general

Chirurgeon – surgeon, ship's doctor (a chirurgeon was not university-trained)

Cinqüenta – Portuguese: fifty

Classis – the regional governing body of a Protestant church denomination

Cleat – wooden bracket, hook, or clamp to secure a line, available in various types

Commis – rank within the WIC or VOC: clerk, assistant

Contemplari et contemplare aliis tradere – Thomas Aquinas: "To contemplate and to pass on to others what is contemplated."

Contraband runner – smuggling ship

Cowrie shells – Dutch: 'boesjes'. Used as currency by West African tribes

Crisiapalm – palm tree on the West African coast; source of palm wine

Curtain wall – fortified wall connecting two roundels or bastions

Deadeye – a ship's block with three holes used to tighten the standing rigging

Dinghy – small rowboat, often carried or towed by a larger vessel for use as a tender

Djinn – Arabic: spirit, supernatural being

Dockside dolly – prostitute, whore

Dog watch – ship's watch from 4:00 PM to 8:00 PM

Donka – inhabitant from northern West Africa, present-day Guinea

East Countrymen – English translation for Dutch 'noordsvaarder' (north trader), referring to ships that typically traded with the Baltic. The Baltic trade was highly significant for both England and Holland during the 17th and 18th centuries, as both nations relied on timber and grain from the region. In England, the trade route to the Baltic was commonly referred to as the East Country trade, in Holland as the 'mother trade.'

Efendi – Turkish/Arabic honorific title

Enfilade – to fire at a target along its length

Factory – overseas trading post

Faience – thin earthenware mixed with marl and covered with a layer of tin glaze (e.g., Delftware)

Fathom – a maritime unit of length used to measure water depth and rope length, approximately 1.8 meters or 6 feet (1/1000th of a nautical mile)

First watch – ship's watch from 8:00 PM to midnight

Fleurs de lis – three golden lilies on a blue background, symbol of the French kings

Flute/flute ship – a typical Dutch merchant ship from the 17th century, a three-masted vessel characterized by a rounded shape and inward-sloping sides

Flux, the – slang: severe diarrhea. The 'bloody flux' for dysentery with blood

Forecastle – raised foredeck on a ship

Foremast – the front mast on a three-masted ship

Foresail – the lowest square sail on the foremast

Fufu – a staple food in West Africa: a porridge made from pounded cassava, bananas, or yams

Gallion – the section of the ship between the forecastle and the bowsprit

Genièvre – Dutch gin

Grapeshot – ammunition for naval artillery, consisting of small balls or shrapnel stacked on a round disc in the shape of a grape cluster, tied together with sailcloth and cord

Griffin – a mythical creature (from Babylon, Persia, and Egypt) with the upper body of an eagle and the lower body of a lion; ruler of land and sky

Grommet – a young apprentice sailor or ship's boy. Traditionally, grommets were young boys serving on a ship, often tasked with basic duties such as carrying messages, assisting the crew, and learning the ropes of seamanship

Guava – an edible, green-yellow fruit

Guinea – the coasts of present-day Sierra Leone, Liberia, Ivory Coast and Ghana in West Africa. Known at the time (from north to south) as Upper Coast, Grain Coast/Pepper Coast, Ivory Coast/Tooth Coast, Gold Coast and Slave Coast. Not to be confused with the current country of Guinea

Guinean – adjective: "of Guinea." Also, the Dutch collective term for all Indigenous languages on the Gold and Slave Coasts

Gun carriage – wooden mount for a ship's cannon

Gun deck – (also: gangway) covered, continuous deck between the bow and stern, served as below-deck battery deck and also as sleeping quarters for the crew

Half-pike – short spear

Hamite – the descendant of Ham, the son cursed by Noah, referring to anyone, not of Jewish or European descent, thus considered inferior and condemned to slavery

Hammock – sailor's berth: a piece of canvas edged with rope, fitted with cross-wood at the narrow ends and set up to hang from the ceiling. A hammock always hung lengthwise

Hooker – a small, then-popular two-masted sailing vessel used for fishing and coastal trade

Housemother – matron (head of an institution)

Hulandi – Arabic: the Dutch

Indian corn – maize

Inglizia – Arabic: the English

Inna lillahi wa inna ilaihi radjioen – Arabic: "We belong to God, and to Him we shall return"

Insha'Allah – Arabic: "God willing"

Kafir – Arabic: unbeliever

Kaftan – Arabic garment

Keffiyeh – Arabic headscarf

Kenkey – fermented dough (Ghana)

Kente – precious, traditionally woven fabric (Ghana)

Kombe arrow poison – rope flower: Strophanthus Kombe, a vine that grows in the tropical regions of Eastern Africa. Contains a cardiac glycoside that directly affects the heart

Krak – Dutch slang: corn brandy or Dutch gin

La ilaha illa Allah, Muhammadun rasulullah – Arabic: "There is no deity but Allah, and Muhammad is His prophet"

Landlubber – someone who is inexperienced with life at sea

Leeward – the direction the wind is blowing towards

Mainmast – the central mast on a three-masted vessel

Mampam – coastal lizard. Mentioned by Willem Bosman in his books, but I have not been able to identify the species

Mark – used by the Dutch as a standard unit for gold, measuring 800 grams. The troy ounce (approximately 31 grams) and the troy pound (12 troy ounces, roughly 370 grams) were the standard units in England for such purposes

Masha Allah – Arabic: "God has willed it"

Master gunner – petty officer on board, responsible for ammunition, weapons and artillery

Messmates – sailors grouped by skill or profession who ate together

Middle passage – the second part of the triangular trade: the journey (with a cargo of slaves) from West Africa to the Caribbean

Middle watch – ship's watch from midnight to 4:00 AM

Mizzen – rearmost mast on a ship, or the triangular sail on it

Morning watch – ship's watch from 4:00 AM to 8:00 AM

Muadhdhin – Arabic: the caller to prayer (muezzin)

Mulatto – child of a white father and African mother

Musket – long firearm (muzzle-loader) from the 16th and 17th centuries, with matchlock ignition

Mussulman – Muslim

Nautical mile – refers to the international nautical mile of 1,852 meters (1/60th of a degree of latitude at the equator, or 1 minute of a meridian). At that time, the Dutch mile was also in use: 7.4 km (1/15th of a degree of longitude)

Navigation report – ship's position log (daily determination of a ship's position based on course, speed, and time traveled, as well as celestial navigation)

Nsafufuo – palm wine (Ghana)

Odomankoma Nana Nyankopon, Nyame mu Enyame – from Akan: "God Almighty Creator, Lord of all gods"

Onyame – from Akan: creator/supreme god

Orlop deck – extra, lowered deck between the gun deck and hold, used for storing gear or as quarters for soldiers or slaves

Padauk – wood from the African padauk tree (Pterocarpus soyauxii); highly valued for its hardness and color (ranging from deep red to black)

Patrão – Portuguese: boss/master

Patria – the homeland

Pawn – debtor detained until their debt is paid off

Peruvian bark – quinine: antipyretic (fever-reducing) medicine, later known as Jesuit's powder

Pinnace – small, fast sailing ship from the 17th century, with two or three masts, spritsail, and topsail

Plantation – a large-scale agricultural enterprise, usually growing a single crop (monoculture)

Poleponze – a drink made of brandy, sugar, nutmeg, and lime juice: used against seasickness

Pomander – a spherical jewel worn by wealthy ladies as a fragrance diffuser

Poop deck – second raised deck behind the mainmast, the domain of the skipper/captain

Port side – left side of the ship, facing the bow

Prince's flag – (originally orange, white, and blue, but the orange was replaced by red around 1650); based on the livery colors of Prince William I of Orange-Nassau (1533-1584), stadtholder of several of the Dutch provinces and leader of the revolt against the Spanish occupation

Provost – (or fiscal prosecutor) responsible not only for financial matters but also for law enforcement, justice, and maintaining order in overseas settlements

Qat – leaf of the plant Catha edulis: chewed to ward off fatigue and hunger

Qua-qua-coast – Liberia

Quarterdeck – the first raised deck behind the mainmast, reserved for officers and distinguished crew, unlike the common sailors who had to remain forward of the mast

Reef/To reef – to shorten a sail using ropes, reducing the sail area. The sail is tied up using reef lines or seizings

Return ship – in this context: a merchant ship of the WIC that shuttled between Holland and the West African coast (3 months out, 3 months back). On average, about five ships were outfitted per year. A slave ship did not fall under this category

Salatoel-'Asr – Arabic: the afternoon prayer

Salatoel-Duhr – Arabic: the midday prayer

Salatoel-Isja – Arabic: the evening/night prayer

Seasoning – or seasoning sickness. General term for the fever and diarrhea that almost every European had to endure after arriving in West Africa

Seizing – band of sewn canvas used to tie up sails

Sessenta – Portuguese: sixty

Ship's articles – detailed provisions and rules for the entire crew of a ship issued by the shipping company

Shroud cleat – beam on the outside of a sailing ship for securing the standing rigging

Shrouds – the standing rigging used to secure the masts laterally (side to side)

Snaphaunce – a more modern version of the musket, equipped with a flintlock. Fired faster, more reliably, and accurately

Sprit sail – auxiliary sail set under the bowsprit

Sprit topsail – auxiliary sail above the bowsprit

Squad – a group of 8-12 soldiers led by a corporal. Two squads formed a section under the command of a sergeant

Starboard – the right side of the ship, with the bow facing forward

Stay – rope providing additional support to a mast section, running directly to the deck

Steward – petty officer responsible for food and drink supplies

Subhan'Allah – Arabic: "Praise God"

Swivel gun – small rotatable cannon rotating on an iron pivot

Tacking – also: coming about. A maneuver by which a sailing craft turns its bow toward and through the wind so that the direction from which the wind blows changes from one side of the boat to the other

Taffrail – the upper part of the stern, often richly decorated

Takoelah wood – dyewood

Tamarind – paste from the fruit of the tamarind tree with a tangy taste, used as a substitute for lime or lemon juice

Third mate – third-ranking officer responsible for navigation on a ship, after the second and first mate; there could be multiple third mates

Thwart – transverse seat plank in a small, open boat

Top – a platform located around the top of the lower masts, used both for lookout purposes and as a position for armed sailors during naval engagements

Topgallant sail – uppermost, third layer of square sail on a full-rigged ship

Topmast – a removable extension of a mast

Topsail – the second layer of square sails on a full-rigged ship

Transom – the often elaborately decorated rear of a 17th-century ship

Triangular trade – Transatlantic triangular trade: 1. Ships departed from Western Europe with trade goods, mainly firearms, gunpowder, iron, and textiles. These were exchanged in West Africa with local rulers for slaves, gold, and ivory. 2. From West Africa, ships carrying slaves then sailed to the Caribbean. 3. Return journey to Western Europe with luxury goods such as sugar, rum, coffee, cotton, silver, and tobacco

Trots, the – slang: diarrhea.

Tufohen – from Akan: supreme commander of all Indigenous militias (see Asafo)

Twi – one of the dialects of the Akan language

Uncle – (Dutch: 'ome') a title typically used between Dutch seasoned sailors to address each other

Voacanga – a small tropical tree in Africa whose bark and seeds contain iboga alkaloids, ingested for their stimulating, aphrodisiac and psychedelic effects

Waist deck (or waist) – the open, central section of a ship between the forecastle (forward part) and the quarterdeck (aft part)

Weather glass – the precursor of the barometer

Whipstaff – on large ships, the rudder was operated by a long tiller below deck, connected to the whipstaff (a vertical pivoting rod). This allowed the rudder to move at a very small angle, no more than 5 to 10 degrees. Steering at that time depended largely on sail positioning. The ship's wheel became common only at the beginning of the 18th century

Windward – the direction the wind is coming from

Woolding – tight rope binding used to reinforce composite spars (such as masts and yards)

Yacht – a general term for any fast-sailing, not-too-large vessel; one or two-masted, often equipped with rowing benches

Yam – edible tuber

Yard – a spar that hangs transversely and is movable on the mast to which a sail is attached

Yaws – a tropical disease caused by a bacterium, characterized by raspberry-like growths on the skin

The following excerpt is taken from the second novel in the Sons of Japheth Series:

ON THE BARBARY COAST
By John Meilink

1678. The Dutch trader ship Sint Joris leaves the Dutch Republic in high spirits, bound for Paramaribo (Suriname) with a hold full of Schiedam gin and a handful of unsuspecting passengers. But off the Cape Verde Islands, disaster strikes: Algerian corsairs overwhelm the ship, and every soul on board is thrown into chains. What begins as a routine crossing becomes a nightmare as the Dutch disappear into the brutal world of Moorish slave markets, forced labor, and desperate bargaining for freedom.

In Algiers, envoy Thomas Hees fights a different battle. Tasked with securing a peace treaty to protect Dutch merchant ships from Mediterranean piracy, he enters a city shaped by power struggles, corruption, and political intrigue. But the English and French have the same goal—and they are willing to sabotage negotiations, manipulate rivalries, and spill blood to dominate the region's maritime trade.

Amid shifting alliances, court conspiracies, and the crushing machinery of North African slavery, a darker threat descends upon Algiers: the Black Death, cutting down rich and poor alike and sending the city into chaos.

On the Barbary Coast delivers an unflinching portrayal of a world where diplomacy is as deadly as warfare, where survival depends on calculated loyalty, and where the line between captor and captive is thinner than anyone dares to admit. Meticulously grounded in original seventeenth-century accounts, maritime records, and diplomatic history, the novel recreates the political, economic, and cultural realities of the early modern Mediterranean world.

Hansum Han

"The bird in its cage does not sing out of joy, but from anger."

Arthur Schopenhauer (1788 - 1860)

He is gaunt, always has been—skin stretched over bone—but with tough, sinewy muscles rolling beneath his loose skin. His endurance seems inexhaustible; where others collapse, he remains standing, ever ready to fight, fearing no one. His battered face is a mask, his eyes blazing with a feverish, wild fire. His credo is simple, yet unmistakable: "Bring it on."

ن

"Hansum Han?" asks the old salt as he downs his grog. "By God, he's uglier than I am." He laughs and slaps the table with a flat hand for emphasis. "Fell twenty fathoms out of the main topgallant, landed headfirst on the rail, split his skull wide open from here to ..." He puts his mug down, pointing with one finger at his right temple and the other at the back of his head. "... here. A hole as big as an inch and a half across. You could see his brains sittin' there. Ask Cross-Eyed Gus over there. Gus! Gus! How big was that hole in Hansum Han's head?"

Cross-Eyed Gus, slouched at the makeshift bar, glances back lazily, one eye drifting left and the other right. "Two inches and a bit," he answers flatly.

"Aw, shut it, for God's sake, mate, no need to exaggerate, eh?" The old sailor crows with laughter. "An inch and a half, and the cook and the barber patched it all up—hair, bone, the whole bloody mess—and stitched it back together with a sail needle. No lie. Hansum Han spent two months laid out like a goner. Couldn't say a word, nah, more dead than alive he was."

He drains his mug in one go and grabs the jug. The rum flows with a glugging sound. "Well, he didn't get any better looking, that Han, ha-ha. It was back in '54, right after the surrender of Taborda, when we had to move the Jews out of Paraibo. We did more fighting than sailing in those days, I can tell you that. And after that—God, that poor bastard was born under a bad sign—he took the tip of a rapier clean through his jaw during a scuffle on the Wild Coast. Went in one side, out the other—through his cheek, his tongue, and his lower jaw. I was right there, saw the whole thing. I even shouted, 'Look out!' But does Hansum Han flinch? No, sir. He kicks the bastard holding the rapier right in the stones and, just to make sure, bashes his brains in. I says, 'Your face is half gone, Han.' And he goes, stone cold, 'Reckon it needs a stitch or two.'"

The old sailor howls with laughter. "Can you picture it? Blood squirting out of his mouth. What a man!"

A life full of hardships. During a voyage to Suriname—he's twenty-three at the time—his ship founders in a storm on the western Atlantic Ocean. By sheer chance, he survives, part of a group of just eight men: the third mate, the steward, the carpenter, three able seamen, and two deckhands. He is one of the able seamen. The carpenter is gravely injured, his leg impaled by a splinter of spar. Eight men in a small boat, without a sail, without food, and no land in sight. Fortunately, it rains almost constantly, sparing them the agony of thirst. They collect the water in buckets and small casks.

From a few planks, they fashion paddles and divide into two groups of four: three hours on, three hours off. Two men per side. Paddling until they drop. Luckily, the third mate has managed to save a Jacob's staff. Though he's not particularly skilled, he takes sightings of the sun whenever the rain lets up, giving them a rough idea of their position and direction; the mainland of South America can't be far.

But the paddling quickly wears them down. Without food, their strength ebbs. Onboard the ship, scurvy had already begun to set in, but now the disease strikes swiftly and mercilessly. Three hours of paddling shrinks to two, then to one. By the end of the first week, no one has the strength to row.

Hansum Han lies in the stern of the boat. His teeth are loose, and old wounds ache. Hunger churns through his gaunt body like an untamed dog.

On the eighth night, the carpenter dies from blood loss and shock. Despite outraged protests, Hansum Han takes out his knife and, without hesitation, slices thin strips of flesh from the man's healthy leg, chewing them down laboriously. "Shut your traps," he growls at the others. "Unless you've got a better idea." He feels no remorse; the carpenter was a goner. But the others refuse to eat, and the third mate cries out loudly for God's forgiveness.

By the eleventh day, the corpse begins to bloat. Disgusted, Hansum Han tosses it overboard; even he can't stomach the rotting flesh. But the carpenter doesn't sink. Bloated with gas, he floats belly-up, eerily following the boat downstream, an accusatory presence. Not a shark in sight.

"We're doomed," wails the third mate. "We're finished."

"Never," Hansum Han growls defiantly. The scurvy makes his lower jaw feel like it's barely hanging on, as if it might drop off at any moment.

On the twelfth day, one of the deckhands—a boy of fifteen—dies. Hansum Han cuts strips from his thighs and buttocks. This time, the two able seamen and the steward join in. "No choice," they mutter to each other, looking like living skeletons themselves.

It hasn't rained for three days now, so the water is rationed: two small cups per man a day. The men sink deeper into lethargy.

Hansum Han stays awake. With one hand, he presses against his unsteady jawbone. All his lower teeth are gone now. Scurvy offers no relief. He stares longingly at the western horizon. There must be land out there. There has to be.

On the thirteenth night, the carpenter's bloated corpse finally disappears. Hansum Han, the only one awake, hears the splashing and gurgling overboard in the dark. Sounds like a school of barracuda, he concludes with relief. Despite his misery, he can't help but grin: We eat them, they eat us.

The days and nights that follow blur into a fog. Waning consciousness. Apathy. Sometime in that haze, the steward and another seaman die. No one notices.

It isn't until the seventeenth day that they reach the coast.

"He had a black lass in Berbice," the old sailor continues, pouring the last drops of rum from the jug. "Pretty little thing, an escaped slave from a plantation. She'd taken refuge in a hut on the coast, far from Fort Nassau and Governor Van Pere. Escaped slaves can't count on much mercy, especially not from that bastard Van Pere. Anyway, she found Hansum Han more dead than alive in a mangrove swamp, washed up from the sea with two white corpses nearby. Covered in scurvy from head to toe, skin burnt raw from the sun. But she nursed him back to health, bless her, until he could stand on his feet again. Hansum Han and a black girl—yes, sir, he took a liking to her. Word is, there's still a kid of his somewhere in the West Indies, black as coal. He told me the whole tale himself, hand on heart.

"It went well for two years, living like Adam and Eve in paradise. Maybe that was the only time in his miserable life that he found any happiness, the ugly mutt. But someone must've seen the girl—maybe in a village or at a market. Betrayers are everywhere. One foul day, the sheriff and his thugs show up at Han's place: 'Hello there! By order of Governor Van Pere: hand over the slave!' Poor Han didn't have a leg to stand on."

The old sailor shakes his head sadly, then starts throwing shadow punches at imagined foes. "He tried to resist, of course, but they beat him to the ground—five of them, with clubs. He was lucky they didn't press charges, they said. Left him for dead. And that was the end of his paradise. Later, he heard they'd beaten the girl to death back on the plantation. As a warning to others. That Van Pere's a proper arsehole, make no mistake."

A year later, he suddenly reappears in Holland. No one but himself knows how he made it back, and no one dares ask him because he's utterly unmanageable. In the taverns of Rotterdam, he becomes a feared presence, growling and snarling his way through the day as he drinks himself senseless. And when he's had enough to drink, there's always some unsuspecting boozer to whom he can pour out his story:

"Listen, mate, the chirurgeon examined me and said he'd never seen so much damage. Asked if I could still climb the rigging. Haha! With two fingers up my nose, pal! Nothing can beat me. I've been through it all. But they slaughtered my girl, the filthy bastards, the only woman I ever gave a damn about, even if she was just a black girl and didn't have a soul. Black as tar, she was, but good enough for me. She mattered to me. We could laugh together. Everything's broken now, mate. Everything in my head is dead. I don't care about anything anymore. I laugh at pain and spit on everyone. I bleed as if it's nothing. I bow to the bigwigs, and then – when they're not looking – I slit their fuckin' throats."

Back to the sea. Always the sea. A good able seaman is never turned away, even one who looks like him. The West India Company trades to Suriname and Berbice, and sometimes – when the black coats of the church get a notion in their heads – there are Bibles, weapons, and clothes to be smuggled to the Calvinist Tupi Indians at the Rio Grande do Norte, along secret routes through what is now Portuguese-controlled Brazil.

It's what he likes most: seeking danger. He's always the first to volunteer when they need to paddle silently through the Jaguaribe rivers in the dead of night, the oars wrapped in cloth, muskets at the ready.

"Those were dark times." The old sailor uncorks a new jug. "Those damned Indians are just as untrustworthy as the Portuguese, Judas types who'll switch sides for a handful of lousy coppers." With both hands, he pours the rum into his mug without spilling a drop. "Hansum Han had the bad luck to be the first out of the boat. It was pitch black." He drinks in deep, greedy gulps, his thoughts drifting far back to that night in '62. "He hadn't even touched the ground when one of those rednecks shoots an arrow clean through his jaw. His jaw, again! Damn thing was sticking out on both sides of his head."

He stares sombrely into his empty mug. "They came at us like flies to honey, and we had to fight for our lives. But we beat them off by the skin of our teeth, mate. Pushed the boat back into the river and got the hell out, under a rain of spears and stones. It was a bloody miracle we escaped. Only after an hour did we dare to light a lantern to see what they'd done to us. My God, what a slaughter!" He crosses himself, his fingers gesturing toward the vision in his mind. "Fourteen dead comrades we counted. Twenty-eight wounded, including the skipper."

He shakes his head desolately. "But that's not what stuck with me most. No, what I'll never forget is Hansum Han, sitting there on the gunwale, covered in blood with that arrow still sticking through his jaws. That wasn't a man sitting there, sir. That was the devil himself, I swear on everything I hold dear."

Also available in the 'Sons of Japheth' series:

In preparation:

www.ingramcontent.com/pod-product-compliance
Lightning Source LLC
LaVergne TN
LVHW010147070526
838199LV00062B/4280